CONTENTS

	Page
How to get the most from your guide	II
Key Plan	III
Cape Town Central Plan	IV - V
Main Map Pages	2 - 89
Index to Street Names	90 - 133
Index to Suburbs	133 - 134
Index to Community Services	134 - 136
Index to Education	136 - 138
Index to General Information	138 - 139
Amendments	140

MapStudio

0860 10 50 50

Visit our website: www.mapstudio.co.za

Production: Christine Flemington, Martin Endemann, Ryno Swart
Research: Judy Graham.
Technical: Mark Hedington.
Graphic Design & Index: Martin Endemann.

HOW TO GET THE MOST FROM YOUR STREETFINDER

The key plan

On page III the Key Plan gives an overall view of the area covered by this guide. The numbered blue outlines represent the map pages of the book and are used to determine which page covers a particular area. Maps are arranged in double page spreads, with overlaps on three sides, to enable detail to be followed easily from map to map. All maps are arranged with North at the top.

Large scale map

A large scale map of Cape Town Central appear on pages IV & V.

Index pages

The Index pages, starting on page 90, feature both Street and Suburb Indexes. There are also sections indexing Schools, Police Stations, Sports Facilities and other features.

Datum

The datum used on this street guide is WGS 84 (World Geodetic System).

Grid reference system

Look up the required Street, Suburb or Feature in the index at the back of the book, and note the grid reference. Turn to the appropriate page and identify the grid block.

Example: Aandwind St   Kirstenhof   63   DA 31

In the order of: Street Name, Suburb, Page No., Grid Letter, Grid number

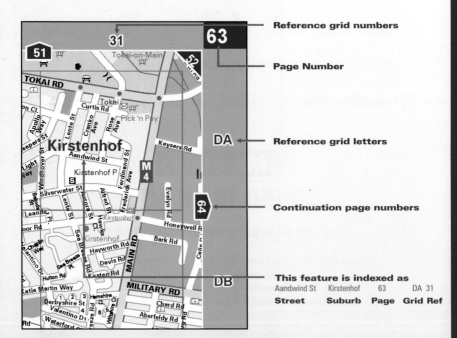

Reference grid numbers

Page Number

Reference grid letters

Continuation page numbers

This feature is indexed as

Aandwind St   Kirstenhof   63   DA 31

Street   Suburb   Page   Grid Ref

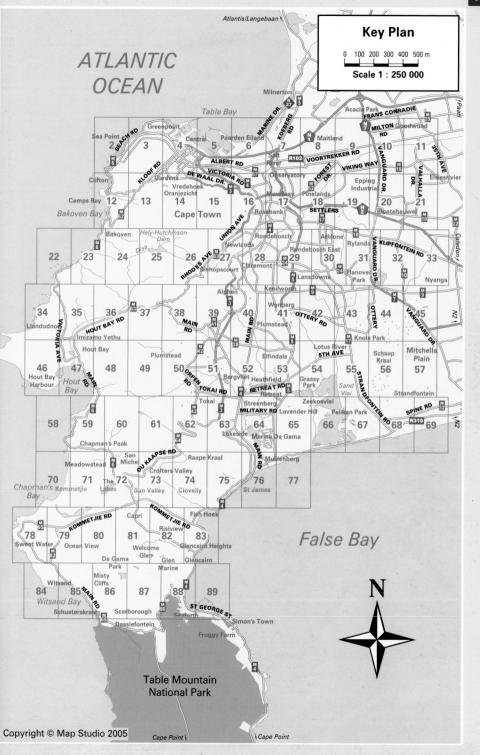

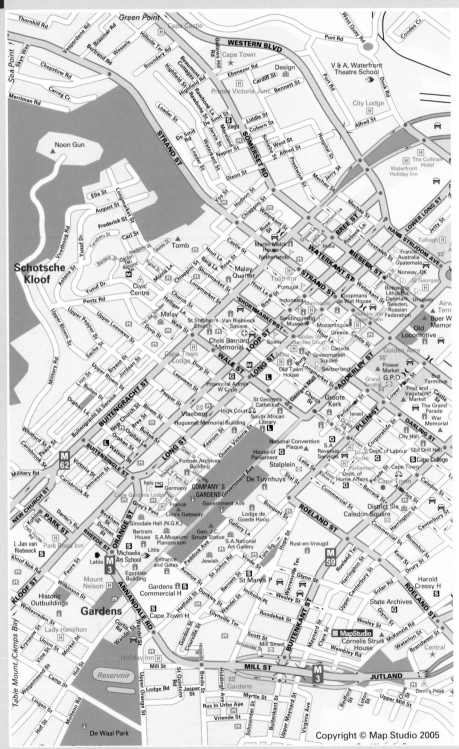

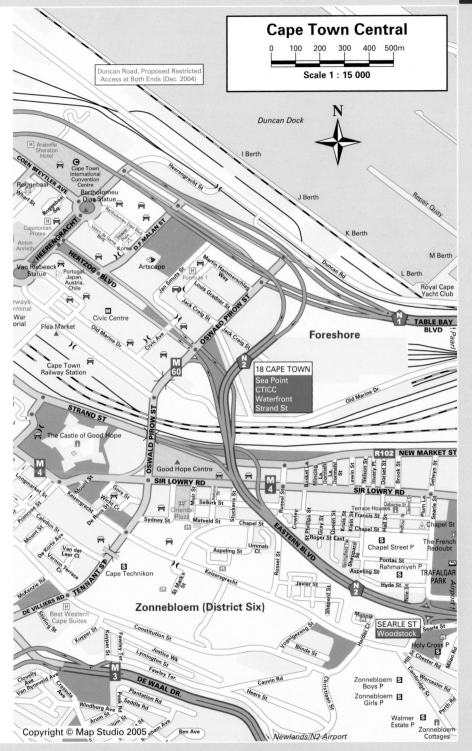

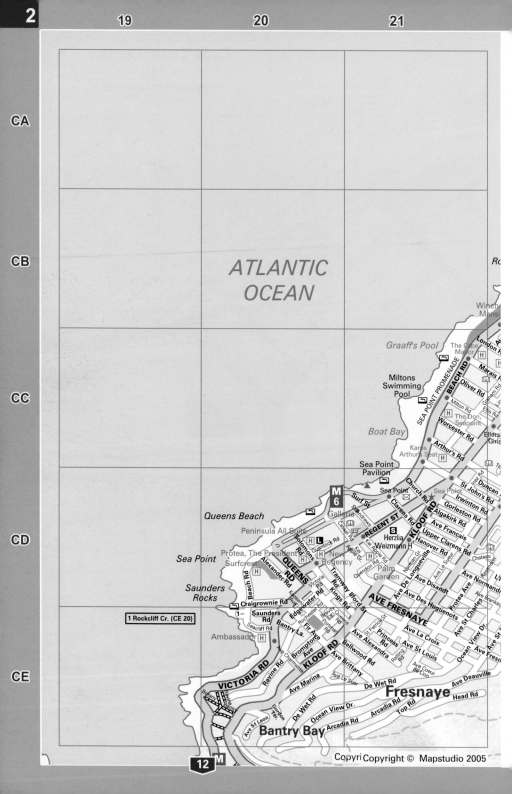

CA

CB

CC

CD

CE

ATLANTIC
OCEAN

ATLANTIC OCEAN

Graaff's Pool   The Cape
                 Manor

Miltons
Swimming
Pool

Boat Bay

Sea Point
Pavilion

Queens Beach

Peninsula All Suite

Sea Point

Protea, The President
Surfcrest

Saunders
Rocks

1 Rockcliff Cr. (CE 20)

Craigrownie Rd

Saunders
Rd

Ambassador

Graaff's Pool

Winch
Mansi

London R

Marais

Oliver Rd

Milton Rd
The Don,
Seapoint

Worcester Rd

Ellers
Girls

Karos
Arthurs Seat

Arthur's Rd

St Duncan
Rd

Sea Point

Irwinton Rd

Gorleston Rd

Surf St

Galleria

St Andrews

Herzlia
Weizmann H

Algakirk Rd

Ave Francais

Upper Clarens Rd

Hanover Rd

New
Regency

Ave De Longueville

Palm
Garden

Ave Disandt

Chateau

Ave Normand

Ave Des Huguenots

Protea Ave

Alexander Rd

AVE FRESNAYE

Beach Rd

Ave St Charles

Ave St Patrick

Ave Alexandra

Ave La Croix

Ave St Louis

Ocean View Rd

Ave Fresn

Bantry La.

Princess

Bellwood Rd

Ave Brittany

Ave Coeur
de Lion

Ave Deauville

KLOOF RD

Bromptom

Edgewater Rd

Kings Rd

VICTORIA RD

Ravine Rd

Ave Marina

De Wet Rd

Fresnaye

Head Rd

Seacliff Rd

Ave St Leon

Gordon
Ter.

De Wet Rd

Ocean View Dr.

Arcadia Rd

Arcadia Rd

Top Rd

Bantry Bay

1

12

S.A.Seafarer (1966)

Green Point

Green Point (1824)

Mouille Point

BEACH RD

Alexandra Pl.
Bay Rd
Rothesay Pl.
Surrey Pl.

Kiewiet La.
Stephan Way

Bay Pl.

Green Point

Park Rd

Serendipity Maze

Fritz Sonnenberg Rd

Sea Point

Three Anchor Bay

Green Point Common

Bill Peters Dr.

Vlei Rd

Green Point Stadium

Three Anchor Bay

Stanley Pl.

Civic Centre

Three Anchor Bay

M 6

WESTERN BLVD

Rocklands Bay
Rocklands Beach

BEACH RD

Marine Rd
Fort Rd
Pedinth

Green Point

Carnaby
Ritz

M 61

MAIN RD

Sleep Easy
Green Point

Graeme
N.S.R.I.

Rocklands Rd

Stone

Glengariff
Avondale

Richmond Rd

Grove Rd
Leicester Rd

Pine Rd

Sydney Rd
Dysart Rd

Norman

Leinster Rd

St James Rd
Capetonian

Homley

Ellerton P

Antrim Rd

St Georges Rd
Croxteth
Clyde Bank Rd

Torbay Rd
Haytor Rd

De Goede Verwachting

Winchester Mansions

Sea Point H

Norfolk Rd

Rhine Rd

Centurion
All-Suite

Adelphi

S

Law
Walter

Maydon

Mutley Rd

Hatfield Rd

St Bede's Rd

Kevin Rd

Romney Rd
Braeside

Sollum Rd

Cheviot Pl.

Modena

Thornhill Rd

Reddam House

London Rd
Aurora

Hall Rd

Wisbeach Rd

Rhine Rd

Mount Nelson S

Sea Point P

Blackheath Rd

Korf St

HIGH LEVEL RD

Joubert Rd
Ocean View Dr.

Ben Nevis Rd

Roos Rd

Skye Way

Chepstow Rd

Ocean View Rd

Carre

Le Vendome
Royal Atlantic

Firmount Rd

Upper Man Dr.

Springbok Rd

Merriman Rd

Marais Rd

Lincoln
Albany Rd
Oldfield Rd
Fleurs Rd
Calais Rd

Battery Cr.

Antwerp Rd
Ocean View Dr.

Ilkley Cr.

Noon Gun

Bellevue Rd

Milner
Tafelberg Training Centre

Dover Rd

HIGH LEVEL RD

Rhine Rd

Ellerslie Girls

The Glen

Heathfield

Holmfirth Rd

Sea Point

Signal Hill
350m

SEE PAGE [V AND V]

Trafalgar

Edward Rd
Clifford Rd
Deane Rd
Firdale Ave

Northumbr

Friars Rd
Dassen Rd

Duncan Rd

Barkly Rd

Arthur's Rd

Ocean View Dr.

Viewpoint

Lion's Rump

St Charles
St Ave
Marcelle

Signal Hill Rd

1 Frere Rd (CB 22)		
2 Rosedene Rd (CC 22)		
3 Winstonia Rd (CC 22)		
4 Herbert Rd (CC 22)		

Schotsche Kloof

Ave Bordeaux

Chateau
Alexander

Ave St Charles

L'Hermite
Ave Fontainebleau

Normandie

Ave Bransome

Ave De Dreilingcourt

Fresnaye Sports Club

Poyser Rd

Kenmore Rd

Whitford St
Carisbrook St
Bryan

Harrington Rd

Devonport Rd
Queens Rd
Brownlow Rd
Milner Rd

Hillside St

Bennington Rd
Military Rd

Ave St Bartholomew
Ave De Berrange
Ave Disandt

Ave De Dreilingcourt

Leeukloof Dr.

Brunswick Rd

Carstens St

S Var Col

Fresnaye

Ave Fresnaye

Tamboerskloof

Frederick Ct.

Burnside Rd

Tamboerskloof St

Hillside St

CE

Hildene Rd

Gilmour Hills

Woodside Rd

Albert Rd
Belle Ombre

Warren St

Tamboerskloof P

UPPER BUITENGRACHT ST

NEW CHURCH ST

PARK ST

Kohling

Deutsche Schule Cape Town

S

Upper Albert Rd

Bond St

Camden St

Bay View St

Rael St

Upper Union St

Hastings St

Eaton Rd

Kloof Nek Rd

Jan v Riebee

L

14

13

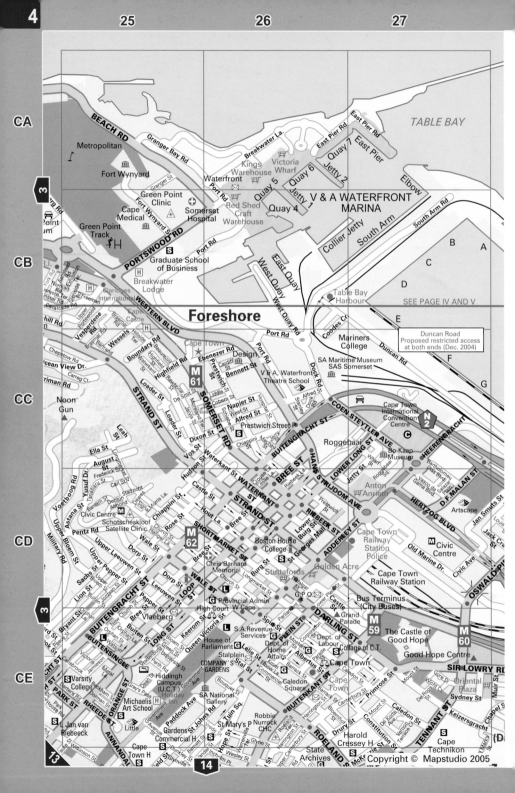

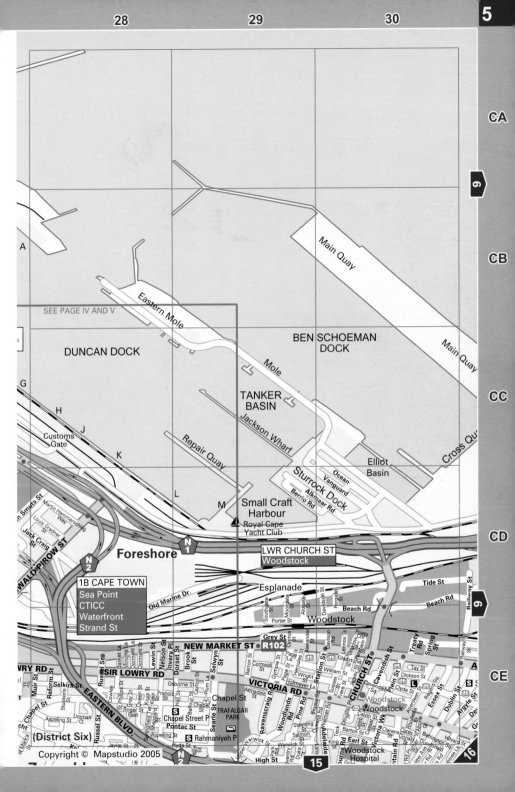

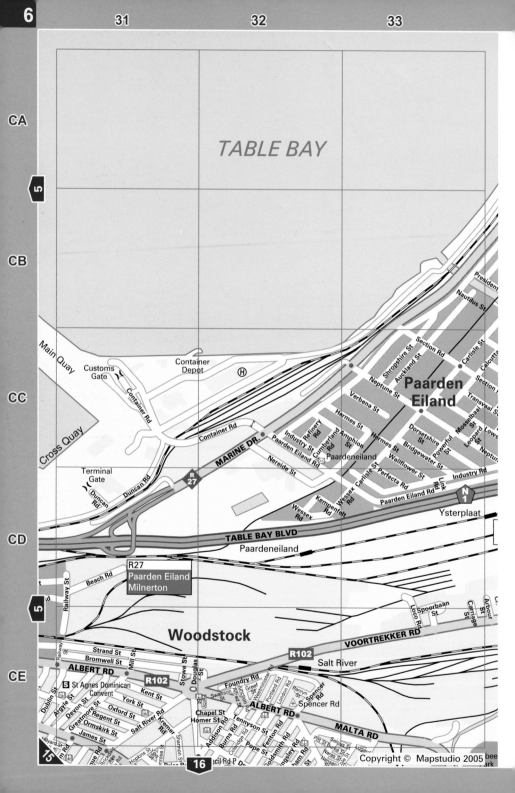

TABLE BAY

Main Quay

Customs Gate

Container Depot

Ⓗ

Cross Quay

Container Rd

Terminal Gate

Duncan Rd

Duncan Rd

MARINE DR.

R27

Container Rd

Paarden Eiland Rd

Nereide St

Industry St

Refinery Rd

Cumberland Rd

Paardeneiland

Hermes Rd

Verbena St

Neptune St

Amphion St

Shropshire St

Auckland St

Section Rd

Paarden Eiland

Carlisle St

Calcutte

Section

Transvaal S

Dorsetshire St

Mosselbaai St

Leopard Lowe

Hermes St

Bridgewater St

Powerful St

Neptu

Wallflower St

Carlisle St

Perfecta Rd

Kempenfelt Rd

Wessex Rd

Wessex Rd

Paarden Eiland Rd

Link Rd

Industry Rd

N1

Ysterplaat

President

Nautilus St

TABLE BAY BLVD

Paardeneiland

R27
Paarden Eiland
Milnerton

Beach Rd

Railway St

Spoorbaan St

Loco Rd

Arbour St

Carriage St

Woodstock

VOORTREKKER RD

Railway St

Strand St

Bromwell St

Mill St

Stowe St

Douglas St

R102

Salt River

ALBERT RD

R102

Ⓢ St Agnes Dominican Convent

Kent St

Foundry Rd

Greef St

Allied St

Duncan Rd

Westminster Rd

Portland Rd

London Rd

Renyn St

Spencer Rd

Dublin St

Argyle St

Devon St

York St

Oxford St

Greatmore St

Regent St

Ormskirk St

Salt River Rd

Kromer Rd

ALBERT RD

Swanson St

Spencer Rd

Chapel St

Homer St

Tennyson St

Burns St

Addison Rd

Pope St

Fenton St

Coleridge Rd

Goldsmith Rd

Kingsley Rd

Latham Rd

Pitt St

Burke St

Seloya St

Nares St

Nassen St

MALTA RD

Hillyard Rd

Blue Rd

Spencer Rd

James St

Hopkins St

Shannon St

Cecil Rd P D

15

16

CA CB CC CD CE

5 5

31 32 33

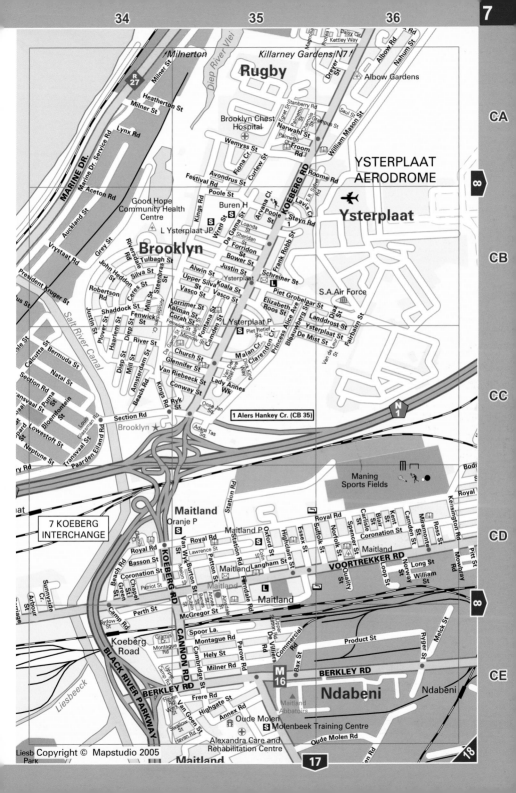

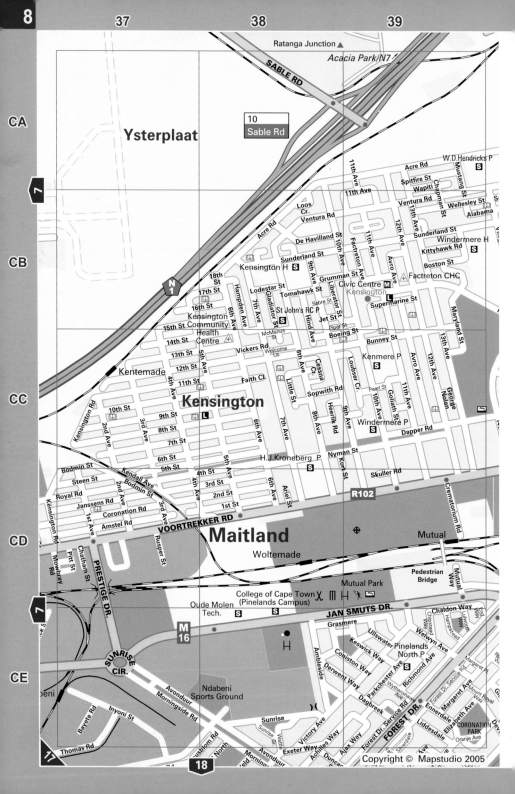

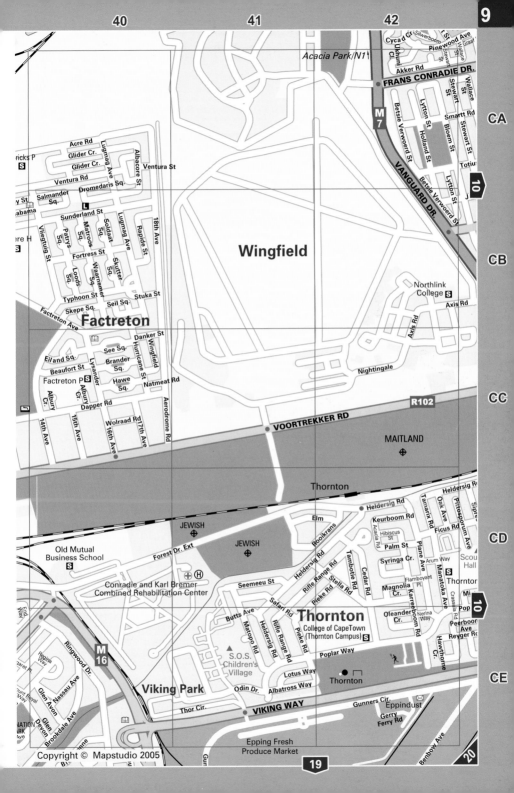

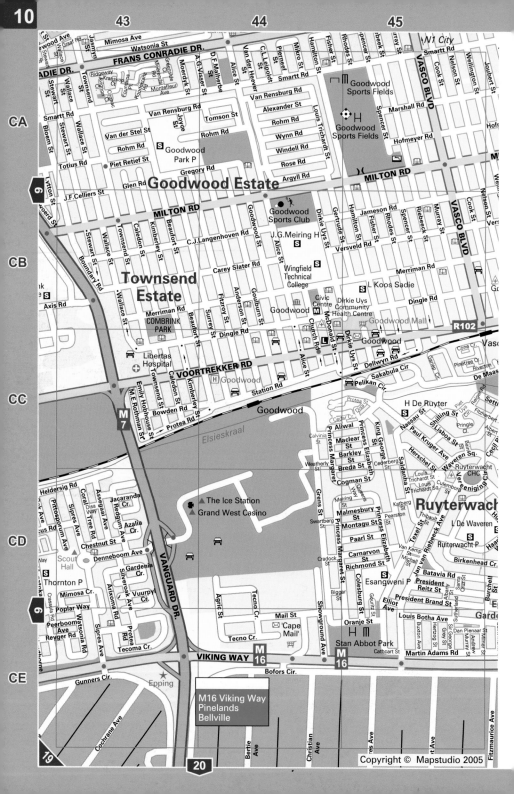

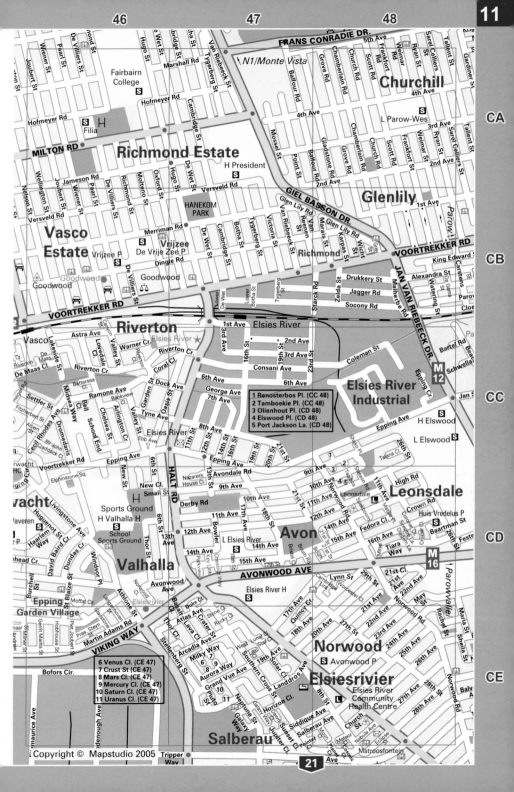

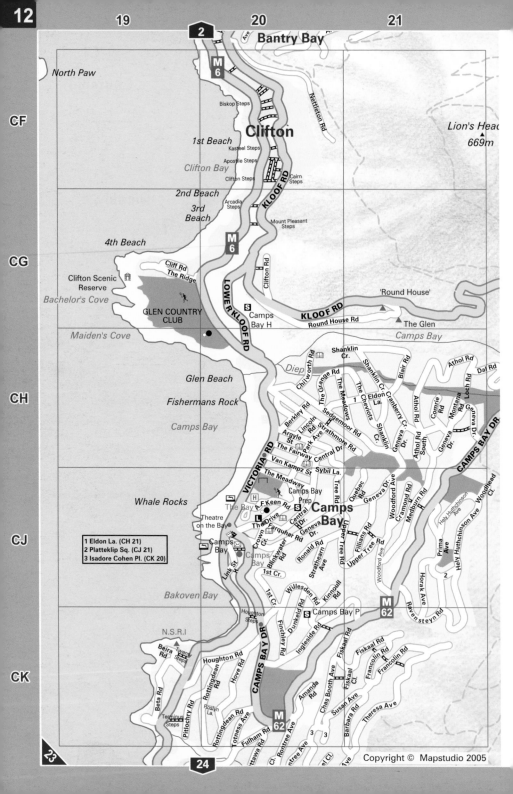

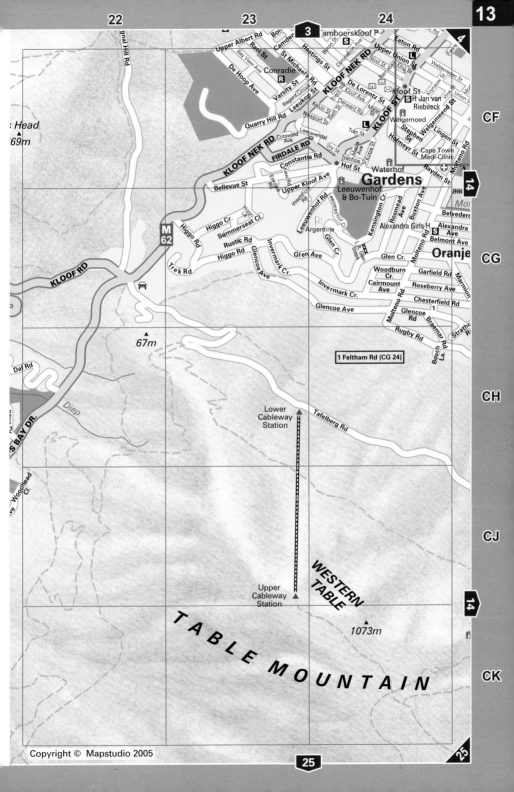

CF

CG

CH

CJ

CK

4

14

14

25

's Head
69m

Upper Albert Rd
Camden
Hastings St
De Hoop Ave
Conradie
Bay View Ave
Rael St
St Michael's Rd
Regent Circus
Varsity St
Leeukop St
Quarry Hill Rd
Leeuwendal
Cotswold Ave

KLOOF NEK RD

FIRDALE RD

Constantia Rd

Bellevue St

Upper Kloof Ave

Eskrole

Rustic Rd

Higgo Rd

Higgo Cr.

Summerseat Cl.

Higgo Rd

Trek Rd

KLOOF RD

M 62

67m

Diep

S BAY DR.

Dal Rd

Woodhead Cl.

Tamboerskloof P
Eaton Rd
Upper Union St
Nicol St
Barnaby
Kloof St
Weltevreden St
Welgemoed
Stephen Welgemeend St
Cape Town
Medi-Clinic
Rayden St
Molteno Rd

KLOOF NEK RD

De Lorentz St

Kloof St

H Jan van
Riebeeck

Waterhof

Gardens

Hof St

Leeuwenhof
& Bo-Tuin

Argentine

Glen Cr.

Glen Ave

Invermark Cr.

Glen Ave

Invermark Cr.

Glencoe Ave

Kensington Cr.

Alexandra Girls H

Glen Cr.

Woodburn
Cr.

Cairmount
Ave

Molteno Rd

Glencoe
Rd

Rugby Rd

Belvedere

Alexandra
Ave

Belmont Ave

Oranje

Garfield Rd

Roseberry Ave

Chesterfield Rd

Bosch La.

Braemar Rd

1 Feltham Rd (CG 24)

Lower
Cableway
Station

Tafelberg Rd

Upper
Cableway
Station

WESTERN
TABLE

1073m

T A B L E   M O U N T A I N

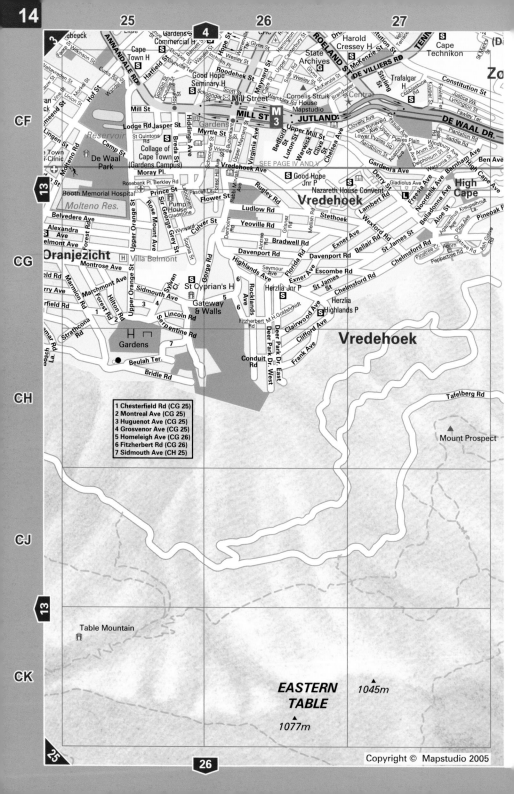

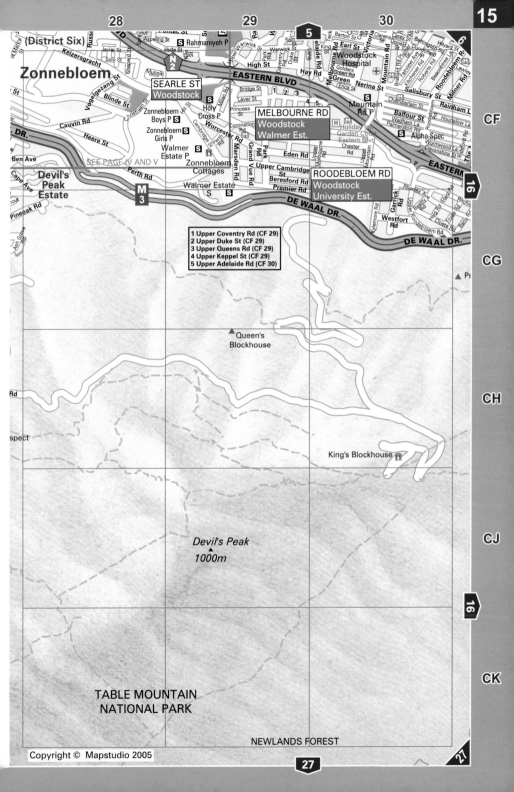

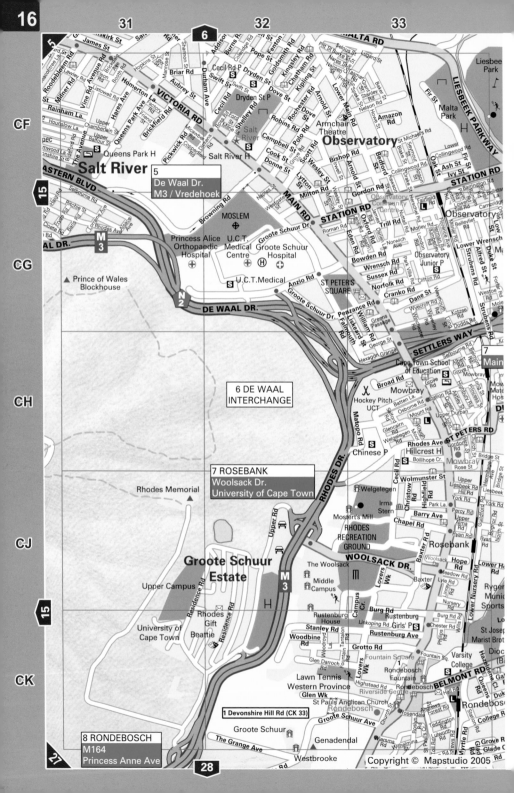

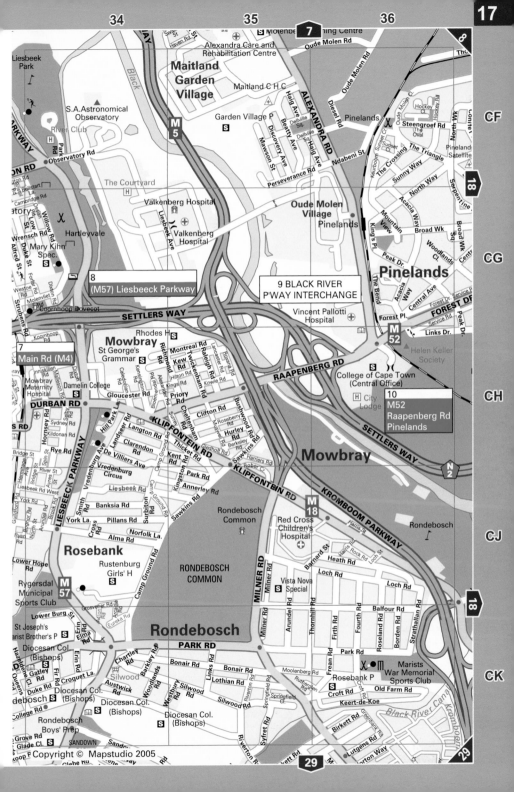

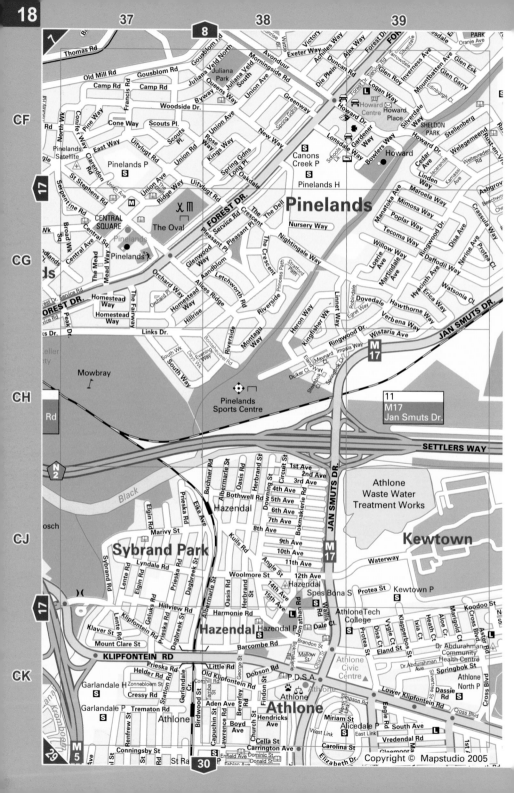

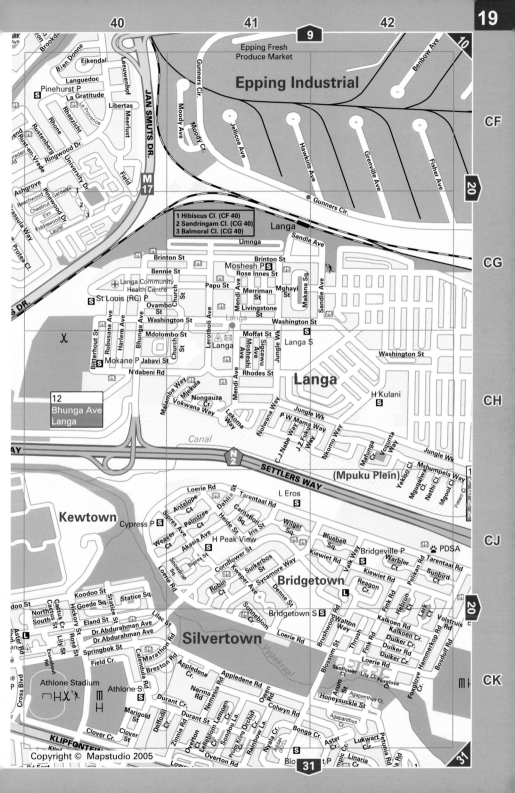

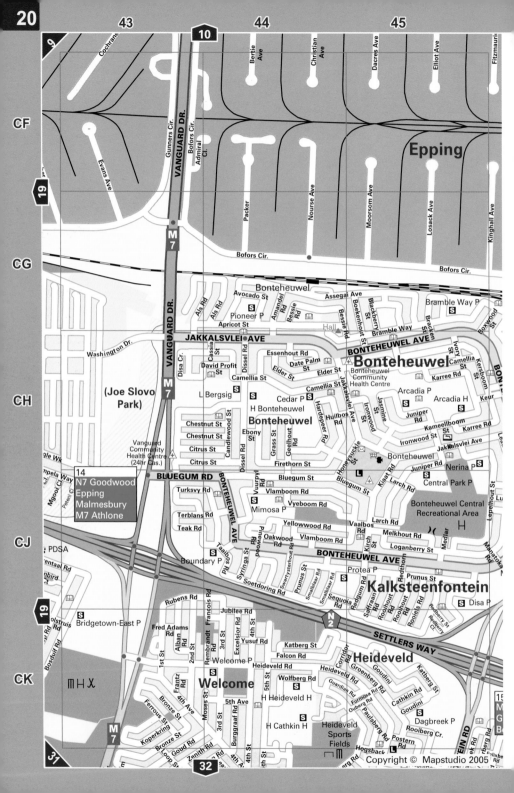

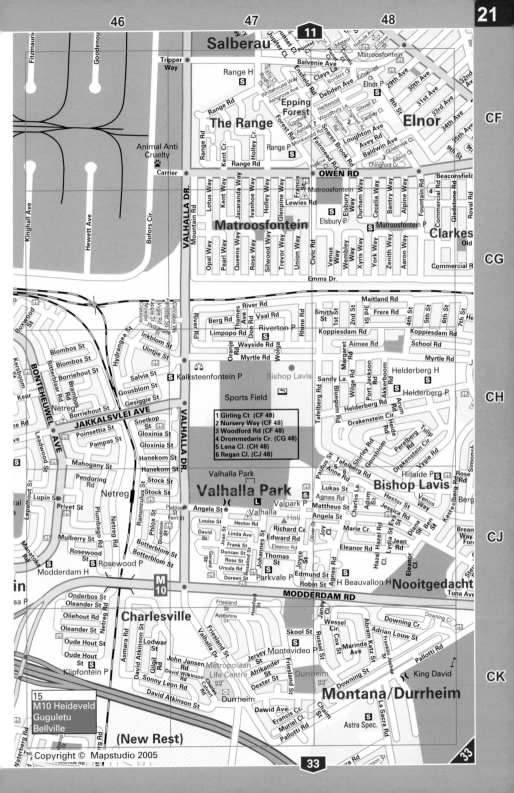

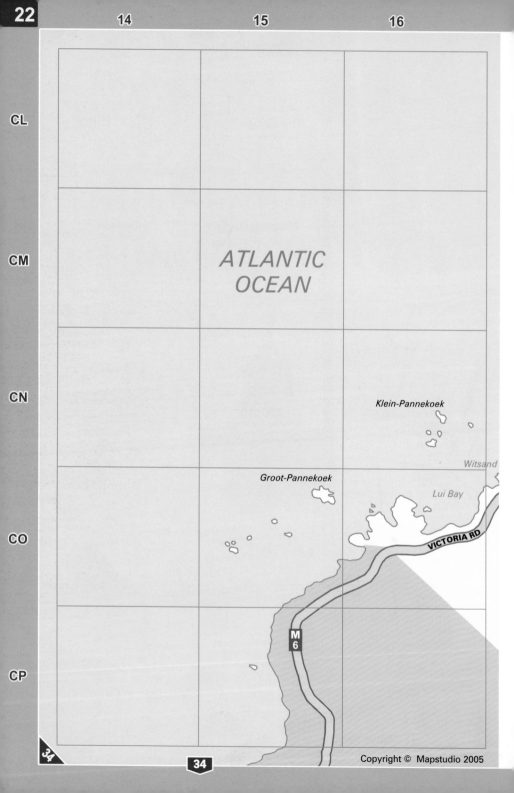

CL

CM

ATLANTIC
OCEAN

CN

Klein-Pannekoek

Witsand

Groot-Pannekoek

Lui Bay

CO

VICTORIA RD

M6

CP

34

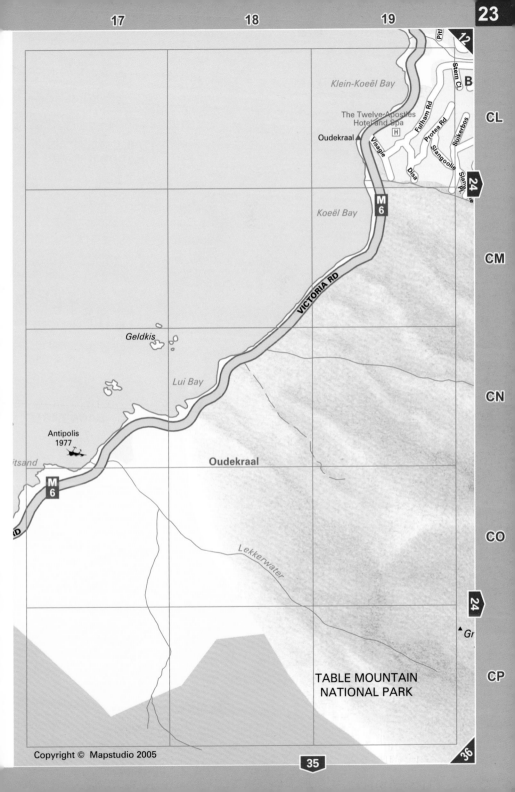

Klein-Koeël Bay

The Twelve-Apostles
Hotel and Spa ⒣

Oudekraal ▲

CL

CM

CN

CO

CP

B

12

Stern Cl

Fulham Rd

Protea Rd

Stikerbos

Slangoolie

Disa

Visagie

Slang Pk

24

Koeël Bay

M6

VICTORIA RD

Geldkis

Lui Bay

Antipolis
1977

itsand

M6

D

Oudekraal

Lekkerwater

24

Gr

TABLE MOUNTAIN
NATIONAL PARK

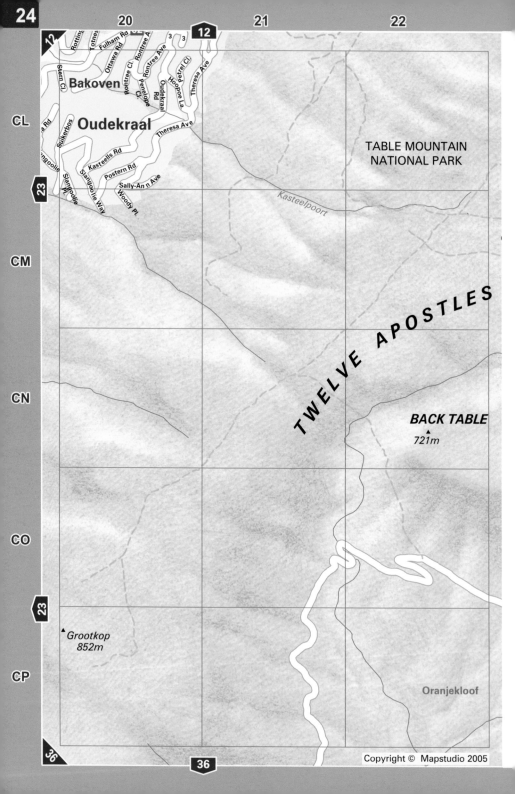

CL

Rottins
Fotnes
Fulham Rd
Ottawa Rd
Rontree Cl
Rontree A
Rontree Ave
3
3
Stem Cl
Penelope Cl
Oudekraal Rd
Hoopoe Petrel Cl
Theresa Ave
Theresa Ave

Bakoven

Oudekraal

a Rd
Suikerbos
Kasteells Rd
Postern Rd
Theresa Ave
ngoolie
Slangoolie
Slangoolie Way
Sally-Ann Ave
Woody Pl.

23

**TABLE MOUNTAIN
NATIONAL PARK**

Kasteelpoort

CM

CN

T W E L V E   A P O S T L E S

BACK TABLE
▲
721m

CO

23

▲*Grootkop*
852m

CP

Oranjekloof

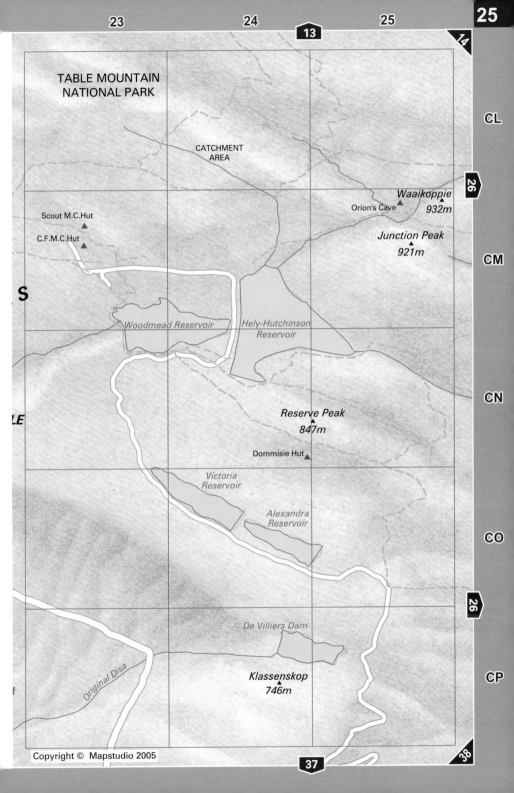

CL

TABLE MOUNTAIN
NATIONAL PARK

CATCHMENT
AREA

26

Scout M.C.Hut

C.F.M.C.Hut

Waaikoppie
932m

Orion's Cave

Junction Peak
921m

CM

S

Woodmead Reservoir

Hely-Hutchinson
Reservoir

CN

LE

Reserve Peak
847m

Dommisie Hut

Victoria
Reservoir

Alexandra
Reservoir

CO

26

De Villiers Dam

Original Disa

CP

Klassenskop
746m

f

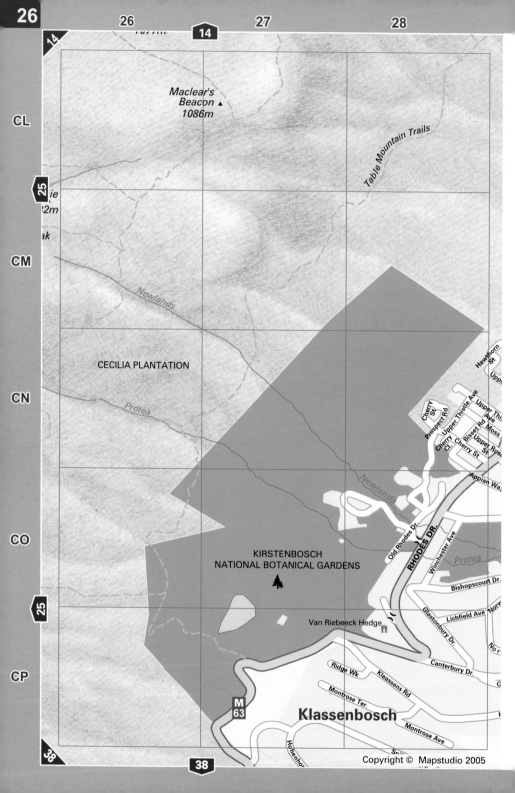

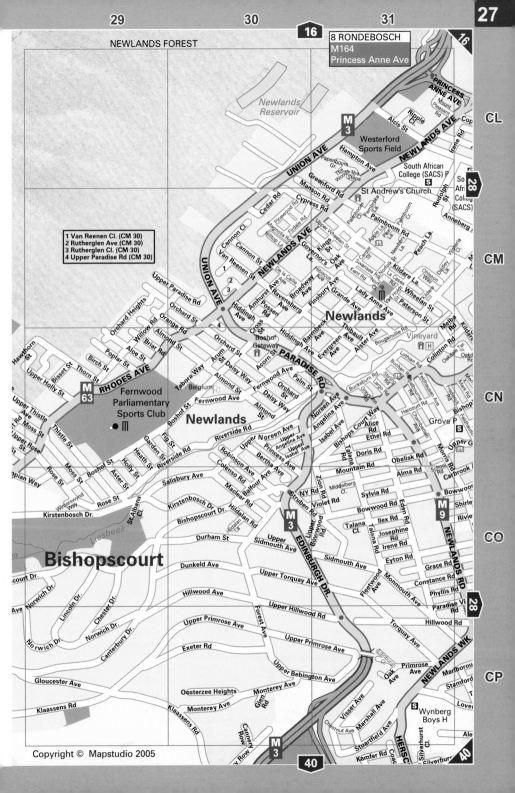

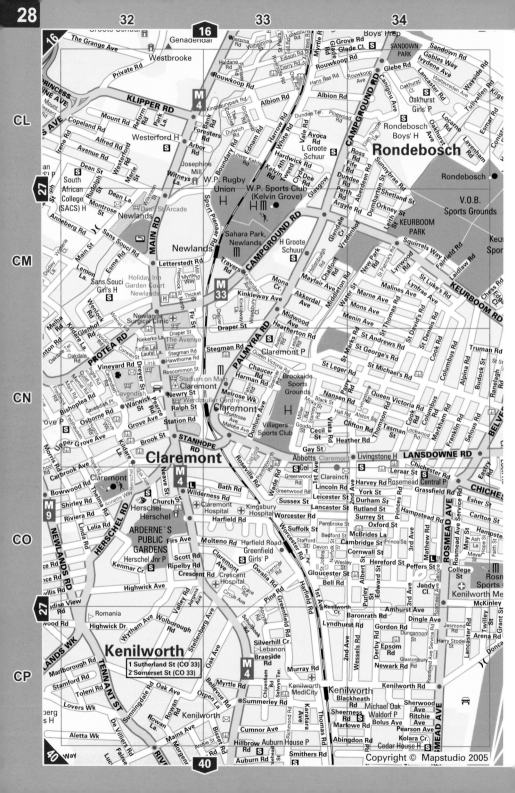

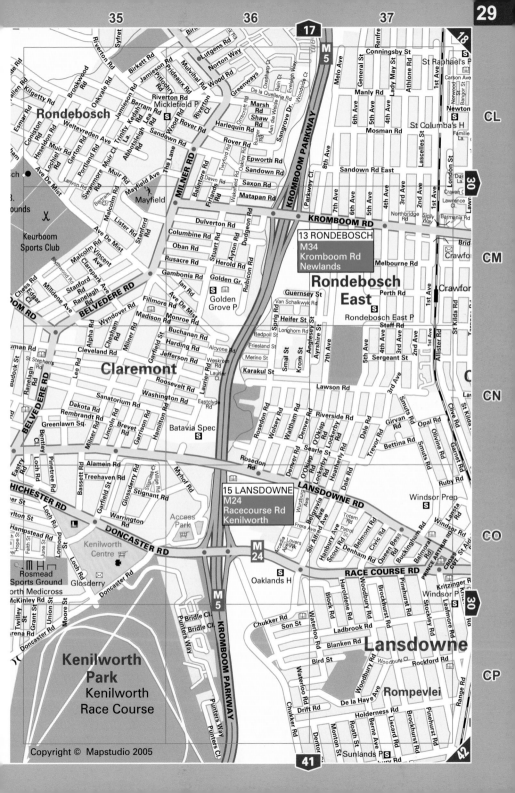

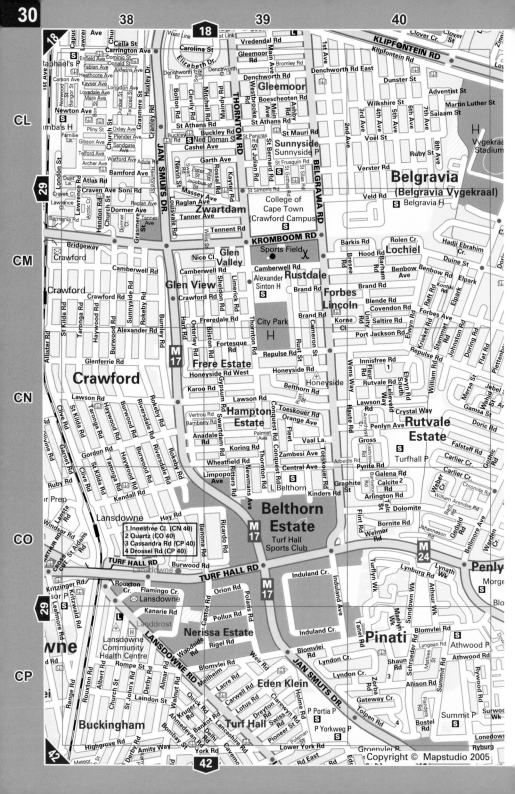

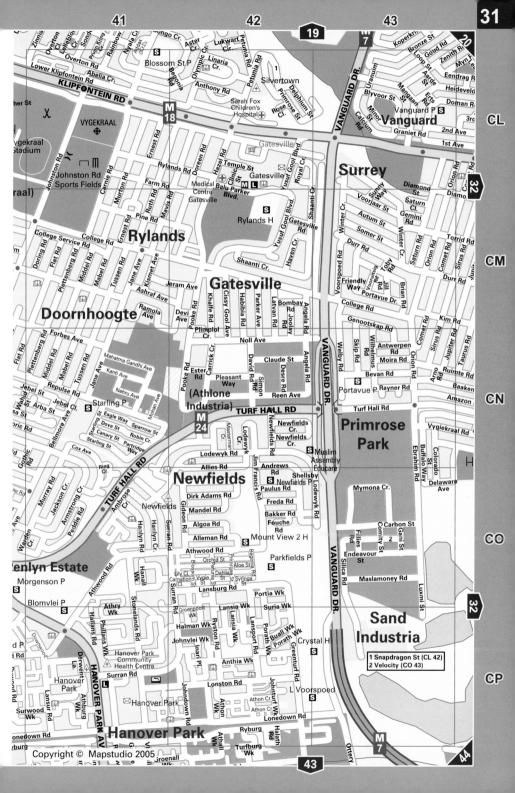

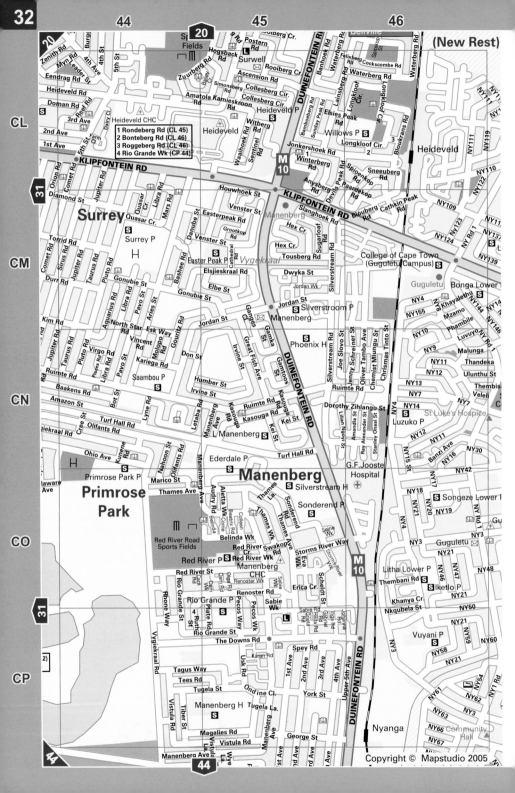

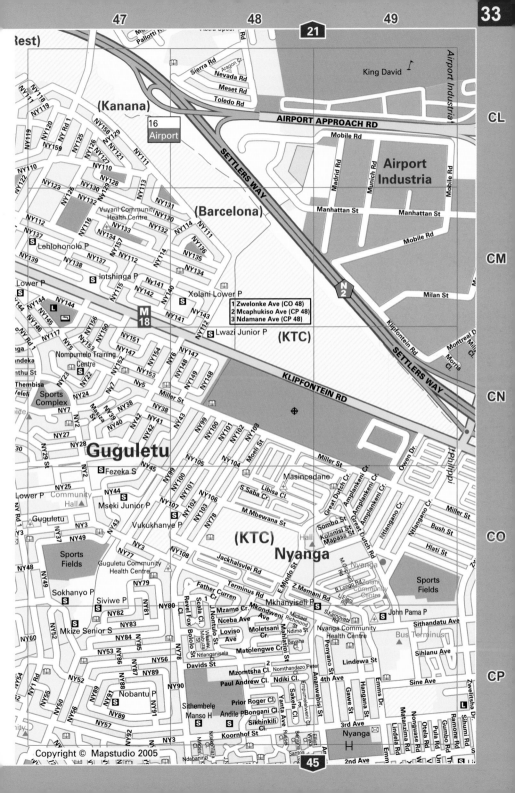

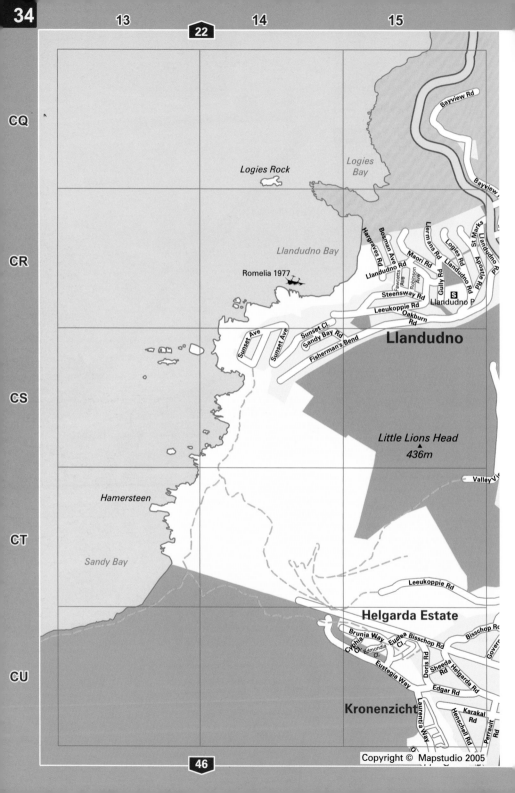

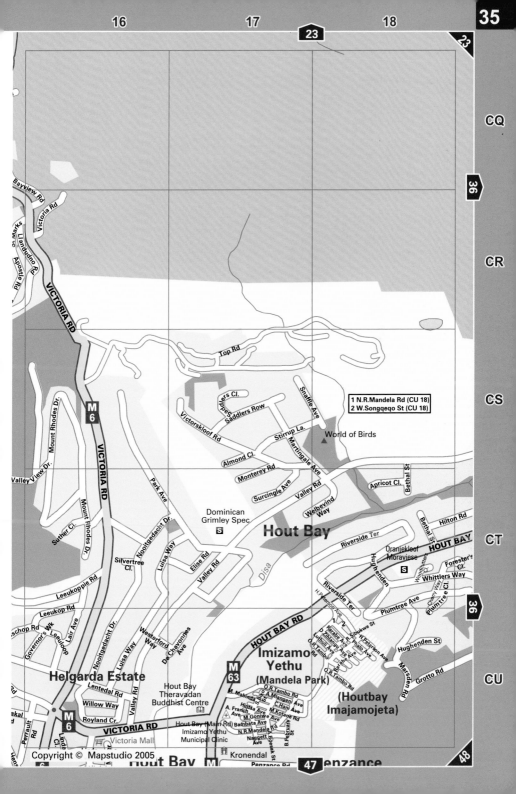

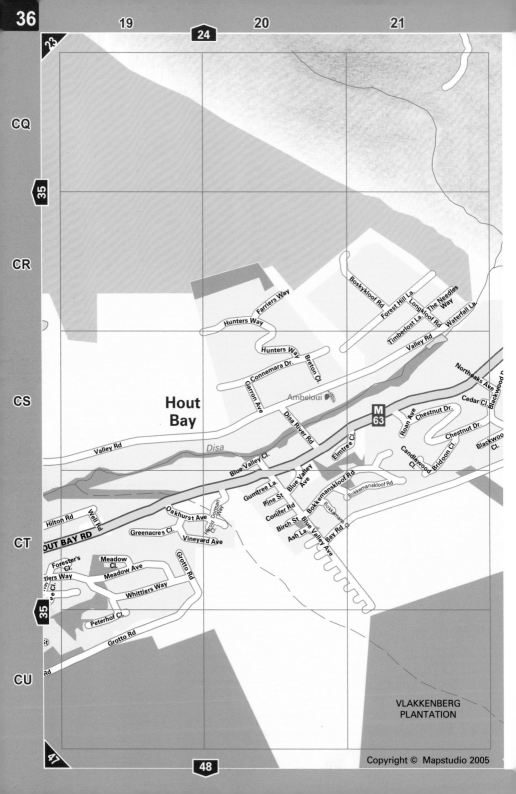

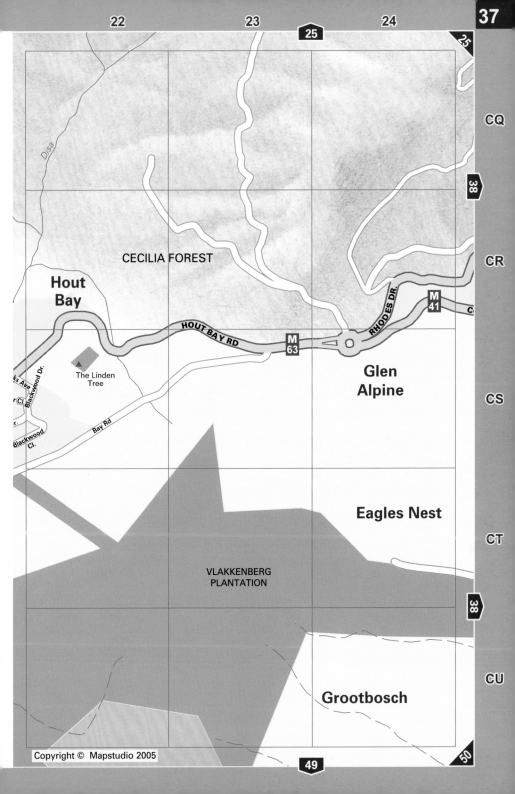

22 23 25 24

CQ

38

CECILIA FOREST

CR

Hout Bay

RHODES DR.

M 41

HOUT BAY RD

M 63

Glen Alpine

CS

The Linden Tree

Blackwood Dr.

Bay Rd

Blackwood Cl.

ts Ave

r Cl.

Disa

Eagles Nest

CT

VLAKKENBERG PLANTATION

38

CU

Grootbosch

49

50

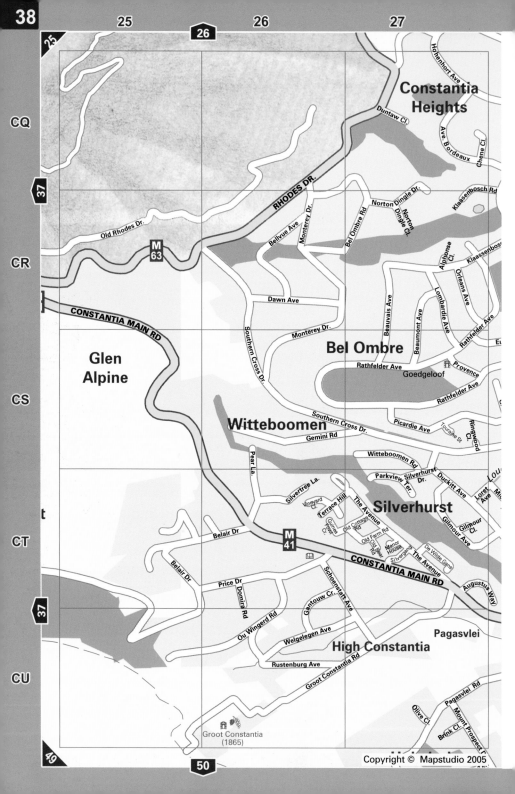

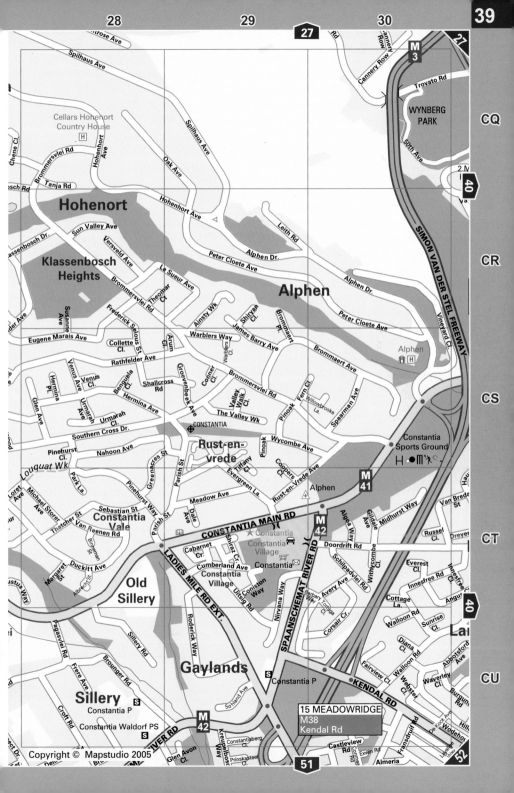

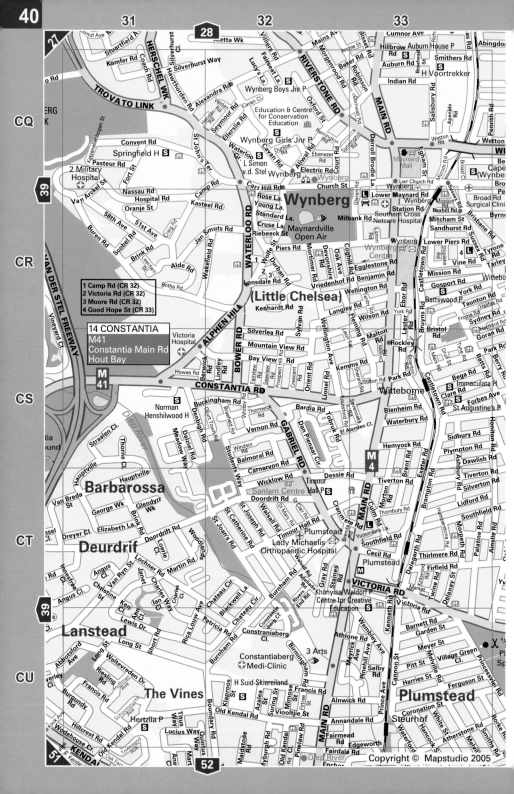

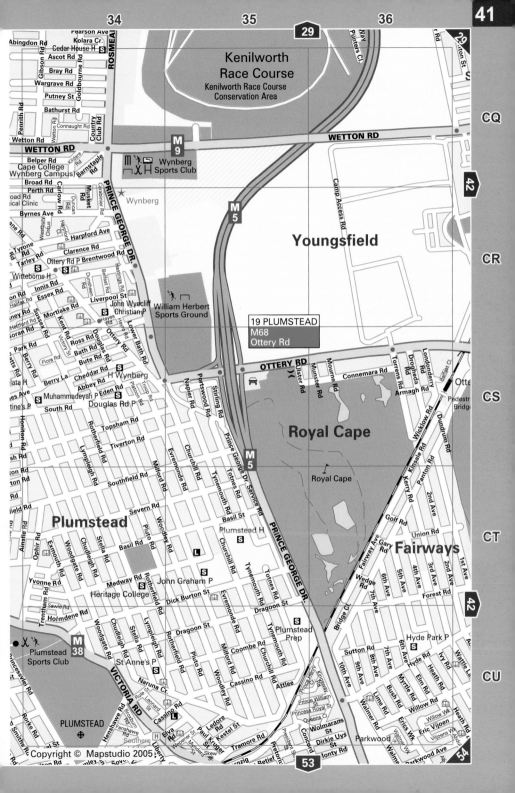

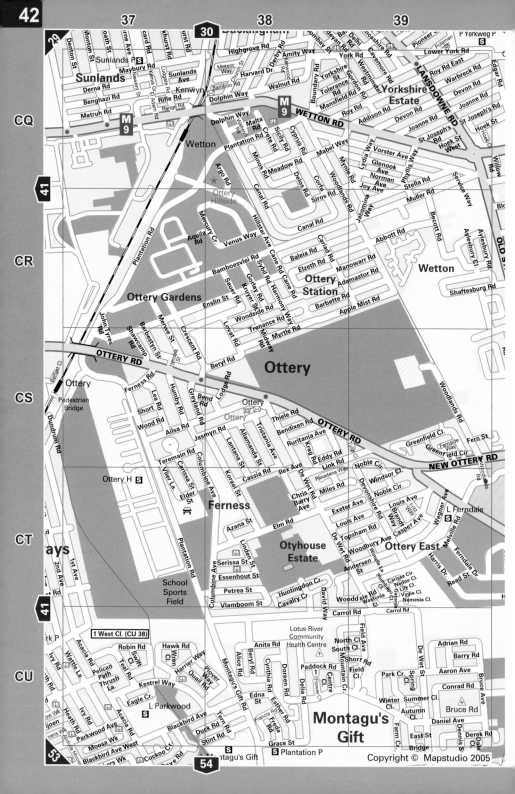

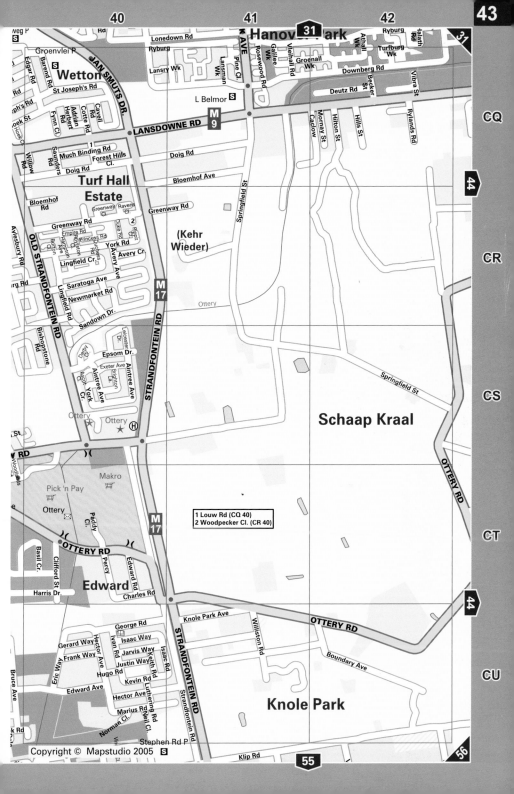

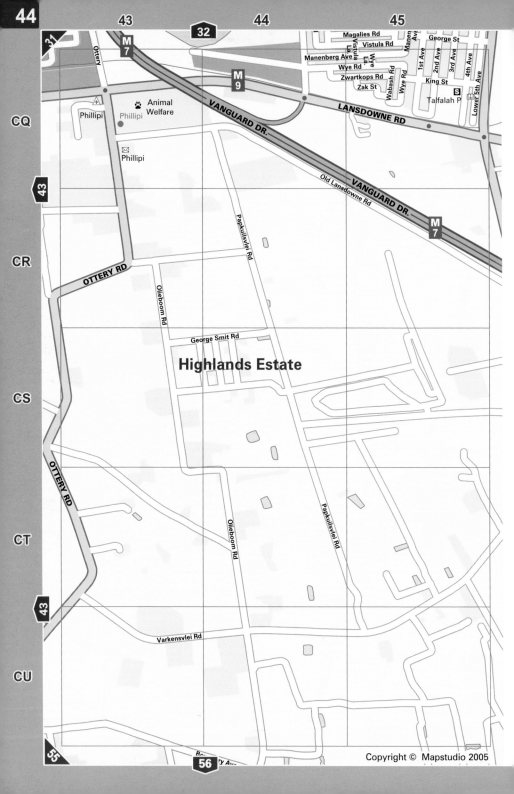

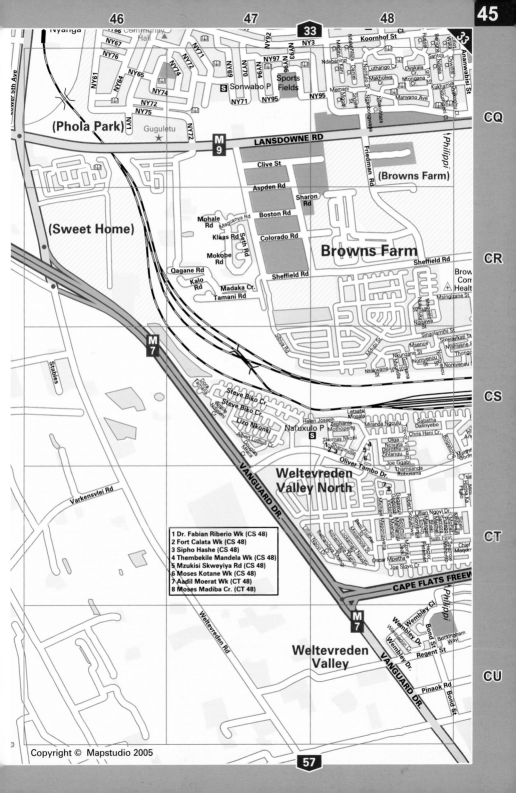

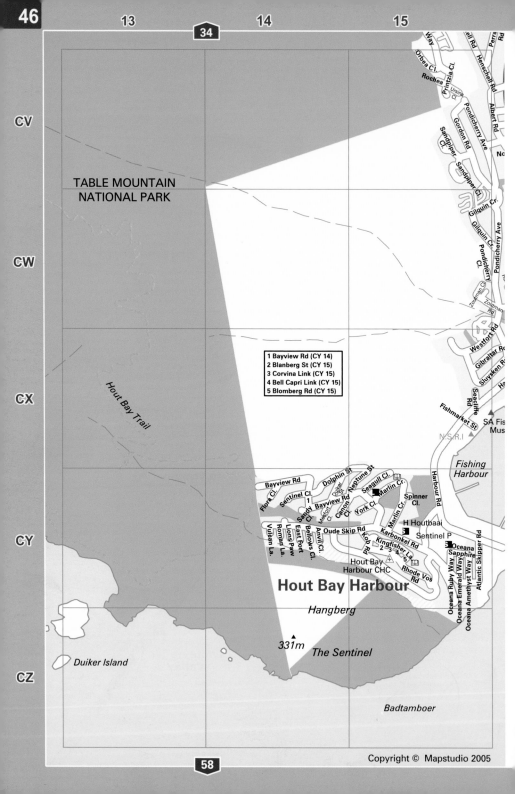

13 **34** 14 15

CV

**TABLE MOUNTAIN
NATIONAL PARK**

CW

Hout Bay Trail

CX

1 Bayview Rd (CY 14)
2 Blanberg St (CY 15)
3 Corvina Link (CY 15)
4 Bell Capri Link (CY 15)
5 Blomberg Rd (CY 15)

Fishmarket St

N.S.R.I

SA Fis
Mus

*Fishing
Harbour*

Bayview Rd

Dolphin St

Neptune St

Seagull Cl.

Marlin Cr.

Spinner
Cl.

Flora Cl.

Sentinel Cl.

Sandy Cl.

Bayview Rd

York Cl.

Marlin Cl.

H Houtbaai

Sentinel P

Harbour Rd

Seacliffe
Rd

Westfort Rd

Gibraltar Rd

Sluysken Rd

CY

Vulcan La.

Romar La.

Lions Paw

East Fort

Bellows Cl.

Anvil Cl.

Oude Skip Rd

Kob Rd

Karbonkel Rd

Kingfisher La.

Oceana
Sapphire

Oceana Ruby Way

Oceana Emerald Way

Oceana Amethyst Way

Atlantic Skipper Rd

Hout Bay
Harbour CHC

Rhode Vos
Rd

Hout Bay Harbour

Hangberg

331m *The Sentinel*

Duiker Island

CZ

Badtamboer

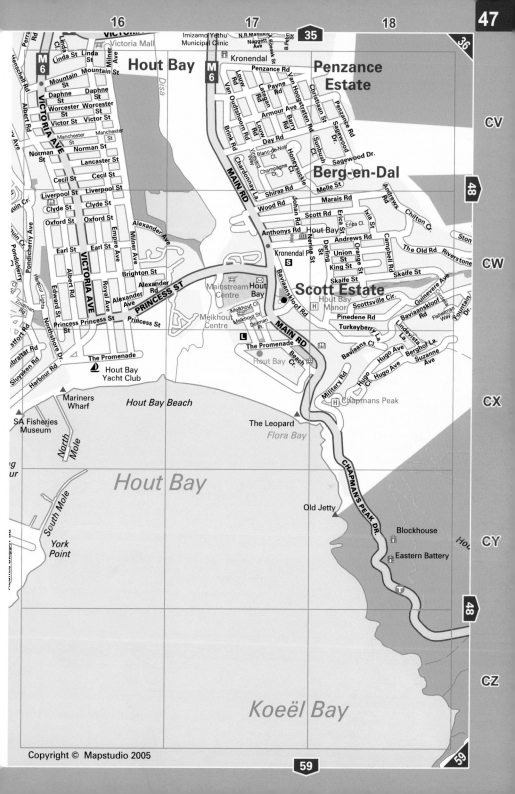

16   17   18

35

36

CV

CW

CX

CY

CZ

48

48

59

59

Hout Bay

Victoria Mall

Imizamo Yethu
Municipal Clinic

N.R Mandela
Naggett Ave

Kronendal

Penzance Rd

**Penzance
Estate**

M6

M6

Pereo
Rd

Glenschell Rd

Linda
Cl.

Linda St

Linda
St

Mountain

Mountain St

Milner
Ave

Disa

Louw
Rd

Van Hoogstraten Rd

Christian St

Penzance Rd

Sagewood
Dr.

Daphne
St

Daphne
St

Worcester

Worcester
St

Latzgan
Rd

Payne
Rd

Armour Ave

Barry
Rd

Sagewood
Dr.

Albert Rd

VICTORIA AVE

Victor St

Victor St

Van Oudtshoorn Rd

Louw
St

Day Rd

Sunbush
St

Honeysuckle

Berg-en-Dal

Manchester

Manchester
St

Brink Rd

Vineyard
Way

Blanc-de-Noir
Cl.

Champagne
Cl.

Champagne
Cl.

Norman
St

Norman St

Chardonnay La.

Shiraz Rd

Melle St

Andrews
Rd

Chilton Cr.

Cecil St

Cecil St

MAIN RD

Wood Rd

Johan
Rd

Marais Rd

Erica
St

Ixia St

Ston

Liverpool St

Liverpool St

Scott Rd

Erica St

Andrews Rd

The Old Rd

Riverstone

Clyde St

Clyde St

Alexander Ave

Anthonys Rd

Hout Bay

Nerine
St

Darling
St

Union
St

Orange
St

Campbell Dr.

Oxford St

Oxford St

Empire Ave

Milner Ave

Kronendal P.

King St

Skaife St

Skaife St

Guinevere Ave

Baviaanskloof
Rd

Earl St

Earl St

Brighton St

S

Hout Bay
Manor

Scottsville Cir.

Linevista
La.

Fisherman
Way

Fountain
Dr.

Pondicherry

Albert Rd

Royal Ave

Alexander
Ave

Alexander
Rd

Scott Estate

H

Pinedene Rd

Baviaanskloof
Rd

Suzanne
Ave

Norman
St

Lancaster St

PRINCESS ST

Mainstream
Centre

Hout
Bay

Bavianskloof Rd

Turkeyberry La.

Linevista
La.

Berghof La.

Hout Bay
Lights

Harbour Rd

Zourman
Rd

Edward St

Princess
St

Princess
St

Alexander
Rd

Princess St

Melkhout Cr.

Melkhout St

MAIN RD

Baviaans Cl.

Hugo
Cl.

Hugo Ave

Hugo Ave

Melkhout
Centre

Dolman
Pl.

Military Rd

Hugo
Cl.

Fountain
Rd

Gibraltar Rd

Sluysken Rd

The Promenade

L

The Promenade

Beach
Cr.

Chapmans Peak

Northshore Dr.

Harbour Rd

Hout Bay
Yacht Club

Hout Bay Cr.

Mariners
Wharf

Hout Bay Beach

H

Chapmans Peak

SA Fisheries
Museum

North
Mole

The Leopard

Flora Bay

Hout Bay

Old Jetty

CHAPMAN'S PEAK DR.

Hou

ng

ur

South Mole

*York
Point*

Blockhouse

Eastern Battery

T

Koeël Bay

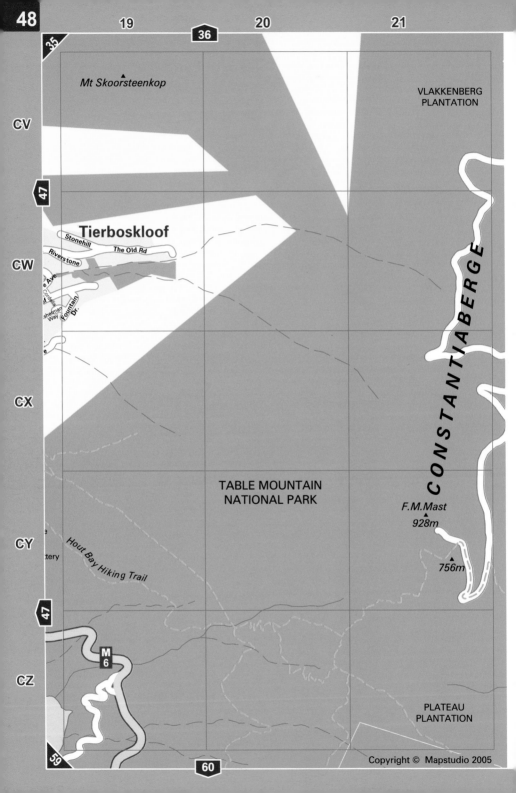

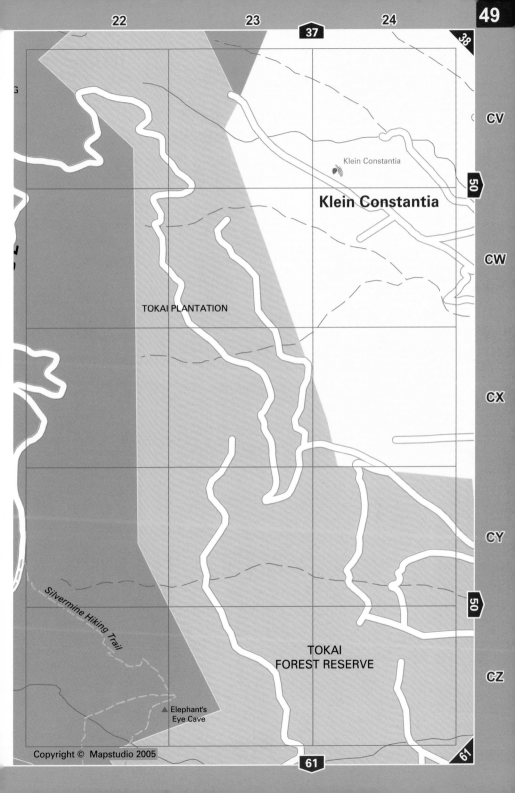

22   23   24

37

38

CV

50

Klein Constantia

Klein Constantia

CW

TOKAI PLANTATION

CX

CY

50

Silvermine Hiking Trail

TOKAI
FOREST RESERVE

CZ

▲ Elephant's
Eye Cave

61

61

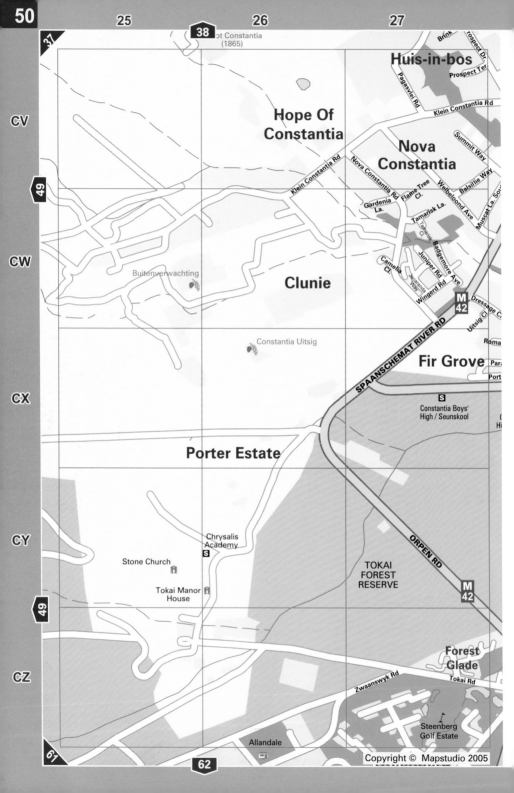

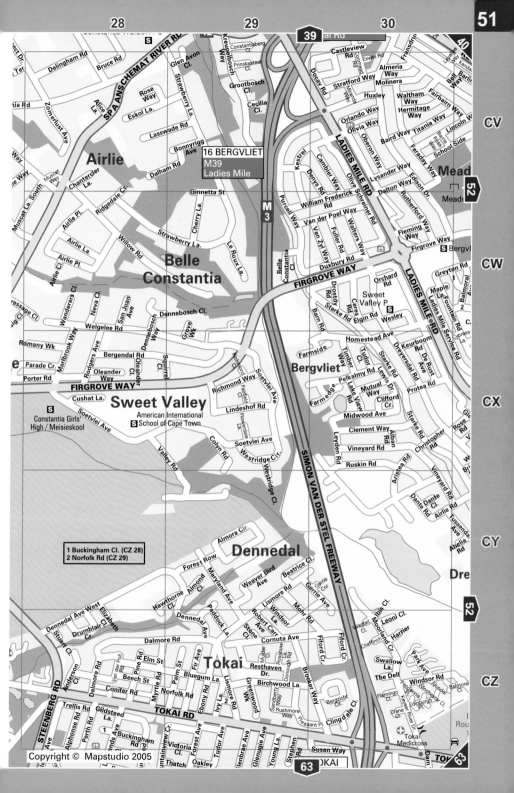

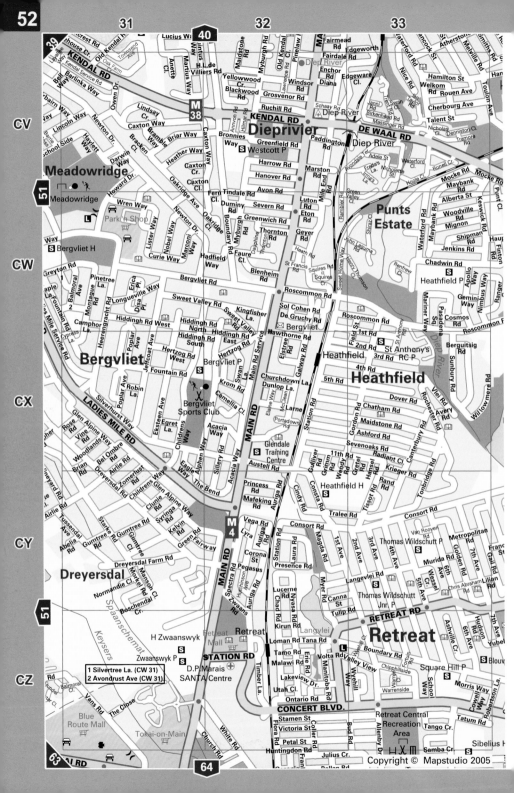

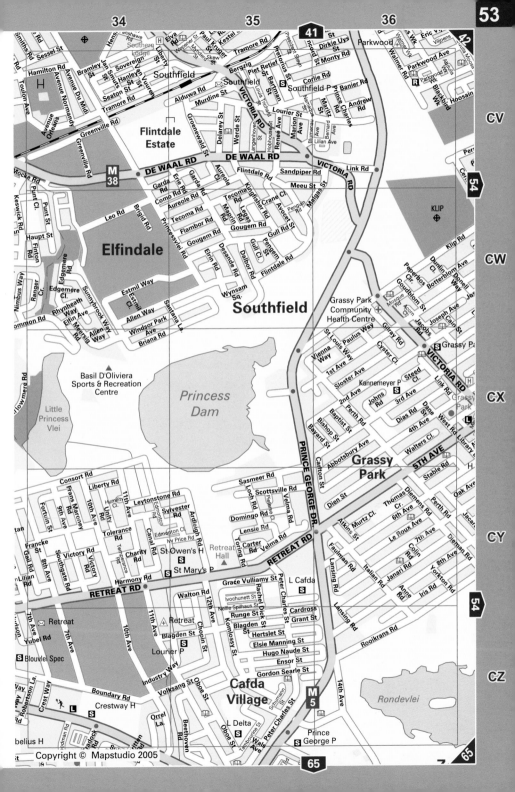

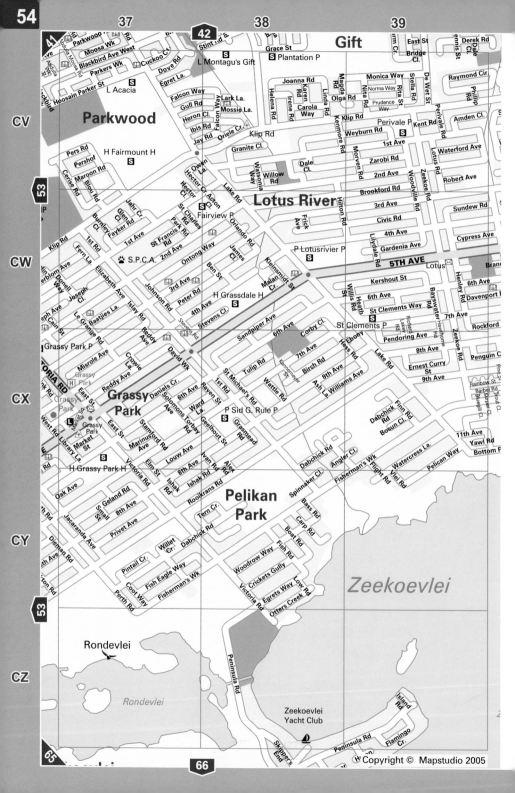

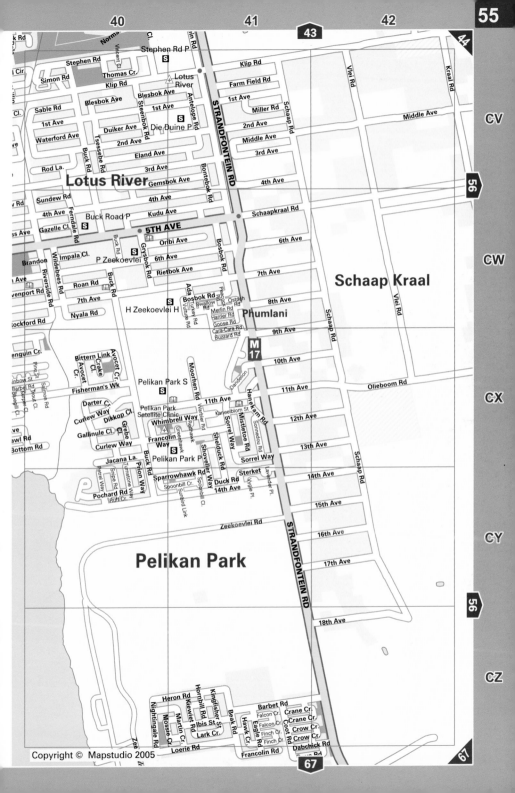

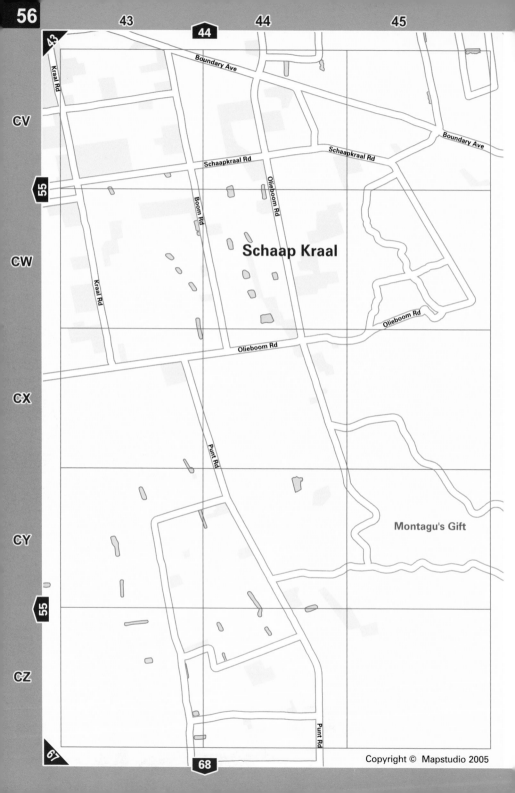

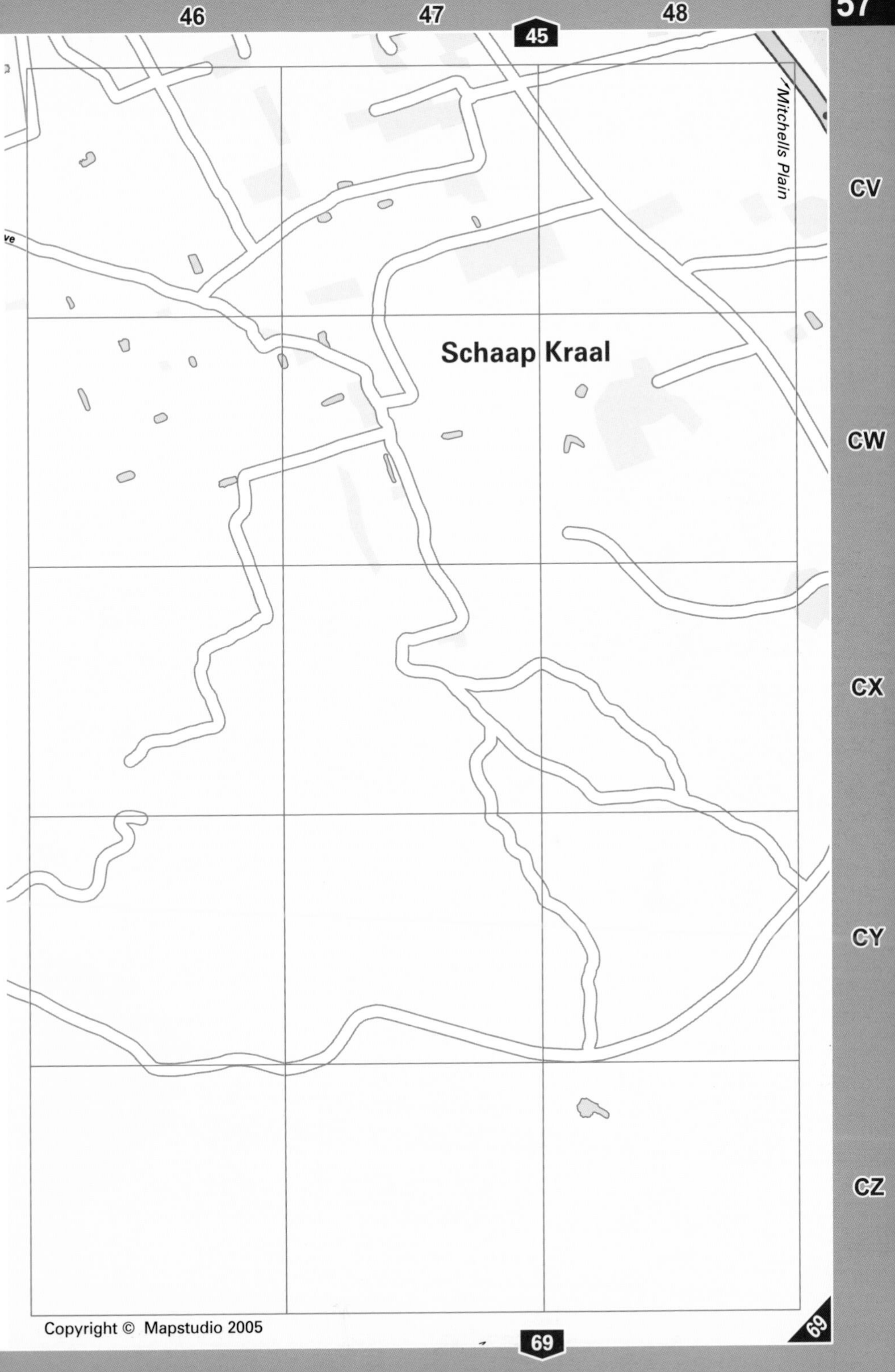
46
47
48
45
Mitchells Plain
ve
Schaap Kraal
CV
CW
CX
CY
CZ
69
69

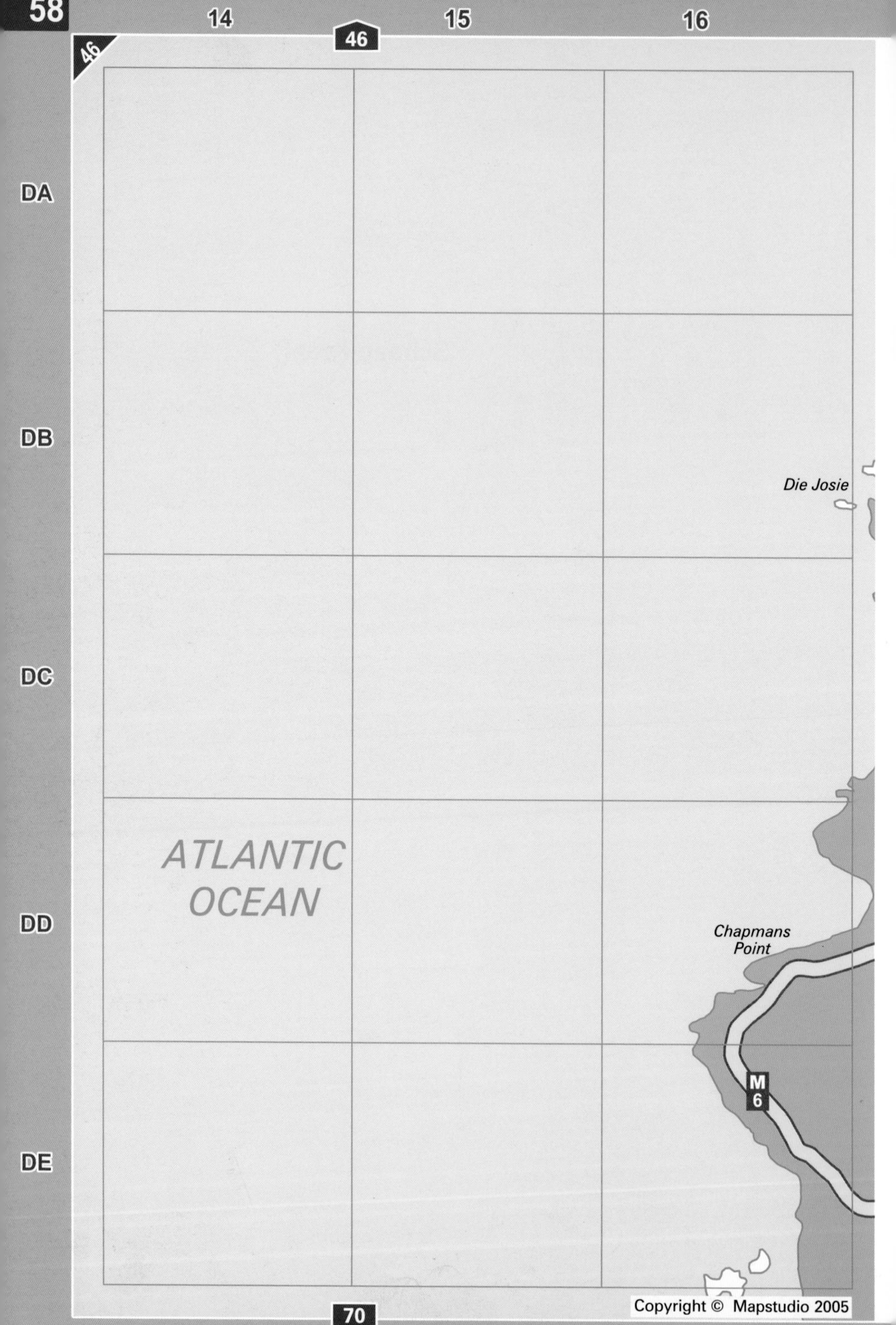

14
15
16
46
46
DA
DB
DC
DD
DE
Die Josie
ATLANTIC
OCEAN
Chapmans
Point
M
6
70
Copyright © Mapstudio 2005

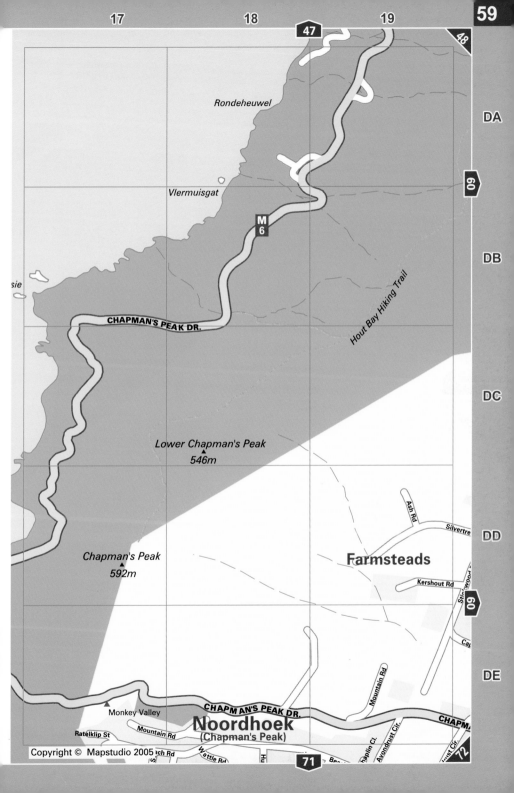

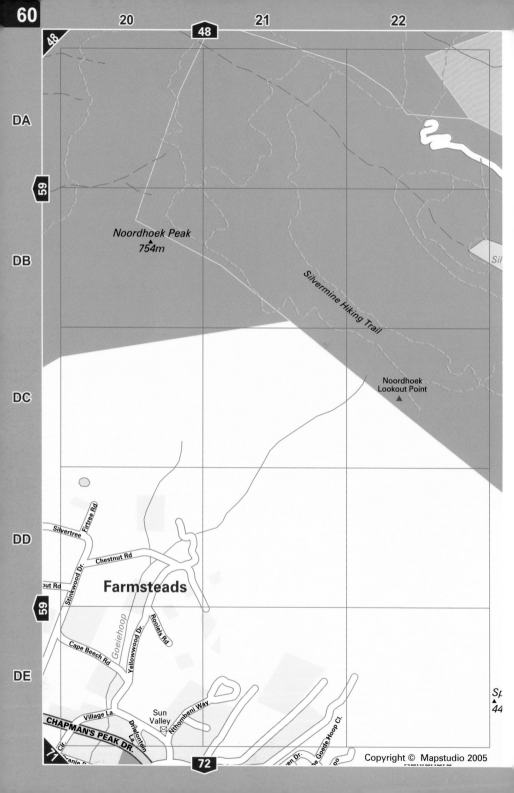

20   21   22

48

48

DA

59

Noordhoek Peak
754m

DB

Silvermine Hiking Trail

Sil

DC

Noordhoek
Lookout Point

Firtree Rd

Silvertree

DD

Chestnut Rd

Stinkwood Dr.

ut Rd

Farmsteads

Goeiehoop

Rooiels Rd

59

Yellowwood Dr.

Cape Beech Rd

DE

Village La.

Sun
Valley

Driefontein La.

Nthombeni Way

CHAPMAN'S PEAK DR.

Ch.

ranje

71

72

Goede Hoop Cl.

en Dr.

no

S
44

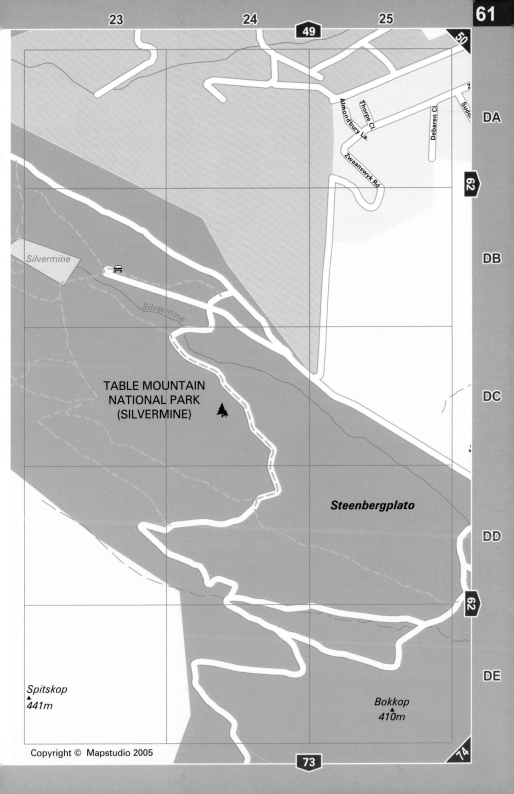

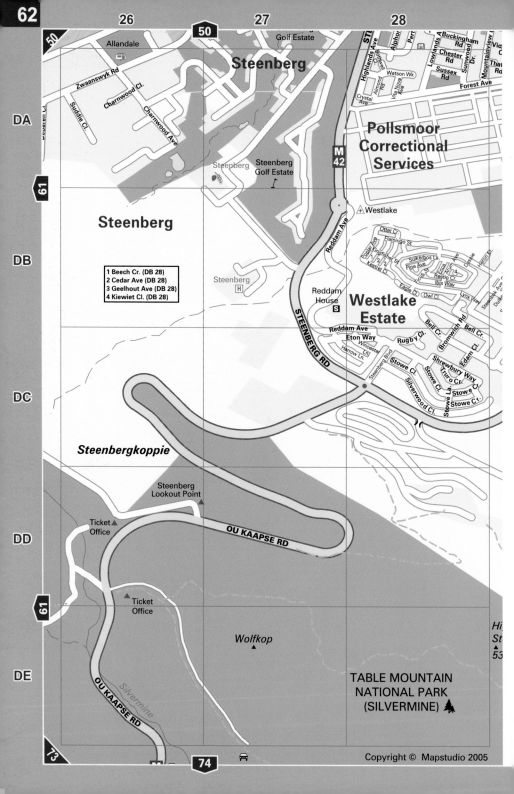

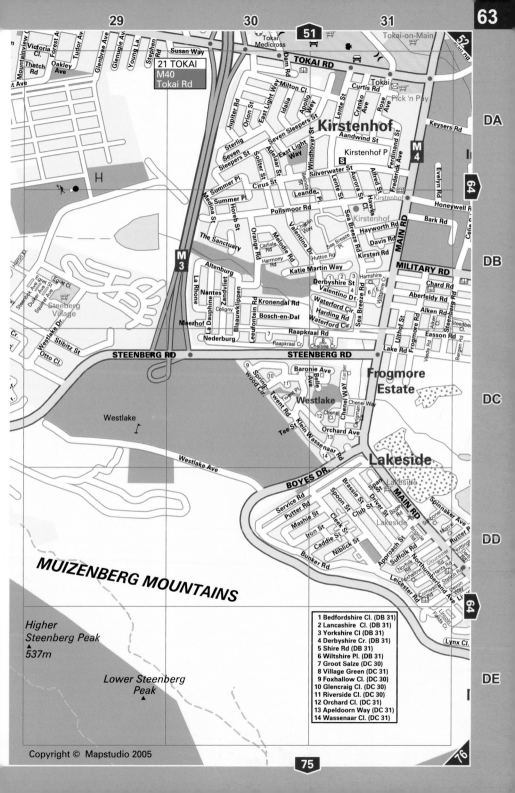

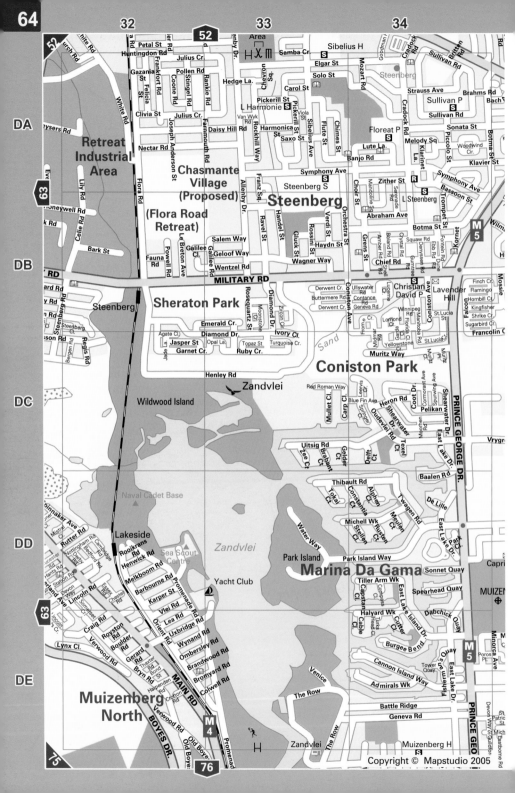

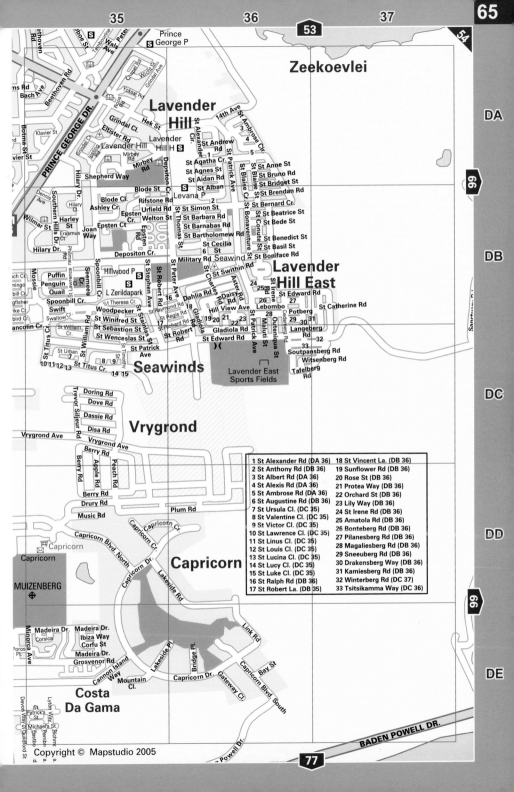

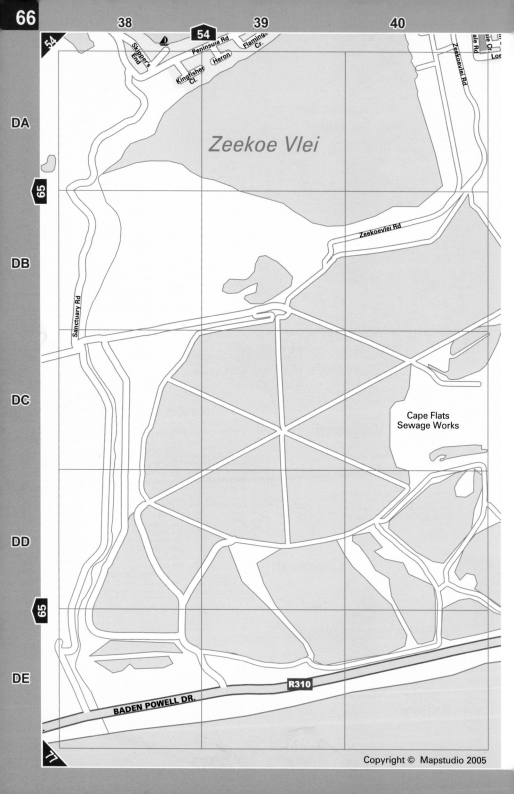

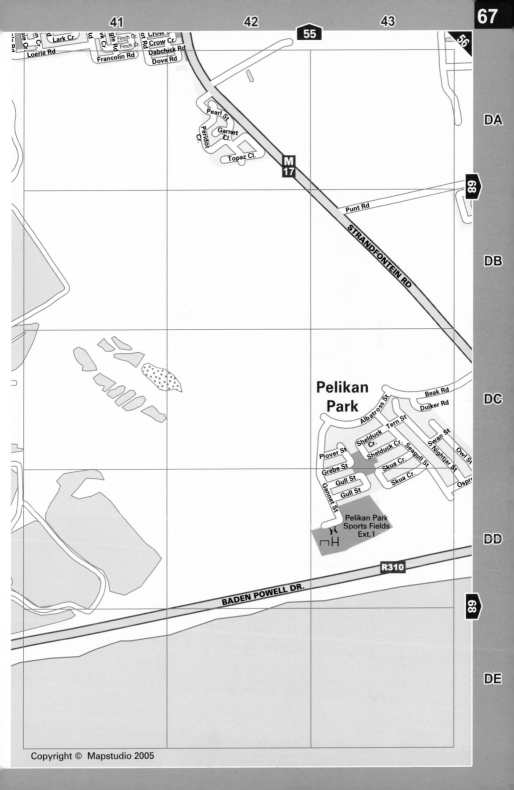

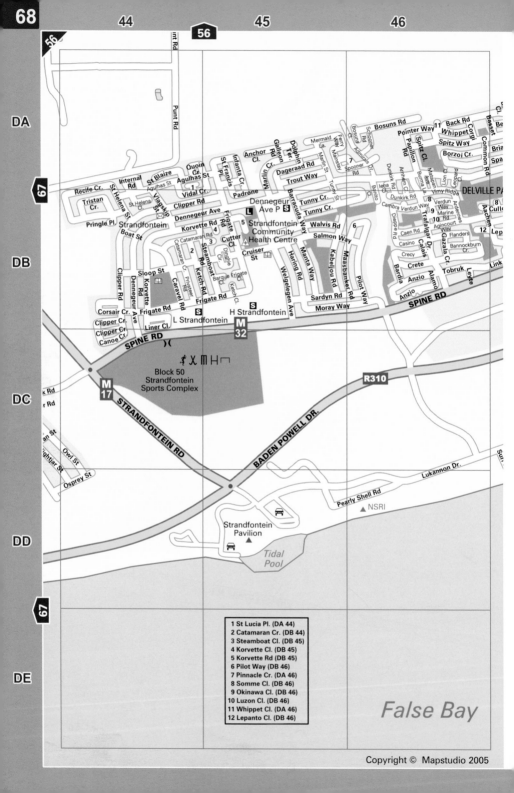

44   **56**   45   46

56

DA

67

Index of places (numbered on map):

1 St Lucia Pl. (DA 44)
2 Catamaran Cr. (DB 44)
3 Steamboat Cl. (DB 45)
4 Korvette Cl. (DB 45)
5 Korvette Rd (DB 45)
6 Pilot Way (DB 46)
7 Pinnacle Cr. (DA 46)
8 Somme Cl. (DB 46)
9 Okinawa Cl. (DB 46)
10 Luzon Cl. (DB 46)
11 Whippet Cl. (DA 46)
12 Lepanto Cl. (DB 46)

False Bay

Tidal Pool

Strandfontein Pavilion

NSRI

Lukannon Dr.

Pearly Shell Rd

BADEN POWELL DR.

R310

SPINE RD

STRANDFONTEIN RD

Block 50
Strandfontein
Sports Complex

M 17

M 32

DB

DC

DD

DE

67

Punt Rd

Recife Cr.
Tristan Cr.
Pringle Pl.
Internal Rd
St Blaize
St Helena Rd
Agulhas Cr.
Vlakskip
Strandfontein
Boat St
Quoin Cr.
Agulhas St
Vidal Cr.
Clipper Rd
Dennegeur Ave
Korvette Rd
Catamaran Rd
Catamaran
Sloop St
Clipper Rd
Dennegeur Ave
Corsair Cr.
Clipper Cr.
Clipper Cr.
Canoe Ct.
Frigate Rd
Korvette
Caravel Rd
Ketch Rd
Liner Cl.
Barque Cr.
Privateer Cr.
Ketch Cr.
Dinghie Circ.
Cutter Cl.
Steamboat Rd
Frigate Rd
Frigate Rd
L Strandfontein
H Strandfontein
Anchor Cl.
St Francis Pl.
Infanta Cr.
Galleon Rd
Marlin Cr.
Dolphin Ter.
Dageraad Rd
Trout Way
Padrone
Dennegeur Ave P
Strandfontein Community Health Centre
Cruiser St
Barracuda Way
Haring Rd
Welgelegen Ave
Sardyn Rd
Manta Way
Tunny Cr.
Tunny Cr.
Walvis Rd
Salmon Way
Moray Way
Kabeljou Rd
Maasbanker Rd
Pilot Way
SPINE RD

Mermaid La.
Ferry La.
Bosuns Rd
Pointer Way
Back Rd
Whippet Cl.
Corgi Cl.
Spitz Way
Borzoi Cr.
Papillon Rd
Spooner Rd
Verdun Way
Marine Rd
Agincourt Way
Flanders
Vimy Ridge
Trafalgar Dr.
Dieppe Rd
Caen Rd
Casino
Crecy
Bardia
Anzio
Anzio
Crete
Tobruk
Gazala Cr.
Bannockburn Cr.
Calais
Verdun Way
Cambrai
Dunkirk Rd
Arnhem Rd
Bunga La.
Masasa Ave
DELVILLE PA
SPINE RD

Copyright © Mapstudio 2005

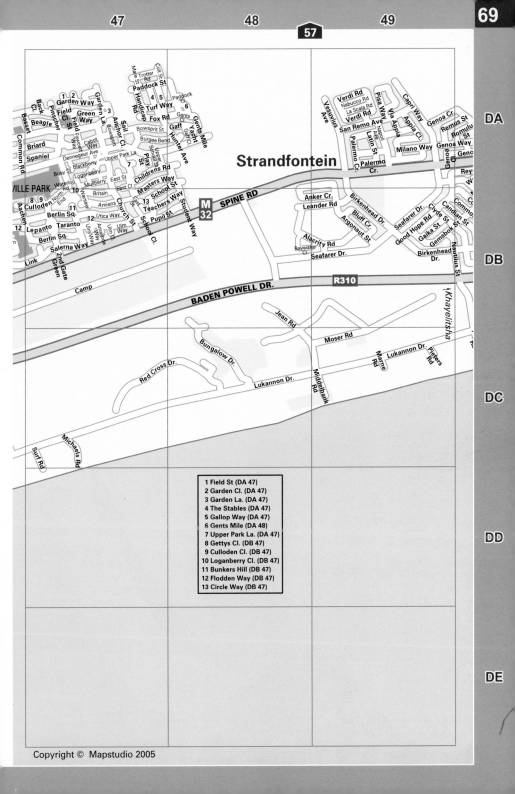

57

Strandfontein

M 32

SPINE RD

R310

BADEN POWELL DR.

DA

DB

DC

DD

DE

1 Field St (DA 47)
2 Garden Cl. (DA 47)
3 Garden La. (DA 47)
4 The Stables (DA 47)
5 Gallop Way (DA 47)
6 Gents Mile (DA 48)
7 Upper Park La. (DA 47)
8 Gettys Cl. (DB 47)
9 Culloden Cl. (DB 47)
10 Loganberry Cl. (DB 47)
11 Bunkers Hill (DB 47)
12 Flodden Way (DB 47)
13 Circle Way (DB 47)

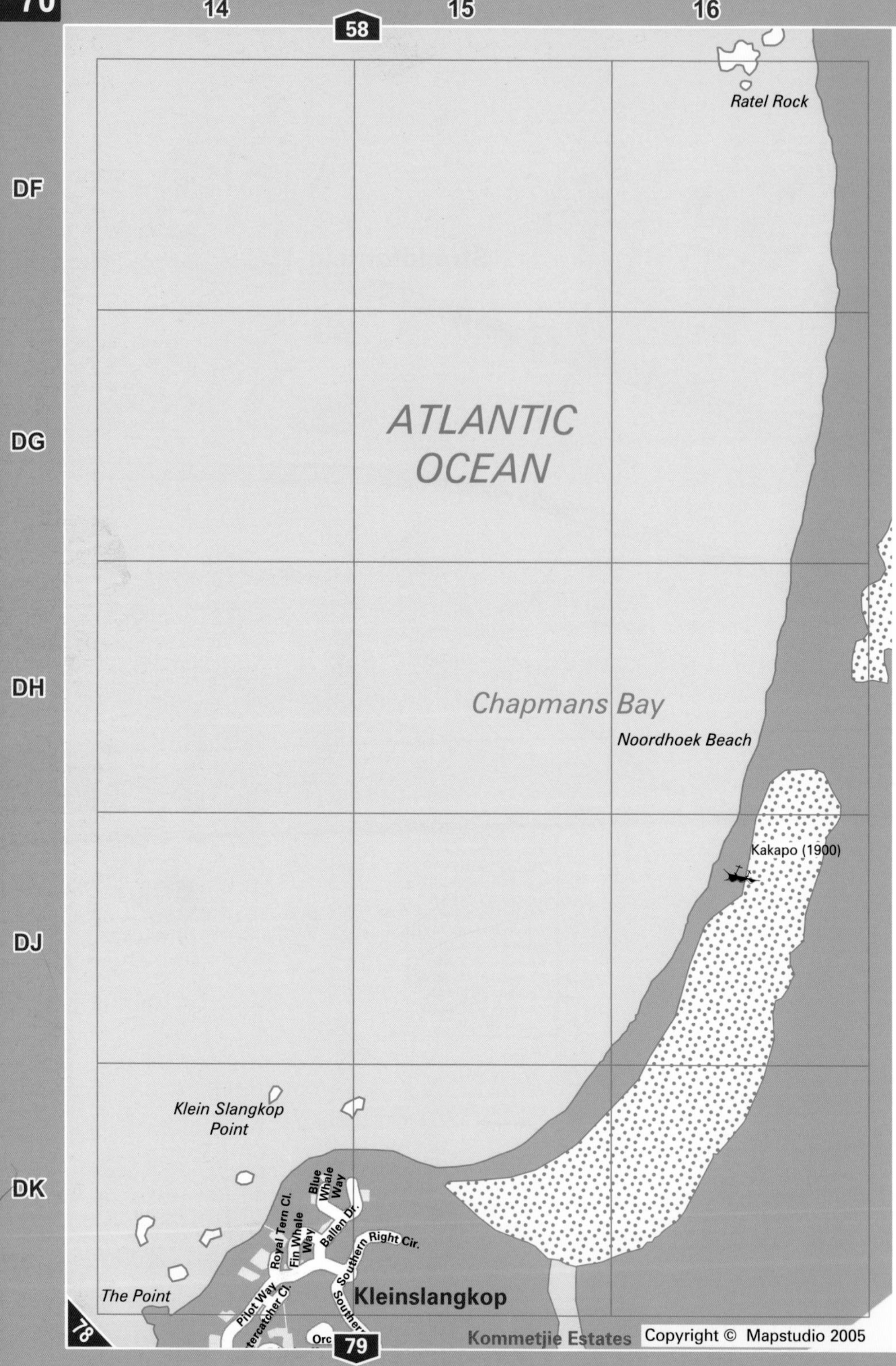

14   15   16

58

Ratel Rock

DF

DG

ATLANTIC OCEAN

DH

Chapmans Bay

Noordhoek Beach

Kakapo (1900)

DJ

Klein Slangkop Point

DK

Blue Whale Way

Royal Tern Cl.

Fin Whale Way

Ballen Dr.

Southern Right Cir.

Pilot Way

stercatcher Cl.

Southern

The Point

Kleinslangkop

Orc

79

78

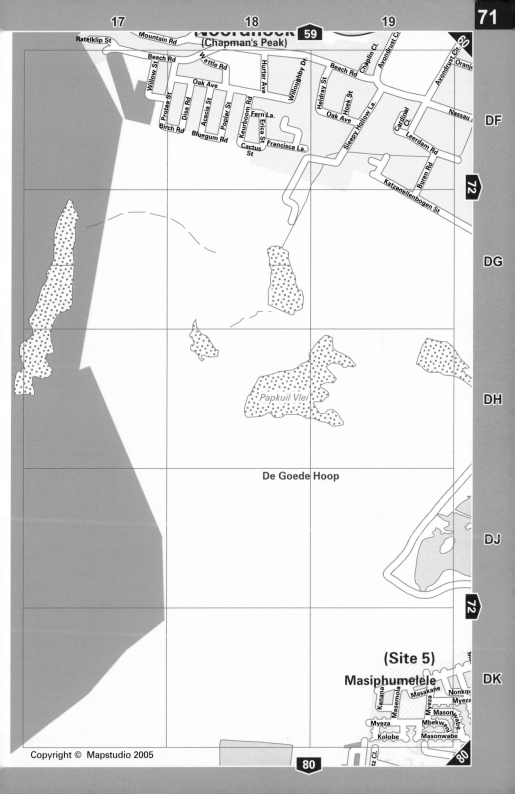

Noordhoek **59**
(Chapman's Peak)

Ratelklip St

Mountain Rd

Beach Rd

Willow St

Wattle Rd

Protea St

Oak Ave

Disa Rd

Birch Rd

Acacia St

Bluegum Rd

Poplar St

Keurboom Rd

Cactus St

Erica St

Fern La.

Francisca La.

Hunter Ave

Willoughby Dr.

Heldray St

Beach Rd

Hoek St

Oak Ave

Sleepy Hollow La.

Chaplin Cl.

Avondrust Cr.

Avondrust Cr.

Oranje

Cardinal Cl.

Leerdam Rd

Nassau

Buren Rd

Katzenellenbogen St

72

DF

DG

Papkuil Vlei

DH

De Goede Hoop

DJ

72

(Site 5)
Masiphumelele

Kanana

Masemola

Nonkqu

Masakane

Myeza

Myeza

Mason

Myeza

Mbekweni

Masonwabe

Kolobe

Masonwabe

DK

80

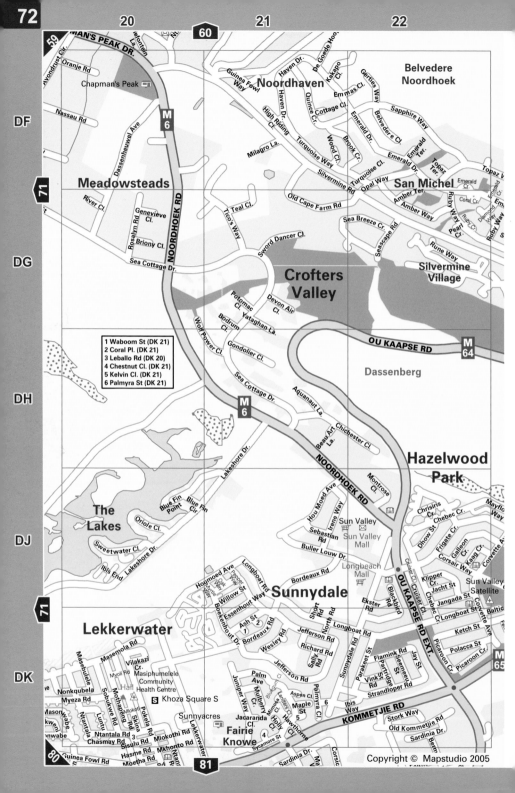

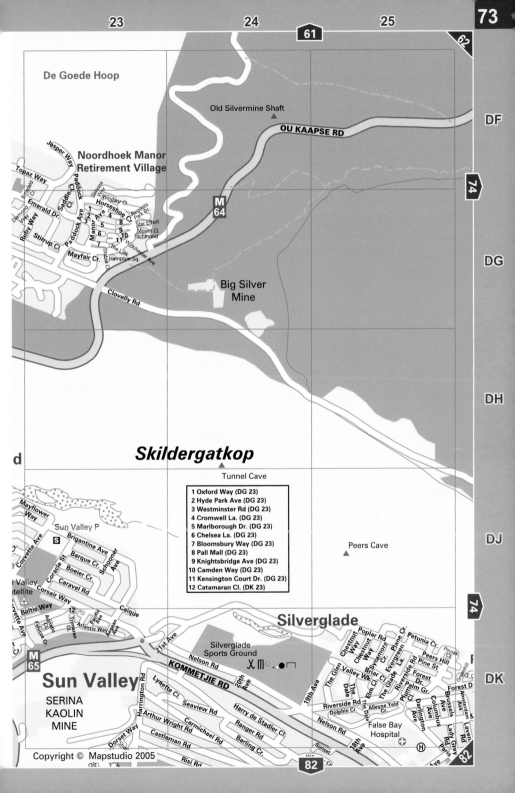

23   24   **61**   25   **62**

De Goede Hoop

Old Silvermine Shaft

OU KAAPSE RD

DF

74

Jasper Way

**Noordhoek Manor
Retirement Village**

Topaz Way

Paddock Cr.

Saddle Cl.

Emerald Cr.

Diamond Way

Emerald Dr.

Ruby Way

Emerald Cr.

Stirrup Cl.

Windsor Cl.

Simons Way

Horseshoe Ave

Paddock Ave

Manor

1 2 3 4 5 6 7 8 9 10 11

Residents Park Dr.

Star Effort

Mount Cl. Richmond

Witchester Ave

Mayfair Cr.

The Link

Hampton Sq.

M 64

Clovelly Rd

**Big Silver
Mine**

DG

DH

Skildergatkop

Tunnel Cave

1 Oxford Way (DG 23)
2 Hyde Park Ave (DG 23)
3 Westminster Rd (DG 23)
4 Cromwell La. (DG 23)
5 Marlborough Dr. (DG 23)
6 Chelsea La. (DG 23)
7 Bloomsbury Way (DG 23)
8 Pall Mall (DG 23)
9 Knightsbridge Ave (DG 23)
10 Camden Way (DG 23)
11 Kensington Court Dr. (DG 23)
12 Catamaran Cl. (DK 23)

Peers Cave

DJ

Mayflower Way

Sun Valley P

S

Brigantine Ave

Corvette Ave

Barque Cr.

Coracle St

Boeier Cr.

Schooner Ave

Caravel Rd

Corsair Way

Baltic Way

12

Pacific Ave

Caique

Trimaran Cr.

Adriatic Cr.

Felucca Cr.

Atlantic Way

Aegean Way

Valley Satellite

Corvette Ave

74

21st Ave

Silverglade

**Silverglade
Sports Ground**

Nelson Rd

M 65

Sun Valley

SERINA
KAOLIN
MINE

Harrington Rd

Lynette Cl.

KOMMETJIE RD

20th Ave

19th Ave

Seaview Rd

Carmichael Rd

Harry de Stadler Cl.

Ranger Rd

Barling Cr.

Dorset Way

Arthur Wright Rd

Castleman Rd

Risi Rd

Riverside Rd

Dolphin Cr.

Nelson Rd

The Glen

The Dale

Valley Wk

The Dale

Elm Cl.

Riverside Rd

Streamway

The Glade

Poplar Rd

Chestnut Way

Chestnut Way

Briar Way

Evergreen Cl.

Plane Cr.

Riverside Rd

Palm Gr.

Forest Dr.

Plumar Cl.

Plane Cr.

Petunia Cr.

Peers Hill

Pine St

Pinoak

Columbus Ave

Brussels Cl.

Forest Dr.

Amsterdam Cr.

Greenhill

Lady Grey

Lavender

Paris

Darlington Ave

The Alleyne Yeld Cr.

**False Bay
Hospital**

H

18th Ave

DK

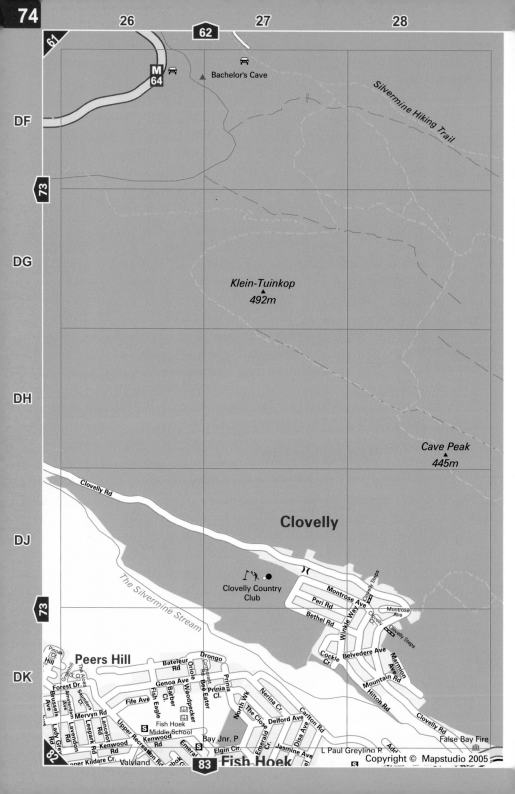

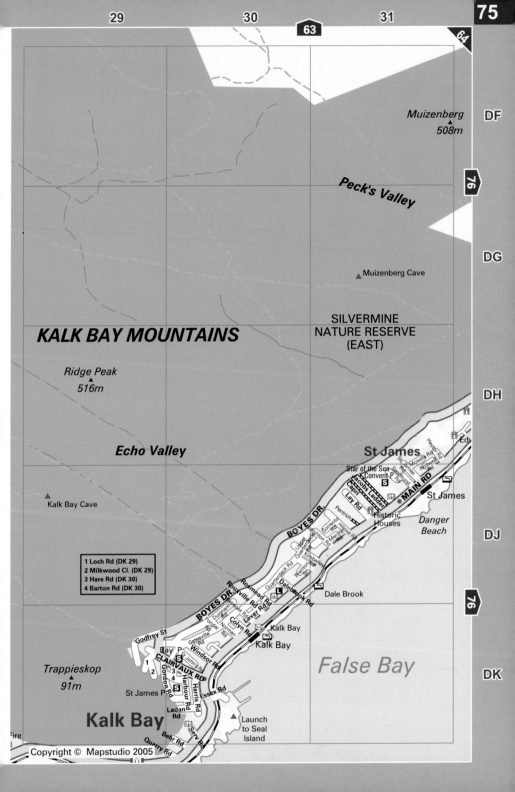

29   30   63   31   64

DF

76

Muizenberg
508m

DG

Peck's Valley

Muizenberg Cave

SILVERMINE
NATURE RESERVE
(EAST)

KALK BAY MOUNTAINS

DH

Ridge Peak
516m

Echo Valley

St James

Star of the Sea
Convent P.

Jacobs Ladder

Ley Rd

MAIN RD

St James

BOYES DR.

Historic
Houses

*Danger
Beach*

DJ

Kalk Bay Cave

Dale Brook

76

1 Loch Rd (DK 29)
2 Milkwood Cl. (DK 29)
3 Hare Rd (DK 30)
4 Barton Rd (DK 30)

BOYES DR.

Rosmead Rd

Rouxville Rd

Dalebrook Rd

Dale Brook

False Bay

Lever Rd

Godfrey St

Kalk Bay

Kalk Bay

*Trappieskop
91m*

CLAIRVAUX RD

Windsor Rd

Covin Rd

Gatesville Rd

St John's Rd

1
2
3
4

Gordon Rd

Harbour Rd

Harris Rd

Essex Rd

DK

St James P.

Ladan
Rd

Behr Rd

Serv Rd

Launch
to Seal
Island

Kalk Bay

Fire

Quarry Rd

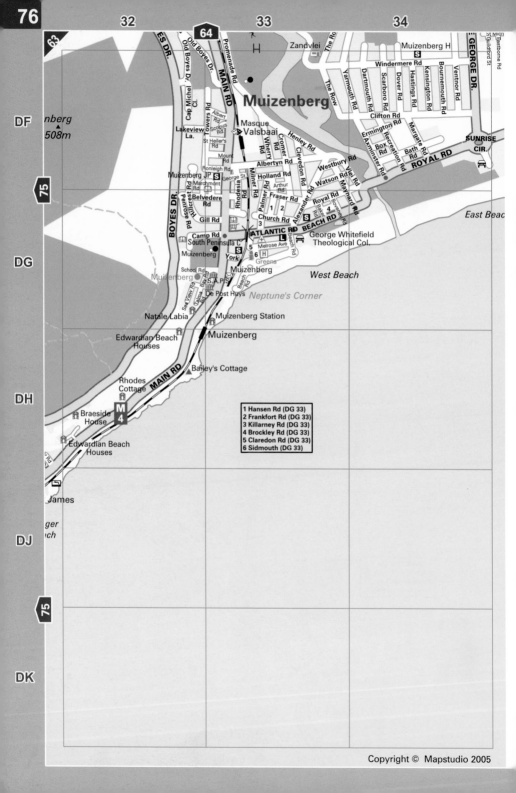

32 33 34

63

64

ES DR.

Old Boyes Dr.

Cap. Michel Cl.

Promenade Rd

MAIN RD

Zandvlei

Muizenberg H

GEORGE DR.

St Mich

St Guildford St

Eastbourne Rd

Windermere Rd

Yarmouth Rd

Dartmouth Rd

Scarboro Rd

Dover Rd

Hastings Rd

Kensington Rd

Bournemouth Rd

Ventnor Rd

The Row

The Row

Muizenberg

Clifton Rd

Ermington Rd

Margate Rd

Recreation Rd

Axminster Rd

Box Rd

Bath Rd

ROYAL RD

SUNRISE CIR.

DF

nberg
▲
508m

Lakeview La.

St Heller's Rd

Towers Rd

Albert Rd

Scobus Rd

Masque
Valsbaai

Henley Rd

Clevedon Rd

Cromer Rd

Wherry Rd

Westbury Rd

Watson Rd

Wiel Rd

75

BOYES DR.

Mount Rd

Ronleigh Rd.

Muizenberg JP S

Marchmont

Belvedere Rd

Gill Rd

George St

Rhodes Rd

Milner Rd

Palmer Rd

Holland Rd

Albertyn Rd

Fraser Rd

1   2

Arthur Rd

3

Church Rd

Alexander Rd

Royal Rd

4

Maynard Rd

Boyes Rd

ATLANTIC RD

BEACH RD

East Beac

Camp Rd

South Peninsula C

Muizenberg

York

5

Melrose Ave

L

6 **H**

George Whitefield
Theological Col.

DG

Muizenberg

School Rd

Sea View Rd

Tauma Rd

Muizenberg S.A.P.

De Post Huys

Muizenberg

Greens

West Beach

Neptune's Corner

Natale Labia

Muizenberg Station

Edwardian Beach
Houses

Muizenberg

DH

Rhodes
Cottage

MAIN RD

Bailey's Cottage

M 4

Braeside
House

Edwardian Beach
Houses

| 1 Hansen Rd (DG 33) |
| 2 Frankfort Rd (DG 33) |
| 3 Killarney Rd (DG 33) |
| 4 Brockley Rd (DG 33) |
| 5 Claredon Rd (DG 33) |
| 6 Sidmouth (DG 33) |

James

ger
ch

DJ

75

DK

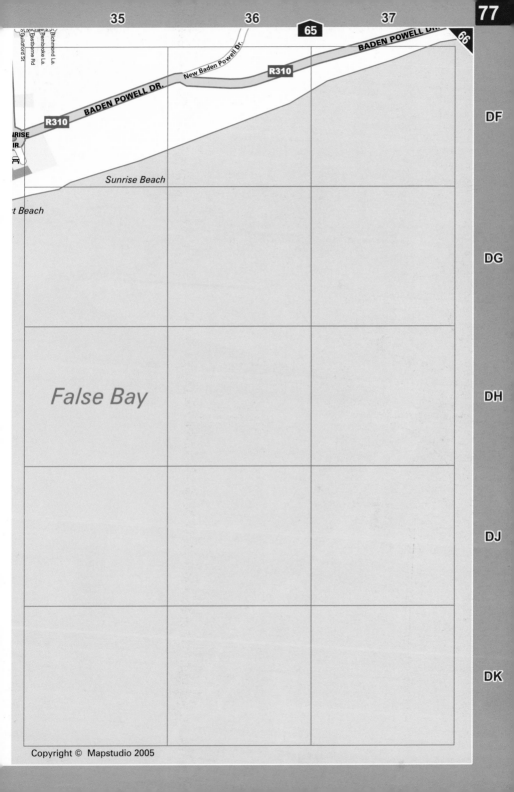

65

66

BADEN POWELL DR.

New Baden Powell Dr.

R310

BADEN POWELL DR.

R310

RISE
R.

Sunrise Beach

t Beach

False Bay

DF

DG

DH

DJ

DK

DL

DM

DN

DO

DP

The Point

Bokram Beach

Long Beach

Imhoff

Orca Cl.

Southern light...

Pilot Way

Oystercatcher Cl.

IMHOFF`S PARK

Pelican Pl.

Gannet Cl.

Wireless Rd

Kingfisher Rd

Duiker Dr.

Pipers Cl.

Seeliger Rd

Oyster Cl.

Bijou Cl.

Fuchsia Cl.

Riverside Dr

Topaz Cl.

Sandstone Rd

Nicholl Ave

Can...

Flamingo Dr.

Weavers End

Swallow La.

Forsyth Rd

Kelp Rd

Melkbout Ave

Ixia Ave

Beach Ave

Diemaar Rd

Surf Way

Benning Dr.

Arum Ave

Gladioli Way

Arum Ave

Africander Ave

Huskisson Way

Van der Horst Ave

Kommetjie

Somerset Way

Beach Rd

Van Imhoff Way

Kommetjie

Kirsten Ave

Jacob Ave

Fisherman's Cove

Mariner's Cl.

Periwinkle Pl.

Periwinkle Cl.

Heron Cir.

Kommetjie Blvd

Sunbird Cl.

Sunbird Cir.

Wireless Rd

Osborne St

Kommetjie P

KOMMETJIE RD

Kommetjie Bay

Dreyer Rd

Teubes Rd

Erica Rd

Van der Poll Ave

De Villiers St

Mountain Rd

Rubbi Rd

Andrews Rd

Maree St

Maree Cl.

Crassula Rd

Protea Ave

Disa Ave

Lighthouse Rd

Strelitzia Rd

Nerina Ave

Clan Monroe Ave

Aloe Cl.

Lookout Wk

Slangkop Point Lighthouse (1919)

Barry's

MAIN RD

M 65

Medusa 977

Tidal Pool

The Anchor

Sweet Water

MAIN RD

M 65

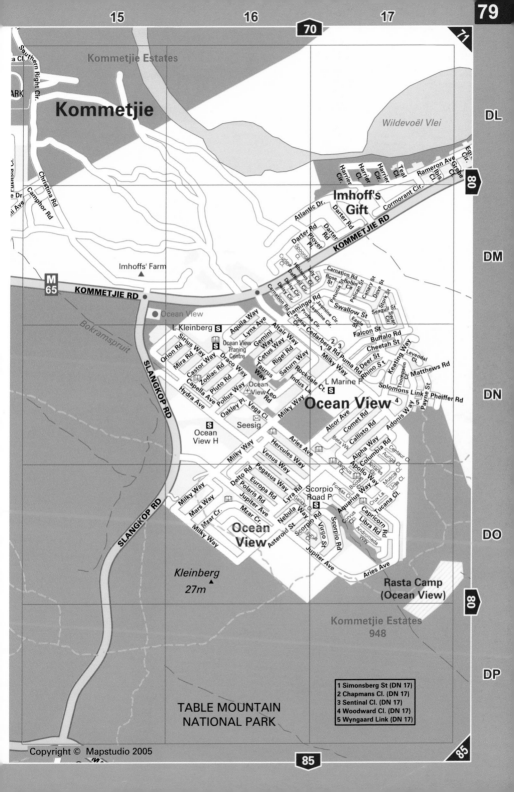

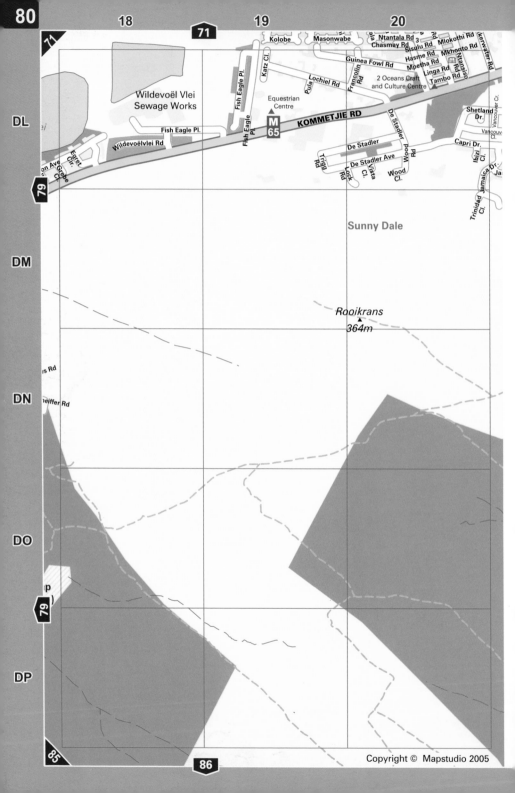

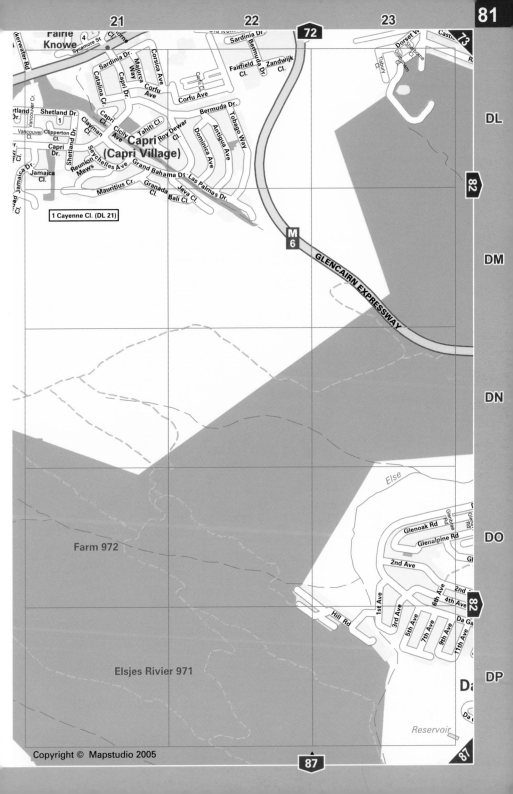

Fairie
Knowe

Sycamore St

21

22

72

23

Old Rum

Sardinia Dr.

Bermuda Dr.

Fairfield Cl.

Zandwijk Cl.

Corsica Ave

Sardinia Dr.

Majorca Way

Capri Dr.

Corfu Ave

Corfu Ave

Catalina Cl.

Bermuda Dr.

Tobago Way

Dorset W

Castle

73

Tisbury

Gillingham

Osborne

DL

Shetland Dr.

Vancouver Cr.

1

Capri Cl.

Clayman Cl.

Tahiti Cl.

Roy Dewar Cl.

Antigua Ave

Dominica Ave

Las Palmas Dr.

82

etland
Dr.

Clipperton Cl.

Cicily Ave

Capri
(Capri Village)

DM

Vancouver
Cl.

Capri Dr.

Shetland Dr.

Seychelles Ave

Reunion Mews

Grand Bahama Dr.

Jamaica Cl.

Jamaica Dr.

Mauritius Cr.

Granada Cl.

Java Cl.

Bali Cl.

Cl.

M
6

GLENCAIRN EXPRESSWAY

1 Cayenne Cl. (DL 21)

DN

Else

DO

Glenoak Rd

Glenalpine Rd

Farm 972

2nd Ave

2nd

Glenblae Rd

6th Ave

4th Ave

82

1st Ave

3rd Ave

5th Ave

7th Ave

9th Ave

11th Ave

Da Ga

Hill Rd

Elsjes Rivier 971

Da

DP

Da

Reservoir

87

87

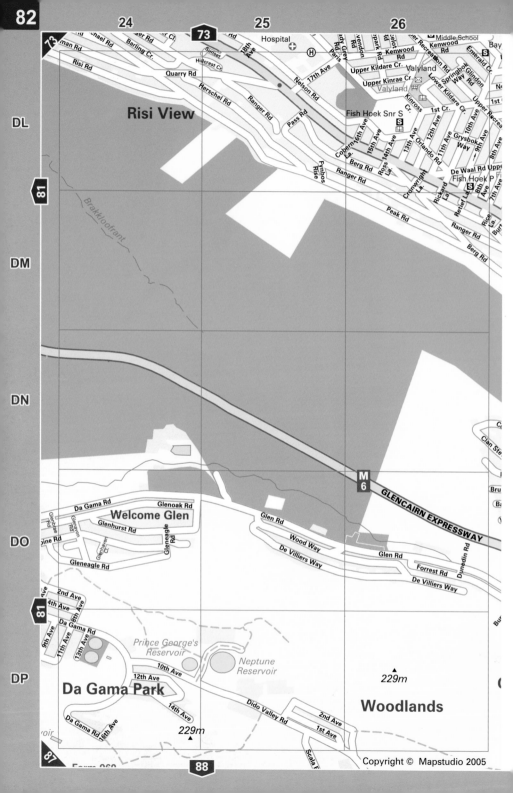

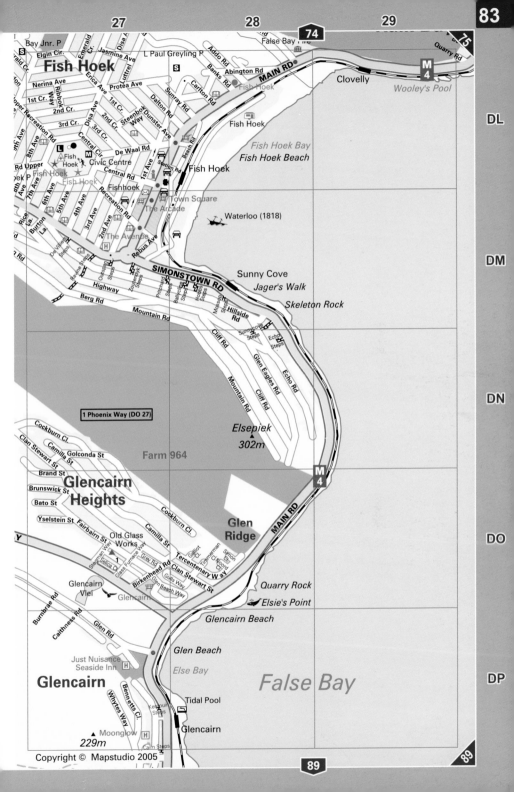

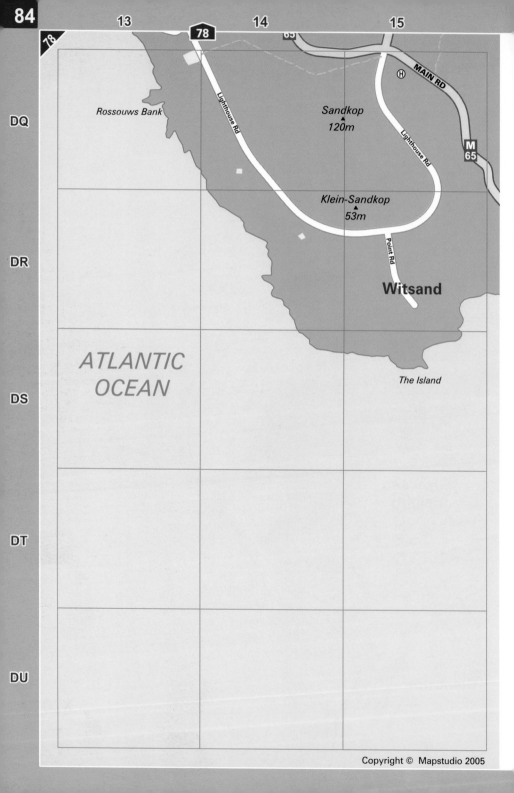

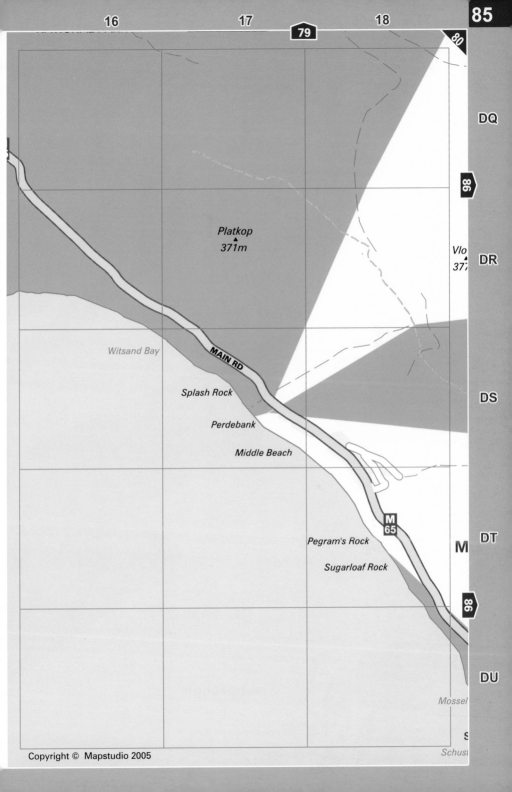

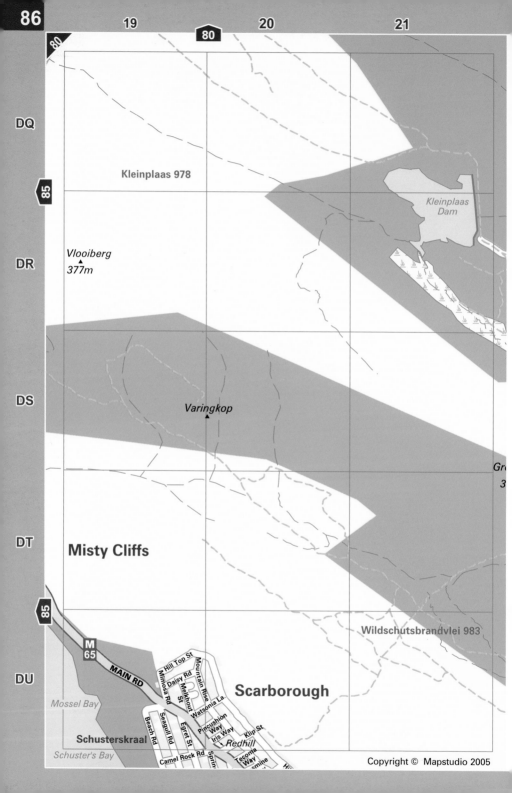

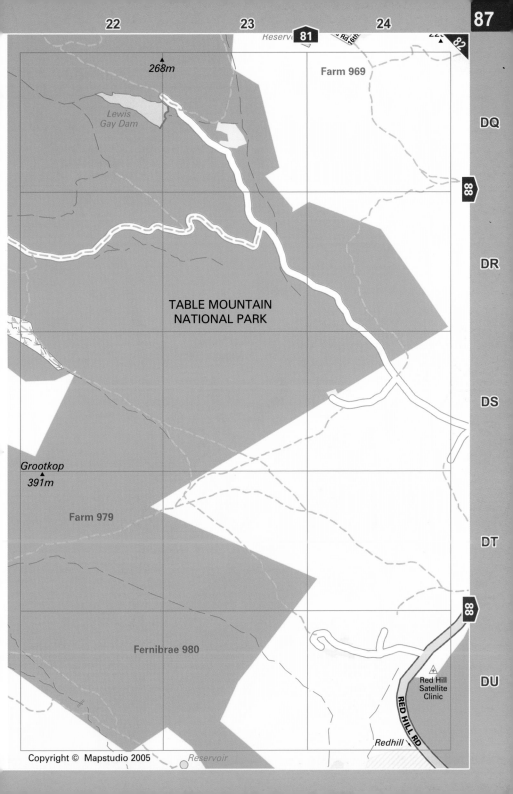

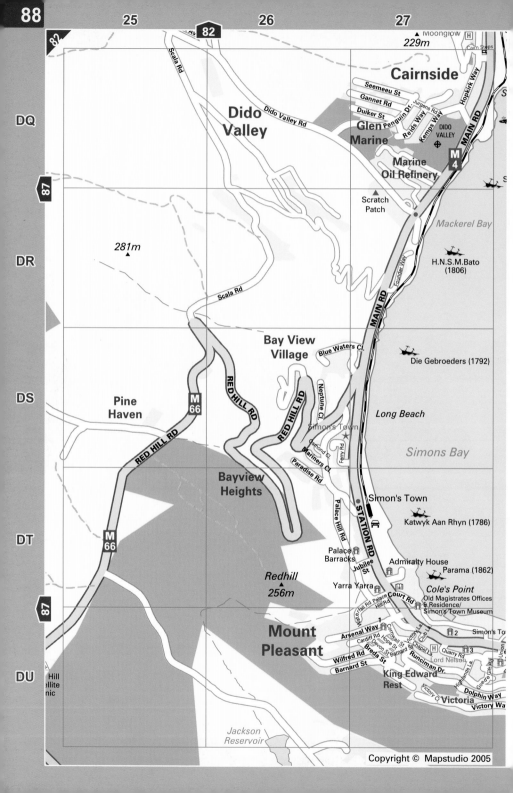

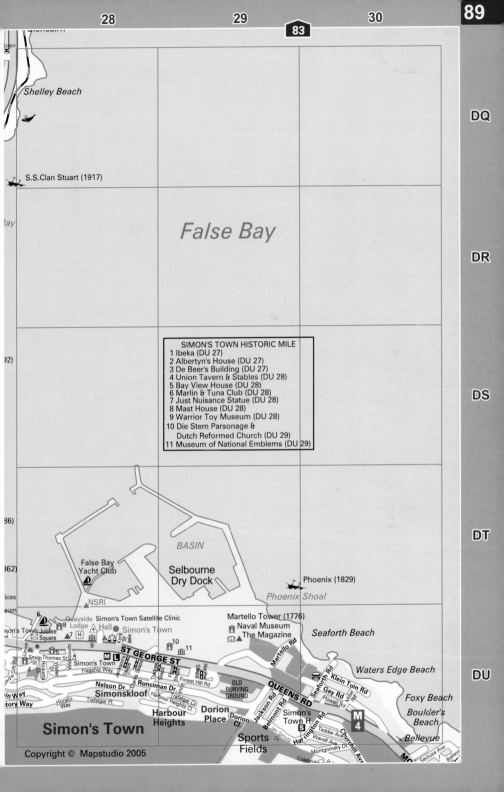

DQ

DR

DS

DT

DU

Shelley Beach

S.S.Clan Stuart (1917)

Bay

False Bay

```
SIMON'S TOWN HISTORIC MILE
 1 Ibeka (DU 27)
 2 Albertyn's House (DU 27)
 3 De Beer's Building (DU 27)
 4 Union Tavern & Stables (DU 28)
 5 Bay View House (DU 28)
 6 Marlin & Tuna Club (DU 28)
 7 Just Nuisance Statue (DU 28)
 8 Mast House (DU 28)
 9 Warrior Toy Museum (DU 28)
10 Die Stem Parsonage &
    Dutch Reformed Church (DU 29)
11 Museum of National Emblems (DU 29)
```

BASIN

False Bay
Yacht Club

Selbourne
Dry Dock

Phoenix (1829)

Phoenix Shoal

NSRI

Quayside   Simon's Town Satellite Clinic
Lodge   Hall   Simon's Town

Martello Tower (1776)
Naval Museum
The Magazine

Seaforth Beach

Simon's Town Jubilee
Square

Simon's Town

ST GEORGE ST

Smith Thomas St
Simon's Town
Flagship Way

Runciman Dr.
Forest Hill Rd

Martello Rd

Waters Edge Beach

Klein Tuin Rd
Seaforth Rd
Gay Rd

Nelson Dr.
Simonskloof
Harbour
Heights

Dorion
Place

Jackson Rd
Belmont Rd

QUEENS RD

OLD
BURYING
GROUND

Simon's
Town H

Harthington Ave

Foxy Beach

*Boulder's
Beach*

M
4

Simon's Town

Sports
Fields

Bellevue

MO

Index to Street Names

Abbreviations: Ave. - Avenue A.H. - Agricultural Holding Blvd - Boulevard Cir. - Circle
Cl. - Close Cr. - Crescent Ct - Court Dr. - Drive Gdns - Gardens Gr. - Grove La. - Lane
Pl. - Place Rd - Road Sq. - Square St - Street Ter. - Terrace Tn - Turn Wk - Walk

A. Franch Ave — Alphen Way

STREET NAME	SUBURB NAME	PG	GRID
	A		
A. Franch Ave	Hout Bay	35	CU 17
A.Boesak St	Hout Bay	35	CU 17
A.F.Keen Dr.	Camps Bay	12	CJ 20
A.G.Visser St ...	Townsend Est.	10	CA 43
A.Mlangeni Ave	Hout Bay	35	CU 17
Aachen	Strandfontein	68	DB 46
Aadil Moerat Wk			
..................Weltevreden Valley ...		45	CT 48
Aadil Moerat Wk			
.... Weltevreden Valley		45	CT 47
Aan die Weide ..	Rondebosch	29	CL 36
Aandblom	Pinelands	18	CG 38
Aandblom St	Devil's Peak Est.	14	CF 27
Aandwind St	Kirstenhof	63	DA 31
Aarde St	Vanguard	31	CL 43
Aaron Ave	Montagu's Gift	42	CU 39
Aaron Way	Matroosfontein	21	CG 48
Abbey Rd	Wynberg	41	CS 34
Abbotsbury Ave ...	Grassy Pk	53	CX 36
Abbotsford Ave ...	Barbarossa	40	CU 31
Abbotsleigh Rd	Rondebosch	29	CL 35
Abbott Rd	Wetton	42	CR 39
Abdulla Moosa Rd ..	Parkwood	54	CV 37
Abdulla Wk	Parkwood	53	CV 36
Abelia Cr.	Silvertown	31	CL 41
Abelia Rd	Dreyersdal	52	CY 31
Aberdeen Rd	Rondebosch	28	CL 34
Aberdeen St	Woodstock	5	CE 30
Aberfeldy Rd	Frogmore Est.	63	DB 31
Abingdon Rd	Kenilworth	28	CP 34
Abington Rd	Fish Hoek	83	DL 28
Aboyne Rd	Kenilworth	28	CP 33
Abraham Ave	Steenberg	64	DB 34
Abram Katz St ..	Montana/Durrheim .	21	CK 48
Acacia Rd	Parkwood	42	CU 37
Acacia Rd	Thornton	9	CD 42
Acacia St ...	Chapman's Peak	71	DF 18
Acacia Way	Bergvliet	52	CX 32
Acacia Way	Pinelands	17	CG 36
Aceton Rd	Paarden Eiland	7	CB 34
Achilles Way	Pinelands	8	CE 38
Acorn Cl.	Devil's Peak Est.	14	CG 27
Acorn Cl.	Grassy Pk	53	CW 36
Acorn St	Newlands	27	CN 30
Acre Rd	Factreton	8	CA 39
Acre Rd	Kensington	8	CB 38
Acton Cl.	Grassy Pk	54	CW 38
Acton Rd	Rosebank	17	CK 34
Ada	Lotus River	55	CW 41
Adam St	Valhalla Pk	21	CJ 48
Adam Tas Sq.	Brooklyn	7	CC 35
Adamastor Rd	Ottery	42	CR 39
Addax Cr.	Silvertown	19	CK 41
Adderley St	Foreshore	4	CD 26
Addison Rd	Lansdowne	42	CQ 39
Addison Rd	Salt River	6	CE 32
Addo Rd	Fish Hoek	83	DL 28
Adelaar St	Kirstenhof	63	DA 30
Adelaide Rd	Plumstead	40	CT 32
Adelaide Rd	Woodstock	15	CF 30
Adele St	Plumstead	52	CV 33
Aden Ave	Athlone	18	CK 38
Admiral Cl.	Epping Ind.	20	CF 44
Admirals Dr.	Strandfontein	68	DA 46
Admirals Wk ..	Marina Da Gama	64	DE 34
Adonis Way	Ocean View	79	DN 17
Adrian Herbert Rd	Lansdowne	43	CQ 40

STREET NAME	SUBURB NAME	PG	GRID
Adrian Louw St ..	Montana/Durrheim..	21	CK 48
Adrian Rd	Montagu's Gift	42	CU 39
Adriatic Cl.	Sun Valley	73	DK 23
Adula Rd	Athlone	30	CL 38
Adventist St	Belgravia	30	CL 40
Aegean Ave	Sun Valley	73	DK 23
Aerodrome Rd	Maitland	9	CC 40
Africander Ave ...	Kommetjie	78	DM 12
Afrikander St ...	Montana/Durrheim..	21	CK 47
Agapanthus Ave ..	Devil's Peak Est. ..	14	CG 27
Agapanthus Cr. ...	Bridgetown	19	CK 42
Agapanthus Cr. ...	Silvertown	19	CK 42
Agate Cl.	Sheraton Pk	64	DC 32
Agincourt Way	Strandfontein	68	DB 46
Agnes Rd	Valhalla Pk	21	CJ 48
Agric St	Epping Ind.	10	CD 44
Agulhas St	Strandfontein	68	DA 44
Ahmedeyan Rd ...	Lansdowne	30	CP 38
Ailsa St	Ottery	42	CS 37
Aimee Rd	Bishop Lavis	21	CH 48
Ainsdale St	Maitland	7	CE 35
Ainslie Rd	Plumstead	41	CT 34
Ainsty Wk	Alphen	39	CR 29
Aintree Ave	Ottery	43	CS 40
Aintree Rd	Vredehoek	14	CG 26
Airlie Cl.	Airlie	51	CW 28
Airlie La.	Airlie	51	CW 28
Airlie Pl.	Airlie	51	CW 28
Airlie Rd	Bergvliet	52	CX 31
Airlie Rd	Dreyersdal	51	CY 30
Airport Approach Rd ..	Airport Ind. .	33	CL 49
Ajax Way	Pinelands	8	CE 39
Akasia Ave	Bridgetown	19	CJ 41
Akker Rd	Tygerdal	9	CA 42
Akkerboom Rd ...	Bishop Lavis	21	CH 48
Akkerdal Ave	Claremont	28	CM 33
Alabama	Factreton	8	CB 39
Alacrity Rd	Strandfontein	69	DB 49
Alamein Rd	Claremont	29	CO 35
Alamo	Strandfontein	68	DB 46
Albacore St	Factreton	9	CA 40
Alban Rd	Bergvliet	51	CX 30
Alban Rd	Welcome	20	CK 43
Albany Rd	Sea Point	3	CC 22
Albany St	Ruyterwacht	10	CD 45
Albatross St	Pelikan Pk	67	DC 43
Albatross Way	Thornton	9	CE 41
Albermarle St ...	Hazendal	18	CJ 38
Albert Luthuli Cr.	Weltevreden Valley..	45	CS 47
Albert Rd	Hout Bay	46	CV 15
Albert Rd	Lansdowne	30	CP 38
Albert Rd	Mowbray	16	CH 33
Albert Rd	Muizenberg	76	DF 33
Albert Rd	Salt River	6	CE 32
Albert Rd	Tamboerskloof	3	CE 23
Albert Rd	Woodstock	6	CE 31
Albert St	Claremont	28	CO 34
Albert St	Ruyterwacht	11	CC 46
Alberta St	Flintdale Est.	52	CW 33
Albertus St .	Cape Town Central ...	4	CE 26
Albertyn Rd	Muizenberg	76	DF 33
Albion Cl.	Epping Forest	21	CF 48
Albion Rd	Rondebosch	28	CL 33
Albow Rd	Rugby	7	CA 36
Albrecht St ..	Constantia Vale	39	CT 28
Albury Cr.	Factreton	9	CC 40
Alcis St	Newlands	27	CL 31
Alcor Ave	Ocean View	79	DN 17
Alcyone Rd	Rondebosch	29	CN 36
Alde Rd	Wynberg	40	CR 31
Aldgate St	Woodstock	5	CD 29

STREET NAME	SUBURB NAME	PG	GRID
Alduwa Rd	Flintdale Est.	53	CV 35
Aldwins Ave	Athlone	30	CL 38
Alers Hankey Cr. ...	Brooklyn	7	CB 35
Alers Hankey Cr. ...	Brooklyn	7	CC 35
Aletta Wk	Manenberg	32	CO 45
Aletta Wk	Wynberg	28	CP 32
Alex Rd	Grassy Pk	54	CY 38
Alexander Ave ...	Hout Bay	47	CW 16
Alexander Rd	Crawford	30	CN 38
Alexander Rd	Hout Bay	47	CW 16
Alexander Rd	Mowbray	17	CH 34
Alexander Rd	Muizenberg	76	DG 33
Alexander Rd	Sea Point	2	CD 20
Alexander St ..	Goodwood Est.	10	CA 44
Alexander St	Woodstock	5	CE 29
Alexandra Ave ..	Oranjezicht	13	CG 24
Alexandra Pl. ...	Mouille Point	3	CA 23
Alexandra Rd ..	Maitland Gdn Village..	17	CF 36
Alexandra Rd	Wynberg	40	CQ 32
Alexandra St	Parow	11	CB 48
Alfred Rd	Rondebosch	28	CL 32
Alfred St	Cape Town Central ...	4	CC 26
Alfred St	Kirstenhof	63	DA 31
Alfred St	Observatory	16	CG 33
Alfred St	Woodstock	6	CE 32
Algakirk Rd	Sea Point	2	CD 21
Algoa Rd	Newfields	31	CO 42
Algoa Way	Barbarossa	39	CT 30
Alice La.	Huis-in-bos	51	CV 28
Alice Rd	Claremont	27	CN 31
Alice Rd	Montagu's Gift	42	CU 38
Alice St	Goodwood Est.	10	CA 44
Alices Ride	Pinelands	18	CG 38
Aliwal	Ruyterwacht	10	CD 45
Aliwal Rd	Wynberg	40	CQ 32
Alken Cl.	Frogmore Est.	63	DB 31
Alken Rd	Frogmore Est.	63	DB 31
Alkmaar Rd	Foreshore	5	CD 30
Allamanda St	Ottery	42	CS 38
Alleman Rd	Newfields	31	CO 42
Allen Way	Elfindale	53	CW 34
Allenby Dr.	Retreat	52	CZ 33
Allenby Dr.	Steenberg	64	DB 33
Alleyne Yeld Cr. ..	Fish Hoek	73	DK 25
Allies Rd	Newfields	31	CO 42
Allison Rd	Pinati	30	CP 40
Allister Rd	Crawford	29	CN 37
Alma Rd	Claremont	27	CO 31
Alma Rd	Rosebank	17	CJ 34
Almar Rd	Lansdowne	30	CP 38
Almeria Way ...	Meadowridge	51	CV 30
Almond Cl.	Dennedal	51	CY 29
Almond Cl.	Hout Bay	35	CS 17
Almond Rd	Tokai	62	DA 28
Almond St	Newlands	27	CN 29
Almond Ter. ..	Schotsche Kloof	4	CD 25
Almondbury La. ...	Streenberg	61	DA 25
Almora Cir.	Dennedal	51	CY 29
Alnwick Rd	Dieprivier	40	CR 31
Aloe Cl.	Sweet Water	78	DN 12
Aloe Cr.	Kewtown	18	CK 39
Aloe St	Devil's Peak Est.	14	CG 27
Aloe St	Hanover Pk	31	CO 42
Aloe St	Newlands	27	CN 29
Alpha Rd	Claremont	29	CN 35
Alpha Way	Ocean View	79	DN 17
Alphen Cl. ...	Marina Da Gama	64	DD 34
Alphen Dr.	Alphen	39	CR 29
Alphen Hill	Wynberg	40	CR 32
Alphen Way	Bergvliet	52	CX 32

Index to Street Names

Alphonse Cl. — Attlee

STREET NAME	SUBURB NAME	PG	GRID
Alphonse Cl.	Bel Ombre	38	CR 27
Alphonse Rd	Tokai	51	CZ 28
Alpina Rd	Claremont	28	CN 34
Alpine Way	Matroosfontein	21	CG 48
Als Rd	Bonteheuwel	20	CG 44
Alsace Ave	Woodstock	16	CG 31
Alster Ave	Newlands	27	CN 31
Alston Sq.	Claremont	28	CN 34
Altair Way	Ocean View	79	DN 16
Altenburg	Kirstenhof	63	DB 30
Altona Gr.	Woodstock	5	CE 30
Alwin St	Brooklyn	7	CB 35
Amalinde Way	Strandfontein	69	DB 47
Amanda Rd	Bakoven	12	CK 20
Amandel Rd	Bonteheuwel	20	CG 44
Amandla St	Manenberg	32	CN 46
Amatola Rd	Heideveld	32	CL 44
Amatola Rd	Lavender Hill East	65	DB 36
Amatola Rd	Lavender Hill East	65	DD 37
Amazon Rd	Observatory	16	CF 33
Amazon St	Primrose Pk	32	CN 44
Amber Rd	Steenberg	64	DB 34
Amber Ter.	San Michel	72	DG 22
Amber Way	San Michel	72	DG 22
Ambleside	Pinelands	8	CE 38
Ambrose Cr.	Newfields	31	CO 41
Amden Cl.	Lotus River	54	CV 39
Amethyst Cr.	Belthorn Est.	30	CN 40
Amhurst Ave	Kenilworth	28	CP 34
Amhurst Ave	Newlands	27	CM 30
Amiens Way	Strandfontein	69	DB 47
Amity Way	Lansdowne	42	CQ 38
Amphion St	Paarden Eiland	6	CC 33
Amplankeni Cr.	Nyanga	33	CO 49
Amstel Rd	Maitland	8	CD 37
Amsterdam Ave	Fish Hoek	74	DK 26
Amsterdam Cr.	Brooklyn	7	CB 35
Amsterdam St	Brooklyn	7	CC 34
Anadale Rd	Belthorn Est.	30	CN 39
Ananwabisi St	Nyanga	33	CP 48
Anchor Cl.	Strandfontein	68	DA 45
Andersen St	Ottery East	42	CT 39
Anderson Cl.	Tokai	51	CZ 28
Anderson St	Townsend Est.	10	CB 44
Andile Ndleleni Cr.			
	Weltevreden Valley	45	CS 47
Andrew Murray St	Ruyterwacht	10	CE 45
Andrew Rd	Flintdale Est.	53	CV 36
Andrews Rd	Hout Bay	47	CW 18
Andrews Rd	Kommetjie	78	DM 14
Andrews Rd	Newfields	31	CO 42
Andromeda Way	Ocean View	79	DO 17
Anemone Ave	Devil's Peak Est.	14	CF 27
Anette Cl.	The Vines	52	CV 31
Angela Rd	Gatesville	31	CM 42
Angela Rd	Newfields	31	CN 42
Angela St	Valhalla Pk	21	CJ 47
Angelina Ave	Claremont	27	CN 31
Angle St	Hazendal	18	CJ 38
Angler Cl.	Pelikan Pk	54	CX 39
Anglesey St	Rondebosch East	29	CN 37
Angus Cl.	Barbarossa	40	CT 31
Anita Rd	Montagu's Gift	42	CU 38
Anker Cr.	Strandfontein	69	DB 49
Ann Cl.	Barbarossa	40	CU 31
Annandale Rd	Central	14	CF 25
Annandale Rd	Dieprivier	40	CU 33
Anne Rd	Grassy Pk	53	CY 36
Anne Rd	Valhalla Pk	21	CJ 48
Anneberg Rd	Newlands	28	CM 32
Annerley Rd	Rosebank	17	CJ 35
Annes St	Maitland	7	CD 35
Annette Way	Claremont	28	CO 32
Annex Rd	Maitland Gdn Village	7	CE 35
Annvon Rd	Dieprivier	52	CV 32
Anson St	Observatory	16	CF 33
Antares Cl.	Ocean View	79	DO 17
Antelope Ct	Bridgetown	19	CJ 41
Antelope Rd	Lotus River	55	CV 41
Anthia Wk	Hanover Pk	31	CP 42
Anthony Rd	Bridgetown	31	CL 42
Anthonys Rd	Hout Bay	47	CW 17
Antigua Ave	Capri	81	DL 22
Antrim Rd	Three Anchor Bay	3	CB 23
Antwerp Rd	Sea Point	3	CC 22
Antwerpen Rd	Surrey Est.	31	CN 43
Anvil Cl.	Hout Bay Harbour	46	CY 14
Anysberg Rd	Heideveld	32	CM 45
Anzio	Strandfontein	68	DB 46
Anzio Rd	Observatory	16	CG 32
Apeldoorn Way	Westlake	63	DC 31
Apeldoorn Way	Westlake	63	DE 31
Apenide Rd	Kenilworth	40	CQ 33
Apollo Way	Elfindale	52	CW 33
Apollo Way	Kirstenhof	63	DA 31
Apollo Way	Ocean View	79	DO 17
Apostile Steps	Clifton	12	CF 20
Apostle Rd	Hout Bay	47	CR 15
Appia Cl.	Strandfontein	69	DA 49
Appian Way	Bishopscourt	26	CO 28
Apple La.	Newlands	27	CM 31
Apple Mist Rd	Ottery	42	CR 39
Apple Rd	Capricorn	65	DD 35
Appledene Cr.	Silvertown	19	CK 41
Appledene Rd	Silvertown	19	CK 41
Approach St	Lakeside	63	DD 31
Apricot Cl.	Hout Bay	35	CT 18
Apricot St	Bonteheuwel	20	CG 44
Aquanaut La.	Crofters Valley	72	DH 21
Aquarius Rd	Surrey Est.	32	CM 44
Aquarius Way	Ocean View	79	DO 17
Aquila Rd	Ottery	42	CR 37
Aquila Way	Ocean View	79	DM 16
Aragon Cr.	Montana/Durrheim	33	CL 48
Arba St	Penlyn Est.	31	CN 41
Arbeids Rd	Belthorn Est.	30	CN 39
Arbor Rd	Newlands	28	CL 32
Arbour St	Woodstock	6	CE 33
Arcadia Ave	Lansdowne	29	CO 36
Arcadia Ave	Salberau	11	CE 47
Arcadia Rd	Bantry Bay	2	CE 20
Arcadia Rd	Fresnaye	2	CE 21
Arcadia Rd	Rosebank	17	CK 34
Arcadia Steps	Clifton	12	CG 20
Archer Ave	Athlone	30	CL 38
Archie St	Kenilworth	28	CP 33
Arctic Cr.	Athlone	30	CM 38
Ardennes	Strandfontein	68	DB 46
Ardleigh Rd	Retreat	53	CY 35
Arena Rd	Kenilworth Pk	28	CP 34
Argo Rd	Ottery	42	CQ 38
Argonaut St	Strandfontein	68	DB 49
Argyle Rd	Rondebosch	28	CM 33
Argyle St	Camps Bay	12	CH 20
Argyle St	Woodstock	6	CE 31
Argyll Rd	Goodwood Est.	10	CA 44
Ariel St	Maitland	8	CD 35
Aries Ave	Ocean View	79	DN 16
Aries St	Manenberg	32	CM 44
Aristea Rd	Dreyersdal	51	CY 30
Arixoma Rd	Thornton	10	CD 43
Arlington Cr.	Riverton	11	CC 46
Arlington Rd	Belthorn Est.	30	CO 40
Armadale St	Woodstock	5	CE 29
Armagh Rd	Royal Cape	41	CS 36
Armour Ave	Hout Bay	47	CV 17
Armstrong Cr.	Penlyn Est.	31	CO 41
Arnhem Cl.	Strandfontein	68	DA 46
Arno Rd	Primrose Pk	31	CN 43
Arnold St	Observatory	16	CF 32
Arsenal Way	Simon's Town	88	DU 27
Arthur Rd	Muizenberg	76	DF 33
Arthur Wright Rd	Fish Hoek	73	DK 23
Arthur's Rd	Sea Point	2	CC 21
Arum Ave	Kommetjie	78	DM 12
Arum Ave	Westlake Est.	62	DB 28
Arum Cl.	Bel Ombre	39	CS 28
Arum Rd	Bishop Lavis	21	CH 48
Arum St	Bridgetown	19	CK 42
Arum St	Devil's Peak Est.	14	CF 27
Arum St	Newlands	27	CN 30
Arum Way	Thornton	9	CD 42
Arundel	Dreyersdal	51	CZ 30
Arundel Rd	Rondebosch	17	CK 35
Arundel Rd	Rosebank	17	CJ 34
Arvana Cl.	Brooklyn	7	CB 35
Ascension Rd	Heideveld	32	CL 45
Ascot Cl.	Ottery	43	CS 40
Ascot Rd	Kenilworth	41	CQ 34
Ash Grove Rd	Devil's Peak Est.	14	CG 27
Ash La.	Claremont	28	CO 34
Ash La.	Grassy Pk	54	CX 38
Ash La.	Hout Bay	36	CT 20
Ash Rd	Farmsteads	59	DD 19
Ash St	Observatory	16	CF 33
Ash St	Sunnydale	72	DK 21
Ashbury Rd	Plumstead	40	CT 33
Ashby Rd	Athlone	30	CL 39
Ashford Rd	Heathfield	52	CX 33
Ashgrove	Pinelands	19	CF 40
Ashgrove Ave	Epping Forest	21	CF 47
Ashley Cl.	Epping Forest	21	CF 47
Ashley Cr.	Lavender Hill	65	DB 35
Ashraf Ave	Gatesville	31	CM 41
Ashstead Rd	Greenpoint	4	CB 25
Ashville Cr.	Retreat	52	CZ 33
Asmara Rd	Charlesville	21	CK 46
Aspden Rd	Browns Farm	45	CR 47
Aspeling St	District Six	5	CE 28
Aspen Cl.	Fairie Knowe	72	DK 21
Assegaai Ave	Thornton	10	CD 43
Assegai Ave	Bonteheuwel	20	CG 44
Astana St	Schotsche Kloof	4	CD 25
Aster Cr.	Silvertown	31	CL 42
Aster Rd	Kewtown	18	CK 39
Aster Rd	Lavender Hill East	65	DB 36
Aster St	Newlands	27	CO 29
Asteroid St	Ocean View	79	DO 16
Astley St	Mowbray	16	CH 33
Astra Ave	Riverton	11	CC 46
Athall Wk	Hanover Pk	31	CP 42
Athburg Wk	Hanover Pk	31	CP 41
Atherstone Rd	Plumstead	40	CU 33
Athlone Rd	Athlone	29	CL 37
Athlone Rd	Plumstead	40	CU 33
Athlone St	Ruyterwacht	11	CD 46
Athol Rd	Camps Bay	12	CH 21
Athol Rd South	Camps Bay	12	CH 21
Athon Cr.	Hanover Pk	31	CP 42
Athon Wk	Hanover Pk	31	CP 42
Athry Wk	Hanover Pk	31	CP 41
Athsur Wk	Pinati	30	CO 40
Athwood Rd	Hanover Pk	30	CP 40
Atkins St	Grassy Pk	53	CY 36
Atlantic Dr.	Imhoff's Gift	79	DM 17
Atlantic Rd	Muizenberg	76	DG 33
Atlantic Skipper Rd			
	Hout Bay Harbour	46	CY 15
Atlantic Way	Sun Valley	73	DK 23
Atlas Ave	Salberau	11	CE 47
Atlas Rd	Athlone	30	CL 38
Attlee	Plumstead	41	CU 35

Index to Street Names

STREET NAME	SUBURB NAME	PG	GRID
Aubrey St	Salt River	16	CF 31
Auburn Rd	Kenilworth	40	CQ 33
Auckland St	Paarden Eiland	6	CC 22
Audry Rd	Manenberg	32	CO 45
August St	Schotsche Kloof	4	CD 25
Augustus Way	Constantia Vale	38	CT 27
Aureole Cl.	Flintdale Est.	53	CV 35
Aureole Rd	Flintdale Est.	53	CW 35
Auriga Cl.	Ocean View	79	DN 17
Auriga Rd	Retreat	52	CY 32
Aurora La.	Sea Point	3	CC 22
Aurora St	Kirstenhof	63	DA 31
Aurora Way	Salberau	11	CE 47
Austell Rd	Retreat	52	CX 32
Austwick Rd	Rondebosch	17	CK 34
Autum St	Surrey Est.	31	CM 43
Autumn Cl.	Montagu's Gift	42	CU 39
Avalon Rd	Claremont	28	CN 33
Ave Alexandra	Fresnaye	2	CE 21
Ave Bordeaux	Sea Point	3	CD 22
Ave Branksome	Fresnaye	3	CD 22
Ave Brittany	Fresnaye	2	CE 21
Ave Charmante	Bantry Bay	2	CE 20
Ave Coeur de Lion	Fresnaye	2	CE 21
Ave De Berrange	Fresnaye	3	CE 22
Ave De L'Hermite	Fresnaye	3	CD 22
Ave De Longueville	Fresnaye	2	CD 21
Ave De Mist	Claremont	29	CM 36
Ave De Mist	Rondebosch	29	CL 35
Ave Deauville	Fresnaye	2	CE 21
Ave Des Huguenots	Fresnaye	2	CE 21
Ave Disandt	Fresnaye	2	CD 21
Ave Drelingcourt	Fresnaye	3	CD 22
Ave Fontainebleau	Sea Point	3	CD 22
Ave Francais	Fresnaye	2	CD 21
Ave Fresnaye	Fresnaye	2	CE 21
Ave La Croix	Fresnaye	2	CE 21
Ave Le Suer	Fresnaye	2	CE 21
Ave Le Sueur	Fresnaye	2	CD 21
Ave Marina	Bantry Bay	2	CE 20
Ave Marseilles	Sea Point	3	CD 22
Ave Normandie	Fresnaye	2	CD 21
Ave St Bartholomew	Fresnaye	3	CE 22
Ave St Charles	Fresnaye	2	CE 21
Ave St Charles	Sea Point	3	CD 22
Ave St Denis	Sea Point	3	CD 22
Ave St Leon	Bantry Bay	2	CE 20
Ave St Louis	Fresnaye	2	CE 21
Ave Bordeaux	Hohenort	38	CQ 27
Ave Du Midi	Plumstead	53	CV 34
Ave Normandy	Plumstead	53	CV 34
Ave Orleans	Plumstead	53	CV 34
Avenue Rd	Rondebosch	28	CL 32
Avenue Rd	Woodstock	16	CF 31
Avenue St	Cape Town Central	4	CE 25
Avery Ave	Barbarossa	39	CT 30
Avery Ave	Ottery	43	CR 40
Avery Cr.	Ottery	43	CR 40
Avery Rd	Heathfield	52	CX 33
Avey Rd	Epping Forest	21	CF 48
Avignon Cr.	Townsend Est.	10	CA 43
Avoca Rd	Rondebosch	28	CL 33
Avocado St	Bonteheuwel	20	CG 44
Avocet Cr.	Pelikan Pk	55	CX 40
Avocet St	Flintdale Est.	53	CW 35
Avon Rd	Dieprivier	52	CW 32
Avondale Rd	Avon	11	CD 47
Avondale Rd	Three Anchor Bay	3	CB 23
Avondale Ter.	Plumstead	52	CV 33
Avondrus Dr.	Brooklyn	7	CA 35
Avondrust Ave	Bergvliet	52	CW 31
Avondrust Ave	Bergvliet	52	CZ 31
Avondrust Cir.	Chapman's Peak	59	DE 19
Avonduur	Ndabeni	8	CE 37
Avonduur	Pinelands	18	CF 38
Avonwood Ave	Norwood	11	CD 47
Avonwood Ave	Valhalla	11	CD 46
Avro Ave	Kensington	8	CB 39
Axis Rd	Wingfield	9	CB 42
Axminster Rd	Muizenberg	76	DF 34
Aylesbury Cl.	Wetton	42	CR 39
Aylesbury Rd	Wetton	42	CR 39
Ayres St	Rosebank	17	CJ 34
Ayreshire St	Montana/Durrheim	21	CK 47
Ayrshire St	Rondebosch East	29	CN 37
Ayton Rd	Rondebosch	29	CM 36
Azalea St	Plumstead	40	CU 32
Azalia Cr.	Thornton	10	CD 43
Azana St	Ottery	42	CT 38

B

STREET NAME	SUBURB NAME	PG	GRID
B.February St	Hout Bay	35	CU 17
B.Longo Rd	Nyanga	33	CO 49
Baakens Rd	Primrose Pk	32	CN 44
Baalen Rd	Marina Da Gama	64	DD 34
Baartman St	Leonsdale	11	CD 48
Baatjies La.	Grassy Pk	54	CW 37
Bach Ave	Retreat	65	DA 35
Back Cl.	Strandfontein	69	DB 47
Back Rd	Strandfontein	68	DA 46
Baden Powell Dr.	Capricorn	65	DE 37
Baden Powell Dr.	Capricorn	66	DE 38
Baden Powell Dr.	Strandfontein	69	DB 48
Badgemore Ave	Nova Constantia	50	CW 27
Bailey Cr.	Heideveld	32	CL 45
Bain Ct	Rondebosch	29	CL 36
Bain St	Ruyterwacht	10	CC 45
Baird Way	Meadowridge	51	CV 30
Baker Rd	Kenilworth	40	CQ 33
Baker Rd	Muizenberg	76	DG 33
Baker St	Observatory	16	CF 33
Bakker Rd	Newfields	31	CO 42
Baldwin Ave	Epping Forest	21	CF 48
Baleia Rd	Ottery	42	CR 38
Balfour Ave	Bishopscourt	27	CO 30
Balfour Rd	Churchill	11	CA 47
Balfour Rd	Glenlily	11	CA 47
Balfour Rd	Rondebosch	17	CK 36
Balfour Rd	Woodstock	15	CF 30
Balfour St	District Six	5	CE 29
Bali Cl.	Capri	81	DM 22
Balintore Rd	Rondebosch	29	CL 36
Ballcline Steps	Fish Hoek	83	DM 28
Balmoral Ave	Bergvliet	52	CW 31
Balmoral Cl.	Dreyersdal	52	CZ 31
Balmoral Cl.	Pinelands	19	CG 40
Balmoral Cl.	Pinelands	19	CG 41
Balmoral Rd	Lansdowne	29	CO 37
Balmoral Rd	Plumstead	40	CS 32
Balsillie Way	Nova Constantia	50	CV 27
Baltic Way	Sun Valley	73	DK 23
Balu Parker Blvd.	Gatesville	31	CM 42
Balvenie Ave	Epping Forest	21	CF 48
Bambata Ave	Hout Bay	35	CU 17
Bamberry Rd	Belthorn Est.	30	CN 38
Bamboeberg Rd	Heideveld	32	CL 45
Bamboesvlei Rd	Ottery	42	CR 38
Bamboo Rd	Lansdowne	42	CQ 38
Bangor St	Athlone	30	CL 38
Banhoek Rd	Heideveld	32	CL 45
Banier Rd	Flintdale Est.	53	CV 36
Banjo Rd	Retreat	64	DA 34
Bank Rd	Rondebosch	28	CL 33
Bankot Rd	Lansdowne	30	CP 39

STREET NAME	SUBURB NAME	PG	GRID
Banks Rd	Fish Hoek	83	DL 28
Banksia Rd	Rosebank	17	CJ 34
Bankview Cl.	Riverton	11	CC 46
Bannockburn Cr.	Strandfontein	68	DB 46
Bantam St	Schotsche Kloof	4	CD 25
Bantry La.	Bantry Bay	2	CE 20
Bantry Steps	Bantry Bay	2	CE 20
Bantry Way	Matroosfontein	21	CG 48
Banzi Ave	Guguletu	32	CN 46
Baptist St	Grassy Pk	53	CX 36
Barbara Rd	Bakoven	12	CK 21
Barbary Way	Barbarossa	39	CT 30
Barbel Rd	Pelikan Pk	54	CX 39
Barber Cl.	Fish Hoek	74	DK 26
Barbestyn St	Ottery	42	CS 37
Barbet Rd	Pelikan Pk	55	CZ 41
Barbeton Rd	Belthorn Est.	30	CO 40
Barbette Rd	Ottery	42	CR 38
Barbourne Rd	Muizenberg Nth	64	DD 32
Barcombe Rd	Hazendal	18	CK 38
Bardia	Strandfontein	68	DB 46
Bardia Rd	Plumstead	40	CS 32
Barend Rd	Lansdowne	43	CQ 40
Barham Rd	Belgravia	30	CM 40
Baris Rd	Woodstock	16	CG 31
Barit Rd	Penlyn Est.	30	CO 40
Bark Rd	Retreat Ind. Area	63	DB 31
Bark St	Retreat Ind. Area	64	DB 32
Barkis Rd	Belgravia	30	CM 40
Barkley Rd	Rondebosch	17	CK 34
Barkley St	Ruyterwacht	10	CC 45
Barkly Rd	Sea Point	3	CD 22
Barling Cr.	Fish Hoek	82	DL 24
Barlinka Way	Meadowridge	52	CV 31
Barmania Rd	Athlone	30	CM 38
Barmbeck Ave	Newlands	27	CN 31
Barn Rd	Bergvliet	51	CW 30
Barnabas St	Gardens	13	CF 24
Barnard St	Rondebosch	17	CJ 36
Barnard St	Simon's Town	88	DU 27
Barnett Rd	Plumstead	40	CU 33
Barnett St	Gardens	4	CE 25
Barnham Ave	Devil's Peak Est.	14	CF 27
Barnstaple Rd	Wynberg	41	CQ 34
Baronie Ave	Westlake	63	DC 31
Baronrath Rd	Kenilworth	28	CP 34
Barque Cl.	Strandfontein	68	DB 45
Barque Cr.	Sun Valley	73	DJ 23
Barrack St	Cape Town Central	4	CE 26
Barrack St	District Six	4	CE 26
Barracuda Way	Strandfontein	68	DB 45
Barrie Ross Way	Meadowridge	51	CV 30
Barrington Rd	Observatory	16	CF 33
Barron St	Woodstock	5	CE 29
Barry Ave	Rosebank	16	CJ 33
Barry Rd	Hout Bay	47	CV 17
Barry Rd	Montagu's Gift	42	CU 39
Bartel Rd	Beaconvale	11	CC 48
Bartholomeu Dias Blvd			
	Cape Town Central	4	CD 27
Bartman St	Flintdale Est.	53	CV 35
Barton Rd	Kalk Bay	75	DK 30
Barton Rd	Kalk Bay	75	DJ 29
Barton St	Woodstock	5	CE 30
Basalt Cl.	Salberau	11	CE 47
Bashee Rd	Manenberg	32	CM 44
Basil Cr.	Ottery East	43	CT 40
Basil Fischer St	Weltevreden Valley	45	CT 48
Basil Rd	Plumstead	41	CT 34
Basil Rd	Plumstead	41	CT 35
Basket La.	Foreshore	5	CE 28
Bass Rd	Pelikan Pk	54	CY 38
Basset	Strandfontein	68	DA 46
Bassett Rd	Claremont	29	CO 35

STREET NAME	SUBURB NAME	PG	GRID
Basson St	Maitland	7	CD 34
Bassoon St	Steenberg	64	DB 34
Batavia Rd	Ruyterwacht	10	CD 45
Bateleur Rd	Fish Hoek	74	DK 26
Bath Rd	Claremont	28	CO 33
Bath Rd	Muizenberg	76	DF 34
Bath Rd	Wynberg	41	CS 34
Bath St	Gardens	13	CF 24
Bathandwa Mdingi Cr.			
	Weltevreden Valley	45	CT 48
Bathurst Rd	Kenilworth	41	CQ 34
Bato St	Glencairn Hgts	83	DO 27
Batten La.	Mowbray	16	CH 33
Battersea Cl.	Riverton	11	CC 46
Battery Cr.	Sea Point	3	CC 23
Battle Ridge	Marina Da Gama	64	DE 34
Batts Rd	Wynberg	40	CS 33
Baviaans Cl.	Hout Bay	47	CX 18
Baviaanskloof Rd	Hout Bay	47	CW 17
Bax St	Ndabeni	7	CE 35
Baxter Rd	Rosebank	16	CJ 33
Bay St	Capricorn	65	DE 36
Bay Rd	Greenpoint	3	CA 23
Bay Rd	Hout Bay	36	CT 20
Bay Rd	Muizenberg	76	DG 32
Bay View Ave	Tamboerskloof	13	CF 23
Bay View Rd	Wynberg	40	CS 32
Bayana Cl.	Nyanga	33	CP 48
Bayard St	Grassy Pk	53	CX 36
Bayete Rd	Ndabeni	8	CE 37
Bayswater Rd	Lotus River	54	CW 39
Bayview Rd	Hout Bay	35	CR 16
Bayview Rd	Hout Bay Harbour	46	CY 14
Bayview Rd	Hout Bay Harbour	46	CX 14
Bayview Rd	Hout Bay Harbour	46	CY 14
Baywater Cr.	Strandfontein	69	DB 48
Beach	Kommetjie	78	DL 13
Beach Cr.	Hout Bay	47	CX 17
Beach Rd	Brooklyn	7	CC 34
Beach Rd	Chapman's Peak	71	DF 17
Beach Rd	Fish Hoek	83	DL 28
Beach Rd	Greenpoint	4	CA 25
Beach Rd	Kommetjie	78	DM 12
Beach Rd	Maitland	7	CD 34
Beach Rd	Misty Cliffs	86	DU 19
Beach Rd	Mouille Point	3	CA 23
Beach Rd	Muizenberg	76	DG 33
Beach Rd	Sea Point	2	CC 21
Beach Rd	Three Anchor Bay	3	CB 22
Beach Rd	Woodstock	5	CD 30
Beacontree La.	Woodstock	15	CF 30
Beagle	Strandfontein	69	DA 47
Beak Rd	Pelikan Pk	55	CZ 41
Beatrice Cl.	Dennedal	51	CY 29
Beatrix Rd	Manenberg	32	CO 45
Beatty Ave	Maitland Gdn Village	17	CF 35
Beatty Rd	Woodstock	15	CG 30
Beau Art La.	Crofters Valley	72	DH 21
Beaufort Rd	Factreton	9	CC 40
Beaufort St	Townsend Est.	10	CB 43
Beaumont Ave	Bel Ombre	38	CR 27
Beaumont Cottages	Greenpoint	4	CC 25
Beauvais Ave	Bel Ombre	38	CR 27
Becker Rd	Hanover Pk	43	CQ 42
Beckham St	Gardens	4	CE 25
Becott Rd	Wetton	42	CR 39
Bedford Rd	Lakeside	64	DD 32
Bedford St	Claremont	28	CO 33
Bedford St	Observatory	16	CF 33
Bedford St	Vredehoek	14	CF 26
Bedfordshire Cl.	Kirstenhof	63	DB 31
Bedfordshire Cl.	Kirstenhof	63	DE 31
Bee Eater	Fish Hoek	74	DK 26
Beech Cr.	Westlake Est.	62	DB 28
Beech Cr.	Westlake Est.	62	DB 26
Beech St	Tokai	51	CZ 28
Beechwood	Pinelands	19	CG 40
Beethoven Rd	Cafda Village	53	CZ 35
Beethoven Rd	Retreat	65	DA 35
Bega Rd	Wynberg	40	CS 33
Begonia Rd	Hanover Pk	31	CO 42
Begonia Rd	Silvertown	31	CL 41
Behr Rd	Kalk Bay	75	DK 30
Beira Rd	Bakoven	12	CK 19
Bel Ombre Rd	Bel Ombre	38	CR 27
Bel Ombre Rd	Bergvliet	52	CX 31
Belair Dr.	Witteboomen	38	CT 25
Belfast Cl.	Royal Cape	41	CS 36
Belfast Rd	Wynberg	41	CR 34
Belgravia Ave	Lansdowne	29	CO 37
Belgravia Rd	Belgravia	30	CM 39
Belinda Rd	Manenberg	32	CO 45
Belinda St	Kirstenhof	63	DA 30
Belinda Wk	Manenberg	32	CO 45
Bell Capri Link	Hout Bay Harbour	46	CY 15
Bell Capri Link	Hout Bay Harbour	46	CX 14
Bell Cl.	Riverton	11	CC 46
Bell Cr	Westlake Est.	62	DC 28
Bell Rd	Kenilworth	28	CO 33
Bell Way	Meadowridge	52	CV 31
Belladonna Ave	Devil's Peak Est.	14	CG 27
Bellair Rd	Vredehoek	14	CG 27
Belle Ave	Westlake	63	DC 30
Belle Constantia Cl.	Bergvliet	51	CW 29
Belle Ombre Rd	Tamboerskloof	3	CE 23
Bellevliet Rd	Observatory	16	CG 33
Bellevue Rd	Kenilworth	28	CP 33
Bellevue Rd	Sea Point	3	CC 22
Bellevue St	Gardens	13	CG 23
Bellmore Ave	Penlyn Est.	30	CO 40
Bellows Cl.	Hout Bay Harbour	46	CY 14
Bellstart La.	Observatory	17	CG 34
Bellvue Ave	Bel Ombre	38	CR 26
Bellwood Rd	Fresnaye	2	CE 21
Belmont Ave	Oranjezicht	13	CG 24
Belmont Rd	Kalk Bay	75	DK 30
Belmont Rd	Lansdowne	30	CO 37
Belmont Rd	Mowbray	16	CH 33
Belmont Rd	Rondebosch	16	CK 33
Belmont Rd	Simon's Town	89	DU 29
Belper Rd	Wynberg	41	CQ 34
Belthorn Rd	Belthorn Est.	30	CN 39
Belvedere Ave	Clovelly	74	DK 28
Belvedere Av	Oranjezicht	14	CG 25
Belvedere Cl.	Belvedere (Noordhoek)	72	DF 22
Belvedere Rd	Claremont	29	CM 35
Belvedere Rd	Muizenberg	76	DG 33
Ben Ave	Devil's Peak Est.	15	CF 28
Ben Nevis Rd	Sea Point	3	CC 24
Ben St	Grassy Pk	54	CW 38
Ben St	Nooitgedacht	21	CJ 48
Benbow Ave	Belgravia	30	CM 40
Benbow Ave	Epping Ind.	19	CF 42
Benbow Rd	Penlyn Est.	30	CM 40
Bend Rd	Ottery	42	CS 37
Bendixen Rd	Ottery East	42	CS 38
Benes St	Maitland	7	CD 35
Benghazi Rd	Lansdowne	42	CQ 37
Benguela Cl.	Bel Ombre	39	CS 28
Benigna Cl.	Nyanga	33	CP 48
Benjamin Rd	Wynberg	40	CR 33
Bennett St	Cape Town Central	4	CC 26
Bennetts Cl.	Simon's Town	83	DP 27
Bennie St	Langa	19	CG 40
Benning Dr.	Kommetjie	78	DM 13
Bennington Rd	Tamboerskloof	3	CE 24
Benona Rd	Lansdowne	30	CO 38
Bentley Cl.	Claremont	29	CN 35
Beresford Rd	Woodstock	15	CF 29
Berg Rd	Bishop Lavis	21	CG 47
Berg Rd	Fish Hoek	82	DL 26
Bergen Rd	Frogmore Est.	64	DC 32
Bergendal Rd	Fir Grove	51	CX 28
Berghof La.	Hout Bay	47	CX 18
Berguitsig Rd	Elfindale	52	CX 33
Bergvliet Rd	Bergvliet	52	CW 31
Bergzicht Cir.	Tokai	51	CZ 30
Bergzig	Flintdale Est.	53	CV 35
Berkeley Rd	Mowbray	17	CH 35
Berkley Rd	Camps Bay	12	CH 20
Berkley Rd	Ndabeni	7	CE 34
Berkley Rd	Oranjezicht	14	CF 25
Berlin Sq.	Strandfontein	69	DB 47
Bermuda Dr.	Capri	81	DL 22
Bermuda Dr.	Sunnydale	81	DL 22
Bermuda St	Paarden Eiland	7	CC 34
Bernard Ave	Flintdale Est.	53	CV 36
Berne Ave	Lansdowne	29	CP 37
Berram Rd	Rondebosch	29	CL 35
Berrio Rd	Foreshore	5	CD 29
Berry La.	Wynberg	41	CS 34
Berry Rd	Capricorn	65	DC 35
Berry Rd	Wynberg	41	CS 34
Bertha Ave	Bishopscourt	27	CO 30
Bertie Ave	Epping Ind.	20	CF 44
Bertram Cr.	Rondebosch	29	CM 35
Bertram Rd	Sea Point	3	CC 22
Bertrand Rd	Greenpoint	4	CC 25
Berwick Rd	Wynberg	40	CS 32
Beryl Rd	Montagu's Gift	42	CU 38
Beryl Rd	Ottery	42	CS 38
Bessie Rd	Bonteheuwel	20	CG 44
Beta Rd	Bakoven	12	CK 19
Beta Wk	Ocean View	79	DN 17
Bethal St	Hout Bay	35	CT 18
Bethel Rd	Clovelly	74	DK 27
Betsie Verwoerd St	Townsend Est.	9	CA 42
Bettina Rd	Lansdowne	29	CN 37
Bettington Sq.	Woodstock	5	CE 30
Beulah Ter.	Oranjezicht	14	CH 25
Bevan Rd	Surrey Est.	31	CN 43
Beverley Rd	Athlone	18	CK 38
Bexhill Rd	Wynberg	40	CR 33
Beyers Rd	Woodstock	5	CE 29
Bheki Mlangeni	Weltevreden Valley	45	CT 48
Bhunga Ave	Langa	19	CG 40
Bickley Rd	Sea Point	3	CC 22
Bideford Rd	Woodstock	5	CF 40
Bien Donne	Pinelands	19	CF 40
Biggar St	Ruyterwacht	10	CD 44
Bill Peters Dr.	Greenpoint	3	CB 24
Bilston Rd	Crawford	30	CN 39
Binneman St	Constantia Vale	39	CT 28
Birch Rd	Chapman's Peak	71	DF 18
Birch Rd	Grassy Pk	54	CX 38
Birch St	Hout Bay	36	CT 20
Birch St	Newlands	27	CN 29
Birchwood La.	Tokai	51	CZ 29
Bird St	Lansdowne	29	CP 37
Birdwood St	Athlone	18	CK 37
Birkenhead Cr.	Ruyterwacht	10	CD 45
Birkenhead Dr.	Strandfontein	69	DB 49
Birkenhead Rd	Glencairn Hgts	83	DO 27
Birkenhead Rd	Plumstead	52	CV 33
Birkett Rd	Rondebosch	17	CK 36
Birmingham Rd	Plumstead	40	CU 32
Bishop Rd	Observatory	16	CF 32
Bishop St	Grassy Pk	53	CX 36
Bishops Court Way	Claremont	27	CN 31
Bishopscourt Dr.	Bishopscourt	26	CO 28
Bishopstone Rd	Wetton	43	CS 40

STREET NAME	SUBURB NAME	PG	GRID
Biskop Steps	Clifton	12	CF 20
Bisschop Rd	Hout Bay	34	CU 15
Bisset Rd	Kenilworth	28	CP 33
Bisset Rd	Newlands	26	CN 28
Bisset St	Newlands	27	CN 29
Bitou Cl.	Kommetjie	78	DL 14
Bitterblaar Rd	Bonteheuwel	21	CH 46
Bitterhout St	Langa	19	CH 40
Bittern Link	Pelikan Pk	55	CX 40
Blaauwberg St	Brooklyn	7	CC 35
Blaauwklippen	Kirstenhof	63	DB 30
Black River Parkway	Ndabeni	7	CE 34
Black St	Claremont	28	CN 33
Blackberry Mall	Strandfontein	69	DA 47
Blackberry St	Bonteheuwel	20	CG 45
Blackbird Ave	Montagu's Gift	42	CU 37
Blackbird Ave West	Parkwood	54	CV 37
Blackbird Rd	Sunnydale	72	DJ 22
Blackbird Wk	Parkwood	53	CV 36
Blackheath Rd	Kenilworth	28	CP 34
Blackheath Rd	Three Anchor Bay	3	CC 22
Blackwell La.	Barbarossa	40	CT 32
Blackwood Cl.	Hout Bay	37	CS 22
Blackwood Dr.	Hout Bay	37	CS 22
Blackwood Rd	Dieprivier	52	CV 32
Blackwood Rd	Dieprivier	52	CV 32
Blagden St	Cafda Village	53	CZ 35
Blair Rd	Camps Bay	12	CH 21
Blair St	Maitland	7	CD 36
Blake St	Observatory	16	CF 33
Blanberg St	Hout Bay Harbour	46	CY 15
Blanberg St	Hout Bay Harbour	46	CX 14
Blanc-de-Noir Cl.	Hout Bay	47	CV 17
Blanken Rd	Lansdowne	29	CP 37
Blende Rd	Belgravia	30	CM 40
Blenheim Rd	Dieprivier	52	CW 32
Blenheim Rd	Plumstead	40	CS 33
Blesbok Ave	Lotus River	55	CV 40
Blinde St	District Six	15	CF 28
Block Rd	Lansdowne	29	CP 37
Blode Cl.	Lavender Hill	65	DB 35
Blode St	Lavender Hill	65	DB 35
Bloem St	Cape Town Central	4	CE 25
Bloem St	Townsend Est.	9	CA 42
Bloemendal Rd	Mowbray	17	CH 34
Bloemfontein St	Paarden Eiland	7	CC 34
Bloemhof Ave	Schaap Kraal	43	CQ 41
Bloemhof Rd	Ottery	43	CR 40
Bloemhof St	District Six	4	CE 26
Blomberg Rd	Hout Bay Harbour	46	CY 15
Blomberg Rd	Hout Bay Harbour	46	CX 14
Blombos St	Bonteheuwel	21	CH 46
Blomvlei Rd	Lansdowne	30	CP 39
Blomvlei Rd	Pinati	30	CP 39
Bloomsbury Way	Noordhoek Manor Retirement Village	73	DG 23
Bloomsbury Way	Noordhoek Manor Retirement Village	73	DJ 24
Blossom St	Bridgetown	19	CK 42
Blossom St	Hanover Pk	31	CO 42
Blou Rd	Parkwood	54	CW 37
Blouberg Rd	Heideveld	32	CM 46
Bloukrans Rd	Heideveld	32	CL 46
Blue Fin Ave	Marina Da Gama	64	DC 34
Blue Fin Cir.	The Lakes	72	DJ 20
Blue Fin Point	The Lakes	72	DJ 20
Blue Valley Ave	Hout Bay	36	CT 20
Blue Valley Cl.	Hout Bay	36	CS 20
Blue Waters Cl.	Simon's Town	88	DS 26
Blue Whale Way	Kommetjie	78	DK 14
Bluebell Sq.	Bridgetown	19	CJ 42
Bluegill Cl.	Pelikan Pk	54	CX 39
Bluegum Cl.	Fairie Knowe	72	DK 21
Bluegum La.	Tokai	51	CZ 29

STREET NAME	SUBURB NAME	PG	GRID
Bluegum Rd	Bishop Lavis	21	CH 48
Bluegum Rd	Bonteheuwel	20	CJ 43
Bluegum Rd	Chapman's Peak	71	DF 18
Bluegum St	Bonteheuwel	20	CJ 44
Bluff Cr.	Strandfontein	69	DB 49
Blumenau Ave	Flintdale Est.	53	CW 36
Blythwood Rd	Rondebosch	29	CM 35
Blyvoor St	Vanguard	31	CL 43
Boat Rd	Pelikan Pk	54	CY 38
Boat St	Strandfontein	68	DB 44
Bodmin St	Maitland	8	CD 37
Bodrum Cl.	Crofters Valley	72	DH 21
Boeier Cr.	Sun Valley	73	DJ 23
Boeing St	Kensington	8	CC 39
Boekenhout Dr.	Sunnydale	72	DK 21
Boekenhout St	Bonteheuwel	20	CG 45
Boescheoten Rd	Athlone	30	CL 39
Bofors Cir.	Epping Ind.	10	CE 44
Bogey Rd	Lakeside	63	DD 31
Bognor Rd	Rosebank	17	CJ 34
Boipatong	Weltevreden Valley	45	CS 48
Bokkemanskloof Cl.	Hout Bay	36	CT 20
Bokkemanskloof Rd	Hout Bay	36	CT 20
Bokmakierie Rd	Hazendal	18	CK 38
Bokmakierie Rd	Hazendal	18	CJ 38
Boland Rd	Steenberg	64	DB 34
Bollihope Cr.	Mowbray	16	CH 33
Bololo St	Nyanga	33	CP 48
Bolton Rd	Athlone	30	CL 38
Bolus Ave	Kenilworth	28	CP 34
Bombay Rd	Gatesville	31	CM 42
Bombay St	Lansdowne	30	CP 38
Bon St	Athlone	30	CL 38
Bonair Rd	Rondebosch	17	CK 35
Bond St	Muizenberg Nth	64	DE 32
Bond St	Tamboerskloof	3	CE 23
Bond St	Weltevreden Valley	45	CU 48
Bongani Cl.	Nyanga	33	CP 48
Bongo Dr.	Silvertown	19	CK 41
Bonito Cl.	Strandfontein	68	DA 46
Bonnyrigg Ave	Belle Constantia	51	CV 29
Bonteberg Rd	Heideveld	32	CL 46
Bonteberg Rd	Heideveld	32	CL 44
Bonteberg Rd	Lavender Hill East	65	DB 36
Bonteberg Rd	Lavender Hill East	65	DD 37
Bontebok Rd	Lotus River	55	CV 41
Bonteheuwel Ave	Bonteheuwel	20	CH 45
Bonteheuwel Ave	Bonteheuwel	21	CH 46
Bonteheuwel Ave	Pinelands	18	CH 38
Boom Rd	Schaap Kraal	56	CW 43
Bootes Cl.	Ocean View	79	DO 17
Booth Rd	Woodstock	16	CF 31
Bordeaux Rd	Sunnydale	72	DJ 21
Borden Rd	Rondebosch	17	CK 36
Borders Cl.	Epping Forest	21	CF 48
Bornite Rd	Belthorn Est.	30	CO 40
Borriehout St	Bonteheuwel	21	CH 46
Borzoi Cr.	Strandfontein	68	DA 46
Bosbok Rd	Lotus River	55	CW 41
Bosbok Rd	Phumlani	55	CW 41
Bosch La.	Oranjezicht	13	CH 24
Bosch-en-Dal	Kirstenhof	63	DB 30
Boschendal Cr.	Dreyersdal	52	CZ 31
Bosduif Rd	Bridgetown	19	CK 42
Boshof St	Newlands	27	CN 30
Boskykloof Rd	Hout Bay	36	CR 21
Bosman Ave	Hout Bay	34	CR 15
Bostel Rd	Hanover Pk	30	CP 40
Boston St	Browns Farm	45	CR 47
Boston St	Factreton	8	CB 39
Bosun Cl.	Pelikan Pk	54	CX 39
Bosuns Cl.	Strandfontein	68	DA 46
Bosuns Rd	Strandfontein	68	DA 46
Bot St	Primrose Pk	32	CN 44

STREET NAME	SUBURB NAME	PG	GRID
Botany Steps	Bantry Bay	2	CE 20
Botha Rd	Wynberg	40	CR 31
Botha St	Richmond Est.	11	CB 47
Bothwell Cl.	Tokai	62	DA 28
Bothwell Rd	Hazendal	18	CJ 38
Botma St	Retreat	64	DA 34
Botma St	Steenberg	64	DB 34
Botterblom Ave	Grassy Pk	53	CW 36
Botterblom St	Charlesville	21	CJ 46
Bottom Rd	Pelikan Pk	55	CX 40
Bougainville Rd	Newlands	27	CN 31
Boulder Rd	Muizenberg Nth	64	DE 32
Boulevard	Avon	11	CD 47
Boundary Ave	Knole Pk	43	CU 42
Boundary Ave	Schaap Kraal	56	CV 44
Boundary Rd	Greenpoint	4	CC 25
Boundary Rd	Lansdowne	42	CQ 38
Boundary Rd	Meadowridge	52	CW 32
Boundary Rd	Newlands	28	CL 33
Boundary Rd	Retreat	52	CZ 33
Boundary Rd	The Vines	40	CU 32
Boundary Rd	Townsend Est.	10	CB 43
Bouquet St	Cape Town Central	4	CE 26
Bourn	Avon	11	CD 48
Bournemouth Rd	Muizenberg	76	DF 34
Boveney Rd	Muizenberg	76	DG 33
Bowden Rd	Observatory	16	CG 33
Bowden Rd	Townsend Est.	10	CC 43
Bower Rd	Wynberg	40	CS 32
Bower St	Brooklyn	7	CB 35
Bowler	Avon	11	CD 47
Bowlers Way	Pinelands	18	CF 39
Bowlers Way	Three Anchor Bay	3	CB 23
Bowspirit	Strandfontein	69	DA 47
Bowspirit St	Strandfontein	69	DA 47
Bowwood Rd	Claremont	27	CO 31
Box Rd	Muizenberg	76	DF 34
Boxwood St	Bonteheuwel	21	CG 46
Boyd Ave	Athlone	18	CK 38
Boyes Dr.	Kalk Bay	75	DK 30
Boyes Dr.	Lakeside	63	DD 31
Boyes Dr.	Muizenberg	76	DG 32
Boyes Dr.	Muizenberg Nth	64	DE 32
Brabant Ct	Marina Da Gama	64	DC 33
Brabant Rd	Woodstock	5	CF 30
Bracken Cl.	Meadowridge	52	CV 32
Bracken St	Bonteheuwel	20	CG 45
Bradwell Rd	Vredehoek	14	CG 26
Braefield Rd	Plumstead	40	CS 32
Braehead St	Kenilworth	40	CQ 33
Braemar Rd	Greenpoint	4	CB 25
Braemar Rd	Oranjezicht	13	CH 24
Braeside	Greenpoint	3	CB 24
Braeside Rd	Kenilworth	28	CP 33
Brahms Rd	Retreat	64	DA 34
Bramble Way	Bonteheuwel	20	CH 45
Bramble Way	Meadowridge	52	CV 31
Brambos Rd	Bonteheuwel	21	CH 46
Bramford Ave	Athlone	30	CL 38
Bramley St	Plumstead	53	CV 34
Brampton Rd	Plumstead	40	CT 33
Brand Rd	Belgravia	30	CM 39
Brand St	Glencairn Hgts	83	DO 27
Brander Sq.	Factreton	9	CC 40
Brandon	Lotus River	55	CW 40
Brandon St	Hazendal	18	CK 38
Brandt Way	Ottery East	42	CT 39
Brandweer St	Gardens	14	CF 26
Brandwood Rd	Muizenberg Nth	64	DE 32
Brassie St	Lakeside	63	DD 31
Bray Rd	Kenilworth	41	CQ 34
Breakwater La.	Foreshore	4	CA 26
Breda St	Oranjezicht	14	CF 25
Breda St	Ruyterwacht	10	CD 45

STREET NAME	SUBURB NAME	PG	GRID
Breda St	Simon's Town	88	DU 27
Bree St	Cape Town Central ...	4	CD 26
Brenda Rd	Plumstead	40	CT 32
Brent Rd	Plumstead	40	CS 33
Brentwood Rd	Wynberg	41	CR 34
Bresee Rd	Belgravia	30	CM 39
Breston Rd	Silvertown	19	CK 40
Brevet Rd	Claremont	29	CN 35
Brevity La.	Sea Point	2	CE 20
Brian Rd	Bergvliet	52	CY 31
Brian Rd	Surrey Est.	31	CM 43
Briana Rd	Elfindale	53	CX 34
Briar Cl.	Silverglade	73	DK 25
Briar Rd	Newlands	27	CN 29
Briar Rd	Salt River	16	CF 31
Briar Way	Meadowridge	52	CV 31
Briard	Strandfontein	69	DA 47
Brickdale Ave	Woodstock	16	CF 31
Brickfield Rd	Salt River	16	CF 31
Bridge Cl.	Fairways	41	CU 36
Bridge Cl.	Montagu's Gift	54	CV 39
Bridge Pl.	Capricorn	65	DE 36
Bridge St	Mowbray	16	CH 33
Bridge St	Rosebank	17	CJ 34
Bridge St	District Six	15	CF 29
Bridgewater St	Paarden Eiland	6	CC 33
Bridgeway	Crawford	30	CM 38
Bridle Cl.	Kenilworth Pk	29	CP 36
Bridle Rd	Oranjezicht	14	CH 25
Bridoon Cl.	Hout Bay	36	CS 21
Brigade Rd	Lakeside	63	DD 31
Brigantine Ave	Sun Valley	73	DJ 23
Brighton La.	Ottery	43	CS 40
Brighton St	Hout Bay	47	CW 16
Brigid Rd	Elfindale	53	CW 34
Brink Cl.	Huis-in-bos	38	CU 27
Brink Rd	Barbarossa	40	CS 32
Brink Rd	Hout Bay	47	CV 17
Brink Rd	Wynberg	40	CR 31
Brinton St	Langa	19	CG 41
Briony Cl.	Meadowsteads	72	DG 20
Brisbane Rd	Wynberg	40	CR 33
Bristol Cl.	Avon	11	CD 47
Bristol Rd	Observatory	16	CG 33
Bristol Rd	Wynberg	40	CS 33
Britain Way	Strandfontein	69	DB 47
Britten Rd	Retreat	64	DA 34
Broad Cl.	Wynberg	40	CO 33
Broad Rd	Mowbray	16	CH 33
Broad Rd	Wynberg	41	CQ 34
Broad Walk Sq.	Pinelands	18	CG 37
Broad Wk	Pinelands	17	CG 36
Broadway Ave	Newlands	27	CM 30
Brocker Way	Tokai	51	CZ 29
Brockhurst Rd	Lansdowne	29	CP 37
Brockley Rd	Muizenberg	76	DG 33
Brockley Rd	Muizenberg	76	DH 33
Bromley Rd	Athlone	30	CL 39
Brommaert Ave	Alphen	39	CS 30
Brommaert Pl.	Alphen	39	CS 29
Brommersvlei Rd . Bel Ombre		39	CS 29
Brommersvlei Rd .. Hohenort		39	CQ 28
Brompton Ave	Bantry Bay	2	CE 20
Bromwell St	Woodstock	6	CE 31
Bromwich Rd	Westlake Est.	62	DC 28
Bromyard Rd .. Muizenberg Nth		64	DE 33
Bronnies Way	Dieprivier	52	CV 32
Bronze St	Vanguard	20	CK 43
Brook Cr.	San Michel	72	DF 22
Brook Rd	Rosebank	17	CJ 34
Brook St	Claremont	28	CN 32
Brook St	Foreshore	5	CE 29
Brookdale Ave	Pinelands	9	CE 40
Brookford Rd	Lotus River	54	CW 39
Brookwood Rd	Rondebosch	29	CL 35
Brounger Rd	Sillery	39	CU 28
Browning Rd	Observatory	16	CG 32
Brownlow Rd	Tamboerskloof	3	CE 24
Broxburn Rd	Plumstead	41	CU 34
Bruce Ave	Montagu's Gift	42	CU 39
Bruce Rd	Sillery	51	CV 28
Brunia Way	Hout Bay	34	CU 15
Brunswick Rd .. Tamboerskloof		3	CE 24
Brunswick St .. Glencairn Hgts		83	DO 27
Brushwood Rd	Bridgetown	19	CK 42
Brussels Ave	Fish Hoek	73	DK 25
Bruyns Rd	Wynberg	40	CR 33
Bryant St	Schotsche Kloof	4	CE 25
Bryn Rd	Muizenberg Nth	64	DE 32
Buall Wk	Hanover Pk	31	CP 42
Buchan Rd	Newlands	27	CN 31
Buchanan Rd	Claremont	29	CN 36
Buchner Rd	Hazendal	18	CJ 38
Buck Rd	Lotus River	55	CV 40
Buck Rd	Pelikan Pk	55	CX 40
Buckingham Cl.	Tokai	51	CZ 28
Buckingham Cl.	Tokai	51	CY 28
Buckingham Rd .. Lansdowne		29	CO 37
Buckingham Rd .. Plumstead		40	CS 32
Buckingham Rd	Tokai	51	CZ 28
Buckingham Way			
	Weltevreden Valley ..	45	CU 48
Buckley St	Athlone	30	CL 38
Bucksburn Rd	Newlands	27	CN 31
Bud Rd	Retreat	52	CZ 32
Budock St	Claremont	28	CN 34
Buffalo Rd	Ocean View	79	DN 17
Buffalo Way	Primrose Pk ..	31	CN 43
Buiten St	Cape Town Central ..	4	CE 25
Buiten St	Schotsche Kloof ..	4	CD 25
Buitengracht St ..Cape Town Central..		4	CE 25
Buitenkant St	Vredehoek	14	CF 26
Buitenkant St	District Six	4	CE 26
Buitensingle St ..Cape Town Central ..		4	CE 25
Buller Louw Dr.	Sunnydale	72	DJ 21
Bungalow Dr.	Strandfontein	69	DC 48
Bunker Rd	Lakeside	63	DD 31
Bunkers Hill	Strandfontein	69	DD 48
Bunney St	Kensington	8	CC 39
Burchell St	Ruyterwacht	11	CD 46
Buren Rd	Chapman's Peak	71	DF 19
Buren Rd	Wynberg	40	CR 31
Burg Rd	Rondebosch	16	CK 33
Burg Rd	Rosebank	16	CK 33
Burg St	Cape Town Central	4	CD 26
Burgee Bend .. Marina Da Gama		64	DE 34
Burgee Bend	Strandfontein	69	DA 47
Burger Rd	Rondebosch	29	CL 36
Burggraaf Rd	Welcome	20	CK 44
Burgundy Rd	The Vines	40	CU 31
Burke St	Observatory	16	CF 32
Burma La.	Strandfontein	68	DA 46
Burnam Rd	Observatory	16	CG 33
Burnbrae Rd .. Simon's Town		83	DO 27
Burnham Rd	Plumstead	40	CT 32
Burnley Cl.	Grassy Pk	54	CW 37
Burnley Rd	Crawford	30	CN 38
Burns Rd	Salt River	16	CE 32
Burnside Rd	Tamboerskloof	3	CE 24
Burton Cl.	Ottery	43	CR 40
Burton La.	Fish Hoek	83	DM 27
Burton St	Maitland	7	CD 35
Burwood Rd	Crawford	30	CN 38
Burwood Rd	Lansdowne	30	CO 38
Bush Rd	Parkwood	41	CU 36
Bush St	Nyanga	33	CO 49
Bushwood Rd	Mowbray	17	CH 35
Busy St	Strandfontein	69	DA 47
Bute Rd	Wynberg	41	CS 34
Buttermere Rd .... Coniston Pk		64	DB 33
Butts Ave	Thornton	9	CE 41
Buxton Ave	Gardens	13	CG 24
Buxton Ave	Ruyterwacht	10	CE 45
Buzzard Rd	Phumlani	55	CX 41
Byrnes Ave	Wynberg	41	CR 34
Byron St	Tamboerskloof	3	CE 24
Byway	Pinelands	18	CF 38

C

STREET NAME	SUBURB NAME	PG	GRID
C.Hani Ave	Hout Bay	35	CU 17
C.J.Langenhoven Rd ..Townsend Est. .		10	CB 44
C.J.Nabe Way	Langa	19	CH 41
C.L.Leipoldt St .... Goodwood Est.		10	CA 44
Cabarnet Cr. ... Constantia Village ...		39	CT 29
Cable Cl.	Marina Da Gama	64	DE 34
Cabot Way	Strandfontein	69	DA 47
Caclow	Schaap Kraal	43	CQ 41
Cactus Cr.	Kewtown	19	CK 40
Cactus St	Chapman's Peak	71	DF 18
Cactus St	Kewtown	19	CK 40
Caddie St	Lakeside	63	DD 31
Caen Rd	Strandfontein	68	DB 46
Caesar St	Woodstock	5	CE 30
Cain St	Grassy Pk	53	CW 36
Caique	Sun Valley	73	DK 23
Cairmount Ave	Gardens	13	CG 24
Cairn Steps	Clifton	12	CF 20
Cairn Steps	Simon's Town	83	DP 27
Caithness Rd	Simon's Town	83	DP 27
Calais	Strandfontein	68	DB 46
Calais Rd	Sea Point	3	CC 22
Calcite Rd	Belthorn Est.	30	CO 40
Calcium Rd	Vanguard	31	CL 43
Calcutta St	Paarden Eiland	7	CC 34
Caleb St	Woodstock	5	CE 30
Caledon St	Townsend Est.	10	CB 43
Caledon St	District Six	4	CE 27
Caledonian Rd	Mowbray	17	CH 34
Calendula Rd	Silvertown	19	CK 40
Callisto Rd	Ocean View	79	DN 17
Calvin St	Woodstock	5	CE 30
Calvinia St	Ruyterwacht	10	CC 44
Cam Rd	Manenberg	32	CO 44
Camberwell Rd .. Belgravia		30	CM 39
Camberwell Rd .... Crawford		30	CM 38
Camberwell Rd .. Three Anchor Bay..		3	CB 23
Cambier Way	Bergvliet	51	CV 30
Cambra Verdun Way ..Strandfontein..		68	DB 46
Cambridge Link	Norwood	11	CD 48
Cambridge Rd	Lakeside	64	DD 32
Cambridge Rd	Observatory	17	CG 34
Cambridge St	Claremont	28	CO 34
Cambridge St	Maitland	7	CE 35
Cambridge St	Woodstock	15	CF 29
Camden St	Brooklyn	7	CC 35
Camden St	Maitland	7	CD 35
Camden St	Tamboerskloof	3	CE 24
Camden Way	Noordhoek		
Manor Retirement Village		73	DG 23
Camden Way	Noordhoek		
Manor Retirement Village		73	DJ 24
Camelia Cl.	Clunie	50	CW 27
Camellia Cl.	Strandfontein	52	CX 32
Camellia St	Bonteheuwel	20	CH 44
Cameron St	Belgravia	30	CN 39
Camilla St	Glencairn Hgts	83	DN 27
Camp	Strandfontein	69	DB 47
Camp Access Rd	Youngsfield	41	CR 36

STREET NAME	SUBURB NAME	PG	GRID
Camp Ground Rd ...	Mowbray	17	CH 34
Camp Ground Rd ...	Rondebosch	17	CJ 34
Camp Ground Rd ...	Rosebank	17	CJ 34
Camp Rd	Maitland	7	CE 34
Camp Rd	Muizenberg	76	DG 33
Camp Rd	Pinelands	18	CF 37
Camp Rd	Wynberg	40	CR 32
Camp Rd	Wynberg	40	CR 31
Camp St	Oranjezicht	14	CF 25
Campbell Rd	Hout Bay	47	CW 18
Campbell St	Observatory	16	CF 32
Campground Rd ...	Claremont	28	CM 33
Campground Rd ...	Rondebosch	28	CL 34
Camphor La.	Bergvliet	52	CX 31
Camphor Rd	Kommetjie	79	DM 15
Camps Bay Dr.	Camps Bay	12	CK 20
Camps Bay Dr.	Camps Bay	12	CH 21
Campus Cr.	Rondebosch	16	CJ 33
Canal Rd	Ottery	42	CR 38
Canal Rd	Retreat	53	CY 34
Canary St	Ocean View	79	DM 17
Canary St	Penlyn Est.	31	CN 41
Candian St	Strandfontein	69	DB 49
Candlewood Cl.	Hout Bay	36	CS 21
Candlewood St	Bonteheuwel	20	CH 44
Cane Rd	Ottery	42	CR 38
Canigou Ave	Rondebosch	28	CL 34
Canna St	Retreat	52	CY 32
Cannabis Wk	Matroosfontein	21	CG 47
Cannery Row	Wynberg	27	CP 30
Cannon Cl.	Newlands	27	CM 30
Cannon Island Way ...	Capricorn	65	DE 35
Cannon Island Way ..	Marina Da Gama.	64	DE 34
Cannon Rd	Maitland	7	CE 35
Cannon St	Newlands	27	CM 30
Cannon St	Plumstead	40	CU 33
Canoe Cr.	Strandfontein	68	DC 44
Canon Cl.	Hout Bay Harbour	46	CY 15
Canterbury Dr.	Bishopscourt	26	CP 28
Canterbury Rd	Heathfield	52	CX 33
Canterbury St	District Six	4	CE 27
Canyon St	Riverton	11	CB 46
Cap Michel Cl.	Muizenberg	76	DF 32
Cape Beech Rd	Farmsteads	60	DE 20
Cape Flats Freeway	Weltevreden Valley	45	CT 48
Capella Ave	Ocean View	79	DN 16
Capri	St James	75	DJ 31
Capri Cl.	Capri	81	DL 21
Capri Dr.	Capri	80	DL 20
Capri Way	Strandfontein	69	DA 49
Capricorn Dr.	Capricorn	65	DD 35
Capricorn Blvd. North ...	Capricorn	65	DD 35
Capricorn Blvd. South ...	Capricorn	65	DE 36
Capricorn Cr.	Capricorn	65	DD 35
Capricorn Dr.	Capricorn	65	DE 36
Capricorn Rd	Ocean View	79	DO 17
Capstan Cl.	Marina Da Gama	64	DD 34
Capuchin St	Athlone	18	CK 38
Carabinier Rd	Wynberg	41	CR 34
Cara-Cara Rd	Phumlani	55	CX 41
Caravel Rd	Strandfontein	68	DA 44
Caravel Rd	Sun Valley	73	DJ 23
Carbon St	Primrose Pk	31	CO 43
Carbrook Ave	Claremont	28	CO 32
Cardiff Rd	Simon's Town	88	DU 27
Cardiff St	Cape Town Central	4	CC 26
Cardiff St	Newlands	27	CM 31
Cardinal Cl.	Chapman's Peak	71	DF 19
Cardross Grant St ...	Cafda Village	53	CZ 35
Carey Slater Rd ...	Townsend Est.	10	CB 44
Carey St	Woodstock	5	CE 30
Cariad Rd	Ottery	42	CR 38
Carigman La.	Westlake	63	DC 31
Carisbrook St	Gardens	4	CE 25
Carisbrook St	Tamboerskloof	3	CE 24
Carissa Cir.	Ottery East	42	CT 39
Carissa St	Ottery	42	CT 37
Carl St	Schotsche Kloof	4	CD 25
Carlier Cr.	Penlyn Est.	30	CN 40
Carlisle Rd	Kirstenhof	63	DB 30
Carlisle St	Maitland	7	CD 36
Carlisle St	Paarden Eiland	6	CC 33
Carlow Rd	Wynberg	41	CR 34
Carlton Rd	Fish Hoek	74	DK 27
Carlton St	Claremont	28	CO 34
Carlton St	Grassy Pk	53	CY 36
Carmichael Rd	Fish Hoek	73	DK 24
Carnarvon Rd	Plumstead	40	CT 32
Carnarvon St	Ruyterwacht	10	CD 45
Carnation Cl.	Hanover Pk	31	CO 42
Carnation Rd	Ocean View	79	DM 16
Carnation Sq.	Bridgetown	19	CJ 41
Carnie Rd	Doornhoogte	31	CL 41
Carol St	Retreat	64	DA 33
Carola Way	Montagu's Gift	54	CV 38
Carolina St	Athlone	30	CL 38
Carp Cl.	Marina Da Gama	64	DC 33
Carp Rd	Pelikan Pk	54	CY 38
Carr Hill Rd	Wynberg	40	CR 32
Carreg Cr.	Greenpoint	4	CC 25
Carriage St	Woodstock	6	CE 33
Carrick Cr.	Newfields	31	CN 42
Carrier	Epping Ind.	21	CF 47
Carrington Ave	Athlone	30	CL 38
Carrol Rd	Montagu's Gift	42	CU 38
Carrol Rd	Ottery East	42	CU 39
Carson Ave	Athlone	30	CL 38
Carstens St	Tamboerskloof	3	CE 24
Carter Rd	Retreat	53	CY 35
Carwell Rd	Lansdowne	30	CP 39
Cashel Ave	Athlone	30	CL 38
Casino	Strandfontein	68	DB 46
Casper Ave	Ottery East	42	CT 39
Cassandra Rd	Pinati	30	CP 40
Cassandra Rd	Pinati	30	CO 38
Cassel Rd	Sea Point	2	CD 21
Cassia Rd	Ottery	42	CT 38
Cassia St	Bonteheuwel	20	CH 44
Cassino Rd	Plumstead	41	CU 35
Castle St	Cape Town Central	4	CD 25
Castleman Rd	Fish Hoek	73	DK 24
Castletown Rd	Plumstead	40	CS 33
Castletown Rd	Wynberg	40	CR 33
Castleview Rd	Meadowridge	51	CV 30
Castor Rd	Lansdowne	30	CP 39
Castor Way	Ocean View	79	DN 16
Catalina St	Capri	81	DL 21
Catamaran Cl.	Sun Valley	73	DK 23
Catamaran Cl.	Sun Valley	73	DJ 24
Catamaran Cr.	Strandfontein	68	DB 44
Catamaran Cr.	Strandfontein	68	DE 45
Catamaran Rd	Strandfontein	68	DB 44
Cathcart St	Ruyterwacht	10	CE 45
Cathedral Rd	Manenberg	32	CM 45
Cathkin Peak Rd ..	Heideveld	32	CM 46
Cathkin Rd	Heideveld	20	CK 45
Cauvin Rd	District Six	15	CF 28
Cavalcade Rd	Greenpoint	3	CB 24
Cavalry Cr.	Ottery East	42	CT 38
Cavan Cl.	Wynberg	40	CQ 32
Cavan Rd	Wynberg	40	CQ 32
Cavell Rd	Lansdowne	43	CQ 40
Cavemore Rd	Lansdowne	30	CQ 39
Cavendish Pl.	Claremont	28	CN 32
Cavendish Rd	Claremont	28	CN 32
Cavendish Sq.	Woodstock	5	CE 30
Cavendish St	Woodstock	5	CE 30
Caxton Cl.	Meadowridge	52	CW 31
Caxton Cr.	Meadowridge	52	CV 31
Caxton St	Foreshore	5	CE 29
Caxton Way	Meadowridge	52	CV 31
Cayenne Cl.	Capri	81	DL 21
Cayenne Cl.	Capri	81	DM 21
Cecelia Way	Matroosfontein	21	CG 48
Cecil Rd	Mowbray	16	CJ 33
Cecil Rd	Plumstead	40	CT 33
Cecil Rd	Salt River	16	CF 32
Cecil Rhodes Ave ...	Ruyterwacht	11	CC 44
Cecil St	Claremont	28	CN 33
Cecil St	Hout Bay	47	CV 16
Cecilia Cl.	Belle Constantia	51	CV 29
Cedar Ave	Pinelands	18	CF 39
Cedar Ave	Westlake Est.	62	DB 26
Cedar Ave	Westlake Est.	62	DB 26
Cedar Cl.	Hout Bay	36	CS 21
Cedar Cr.	Ruyterwacht	10	CC 45
Cedar Rd	Newlands	27	CM 30
Cedar Rd	Thornton	9	CD 42
Cedarberg Rd	Lavender Hill East	65	DC 36
Cedarberg Rd	Ocean View	79	DN 17
Cedarberg St	Ruyterwacht	10	CC 45
Celie Rd	Retreat Ind. Area	64	DB 32
Cella St	Athlone	18	CK 38
Centaur Cl.	Ocean View	79	DN 17
Central Ave	Belthorn Est.	30	CO 39
Central Ave	Pinelands	17	CG 36
Central Cir.	Fish Hoek	83	DL 27
Central Dr.	Camps Bay	12	CH 20
Central Rd	Fish Hoek	83	DL 27
Central Sq.	Pinelands	18	CG 37
Centre Cl.	Montagu's Gift	42	CU 38
Ceres Rd	Bergvliet	51	CW 30
Ceres St	Brooklyn	7	CB 34
Cerise Rd	Parkwood	54	CV 37
Cessna Cr.	Kensington	8	CC 38
Cetus Way	Ocean View	79	DN 16
Chad Rd	Retreat	52	CY 32
Chadwin Rd	Elfindale	52	CW 32
Chaffinch	Dreyersdal	51	CZ 30
Chaim St	Montana/Durrheim	21	CK 48
Chaldon Way	Pinelands	18	CE 39
Chalfont Rd	Claremont	28	CM 33
Chamberlain Av	Claremont	27	CN 31
Chamberlain Rd	Churchill	11	CA 48
Chamberlain Rd	Glenlily	11	CA 48
Chamberlain St	Woodstock	15	CF 30
Chamois St	Rugby	7	CA 35
Champagne Cr.	Hout Bay	47	CV 17
Chantercler La.	Airlie	51	CV 28
Chapel La.	Simon's Town	88	DU 27
Chapel Rd	Lavender Hill	65	DA 35
Chapel Rd	Rosebank	16	CJ 33
Chapel St	Maitland	7	CD 34
Chapel St	Salt River	6	CE 32
Chapel St	District Six	5	CE 28
Chaplin Cl.	Chapman's Peak	71	DF 19
Chaplin Way	Kirstenhof	63	DB 30
Chapman St	Factreton	8	CB 39
Chapmans Cl.	Ocean View	79	DN 17
Chapmans Cl.	Ocean View	79	DP 17
Chapman's Peak Dr. ...	Hout Bay	47	CV 18
Chapman's Peak Dr. ...	Noordhoek	59	DB 17
Chard Rd	Frogmore Est.	63	DB 31
Chardonnay La.	Hout Bay	47	CV 17
Charity Rd	Retreat	53	CY 34
Charles Calvert Rd ...	Charlesville	21	CK 47
Charles Cl.	Barbarossa	40	CT 31
Charles La.	Valhalla Pk	21	CJ 48
Charles Rd	Edward	43	CT 40
Charles Way	Barbarossa	40	CT 31
Charnwood Ave ...	Steenberg	62	DA 26

STREET NAME	SUBURB NAME	PG	GRID
Charnwood Cl.	Steenberg	62	DA 26
Chartley Rd	Rondebosch	17	CK 34
Chas Booth Ave	Bakoven	12	CK 20
Chasmay Rd	Lekkerwater	72	DK 20
Chateau Ave	Fresnaye	2	CD 21
Chateau Cir.	Barbarossa	40	CT 32
Chatham Rd	Heathfield	52	CX 33
Chatham Rd	Salt River	16	CF 32
Chatham St	Maitland	8	CD 37
Chaucer Rd	Claremont	28	CN 33
Chebec Cr.	Sun Valley	72	DJ 22
Cheddar Rd	Wynberg	41	CS 34
Cheetah St	Ocean View	79	DN 17
Chelmsford Rd	Vredehoek	14	CG 27
Chelsea Ave	Vredehoek	14	CF 26
Chelsea Cr.	Kirstenhof	63	DC 31
Chelsea La.	Noordhoek		
Manor Retirement Village		73	DG 23
Chelsea La.	Noordhoek		
Manor Retirement Village		73	DJ 24
Chelsea St	Riverton	11	CC 46
Cheltenham Rd	Mowbray	17	CH 35
Chemist Mlungu St	Manenberg	32	CN 46
Chene Cl.	Hohenort	38	CQ 27
Chenel Cl.	Westlake	63	DC 31
Chenel Way	Westlake	63	DC 31
Chepstow Rd	Greenpoint	4	CC 25
Cherbourg Ave	Plumstead	52	CV 33
Cherry Cl.	Newlands	26	CN 28
Cherry La.	Belle Constantia	51	CW 29
Cherry St	Newlands	26	CN 28
Cherry Way	Hout Bay	35	CT 18
Chesham Rd	Claremont	29	CN 35
Chess Rd	Rondebosch	29	CM 35
Chester Dr.	Bishopscourt	27	CP 29
Chester Rd	Lakeside	64	DD 32
Chester Rd	Rosebank	16	CK 33
Chester Rd	Tokai	62	DA 28
Chester Rd	Woodstock	15	CF 30
Chesterfield Rd	Oranjezicht	13	CG 24
Chesterfield Rd	Oranjezicht	14	CH 25
Chestnut	Pinelands	19	CG 40
Chestnut Ave	Wynberg	27	CP 31
Chestnut Cl.	Fairie Knowe	72	DK 21
Chestnut Cl.	Fairie Knowe	72	DH 20
Chestnut Dr.	Hout Bay	36	CS 21
Chestnut Rd	Farmsteads	60	DD 20
Chestnut St	Bonteheuwel	20	CH 44
Chestnut St	Thornton	10	CD 43
Chestnut Way	Avon	11	CD 47
Chestnut Way	Silverglade	73	DK 25
Cheviot Pl.	Greenpoint	3	CB 24
Chevron Sq.	Retreat	64	DA 33
Chiappini St	Cape Town Central	4	CC 26
Chiappini St	Schotsche Kloof	4	CD 25
Chichester Rd	Crofters Valley	72	DH 22
Chichester Cl.	Claremont	28	CO 34
Chief Rd	Steenberg	64	DB 34
Chigwell Rd	Epping Forest	21	CF 48
Childrens Rd	Strandfontein	69	DA 47
Childrens Way	Bergvliet	52	CX 31
Chilton Cr.	Hout Bay	47	CW 18
Chilworth Rd	Camps Bay	12	CH 20
Chimes St	Retreat	64	DA 33
Chingford Cr.	Epping Forest	21	CF 48
Chipenham Rd	Kenilworth	28	CP 33
Chipphillside	Retreat	52	CZ 33
Chipstead Way	Pinelands	8	CE 39
Choir St	Steenberg	64	DB 34
Chopin St	Cafda Village	53	CZ 35
Chris Abraham Rd	Retreat	52	CY 33
Chris Barry Ave	Retreat	52	CY 33
Chris Hani Cr.	Weltevreden Valley.	45	CS 48
Chrisiris Cr.	Hazelwood Pk	72	DJ 22
Chrismas Tinto St	Manenberg	32	CN 46
Christiaan St	Hout Bay	47	CV 18
Christiaan St	District Six	15	CF 28
Christian Ave	Epping Ind.	10	CE 44
Christina Rd	Kommetjie	79	DM 15
Christine St	Barbarossa	40	CT 31
Christopher Rd	Bergvliet	51	CX 30
Christow Rd	Rosebank	16	CJ 33
Chromite Rd	Penlyn Est.	30	CO 40
Chudleigh Rd	Plumstead	41	CT 34
Chukker Rd	Lansdowne	29	CP 36
Church Rd	Churchill	11	CA 48
Church Rd	Glenlily	11	CA 48
Church Rd	Goodwood Est.	10	CC 44
Church Rd	Muizenberg	76	DG 33
Church Rd	Retreat Ind. Area	52	CZ 32
Church Rd	Sea Point	2	CD 21
Church St	Athlone	18	CK 38
Church St	Brooklyn	7	CS 26
Church St	Cape Town Central	4	CD 25
Church St	Claremont	28	CO 32
Church St	Langa	19	CG 41
Church St	Lansdowne	30	CP 38
Church St	Mowbray	16	CH 33
Church St	Rondebosch	16	CK 33
Church St	Salberau	11	CE 48
Church St	Strandfontein	69	DB 47
Church St	Woodstock	5	CE 30
Church St	Wynberg	40	CR 32
Churchdown La.	Heathfield	52	CX 32
Churchill Rd	Plumstead	41	CS 35
Cicily Ave	Capri	81	DL 21
Cindy Rd	Heathfield	52	CY 32
Circle Way	Strandfontein	69	DB 47
Circle Way	Strandfontein	69	DD 48
Circuit St	Hazendal	18	CJ 38
Circus Ave	Claremont	28	CO 33
Cirus St	Kirstenhof	63	DA 30
Cissy Gool Ave	Gatesville	31	CM 42
Citrus St	Bonteheuwel	20	CH 43
Civic Ave	Foreshore	4	CD 27
Civic Rd	Lansdowne	29	CO 37
Civic Rd	Lotus River	54	CW 39
Civic Rd	Matroosfontein	21	CG 48
Clairvaux Rd	Kalk Bay	75	DK 30
Clan Monroe Ave	Kommetjie	78	DN 12
Clan Stewart St	Glencairn Hgts	83	DN 27
Clare Rd	Wynberg	40	CS 33
Clare St	Gardens	14	CF 26
Claremont Ave	Claremont	28	CO 33
Clarence Rd	Wynberg	41	CR 34
Clarendon Cr.	Brooklyn	7	CC 35
Clarendon Rd	Mowbray	17	CH 34
Clarendon Rd	Muizenberg	76	DG 33
Clarendon Rd	Muizenberg	76	DH 33
Clarendon Rd	Pinelands	18	CF 37
Clarens Rd	Sea Point	2	CD 21
Clarens St	Woodstock	5	CE 30
Clarepark Ave	Rondebosch	29	CM 35
Clarewyn Rd	Lansdowne	30	CP 39
Clarks Steps	Simon's Town	89	DU 28
Claude St	Newfields	31	CN 42
Clayman Cl.	Capri	81	DL 21
Clays La.	Epping Forest	21	CF 48
Cleek St	Lakeside	63	DD 31
Clement Way	Bergvliet	51	CX 30
Clevedon Rd	Muizenberg	76	DF 33
Cleveland Rd	Claremont	29	CN 35
Clevily Rd	Athlone	30	CL 38
Cliff Rd	Clifton	12	CG 19
Cliff Rd	Fish Hoek	83	DN 28
Clifford Ave	Vredehoek	14	CH 26
Clifford Cr.	Bergvliet	51	CX 30
Clifford Rd	Sea Point	3	CC 22
Clifford St	Ottery East	43	CT 40
Clifton Rd	Camps Bay	12	CG 20
Clifton Rd	Claremont	28	CN 34
Clifton Rd	Mowbray	17	CH 35
Clifton Rd	Muizenberg	76	DF 34
Clifton Rd	Observatory	16	CG 33
Clifton Steps	Clifton	12	CF 20
Clingdale Cl.	Tokai	51	CZ 30
Clinic St	Gatesville	31	CL 42
Clipper Cr.	Strandfontein	68	DB 44
Clipper Rd	Strandfontein	68	DB 44
Clipperton Cl.	Capri	81	DL 21
Clive Rd	Crawford	29	CN 37
Clive St	Browns Farm	45	CQ 47
Clive St	Vredehoek	14	CF 26
Clivia St	Retreat	64	DA 32
Cloete Rd	Woodstock	15	CG 30
Clovelly Ave	Devil's Peak Est.	14	CF 27
Clovelly Cl.	Clovelly	74	DK 28
Clovelly Rd	Clovelly	74	DJ 26
Clovelly Rd	Noordhoek		
Manor Retirement Village		73	DG 23
Clovelly Steps	Clovelly	74	DJ 28
Clover Cr.	Silvertown	19	CK 40
Clover St	Silvertown	19	CK 40
Club La.	Simon's Town	88	DU 27
Club St	Lakeside	63	DD 31
Clunie Rd	Bergvliet	52	CY 31
Clyde Rd	Greenpoint	3	CB 24
Clyde Rd	Rondebosch	28	CL 33
Clyde St	Hout Bay	47	CW 16
Clyde St	Strandfontein	69	DB 49
Clyde St	Woodstock	5	CE 30
Clydebank Rd	Greenpoint	3	CB 24
Coach Rd	Wynberg	40	CQ 31
Cobblestone Rd	District Six	14	CF 27
Cobern La.	Fish Hoek	82	DL 26
Cobern St	Cape Town Central	4	CC 26
Cochrane Ave	Epping Ind.	10	CE 43
Cockburn Cl.	Glencairn Hgts	83	DN 27
Cockle Cr.	Clovelly	74	DK 27
Cockscombe Rd	Heideveld	32	CL 46
Coen Steytler Ave	Cape Town Cen.	4	CC 27
Coghill Rd	Wynberg	40	CR 32
Cogman St	Ruyterwacht	10	CD 45
Cognac Cl.	Townsend Est.	10	CA 43
Cole St	Observatory	16	CF 33
Colebrook Cl.	Elnor	21	CF 48
Coleman St	Elsies River Ind.	11	CC 48
Colenso Rd	Bishopscourt	27	CO 30
Coleridge Rd	Salt River	6	CE 32
Colesburg St	Ruyterwacht	10	CD 45
Coligny	Kirstenhof	63	DB 30
Colin Rd	Grassy Pk	53	CY 36
Colin St	Maitland	7	CD 35
Colinton Rd	Newlands	27	CN 31
Colleen Rd	Manenberg	32	CO 45
College Rd	Doornhoogte	31	CM 41
College Rd	Rondebosch	17	CK 34
College Rd	Surrey Est.	31	CM 43
College Service Rd	Doornhoogte	31	CM 41
College St	Claremont	28	CO 34
Coller Rd	Retreat	52	CZ 32
Collesberg Cir.	Heideveld	32	CL 45
Collette Cl.	Bel Ombre	39	CS 28
Collingwood Rd	Observatory	16	CF 33
Colorado Rd	Browns Farm	45	CR 47
Colorado St	Primrose Pk	31	CN 43
Colt St	Strandfontein	69	DA 47
Columbia Rd	Ocean View	79	DN 17
Columbine Ave	Ottery	43	CT 37
Columbine Rd	Rondebosch	29	CM 36
Columbus Ave	Fish Hoek	73	DK 25

STREET NAME	SUBURB NAME	PG	GRID
Columbus Rd	Claremont	28	CN 34
Colwell Rd	Muizenberg Nth	64	DE 33
Colwyn Rd	Silvertown	19	CK 41
Colyn Rd	Kalk Bay	75	DK 30
Colyn Rd	Sweet Valley	51	CX 29
Comet Rd	Ocean View	79	DN 17
Comet Rd	Surrey Est.	31	CM 43
Comity St	Primrose Pk	31	CO 43
Commercial Rd	Clarkes	21	CG 48
Commercial Rd	Ndabeni	7	CE 35
Commercial St	Cape Town Cen.	4	CE 26
Common Rd	Strandfontein	68	DA 46
Como Rd	Flintdale Est.	53	CW 35
Compass Cl.	Marina Da Gama	64	DD 34
Comrie Rd	Camps Bay	12	CH 21
Concert Blvd.	Retreat	52	CZ 32
Concord St	Flintdale Est.	53	CV 35
Conduit St	Vredehoek	14	CH 26
Cone Cr.	Ruyterwacht	10	CC 45
Cone Way	Pinelands	18	CF 37
Conifer Rd	Hout Bay	36	CT 20
Conifer Rd	Sea Point	3	CC 22
Conifer Rd	Tokai	51	CZ 28
Conifer Way	Pinelands	18	CF 37
Coniston Ave	Coniston Pk	64	DB 33
Coniston Rd	Rondebosch	29	CL 35
Coniston Way	Pinelands	8	CE 39
Coniston Way	Silverhurst	39	CT 29
Conmead Rd	Meadowridge	51	CV 30
Connaught Rd	Kenilworth	41	CQ 34
Connemara Dr.	Hout Bay	36	CS 20
Connemara Rd	Royal Cape	41	CS 36
Conner Cl.	Bel Ombre	39	CS 29
Conningsby St	Athlone	29	CL 37
Conquest Rd	Belthorn Est.	30	CN 39
Conrad Rd	Montagu's Gift	42	CU 39
Consani Ave	Elsies River Ind.	11	CC 47
Consort Rd	Retreat	52	CY 32
Consta Rd	Heathfield	52	CY 32
Constance Rd	Claremont	27	CO 31
Constantia Ct	Marina Da Gama	64	DD 34
Constantia Main Rd	High Constantia	38	CT 27
Constantia Main Rd	Silverhurst	39	CT 29
Constantia Main Rd	Wittebloomen	38	CR 25
Constantia Rd	Gardens	13	CF 23
Constantia Rd	Plumstead	40	CS 32
Constantiaberg Cl.	Belle Constantia.	39	CU 29
Constantiaberg Cl.	Plumstead	40	CU 32
Constitution St	District Six	14	CF 27
Constraniaberg Cl.	Plumstead	40	CU 32
Container Rd	Foreshore	6	CC 31
Contance Rd	Coniston Pk	64	DB 34
Convent Rd	Wynberg	40	CQ 31
Conway St	Brooklyn	7	CC 35
Coodes Cr.	Foreshore	4	CB 26
Cook Rd	Claremont	28	CN 34
Cook St	Observatory	16	CF 32
Cook St	Vasco Est.	10	CA 45
Coombe Rd	Plumstead	41	CU 35
Coone Rd	Retreat	64	DA 32
Coopers Cl.	Rust-en-vrede	39	CT 29
Coot Dr.	Marina Da Gama	64	DC 34
Coot Rd	Pelikan Pk	55	CZ 41
Coot Way	Pelikan Pk	54	CY 37
Copeland Rd	Rondebosch	28	CL 32
Copperfield Rd	Salt River	16	CF 31
Coracle St	Sun Valley	73	DJ 23
Corah St	Brooklyn	7	CB 35
Coral Cl.	Riverton	11	CC 46
Coral Cr.	San Michel	72	DG 22
Coral Pl.	Sunnydale	72	DK 21
Coral Pl.	Sunnydale	72	DH 20
Coral Tree Rd	Thornton	10	CD 43
Corby Cl.	Grassy Pk	54	CX 38
Cordelia	Hout Bay	47	CW 18
Corfu	Ottery	42	CQ 38
Corfu Ave	Capri	81	DL 21
Corfu Ave	Sunnydale	81	DL 22
Corfu Cl.	Sunnydale	81	DL 22
Corfu St	Capricorn	65	DE 35
Corgi	Strandfontein	68	DA 46
Corlie Rd	Flintdale Est.	53	CV 36
Cormorant Ave	Marina Da Gama	64	DC 34
Cormorant Cir.	Imhoff's Gift	79	DM 17
Cormorant Rd	Fish Hoek	74	DK 27
Cornflower St	Bridgetown	19	CJ 41
Cornhill Rd	Athlone	18	CK 38
Cornuta Ave	Tokai	51	CZ 29
Cornwall Rd	Kenilworth	40	CQ 33
Cornwall Rd	Lakeside	63	DD 31
Cornwall St	Claremont	28	CO 34
Cornwall St	Simon's Town	88	DU 27
Cornwall St	Woodstock	5	CE 29
Corona St	Retreat	52	CY 32
Coronation Ave	Tamboerskloof	13	CF 24
Coronation Rd	Maitland	8	CD 37
Coronation Rd	Woodstock	15	CF 29
Coronation St	Maitland	7	CD 34
Coronation St	Plumstead	40	CU 33
Coronet Ct	Leonsdale	11	CD 48
Corporation St	Cape Town Central	4	CE 26
Corridor Rd	Heideveld	20	CK 45
Corrie Rd	Manenberg	32	CO 45
Corsair Cr.	Barbarossa	39	CU 30
Corsair Cr.	Strandfontein	68	DB 44
Corsair Way	Sun Valley	72	DJ 22
Corsica	Capricorn	65	DE 35
Corsica Ave	Capri	81	DL 21
Corvette Ave	Sun Valley	72	DK 22
Corvina Link	Hout Bay Harbour	46	CY 15
Corvina Link	Hout Bay Harbour	46	CX 14
Corvus Cl.	Ocean View	79	DO 17
Corwen St	Claremont	28	CN 32
Cosmic Cl.	Salberau	21	CF 48
Cosmos Rd	Elfindale	52	CW 33
Cotswold Ave	Gardens	13	CF 23
Cottage Cl.	Noordhaven	72	DF 21
Cottage La.	Barbarossa	39	CU 30
Cotte Rd	Lansdowne	43	CQ 40
Country Club Rd	Kenilworth	41	CQ 34
Court Rd	Simon's Town	88	DT 27
Court Rd	Wynberg	40	CQ 32
Court Town Rd	Plumstead	40	CS 32
Courville St	Gardens	14	CF 25
Covendon Rd	Belgravia	30	CM 40
Coventry Rd	Woodstock	15	CF 29
Cowell Way	Retreat	52	CZ 33
Cowley	District Six	5	CE 28
Cox Ave	Penlyn Est.	31	CN 41
Cox St	Montana/Durrheim	21	CK 48
Cradock Rd	Retreat	53	CZ 34
Cradock St	Ruyterwacht	10	CD 44
Craig Rd	Muizenberg Nth	64	DE 32
Craig Rd	Wynberg	40	CR 31
Craigrownie Rd	Bantry Bay	2	CD 20
Crake Cl.	Pelikan Pk	55	CX 40
Cramond Rd	Camps Bay	12	CJ 21
Cranberry Cr.	Camps Bay	12	CH 21
Crane Cl.	Dreyersdal	51	CZ 30
Crane Cl.	Flintdale Est.	53	CW 35
Crane Cr.	Pelikan Pk	55	CZ 41
Cranko Ave	Kirstenhof	63	DA 31
Cranko Rd	Observatory	16	CG 33
Cranley Rd	Athlone	30	CL 38
Cranmere Rd	Plumstead	40	CT 32
Crassula Ave	Devil's Peak Est.	14	CF 27
Crassula Rd	Kommetjie	78	DM 12
Crassula Rd	Thornton	9	CD 42
Crassula Way	Pinelands	18	CG 39
Crater St	Salberau	11	CE 47
Craven Ave	Athlone	30	CM 38
Craven Cl.	Athlone	30	CM 38
Crawford Rd	Crawford	30	CM 38
Crecy	Strandfontein	68	DB 46
Cree St	Primrose Pk	32	CN 44
Crematorium Rd	Maitland	8	CD 39
Crescent Rd	Claremont	28	CO 32
Crescent Rd	Ottery	42	CS 37
Crescent Rd	Wynberg	40	CS 32
Cressy Rd	Athlone	18	CK 37
Crest Way	Retreat	53	CZ 34
Crete	Strandfontein	68	DB 46
Crete Rd	Ottery	42	CQ 38
Crickets Gully	Pelikan Pk	54	CY 38
Croft Cl.	Rondebosch	17	CK 36
Croft Rd	Sillery	39	CU 28
Crofton Rd	Muizenberg Nth	64	DE 32
Cromer Rd	Muizenberg	76	DF 33
Cromwell La.	Noordhoek Manor Retirement Village	73	DG 23
Cromwell La.	Noordhoek Manor Retirement Village	73	DJ 24
Cronwright La.	Fish Hoek	82	DL 26
Croquet La.	Rondebosch	17	CK 34
Cross Blvd	Silvertown	18	CK 39
Cross Blvd.	Kewtown	18	CK 39
Cross Cut	Lansdowne	30	CO 38
Cross Rd	Rosebank	17	CJ 34
Cross Rd	Sea Point	3	CC 22
Cross St	Newlands	27	CN 30
Crouse La.	Cape Town Central	4	CD 26
Crow Cr.	Pelikan Pk	55	CZ 41
Crowie La.	Grassy Pk	54	CX 37
Crown Cr.	Camps Bay	12	CJ 20
Crown Rd	Leonsdale	11	CD 48
Croxteth Rd	Greenpoint	3	CB 24
Crozier Cl.	Leonsdale	11	CD 48
Cruiser Cl.	Sun Valley	72	DJ 22
Cruiser St	Strandfontein	68	DB 45
Cruse La.	Wynberg	40	CR 32
Crust St	Salberau	11	CE 47
Crust St	Salberau	11	CE 46
Crux La.	Ocean View	79	DO 17
Crystal Ave	Pollsmoor	62	DA 28
Crystal Cl.	Steenberg	64	DB 34
Crystal Way	Belthorn Est.	30	CN 40
Cuckoo Cr.	Montagu's Gift	54	CV 37
Culemborg St	Ruyterwacht	10	CD 45
Culloden	Strandfontein	69	DB 47
Culloden Cl.	Strandfontein	69	DB 48
Culm Rd	Plumstead	40	CT 33
Culver St	Oranjezicht	14	CG 26
Cumberland Ave	Constantia Village	39	CT 29
Cumberland Rd	Paarden Eiland	6	CC 32
Cumnor Ave	Kenilworth	28	CP 33
Curie Way	Meadowridge	52	CW 31
Curlew Cl.	Imhoff's Gift	79	DM 16
Curlew St	Brooklyn	7	CA 35
Curlew Way	Pelikan Pk	55	CX 40
Curtis Rd	Gardens	14	CF 25
Curtis Rd	Kirstenhof	63	DA 31
Cushat La.	Sweet Valley	51	CX 28
Cutter Cl.	Marina Da Gama	64	DE 34
Cutter Cl.	Strandfontein	68	DB 45
Cygnus Cl.	Ocean View	79	DO 17
Cynthia Rd	Montagu's Gift	54	CU 38
Cyphia Cl.	Hout Bay	34	CU 15
Cypress Ave	Lotus River	54	CW 39
Cypress La.	Bergvliet	52	CX 31
Cypress Rd	Newlands	27	CM 30
Cyprus Rd	Ottery	42	CQ 38

STREET NAME	SUBURB NAME	PG	GRID
Cyprus St	Woodstock	5	CE 29
Cyster Cl.	Grassy Pk	53	CX 36

D

STREET NAME	SUBURB NAME	PG	GRID
D.F.Malan St	Cape Town Central	4	CD 27
D.F.Malherbe St	Townsend Est.	10	CA 44
D.Zihlangu Ave	Hout Bay	35	CU 18
Da Gama Rd	Da Gama Pk	82	DP 24
Da Gama Rd	Welcome Glen	82	DO 24
Da Gama St	Brooklyn	7	CB 35
Da Gama St	Parow	11	CB 48
Dabchick Quay	Marina Da Gama	64	DE 34
Dabchick Rd	Pelikan Pk	54	CX 38
Dacres Ave	Epping Ind.	20	CF 45
Daffodil Cir.	Ocean View	79	DM 16
Daffodil Cr.	Silvertown	19	CK 41
Daffodil Way	Pinelands	18	CG 39
Dagbreek	Pinelands	8	CE 39
Dagbreek St	Sybrand Pk	18	CJ 37
Dageraad Rd	Strandfontein	68	DA 45
Dahlia Rd	Lavender Hill East	65	DB 36
Dahlia St	Bridgetown	19	CJ 41
Dahlia St	Hanover Pk	31	CO 42
Dairy Cl.	Heideveld	32	CL 44
Daisy Cir.	Ocean View	79	DM 16
Daisy Hill Rd	Retreat	64	DA 33
Daisy Rd	Lavender Hill East	65	DB 36
Daisy Rd	Scarborough	86	DU 19
Daisy Way	Newlands	27	CN 30
Dakota Rd	Claremont	29	CN 35
Dal Rd	Camps Bay	13	CH 22
Dalbor Rd	Flintdale Est.	53	CW 35
Dale Ave	Silverhurst	39	CT 29
Dale Cl.	Hazendal	18	CK 38
Dale Cl.	Lotus River	54	CU 38
Dale Cl.	Montagu's Gift	42	CU 39
Dale Rd	Lansdowne	29	CN 37
Dalebrook Rd	Kalk Bay	75	DJ 30
Dalegarth Rd	Plumstead	40	CT 33
Dalham Rd	Belle Constantia	51	CV 28
Dalmore Rd	Tokai	51	CU 30
Dalton Rd	Fish Hoek	83	DL 27
Dalton Way	Meadowridge	51	CV 30
Dalziel Rd	Plumstead	40	CS 31
Dam Rd	Kirstenhof	63	DA 30
Dam Rd	Manenberg	32	CO 45
Dam Wk	Manenberg	32	CO 45
Dan Pienaar Cir.	Plumstead	40	CS 32
Dan Pienaar St	Ruytewacht	10	CE 45
Dandelion	Pelikan Pk	55	CX 41
Dane St	Grassy Pk	53	CX 36
Dane St	Observatory	16	CG 33
Daniel Ave	Montagu's Gift	42	CU 39
Daniel Cl.	Nyanga	45	CQ 48
Daniels Cr.	Grassy Pk	54	CX 37
Danker St	Factreton	9	CC 40
Dante Cl.	Dreyersdal	51	CY 30
Dante Rd	Dreyersdal	51	CY 30
Danube St	Manenberg	32	CM 44
Daphne St	Hout Bay	47	CV 16
Dapper Rd	Maitland	8	CC 39
Darien La.	Observatory	16	CG 33
Darling St	Cape Town Central	4	CE 26
Darling St	Hout Bay	47	CW 18
Darlington Ave	Fish Hoek	73	DK 25
Darroll Brodie La.	Wynberg	40	CQ 33
Darter Cr.	Pelikan Pk	55	CX 40
Darter Rd	Imhoff's Gift	79	DM 16
Darter's Rd	Gardens	4	CE 25
Dartmouth Rd	Muizenberg	76	DF 34
Darwin Way	Meadowridge	52	CV 31

STREET NAME	SUBURB NAME	PG	GRID
Dassen Rd	Sea Point	3	CD 22
Dassenheuwel Ave	Meadowsteads	72	DF 20
Dassie	Westlake Est.	62	DB 28
Dassie Rd	Capricorn	65	DC 35
Dassie Rd	Silvertown	18	CK 39
Date Palm St	Bonteheuwel	20	CH 44
Dauphine Way	Dieprivier	52	CW 32
Davenport Rd	Lotus River	54	CW 39
Davenport Rd	Vredehoek	14	CG 26
David Atkinson St	Charlesville	21	CK 46
David Baird Cr.	Ruytewacht	11	CD 46
David Profit St	Bonteheuwel	20	CH 44
David Rd	Newfields	31	CN 42
David St	Valhalla Pk	21	CJ 47
David Way	Ottery East	42	CT 38
David Wilkinson Rd	Charlesville	21	CK 47
David Wk	Grassy Pk	54	CX 37
Davids St	Nyanga	33	CP 48
Davidson St	Woodstock	5	CD 30
Davies Rd	Kirstenhof	63	DB 31
Davison Rd	Woodstock	5	CE 30
Dawes St	Schotsche Kloof	4	CD 25
Dawid Ave	Montana	21	CK 47
Dawlish Rd	Plumstead	40	CS 33
Dawn Ave	Bel Ombre	38	CR 26
Dawn Cl.	Salberau	11	CE 47
Dawn Rd	Rondebosch	29	CL 36
Day Rd	Hout Bay	47	CV 17
Days Wk	Pinelands	18	CH 37
De Chavonnes Ave	Hout Bay	35	CU 17
De Goede Hoop Cl.	Noordhaven	60	DE 21
De Gruchy Rd	Heathfield	52	CW 32
De Havilland St	Kensington	8	CB 38
De Hoop Ave	Tamboerskloof	13	CF 23
De Kock Ave	The Vines	39	CU 30
De Korte Ave	District Six	4	CE 27
De la Caille Ave	Newlands	27	CM 30
De la Haye Ave	Lansdowne	29	CP 37
De la Quellerie Rd	Rondebosch	29	CL 36
De Lille	Marina Da Gama	64	DD 34
De Lorentz St	Gardens	13	CF 24
De Maas Cl.	Ruytewacht	11	CC 46
De Maas Cr.	Ruytewacht	11	CC 46
De Mist St	Brooklyn	7	CC 35
De Roos St	District Six	4	CE 27
De Rust Ave	Bergvliet	51	CX 30
De Smit St	Greenpoint	4	CC 25
De Stadler	Capri	80	DL 20
De Stadler Ave	Capri	80	DL 20
De Villiers Ave	Rosebank	17	CH 34
De Villiers Rd	District Six	14	CF 27
De Villiers Rd	Maitland	7	CE 35
De Villiers Rd	Wynberg	28	CP 32
De Villiers St	Kommetjie	78	DM 13
De Villiers St	Vasco Est.	11	CA 46
De Villiers Steps	Fish Hoek	83	DM 27
De Villiers Way	Simon's Town	82	DO 25
De Waal Dr.	Devil's Peak Est.	14	CF 27
De Waal Dr.	Woodstock	15	CG 30
De Waal Rd	Fish Hoek	83	DL 27
De Waal Rd	Flintdale Est.	53	CV 35
De Waal Rd	Plumstead	52	CV 33
De Waal Rd Upper	Fish Hoek	82	DL 26
De Wet Rd	Bantry Bay	2	CE 20
De Wet Rd	Fresnaye	2	CE 21
De Wet Rd	Ottery	42	CT 38
De Wet Rd	Ottery East	42	CT 38
De Wet St	Montagu's Gift	42	CU 39
De Wilde Gans	Silverhurst	38	CT 27
Dean La.	Newlands	28	CM 32
Dean St	Cape Town Central	4	CE 25
Dean St	Newlands	28	CL 32
Deane Rd	Sea Point	3	CC 22
Debaren Cl.	Steenberg	61	DA 25

STREET NAME	SUBURB NAME	PG	GRID
Debden Ave	Epping Forest	21	CF 48
Dee Rd	Rondebosch	28	CL 33
Deer Park Dr. East	Vredehoek	14	CH 26
Deer Park Dr. West	Vredehoek	14	CH 26
Deer St	Ocean View	79	DN 17
Delaney St	Plumstead	40	CT 33
Delarey St	Flintdale Est.	53	CV 35
Delaware Ave	Primrose Pk	31	CO 43
Delford Ave	Fish Hoek	74	DK 27
Delia Rd	Marina Da Gama	64	DC 34
Delhi Rd	Lansdowne	30	CP 38
Delia Rd	Montagu's Gift	42	CU 38
Delingham Rd	Sillery	51	CV 28
Dellville Sq.	Maitland Gdn Village	17	CF 35
Dellwyn Rd	Ruytewacht	10	CC 45
Delmore Rd	Dennedal	51	CZ 28
Delos Rd	Ottery	42	CQ 38
Delphinium St	Devil's Peak Est.	14	CF 27
Delphium St	Bridgetown	31	CL 42
Delto Rd	Ocean View	79	DO 16
Denbigh Rd	Plumstead	40	CS 31
Denchworth Cl.	Athlone	30	CL 39
Denchworth Cr.	Athlone	30	CL 38
Denchworth Rd	Athlone	30	CL 39
Denchworth Rd East	Belgravia	30	CL 39
Denham Rd	Lansdowne	29	CO 37
Denholm Rd	Vredehoek	14	CG 26
Denne St	Bridgetown	19	CJ 41
Denneboom Ave	Thornton	10	CD 43
Dennebosch Cl.	Fir Grove	51	CW 29
Dennebosch Way	Fir Grove	51	CX 28
Dennedal Ave East	Dennedal	51	CZ 29
Dennedal Ave West	Dennedal	51	CZ 28
Denneguer Ave	Strandfontein	68	DB 44
Dennis Ave	Lavender Hill	65	DB 35
Dennis St	Montagu's Gift	42	CU 39
Denniston Cl.	Plumstead	52	CV 33
Denton St	Lansdowne	42	CQ 37
Denton Ter.	Schotsche Kloof	4	CD 25
Denver Rd	Lansdowne	29	CN 36
Denys Rd	Bergvliet	51	CV 30
Denyssen Rd	Steenberg	64	DB 34
Depositon Cr.	Lavender Hill	65	DB 35
Derby Cr.	Ottery	43	CS 40
Derby Rd	Avon	11	CD 47
Derby Rd	Kenilworth	28	CP 34
Derby Rd	Lakeside	64	DD 32
Derby Rd	Lansdowne	30	CP 38
Derbyshire Cr.	Kirstenhof	63	DB 31
Derbyshire Cr.	Kirstenhof	63	DE 31
Derbyshire St	Kirstenhof	63	DB 31
Derek Rd	Montagu's Gift	42	CU 39
Derna Rd	Lansdowne	42	CQ 37
Derry Rd	Rondebosch	28	CL 33
Derry St	Vredehoek	14	CF 27
Derwent Cr.	Coniston Pk	64	DB 33
Derwent La.	Hanover Pk	31	CP 41
Derwent Rd	Gardens	13	CF 24
Derwent Way	Pinelands	8	CE 38
Desande Rd	Flintdale Est.	53	CW 35
Desre Rd	Newfields	31	CN 42
Dessie Rd	Plumstead	40	CT 32
Deutz Rd	Hanover Pk	43	CQ 42
Devi Ave	Gatesville	31	CM 42
Devils Peak Rd	Heideveld	32	CL 45
Devon Air Cl.	Crofters Valley	72	DG 21
Devon Rd	Lansdowne	42	CQ 39
Devon St	Claremont	28	CO 33
Devon St	Simon's Town	88	DU 27
Devon St	Woodstock	6	CE 31
Devon Way	Capricorn	64	DE 34
Devon Way	Lakeside	64	DD 32
Devonport Rd	Tamboerskloof	3	CE 24
Devonshire Hill Rd	Rondebosch	16	CK 33

STREET NAME	SUBURB NAME	PG	GRID
Devonshire Hill Rd ...	Rondebosch ...	16	CK 32
Devonshire Rd	Ottery East	42	CT 39
Devonshire Rd	Wynberg	40	CR 32
Devonshire St	Woodstock	15	CF 30
Dexter St	Montana	21	CK 47
Dhow St	Sun Valley	72	DJ 22
Diadem La.	Leonsdale	11	CD 48
Diamond Dr.	Sheraton Pk	64	DB 33
Diamond St	Surrey Est.	31	CM 43
Diamond Way	San Michel	72	DG 22
Diana	Dieprivier	52	CV 32
Diana Cl.	Barbarossa	39	CU 30
Diana St	Valhalla Pk	21	CJ 48
Dias Rd	Grassy Pk	53	CX 36
Diaz St	Brooklyn	7	CB 36
Dick Burton St	Plumstead	41	CT 35
Dick King Way	Brooklyn	7	CC 35
Dickens St	Salt River	16	CF 32
Dickson St	Woodstock	5	CE 30
Dido Valley Rd ...	Simon's Town ...	82	DP 25
Die Plein	Pinelands	18	CF 38
Diemaar Rd	Kommetjie	78	DL 13
Dieman Rd	Grassy Pk	54	CY 37
Diemens Rd	Grassy Pk	53	CY 36
Dien St	Grassy Pk	53	CY 36
Diep St	Brooklyn	7	CC 34
Dieppe Rd	Strandfontein ...	68	DB 46
Diesel Rd	Ndabeni	17	CF 36
Dikkop Cl.	Pelikan Pk	55	CX 40
Dinghie Cir.	Strandfontein ...	68	DB 45
Dingle Ave	Kenilworth	28	CP 34
Dingle Rd	Goodwood Est.	10	CB 45
Dingle Rd	Richmond Est.	11	CB 47
Dingle Rd	Townsend Est.	10	CC 44
Dinsley Rd	Wynberg	40	CS 33
Dirk Adams Rd	Newfields	31	CO 42
Dirkie Uys St	Flintdale Est.	53	CV 36
Dirkie Uys St	Goodwood Est.	10	CB 44
Disa	Oudekraal	23	CL 19
Disa Ave	Fish Hoek	74	DK 27
Disa Ave	Kommetjie	78	DM 12
Disa Ave	Pinelands	18	CG 39
Disa Cl.	Ruyterwacht	10	CD 47
Disa Cr.	Bonteheuwel	20	CH 43
Disa Ct	Kewtown	18	CK 39
Disa Pl.	Bergvliet	52	CW 31
Disa Rd	Capricorn	65	DC 35
Disa Rd	Chapman's Peak	71	DF 18
Disa River Rd	Hout Bay	36	CS 20
Disa Way	Thornton	10	CD 43
Discovery Ave	Maitland Gdn Village..	17	CF 35
Dissel Rd	Bonteheuwel	20	CH 44
Dixon St	Cape Town Central ...	4	CC 25
Dixton Rd	Mowbray	17	CH 34
Dixton Rd	Observatory	17	CG 34
Dobson Rd	Athlone	18	CK 38
Docav Rd	Meadowridge	51	CV 30
Dock Ave	Riverton	11	CC 46
Dock Rd	Cape Town Central ...	4	CC 26
Dock Rd	Foreshore	4	CC 26
Dodds Rd	Observatory	16	CG 33
Doig Rd	Ottery	43	CQ 40
Doig Rd	Schaap Kraal ...	43	CQ 41
Dolomite	Belthorn Est.	30	CO 40
Dolphin Cr.	Fish Hoek	73	DK 25
Dolphin St	Hout Bay Harbour ..	46	CY 14
Dolphin Ter.	Strandfontein ...	68	DA 45
Dolphin Way	Lansdowne	42	CQ 38
Dolphin Way	Ottery	42	CQ 38
Dolphin Way	Victoria	88	DU 27
Doman Rd	Vanguard	32	CL 44
Domingo Rd	Retreat	53	CY 35
Dominic St	Athlone	30	CL 38
Dominica Ave	Capri	81	DL 22

STREET NAME	SUBURB NAME	PG	GRID
Domira Rd	High Constantia	38	CT 26
Don Rd	Bishop Lavis	21	CG 47
Don St	Manenberg	32	CN 44
Donald St	Athlone	30	CL 38
Donald St	Woodstock	5	CE 30
Doncaster Rd	Claremont	29	CO 35
Doncaster Rd	Kenilworth Pk	29	CO 35
Donell Way	Grassy Pk	53	CW 36
Donne St	Observatory	16	CF 32
Donough Rd	Tokai	51	CZ 29
Doordrift Rd	Barbarossa	39	CT 30
Doordrift Rd	Plumstead	40	CT 32
Dora Tamana ..	Weltevreden Valley ..	45	CS 47
Doreen Rd	Doornhoogte	31	CL 42
Doreen Rd	Montagu's Gift	42	CU 38
Doreen St	Valhalla Pk	21	CJ 47
Doric Rd	Penlyn Est.	30	CN 40
Doring Rd	Capricorn	65	DC 35
Doring Rd	Doornhoogte	30	CN 40
Dorion Cl.	Simon's Town	89	DU 29
Doris Rd	Claremont	27	CN 31
Doris Rd	Hout Bay	34	CU 15
Dorman Pl.	Hout Bay	47	CW 17
Dorman St	Gardens	4	CE 25
Dorman Way	Hout Bay	36	CT 20
Dormehl La.	Foreshore	5	CE 28
Dormehl St	Foreshore	5	CE 28
Dormer Ave	Athlone	30	CM 38
Dormer Cl.	Athlone	30	CM 38
Dorothy Zihlangu ..	Weltevreden Valley.	45	CS 48
Dorothy Zihlangu St ..	Manenberg	32	CN 46
Dorp St	Cape Town Central ...	4	CD 25
Dorset St	Foreshore	5	CE 29
Dorset Way	Sun Valley	73	DK 23
Dorsetshire St ..	Paarden Eiland	6	CC 33
Doublom St	Charlesville	21	CJ 46
Douglas Mfaca Cr.			
....	Weltevreden Valley ...	45	CS 47
Douglas Pl.	Woodstock	5	CE 30
Douglas Rd	Wynberg	41	CS 34
Douglas St	Woodstock	6	CE 32
Dove Rd	Capricorn	65	DC 35
Dove Rd	Montagu's Gift	54	CV 37
Dove Rd	Pelikan Pk	67	DA 41
Dove St	Observatory	16	CF 32
Dove St	Ocean View	79	DM 17
Dove St	Penlyn Est.	31	CN 41
Dove St	Salt River	16	CF 32
Dovedale	Pinelands	18	CG 39
Dover Rd	Heathfield	52	CX 33
Dover Rd	Muizenberg	76	DF 34
Dover Rd	Sea Point	3	CC 22
Downberg Rd	Hanover Pk	43	CQ 42
Downing Cl.	Nooitgedacht	21	CK 48
Downing Cr.	Nooitgedacht	21	CK 48
Downing St	Hazendal	18	CJ 38
Downing St	Montana	21	CK 48
Downwood	Hanover Pk	31	CP 41
Dr.Abdurahman Ave ...	Kewtown	18	CK 39
Draco Way	Ocean View	79	DN 16
Dragoon St	Plumstead	41	CU 35
Drake St	Observatory	16	CF 33
Drakensberg Way			
....	Lavender Hill East ...	65	DC 36
Drakensberg Way			
....	Lavender Hill East ...	65	DD 37
Drakenstein Cir. ..	Bishop Lavis	21	CH 48
Draklow St	Woodstock	5	CE 30
Draper Cl.	Claremont	28	CM 33
Draper St	Claremont	28	CN 32
Dressage Cl.	Fir Grove	50	CW 27
Dreyer Cl.	Barbarossa	40	CT 31
Dreyer St	Kommetjie	78	DM 12
Dreyer St	Claremont	28	CN 32

STREET NAME	SUBURB NAME	PG	GRID
Dreyer St	Rugby	7	CA 34
Dreyersdal Farm Rd ...	Dreyersdal ...	52	CY 31
Dreyersdal Rd	Dreyersdal	52	CY 31
Dreyton Rd	Lansdowne	30	CP 39
Driefontein La.	Farmsteads	60	DE 20
Drift Rd	Lansdowne	29	CP 37
Driver St	Lakeside	63	DD 31
Drogheda Rd	Royal Cape	41	CS 36
Dromedaris	Ruyterwacht	11	CC 46
Dromedaris Sq.	Factreton	9	CA 40
Drommedaris Cr.	Clarkes	21	CG 48
Drommedaris Cr.	Clarkes	21	CH 47
Drongo	Fish Hoek	74	DK 27
Drossel Rd	Pinati	30	CP 40
Drossel Rd	Pinati	30	CO 38
Drostdy Rd	Bergvliet	51	CW 30
Druif St	Wynberg	40	CS 33
Drukkery St	Elsies River Ind.	11	CB 48
Drumblair Cr.	Dennedal	51	CZ 28
Drury Rd	Capricorn	65	DD 35
Drury St	District Six	4	CE 26
Dryden St	Salt River	16	CF 32
Dublin St	Maitland	7	CD 35
Dublin St	Woodstock	5	CE 30
Duchess Rd	Ottery	43	CR 40
Duck Rd	Montagu's Gift	42	CU 38
Duck Rd	Pelikan Pk	55	CY 41
Duckitt Ave	Constantia Vale	39	CT 28
Duckitt Ave	Silverhurst	38	CT 27
Dudgeon Rd	Rondebosch	29	CM 36
Dudley La.	Newlands	27	CM 31
Dudley Rd	Sea Point	3	CC 22
Duet La.	Athlone	30	CL 38
Duignam Rd	Kalk Bay	75	DK 30
Duiker Ave	Lotus River	55	CV 40
Duiker Ave	Westlake Est.	63	DB 29
Duiker Cl.	Pinelands	18	CH 38
Duiker Cr.	Bridgetown	19	CK 42
Duiker Dr.	Kommetjie	78	DL 13
Duiker Rd	Bridgetown	19	CK 42
Duiker Rd	Pelikan Pk	67	DC 43
Duiker St	Hout Bay Harbour ...	46	CY 14
Duiker St	Simon's Town	88	DQ 27
Duine St	Penlyn Est.	30	CM 40
Duinefontein Rd ...	Heideveld	32	CL 45
Duinefontein Rd ..	Manenberg	32	CN 45
Duke Cl.	Salberau	11	CD 47
Duke Rd	Ottery	43	CR 40
Duke Rd	Rondebosch	17	CK 34
Duke St	Observatory	16	CG 33
Duke St	Woodstock	15	CF 29
Dulverton Rd	Rondebosch	29	CM 36
Dulwich Rd	Rondebosch	28	CL 33
Dumbarton St	Rondebosch	28	CM 34
Duminy Rd	Dieprivier	52	CW 32
Dunbar St	Athlone	30	CL 38
Duncan Rd	Foreshore	4	CC 27
Duncan Rd	Pinelands	18	CF 38
Duncan Rd	Sea Point	3	CD 22
Duncan Rd	Wynberg	41	CR 34
Duncan St	Valhalla Pk	21	CJ 47
Dundas Cr.	Ruyterwacht	11	CD 46
Dundee Rd	Rondebosch	28	CL 33
Dundee Ter.	Rondebosch	28	CL 33
Dundonald St	Woodstock	15	CF 30
Dundrum Rd	Fairways	41	CS 36
Dune Rd	Steenberg	64	DB 34
Dunedin Rd	Simon's Town	82	DO 26
Dungannon St	Nooitgedacht	21	CP 34
Dunkeld Ave	Bishopscourt	27	CO 30
Dunkeld Rd	Camps Bay	12	CK 20
Dunkirk Rd	Strandfontein ...	68	DA 46
Dunkley St	Gardens	14	CF 25
Dunlin Cl.	Grassy Pk	53	CW 36

STREET NAME	SUBURB NAME	PG	GRID
Dunloe Rd	Wynberg	40	CQ 32
Dunlop La.	Heathfield	52	CX 32
Dunluce Ave	Claremont	28	CN 33
Dunrobin Rd	Sea Point	3	CC 22
Dunsheen Rd	Wynberg	41	CR 34
Dunster Ave	Fish Hoek	83	DL 27
Dunster St	Belgravia	30	CL 40
Duntaw Cl.	Hohenort	38	CQ 27
Durant Cr.	Silvertown	19	CK 41
Durant St	Silvertown	19	CK 41
Durban Rd	Mowbray	17	CH 34
Durban Rd	Wynberg	40	CR 32
Durham Ave	Salt River	16	CF 31
Durham St	Bishopscourt	27	CO 30
Durham St	Claremont	28	CO 34
Durham Way	Matroosfontein	21	CG 48
Durr Rd	Surrey Est.	31	CM 43
Duxbury Rd	Bergvliet	51	CW 30
Dwyka St	Manenberg	32	CM 45
Dyakala Cr.	Nyanga	45	CQ 48
Dysart Rd	Greenpoint	3	CB 24
Dywilisi Cl.	Nyanga	45	CQ 48

E

STREET NAME	SUBURB NAME	PG	GRID
E.Mjodo St	Nyanga	33	CO 48
E.R.Syfret Rd	Brooklyn	7	CB 36
Eagle Cl.	Westlake Est.	62	DB 28
Eagle Cr.	Montagu's Gift	42	CU 37
Eagle Rd	Athlone	18	CK 39
Eagle Rd	Pelikan Pk	55	CZ 41
Eagle St	Ocean View	79	DN 17
Eagle Way	Bergvliet	52	CY 31
Eagle Way	Penlyn Est.	31	CN 41
Earl St	Hout Bay	47	CW 16
Earl St	Woodstock	15	CF 30
Easson Rd	Frogmore Est.	63	DC 31
East Cl.	Strandfontein	69	DA 47
East Fort	Hout Bay Harbour	46	CY 14
East Lake Dr.	Marina Da Gama	64	DC 34
East Lake Island Dr.	Marina Da Gama	64	DE 34
East Light Way	Kirstenhof	63	DA 30
East Link	Athlone	18	CK 39
East Pier Rd	Foreshore	4	CA 26
East St	Grassy Pk	54	CX 37
East St	Montagu's Gift	42	CU 39
East St	Strandfontein	69	DA 47
East Way	Pinelands	18	CF 37
Eastborne Rd	Capricorn	77	DF 35
Eastclyde Rd	Claremont	29	CN 36
Eastern Blvd	District Six	15	CF 29
Eastern Blvd	Woodstock	16	CF 31
Easterpeak Rd	Manenberg	32	CM 45
Eastry Rd	Claremont	29	CO 35
Eastview Rd	Belthorn Est.	30	CN 40
Eaton Rd	Gardens	3	CE 24
Ebb Ave	Riverton	11	CC 46
Ebb Rd	Steenberg	64	DB 34
Ebenezer Rd	Cape Town Central	4	CC 26
Ebenezer Rd	Wynberg	40	CQ 32
Ebony	Grassy Pk	54	CX 39
Ebony Rd	Tokai	51	CZ 29
Ebony St	Bonteheuwel	20	CH 44
Ebor Rd	Wynberg	40	CR 33
Ebrahim Rd	Primrose Pk	31	CN 43
Echo Rd	Fish Hoek	83	DN 28
Echo Steps	Fish Hoek	83	DN 28
Eclipse St	Salberau	11	CE 48
Edam Cl.	Westlake Est.	62	DC 28
Eddy Rd	Ottery East	42	CS 38
Eden Rd	Claremont	27	CO 31
Eden Rd	Observatory	16	CG 33
Eden Rd	Woodstock	15	CF 29
Eden Rd	Wynberg	41	CS 34
Edgar Cl.	Rondebosch	29	CM 35
Edgar Rd	Hout Bay	34	CU 15
Edgar Rd	Lansdowne	43	CQ 40
Edgemere Cl.	Elfindale	53	CW 34
Edgemere Rd	Elfindale	53	CW 34
Edgeware Cl.	Dieprivier	52	CV 33
Edgewater Rd	Sea Point	2	CD 20
Edgeworth	Dieprivier	52	CV 33
Edinburgh Cl.	Claremont	27	CP 31
Edinburgh Cl.	Pinelands	18	CF 39
Edinburgh Pl.	Dreyersdal	51	CZ 30
Edison Dr.	Meadowridge	51	CV 30
Edison Rd	Rondebosch	28	CL 33
Edmondia Cl.	Hout Bay	34	CU 15
Edmonton Cl.	Retreat	53	CY 35
Edmonton Rd	Retreat	53	CY 34
Edmund St	Valhalla Pk	21	CJ 47
Edna St	Montagu's Gift	42	CU 38
Ednam Rd	Rondebosch	28	CL 33
Edward Ave	Montagu's Gift	43	CU 40
Edward Rd	Edward	43	CT 40
Edward Rd	Sea Point	3	CC 22
Edward Rd	Valhalla Pk	21	CJ 47
Edward St	Claremont	28	CO 34
Edward St	Hout Bay	47	CW 16
Eendrag Rd	Vanguard	32	CL 44
Egglestone Rd	Wynberg	40	CR 33
Egham St	Wynberg	40	CQ 33
Egret Cir.	Imhoff's Gift	80	DL 18
Egret Cl.	Westlake Est.	63	DB 29
Egret La.	Bergvliet	52	CX 31
Egret La.	Montagu's Gift	54	CV 37
Egret St	Rugby	7	CA 35
Egret St	Scarborough	86	DU 19
Egret St	Westlake Est.	63	DB 29
Egret Way	Pinelands	18	CG 39
Egrets Way	Pelikan Pk	54	CY 38
Eighteenth Ave	Factreton	9	CB 40
Eighteenth Ave	Fish Hoek	82	DL 25
Eighteenth Ave	Norwood	11	CE 47
Eighteenth Ave	Schaap Kraal	55	CZ 42
Eighteenth St	Avon	11	CD 47
Eighteenth St	Kensington	8	CB 38
Eighth Ave	Belgravia	30	CL 40
Eighth Ave	Da Gama Pk	82	DP 24
Eighth Ave	Elsies River Ind.	11	CC 47
Eighth Ave	Fairways	41	CU 36
Eighth Ave	Fish Hoek	82	DL 26
Eighth Ave	Grassy Pk	53	CY 36
Eighth Ave	Hazendal	18	CJ 38
Eighth Ave	Kensington	8	CC 38
Eighth Ave	Lotus River	54	CX 39
Eighth Ave	Maitland	8	CC 38
Eighth Ave	Rondebosch East	29	CL 37
Eighth Ave	Schaap Kraal	55	CW 41
Eighth St	Elnor	21	CF 48
Eighth St	Kensington	8	CC 37
Eighth St	Salberau	11	CE 48
Eike Ave	Sybrand Pk	18	CJ 37
Eikendal	Pinelands	19	CF 40
Eiland Sq.	Factreton	9	CC 40
Eksteen Ave	Bergvliet	52	CX 31
Ekster Rd	Sunnydale	72	DK 22
El Adem Rd	Lansdowne	42	CQ 37
El Alamein Cl.	Plumstead	40	CS 33
Elaine Way	Heathfield	52	CX 32
Eland Ave	Lotus River	55	CV 40
Eland St	Kewtown	18	CK 39
Eland Way	Pinelands	18	CH 38
Elbe St	Manenberg	32	CM 45
Elder St	Bonteheuwel	20	CH 44
Elder St	Ottery	42	CT 37
Eldon La.	Camps Bay	12	CH 21
Eldon La.	Camps Bay	12	CJ 19
Eldon Rd	Valhalla Pk	21	CJ 47
Electric Rd	Wynberg	40	CQ 32
Eleventh Ave	Avon	11	CD 47
Eleventh Ave	Cafda Village	53	CZ 34
Eleventh Ave	Da Gama Pk	82	DP 24
Eleventh Ave	Fish Hoek	82	DL 26
Eleventh Ave	Hazendal	18	CJ 38
Eleventh Ave	Kensington	8	CA 39
Eleventh Ave	Leonsdale	11	CD 48
Eleventh Ave	Pelikan Pk	54	CX 39
Eleventh Ave	Retreat	53	CY 34
Eleventh Ave	Schaap Kraal	55	CX 41
Eleventh Rd	Heathfield	52	CX 32
Eleventh St	Elsies River Ind.	11	CC 47
Eleventh St	Kensington	8	CC 37
Elfin Ave	Elfindale	53	CW 34
Elgar St	Retreat	64	DA 33
Elgin Cir.	Fish Hoek	83	DL 27
Elgin Rd	Bergvliet	51	CW 30
Elgin Rd	Sybrand Pk	18	CJ 37
Elise Rd	Hout Bay	35	CT 17
Elizabeth Ave	Grassy Pk	54	CW 37
Elizabeth Ave	Pinelands	8	CE 39
Elizabeth Cl.	Dennedal	51	CZ 28
Elizabeth Dr.	Athlone	30	CL 38
Elizabeth La.	Barbarossa	40	CT 31
Elizabeth Roos St	Brooklyn	7	CB 35
Ella St	Schotsche Kloof	4	CC 25
Ellerslie Rd	Wynberg	40	CQ 32
Elliot Ave	Epping Ind.	20	CF 45
Elliot Ave	Ruyterwacht	10	CE 45
Elliot Waka Cl.	Nyanga	33	CP 48
Ellis Rd	Sea Point	3	CC 22
Elm	Pinelands	19	CG 40
Elm	Thornton	9	CD 42
Elm Cl.	Silverglade	73	DK 25
Elm Rd	Ottery East	42	CT 38
Elm Rd	Parkwood	41	CU 36
Elm St	Grassy Pk	54	CY 37
Elm St	Tokai	51	CZ 28
Elma Rd	Rondebosch	17	CK 34
Elmtree Cl.	Hout Bay	36	CS 21
Elpark	Penlyn Est.	30	CM 40
Elphinstone Sq.	Ruyterwacht	11	CD 46
Elrin Rd	Flintdale Est.	53	CW 35
Elsbury Way	Matroosfontein	21	CG 48
Elsie Manning St	Cafda Village	53	CZ 35
Elsies Peak Rd	Heideveld	32	CL 45
Elsjieskraal Rd	Manenberg	32	CM 45
Elson Rd	Woodstock	16	CF 31
Elstree Rd	Heathfield	52	CX 32
Elswood Pl.	Leonsdale	11	CD 48
Elswood Pl.	Leonsdale	11	CC 47
Eltister Rd	Lavender Hill	65	DA 35
Elva Rd	Plumstead	41	CU 35
Elwyn Rd	Penlyn Est.	30	CM 40
Elwyn Rd South	Belthorn Est.	30	CN 40
Elzeth Rd	Ottery	42	CR 38
Emerald Dr.	Belvedere Noordhoek	72	DF 22
Emerald Cr.	Fish Hoek	74	DK 27
Emerald Cr.	San Michel	72	DF 22
Emerald Dr.	Sheraton Pk	64	DB 33
Emerald Dr.	San Michel	72	DF 22
Emerald Ter.	San Michel	72	DF 22
Emily Hobhouse St	Townsend Est.	10	CC 43
Emmas Cl.	Belvedere Noordhoek	72	DF 22
Emms Dr.	Matroosfontein	21	CG 48
Emms Dr.	Nyanga	33	CP 49
Empire Ave	Hout Bay	47	CW 16
Empire Rd	Ottery	41	CR 40
Empumelelweni Cl.	Nyanga	33	CP 48

STREET NAME	SUBURB NAME	PG	GRID
Enchor Rd	Dieprivier	52	CV 32
End Way	Pinelands	8	CE 39
Endeavour St	Sand Industria	31	CO 43
Enfield Ave	Athlone	30	CL 38
Ennerdale	Pinelands	8	CE 39
Enoch Sontonga	Weltevreden Valley	45	CT 48
Ensfield Rd	Epping Forest	21	CF 47
Enslin St	Ottery	42	CR 38
Ensor St	Cafda Village	53	CZ 35
Epping Ave	Avon	11	CC 47
Epping Ave	Leonsdale	11	CC 48
Epping Ave	Valhalla	11	CC 46
Epping Cr.	Elsies River Ind.	11	CC 48
Epsom Dr.	Ottery	43	CS 40
Epsom Rd	Kenilworth	28	CP 34
Epsten Cr.	Lavender Hill	65	DB 35
Epsten Cr.	Lavender Hill	65	DB 35
Epsten Ct	Lavender Hill	65	DB 35
Epworth Rd	Rondebosch	29	CL 36
Erasmus Ct	Lavender Hill	65	DB 35
Eric Vijoen	Parkwood	41	CU 36
Eric Way	Montagu's Gift	43	CU 40
Erica Ave	Fish Hoek	83	DL 27
Erica Ave	Westlake Est.	62	DB 28
Erica Cl.	Hout Bay	47	CW 18
Erica Cr.	Manenberg	32	CO 45
Erica Pl.	Bergvliet	52	CW 31
Erica Rd	Kommetjie	78	DM 13
Erica St	Chapman's Peak	71	DF 18
Erica St	Hout Bay	47	CW 18
Erica St	Woodstock	15	CF 30
Erica Way	Pinelands	18	CG 39
Erics Wk	Parkwood	41	CU 36
Erie Rd	Flintdale Est.	53	CV 35
Erie Rd	Retreat	52	CZ 32
Erin Rd	Rondebosch	17	CK 34
Erin Rd	Rosebank	17	CK 34
Ermington Rd	Muizenberg	76	DF 34
Ernest Curry St	Lotus River	54	CX 39
Ernest Rd	Doornhoogte	31	CL 41
Erts Rd	Vanguard	31	CL 43
Escombe Rd	Vredehoek	14	CG 26
Esher St	Claremont	28	CO 34
Esk Way	Manenberg	32	CN 44
Eskdale Rd	Gardens	13	CF 23
Eskol La.	Belle Constantia	51	CV 28
Esmar Rd	Rondebosch	29	CL 35
Esme Rd	Newlands	28	CM 32
Essenhout Rd	Bonteheuwel	20	CH 44
Essenhout Rd	Silvertown	19	CK 40
Essenhout St	Ottery	42	CT 38
Essenhout Way	Sunnydale	72	DK 21
Essex Rd	Kalk Bay	75	DK 30
Essex Rd	Lakeside	64	DD 32
Essex Rd	Wynberg	41	CR 34
Essex St	Maitland	7	CD 35
Essex St	Woodstock	5	CE 30
Ester Rd	Newfields	31	CN 42
Esther Rd	Montagu's Gift	42	CU 38
Estmil Cl.	Elfindale	53	CW 34
Estmil Way	Elfindale	53	CW 34
Ethel Rd	Claremont	27	CN 31
Eton Rd	Heathfield	52	CW 32
Eton Way	Westlake Est.	62	DC 28
Euclea Cl.	Hout Bay	34	CU 15
Eugene Marais Ave	Bel Ombre	39	CS 28
Eureka Rd	Rosebank	17	CK 34
Europa Rd	Ocean View	79	DO 16
Eustegia Way	Hout Bay	34	CU 15
Eva St	Valhalla Pk	21	CJ 48
Eva Wk	Manenberg	32	CO 45
Evans Ave	Epping Ind.	20	CF 43
Eveleigh Way	Rondebosch	29	CL 36
Evelyn Rd	Retreat Ind. Area	63	DA 31
Evening Way	Pinelands	18	CH 38
Everest Cl.	Barbarossa	39	CT 30
Evergreen Ave	Newlands	27	CN 31
Evergreen La.	Rust-en-vrede	39	CT 29
Evergreen La.	Silverglade	73	DK 25
Evremonde Rd	Plumstead	41	CT 35
Excelsior Rd	Welcome	20	CK 44
Exeter Ave	Ottery	43	CS 40
Exeter Ave	Ottery East	42	CT 39
Exeter Ave	Bishopscourt	27	CP 30
Exeter Rd	Plumstead	40	CS 33
Exeter Way	Pinelands	18	CF 38
Exhibition Ter.	Greenpoint	4	CB 25
Exmouth Rd	Plumstead	41	CT 34
Exner Ave	Vredehoek	14	CG 26
Exwin Rd	Meadowridge	51	CV 30
Eyton Rd	Claremont	27	CO 31

F

STREET NAME	SUBURB NAME	PG	GRID
Fabian Ave	Athlone	30	CL 38
Factory Rd	Salt River	16	CF 31
Factreton Ave	Factreton	9	CB 40
Factreton Ave	Kensington	8	CB 39
Fairbairn St	Brooklyn	7	CC 36
Fairbairn St	Glencairn Hgts	83	DO 27
Fairbairn Way	Meadowridge	51	CV 30
Fairdale Rd	Dieprivier	52	CV 32
Fairfield Cl.	Sunnydale	81	DL 22
Fairfield Cl.	Sweet Valley	51	CX 29
Fairfield Rd	Observatory	16	CG 33
Fairfield Rd	Rondebosch	28	CM 34
Fairmead Rd	Dieprivier	40	CU 32
Fairmead Rd	Epping Forest	21	CF 48
Fairseat La.	Wynberg	40	CQ 32
Fairview Ave	Woodstock	15	CF 30
Fairview Cl.	Barbarossa	39	CU 30
Fairview Rd	Wynberg	40	CS 32
Fairway Ave	Bergvliet	52	CY 32
Fairway Ave	Fairways	41	CT 36
Faith Cl.	Kensington	8	CC 38
Faith St	Claremont	29	CO 35
Falcon	Seawinds	64	DB 34
Falcon Cr.	Pelikan Pk	55	CZ 41
Falcon Rd	Heideveld	20	CK 44
Falcon St	Ocean View	79	DN 17
Falcon Way	Montagu's Gift	54	CV 37
Falmouth Rd	Observatory	16	CH 32
Falstaff Rd	Penlyn Est.	30	CN 40
Familie La.	Athlone	30	CL 38
Fanshawe Rd	Plumstead	41	CU 34
Faraday Way	Meadowridge	51	CV 30
Fareham St	Woodstock	5	CE 30
Farm Cl.	Heideveld	32	CL 44
Farm Cr.	Montagu's Gift	42	CU 39
Farm Field Rd	Knole Pk	55	CV 41
Farm Rd	Doornhoogte	31	CL 41
Farmedge	Bergvliet	51	CX 30
Farmside	Bergvliet	51	CX 30
Farmnouth Rd	Retreat	64	DA 33
Farquhar Rd	Camps Bay	12	CJ 20
Farriers Way	Hout Bay	36	CR 20
Father Curren Cr.	Nyanga	33	CO 48
Faulman Rd	Grassy Pk	53	CY 36
Fauna Rd	Steenberg	64	DB 32
Faure Cl.	Dieprivier	52	CW 32
Faure St	Gardens	4	CE 25
Fawcett Way	Strandfontein	69	DA 47
Fawcetts Ave	Hout Bay	34	CR 15
Fawley Ter.	District Six	14	CF 27
Fayker Rd	Grassy Pk	54	CW 37
Fedora Cl.	Leonsdale	11	CD 48
Feldhausen Ave	Claremont	27	CN 31
Feldhausen Rd	Claremont	28	CN 32
Felicia St	Retreat	64	DA 32
Felixberg Rd	Heideveld	32	CL 46
Feltham Rd	Oranjezicht	13	CG 24
Feltham Rd	Oranjezicht	13	CH 24
Felucca Cr.	Sun Valley	73	DK 23
Fenton Rd	Salt River	6	CE 32
Fenwick St	Brooklyn	7	CB 34
Ferdinand St	Kirstenhof	63	DA 31
Ferguson St	Plumstead	40	CU 33
Fern Cl.	Alphen	39	CS 29
Fern Cl.	Meadowridge	52	CW 32
Fern La.	Chapman's Peak	71	DF 18
Fern La.	Grassy Pk	54	CW 37
Fern St	Charlesville	21	CJ 47
Fern St	Ottery East	42	CS 39
Ferndale Dr.	Ottery East	42	CT 39
Ferndale Rd	Lotus River	55	CW 40
Ferndale Rd	Maitland	7	CD 35
Ferness Rd	Ottery	42	CS 37
Fernside Way	Ottery East	42	CS 39
Fernwood Ave	Newlands	27	CN 30
Ferrous St	Vanguard	20	CK 43
Ferry Rd	Simon's Town	88	DS 26
Ferry Way	Strandfontein	68	DA 45
Festival Rd	Brooklyn	7	CA 35
Ficus Rd	Thornton	9	CD 42
Ficus St	Westlake Est.	62	DB 28
Fiddlewood	Pinelands	19	CG 40
Field	Epping Ind.	19	CF 40
Field Ave	Montagu's Gift	42	CU 39
Field Cl.	Montagu's Gift	42	CU 39
Field Cl.	Strandfontein	69	DA 47
Field Cr.	Silvertown	19	CK 40
Field St	Heathfield	52	CX 33
Field St	Strandfontein	69	DD 48
Field St	Strandfontein	69	DA 47
Fife Ave	Fish Hoek	74	DK 26
Fife Rd	Rondebosch	28	CL 34
Fiford Cr.	Tokai	51	CZ 30
Fifteenth Ave	Avon	11	CD 47
Fifteenth Ave	Fish Hoek	82	DL 26
Fifteenth Ave	Hazendal	18	CJ 38
Fifteenth Ave	Leonsdale	11	CD 48
Fifteenth Ave	Schaap Kraal	55	CY 42
Fifteenth St	Avon	11	CD 47
Fifteenth St	Kensington	8	CC 37
Fifth Ave	Athlone	29	CL 37
Fifth Ave	Belgravia	30	CL 40
Fifth Ave	Da Gama Pk	81	DP 23
Fifth Ave	Fairways	41	CT 36
Fifth Ave	Fish Hoek	83	DM 27
Fifth Ave	Grassy Pk	53	CX 36
Fifth Ave	Hazendal	18	CJ 38
Fifth Ave	Kensington	8	CC 38
Fifth Ave	Lotus River	54	CW 39
Fifth Ave	Retreat	52	CY 33
Fifth Ave	Rondebosch East	29	CM 37
Fifth Ave	Welcome	20	CK 44
Fifth Rd	Heathfield	52	CX 32
Fifth St	Bishop Lavis	21	CG 48
Fifth St	Heideveld	20	CK 44
Fifth St	Kensington	8	CD 37
Fiftieth Ave	Wynberg	39	CQ 30
Fifty-Eighth Ave	Wynberg	40	CR 31
Fifty-First Ave	Wynberg	40	CR 31
Fig St	Newlands	27	CN 29
Fillians Rd	Camps Bay	12	CJ 21
Fillies Rd	Primrose Pk	31	CO 43
Fillmore Rd	Claremont	29	CM 35
Fin Whale Way	Kommetjie	70	DK 14
Finch Cr.	Pelikan Pk	55	CZ 41

STREET NAME	SUBURB NAME	PG	GRID
Finch Cr.	Seawinds	64	DB 34
Finchley Rd	Camps Bay	12	CK 20
Findon St	Athlone	18	CK 38
Fink Rd	Bridgetown	19	CJ 42
Finn Rd	Pelikan Pk	54	CX 39
Finsbury Ave	Newlands	27	CM 31
Finton St	Elfindale	52	CW 33
Fiona Cr.	Brooklyn	7	CA 35
Fir Ave	Bantry Bay	2	CE 20
Fir Ave	Tokai	51	CZ 29
Fir Rd	Rondebosch	17	CK 34
Fir St	Claremont	28	CM 32
Fir St	Observatory	16	CF 33
Firdale Ave	Sea Point	3	CC 22
Firdale Rd	Gardens	13	CF 23
Firdale Rd	Newlands	27	CM 30
Firethorn St	Bonteheuwel	20	CH 44
Firfield Rd	Plumstead	40	CT 33
Firgrove Way	Bergvliet	51	CW 30
Firgrove Way	Sweet Valley	51	CX 28
Firlands Rd	Rondebosch	29	CM 36
Firmount Rd	Sea Point	3	CC 22
Firs Ave	Claremont	28	CO 32
First Ave	Athlone	29	CL 37
First Ave	Belgravia	30	CL 39
First Ave	Claremont	28	CO 33
First Ave	Da Gama Pk	81	DO 23
First Ave	Elsies River Ind.	11	CC 47
First Ave	Fairways	42	CT 37
First Ave	Fish Hoek	83	DL 27
First Ave	Glenlily	11	CB 48
First Ave	Grassy Pk	53	CX 36
First Ave	Hazendal	18	CJ 38
First Ave	Kenilworth	28	CO 33
First Ave	Knole Pk	55	CV 41
First Ave	Lotus River	54	CV 39
First Ave	Maitland	8	CD 37
First Ave	Manenberg	32	CP 45
First Ave	Retreat	52	CY 32
First Ave	Rondebosch East	29	CM 37
First Ave	Vanguard	31	CL 43
First Ave	Woodlands	82	DP 25
First Cr.	Camps Bay	12	CJ 20
First Cr.	Fish Hoek	82	DL 26
First Rd	Grassy Pk	54	CW 37
First Rd	Heathfield	52	CX 33
First St	Bishop Lavis	21	CG 48
First St	Maitland	8	CD 38
First St	Welcome	20	CK 43
Firth Rd	Rondebosch	17	CK 36
Firtree Rd	Farmsteads	60	DB 20
Firtree St	Plumstead	40	CU 32
Fish Eagle	Fish Hoek	74	DK 26
Fish Eagle Pl.	Imhoff's Gift	80	DL 18
Fish Eagle Pl.	Masiphumelele	80	DL 19
Fish Eagle Way	Pelikan Pk	54	CY 37
Fish Rd	Pelikan Pk	54	CY 38
Fisher Ave	Epping Ind.	19	CF 42
Fisherman Way	Hout Bay	47	CW 18
Fisherman's Bend	Hout Bay	34	CS 14
Fisherman's Cove	Kommetjie	78	DM 13
Fisherman's Quay	Marina Da Gama	64	DE 34
Fisherman's Wk	Pelikan Pk	54	CY 37
Fishmarket St	Hout Bay	46	CX 15
Fiskaal Cl.	Bakoven	12	CK 21
Fiskaal Rd	Bakoven	12	CK 21
Fitzherbert Rd	Vredehoek	14	CG 26
Fitzherbert Rd	Vredehoek	14	CH 25
Fitzherbert St	Ruyterwacht	11	CC 46
Fitzmaurice Ave	Epping Ind.	11	CE 46
Fitzroy St	Townsend Est.	10	CB 44
Flagship Way	Simon's Town	89	DU 28
Flambor Rd	Flintdale Est.	53	CW 35
Flamboyant Pl.	Thornton	9	CD 42

STREET NAME	SUBURB NAME	PG	GRID
Flame Tree Cl.	Nova Constantia	50	CW 27
Flamingo	Seawinds	64	DB 34
Flamingo Cl.	Dreyersdal	51	CZ 30
Flamingo Cr.	Lansdowne	30	CO 38
Flamingo Cr.	Pelikan Pk	54	CZ 39
Flamingo Dr.	Kommetjie	78	DM 14
Flamingo Rd	Ocean View	79	DM 16
Flamingo St	Westlake Est.	62	DB 28
Flamink Rd	Sunnydale	72	DK 22
Flanders	Strandfontein	68	DB 46
Flanders Rd	Pinati	30	CP 40
Flat Rd	Doornhoogte	30	CN 40
Fleet	Belthorn Est.	30	CN 39
Fleetwood Ave	Claremont	27	CO 31
Fleming Rd	Wynberg	40	CS 33
Fleming Way	Meadowridge	51	CW 30
Fleur Rd	Belthorn Est.	30	CN 40
Flight Rd	Pelikan Pk	54	CY 39
Flint Rd	Belthorn Est.	30	CO 40
Flintdale Rd	Flintdale Est.	53	CV 35
Flodden Way	Strandfontein	69	DD 48
Flora Cl.	Hout Bay Harbour	46	CY 14
Flora Rd	Retreat	52	CZ 32
Flora Rd	Retreat Ind. Area	64	DA 32
Flora Rd	Wynberg	41	CS 34
Flora Steps	Simon's Town	89	DU 29
Florence Ave	Observatory	16	CG 33
Florida Cl.	Coniston Pk	64	DB 34
Florida Rd	Vredehoek	14	CG 26
Flower Cl.	Montagu's Gift	42	CU 38
Flower St	Oranjezicht	14	CG 26
Flowerdale La.	Sweet Valley	51	CX 29
Flute St	Retreat	64	DA 33
Fontana St	Brooklyn	7	CB 35
Fontein Rd	Steenberg	64	DB 34
Forbes Ave	Doornhoogte	31	CN 41
Forbes Ave	Wynberg	40	CS 33
Ford St	Salt River	16	CF 32
Forest Ave	Bishopscourt	27	CP 30
Forest Ave	Pollsmoor	62	DA 28
Forest Ave	Tokai	51	CZ 29
Forest Dr.	Peers Hill	73	DK 25
Forest Dr.	Peers Hill	74	DK 26
Forest Dr.	Pinelands	18	CG 37
Forest Dr. Ext	Thornton	9	CD 41
Forest Dr. Service Rd	Pinelands	17	CG 36
Forest Hill Ave	Oranjezicht	14	CF 26
Forest Hill La.	Hout Bay	36	CR 21
Forest Hill Rd	Simon's Town	89	DU 29
Forest Hills Cl.	Ottery	43	CQ 40
Forest Pl.	Pinelands	17	CG 36
Forest Rd	Fairways	41	CT 36
Forest Rd	Oranjezicht	14	CG 25
Forest Rd	Rondebosch	16	CK 33
Forest Rd	The Range	21	CF 47
Forest Row	Dennedal	51	CY 29
Forester's Cl.	Hout Bay	36	CT 19
Foresters Rd	Rondebosch	28	CL 33
Forfar Rd	Observatory	17	CG 34
Forgate St	Woodstock	5	CD 30
Formosa Rd	Heideveld	20	CK 45
Fornax Cl.	Ocean View	79	DO 17
Forrest Rd	Simon's Town	82	DO 26
Forridon St	Brooklyn	7	CB 35
Forsyth Rd	Kommetjie	78	DL 12
Fort Calata Wk	Weltevreden Valley	45	CS 48
Fort Calata Wk	Weltevreden Valley	45	CT 47
Fort Rd	Three Anchor Bay	3	CB 22
Fort St	Wynberg	40	CQ 31
Fort Wynyard St	Greenpoint	4	CB 25
Fortesque Rd	Crawford	30	CN 39
Fortress St	Factreton	9	CB 40
Fortuin Rd	Retreat	52	CZ 33

STREET NAME	SUBURB NAME	PG	GRID
Fortuin St	Retreat	53	CY 34
Fouche Rd	Newfields	31	CO 42
Founder Way	Simon's Town	88	DR 27
Foundry Rd	Woodstock	6	CE 32
Fountain Dr.	Hout Bay	48	CW 19
Fountain Rd	Bergvliet	51	CW 30
Fountain Rd	Clarkes	21	CG 48
Fountain Rd	Rondebosch	16	CK 32
Fountain Sq.	Rondebosch	16	CK 33
Fountains Pl.	Townsend Est.	10	CA 43
Fourteenth Ave	Avon	11	CD 47
Fourteenth Ave	Da Gama Pk	82	DP 24
Fourteenth Ave	Fish Hoek	82	DL 26
Fourteenth Ave	Hazendal	18	CJ 38
Fourteenth Ave	Lavender Hill	53	CZ 36
Fourteenth Ave	Leonsdale	11	CD 48
Fourteenth Ave	Maitland	9	CC 40
Fourteenth Ave	Pelikan Pk	55	CY 41
Fourteenth Ave	Schaap Kraal	55	CY 42
Fourteenth St	Elsies River Ind.	11	CC 47
Fourteenth St	Kensington	8	CC 37
Fourth Ave	Athlone	29	CL 37
Fourth Ave	Belgravia	30	CL 40
Fourth Ave	Churchill	11	CA 47
Fourth Ave	Da Gama Pk	81	DO 23
Fourth Ave	Fairways	41	CT 36
Fourth Ave	Fish Hoek	83	DM 27
Fourth Ave	Grassy Pk	53	CX 36
Fourth Ave	Hazendal	18	CJ 38
Fourth Ave	Kensington	8	CC 37
Fourth Ave	Lotus River	54	CW 39
Fourth Ave	Manenberg	32	CP 45
Fourth Ave	Nyanga	33	CP 49
Fourth Ave	Retreat	52	CY 33
Fourth Ave	Rondebosch East	29	CM 37
Fourth Ave	Schaap Kraal	55	CV 41
Fourth Ave	Vanguard	20	CK 43
Fourth Rd	Heathfield	52	CX 33
Fourth Rd	Rondebosch	17	CK 36
Fourth Rd	Rondebosch	28	CL 33
Fourth St	Bishop Lavis	21	CG 48
Fourth St	Kensington	8	CD 38
Fourth St	Welcome	20	CK 44
Fox Rd	Strandfontein	69	DA 47
Foxglove Cl.	Bridgetown	19	CK 42
Foxglove Cl.	Bridgetown	19	CK 42
Foxhallow Cl.	Kirstenhof	63	DC 30
Foxhallow Cl.	Kirstenhof	63	DE 31
Foxhallow Cl.	Lakeside	63	DD 31
Foyle Rd	Claremont	28	CN 32
Francis Cr.	Montana	21	CK 47
Francis Rd	Montagu's Gift	42	CU 38
Francis Rd	Pinelands	18	CF 37
Francis Rd	Plumstead	40	CU 32
Francis Rd	The Vines	51	CU 31
Francis St	District Six	5	CE 29
Francis St	Matroosfontein	21	CF 47
Francisca La.	Chapman's Peak	71	DF 18
Francke St	Retreat	53	CY 34
Francois Rd	Welcome	20	CJ 44
Francolin Cr.	Seawinds	64	DC 34
Francolin Rd	Bakoven	12	CK 21
Francolin Rd	Masiphumelele	80	DL 20
Francolin Rd	Pelikan Pk	67	DA 41
Francolin Way	Pelikan Pk	55	CX 40
Frank Ave	Vredehoek	14	CH 26
Frank Robb St	Brooklyn	7	CB 35
Frank St	Valhalla Pk	21	CJ 47
Frank Way	Montagu's Gift	43	CU 40
Frankfort Rd	Churchill	11	CA 48
Frankfort Rd	Muizenberg	76	DG 33
Frankfort Rd	Muizenberg	76	DH 33
Frankfort Rd	Retreat	64	DA 32
Frankfort St	Glenlily	11	CA 48

STREET NAME	SUBURB NAME	PG	GRID	STREET NAME	SUBURB NAME	PG	GRID	STREET NAME	SUBURB NAME	PG	GRID
Franklin Joshua St	Montana	21	CK 48	Gallop Way	Strandfontein	69	DD 48	Genoa Cr.	Strandfontein	69	DA 49
Franklin Rd	Claremont	28	CN 34	Galway Rd	Heathfield	52	CX 32	Genoa Way	Strandfontein	69	DA 49
Franklin St	Observatory	16	CF 32	Gambonia Rd	Rondebosch	29	CM 36	Genootskap Rd	Surrey Est.	31	CM 43
Frans Conradie Dr.	Townsend Est.	10	CA 43	Gamka St	Manenberg	32	CN 45	Gents Cl.	Strandfontein	69	DA 48
Frans Maroney Rd	Retreat	53	CY 34	Gamsa St	Penlyn Est.	30	CN 40	Gents Mile	Strandfontein	69	DD 48
Fransdruif Rd	Meadowridge	39	CU 30	Gamtoos St	Manenberg	32	CN 45	Gents Mile	Strandfontein	69	DA 48
Frantz Rd	Vanguard	20	CK 43	Ganges Cl.	Manenberg	32	CM 45	George Ave	Elsies River Ind.	11	CC 47
Franz Sq.	Steenberg	64	DA 33	Gani St	Primrose Pk	31	CO 43	George Nolan	Factreton	8	CC 39
Fraser Rd	Muizenberg	76	DG 33	Gannet Cl.	Kommetjie	78	DL 14	George Rd	Montagu's Gift	43	CU 40
Frean Rd	Rondebosch	17	CK 36	Gannet Rd	Simon's Town	88	DQ 37	George Smit Rd	Highlands Est.	44	CS 44
Fred Adams Rd	Welcome	20	CK 43	Gannet St	Pelikan Pk	67	DD 43	George St	Athlone	18	CK 38
Freda Rd	Montagu's Gift	42	CU 38	Gantouw Cr.	High Constantia	38	CT 26	George St	Manenberg	32	CP 45
Freda Rd	Newfields	31	CO 42	Gaqawuli Godolozi				George St	Muizenberg	76	DF 33
Freda's La.	Plumstead	52	CV 33		Weltevreden Valley	45	CT 48	George St	Observatory	16	CH 33
Frederick Ave	Kirstenhof	63	DA 31	Garda Cl.	Coniston Pk	64	DC 34	George St	Barbarossa	40	CT 31
Frederick Cl.	Tamboerskloof	3	CE 23	Garda Rd	Flintdale Est.	53	CV 35	Gerald St	Valhalla Pk	21	CJ 47
Frederick Rd	Claremont	27	CN 31	Garden Cl.	Strandfontein	69	DD 48	Gerard Rd	Muizenberg Nth	64	DE 32
Frederick Selous St	Bel Ombre	39	CR 28	Garden La.	Strandfontein	69	DD 48	Gerard Way	Montagu's Gift	43	CU 40
Frederick St	Schotsche Kloof	4	CD 25	Garden La.	Strandfontein	69	DA 47	Gerrie Ave	Dennedal	51	CY 30
Freeman Rd	Greenpoint	4	CB 25	Garden St	Newlands	27	CN 29	Gerrie Cnr	Dennedal	51	CY 30
Freesia Ave	Devil's Peak Est.	14	CG 27	Garden St	Plumstead	40	CU 33	Gerrit Maritz St	Ruyterwacht	11	CE 46
Frere Ave	Lansdowne	29	CO 36	Garden St	Riverton	11	CC 46	Gerry Ferry Rd	Epping Ind.	9	CE 42
Frere Ave	Sillery	39	CU 28	Garden Way	Strandfontein	69	DA 47	Gerties Way	Belvedere (Noordhoek).	72	DF 22
Frere Rd	Bishop Lavis	21	CG 48	Gardener Way	Pinelands	18	CF 39	Gertrude St	Goodwood Est.	10	CB 44
Frere Rd	Ndabeni	7	CE 35	Gardenia	Pinelands	19	CF 40	Gesiggie St	Charlesville	21	CH 46
Frere Rd	Three Anchor Bay	3	CB 22	Gardenia Ave	Devil's Peak Est.	14	CF 27	Gettys Cl.	Strandfontein	69	DD 48
Frere Rd	Three Anchor Bay	3	CD 23	Gardenia Ave	Lotus River	54	CW 39	Geyer Rd	Heathfield	52	CW 32
Frere St	Woodstock	5	CE 30	Gardenia La.	Nova Constantia	50	CW 27	Gibraltar Rd	Hout Bay	46	CX 15
Freredale Rd	Crawford	30	CM 39	Garfield Rd	Oranjezicht	13	CG 24	Gibson Ave	Athlone	30	CL 38
Friars Rd	Sea Point	3	CD 22	Garfield St	Claremont	29	CN 35	Gibson Rd	Kenilworth	41	CQ 34
Frick Ave	Lotus River	54	CW 38	Gariep Cir.	Ruyterwacht	10	CC 45	Gideon Rd	Newfields	31	CO 42
Friedman Rd	Browns Farm	45	CQ 48	Garlandale Cr.	Athlone	18	CK 37	Giel Basson Dr.	Richmond	11	CB 48
Friend St	Salt River	16	CF 31	Garnet Cl.	Pelikan Pk	67	DA 42	Gildale Ave	Barbarossa	39	CT 30
Friendly Way	Surrey Est.	31	CM 43	Garnet Cr.	Sheraton Pk	64	DC 32	Gildsteed La.	Tokai	51	CZ 28
Friesland St	Montana	21	CJ 47	Garnet Rd	Lansdowne	30	CN 38	Gilgil Rd	Charlesville	21	CK 45
Friesland St	Rondebosch East	29	CN 36	Garrick Rd	Woodstock	15	CG 30	Gill Rd	Muizenberg	76	DG 33
Frigate Cl.	Strandfontein	68	DB 45	Garrison Rd	Claremont	29	CN 35	Gillingham Cl.	Sun Valley	81	DL 23
Frigate Cr.	Sun Valley	72	DJ 22	Garron Ave	Hout Bay	36	CS 20	Gilmour Rd	Silverhurst	38	CT 27
Frigate Rd	Strandfontein	68	DB 44	Garth Ave	Athlone	30	CL 39	Gilmour Cl.	Silverhurst	38	CT 27
Fritz Sonnenberg Rd	Greenpoint	3	CB 24	Garton Rd	Rondebosch	29	CL 35	Gilmour Hills Rd	Tamboerskloof	3	CE 24
Fritz Way	Ottery East	42	CT 39	Gary Rd	Fairways	41	CT 36	Gilquin Cr.	Hout Bay	46	CW 15
Frogmore Rd	Frogmore Est.	63	DC 31	Gatesville Rd	Gatesville	31	CM 42	Gilray Rd	Grassy Pk	53	CX 36
Frome Cr.	Coniston Pk	64	DB 34	Gateway Cl.	Kalk Bay	75	DK 30	Gilwell Cl.	Epping Forest	21	CF 48
Frome Rd	Wynberg	40	CR 33	Gateway Cl.	Capricorn	65	DE 36	Ginnetta St	Belle Constantia	51	CW 29
Froom Rd	Rugby	7	CA 35	Gateway Cr.	Pinati	30	CP 40	Girling Cl.	Epping Forest	21	CF 48
Fryde Rd	Woodstock	16	CG 31	Gatley Rd	Rondebosch	17	CK 34	Girling Cr.	Epping Forest	21	CH 47
Fuchsia Cl.	Kommetjie	78	DL 14	Gawe St	Nyanga	33	CP 49	Girvan Rd	Lansdowne	29	CN 37
Fulham Rd	Bakoven	12	CK 20	Gay Rd	Simon's Town	89	DU 30	Glade Cl.	Rondebosch	28	CL 34
Fulham Rd	Oudekraal	23	CL 19	Gay St	Claremont	28	CN 33	Glade Rd	Rondebosch	28	CL 33
Fuller Rd	Bergvliet	51	CW 30	Gazala St	Strandfontein	68	DB 46	Gladiator St	Kensington	8	CB 38
Fynbos Rise	Fish Hoek	82	DL 25	Gazania Cl.	Ottery East	42	CT 39	Gladiola Rd	Lavender Hill East	65	DC 36
Fynn Cl.	Lansdowne	43	CQ 40	Gazania St	Retreat	64	DA 32	Gladiola Rd	Seawinds	65	DB 36
				Gazelle Cl.	Lotus River	55	CW 40	Gladioli Way	Kommetjie	78	DM 12
				Geduld Rd	Penlyn Est.	30	CO 40	Gladiolus Ave	Devil's Peak Est.	14	CF 27
				Geelhout Ave	Westlake Est.	62	DB 26	Gladstone	Ruyterwacht	11	CE 46
	G			Geelhout Ave	Bonteheuwel	20	CH 44	Gladstone Rd	Glenlily	11	CA 48
				Geelhout St	Grassy Pk	54	CX 38	Gladstone St	Oranjezicht	14	CG 25
Gables Way	Rondebosch	28	CL 34	Geland Rd	Grassy Pk	54	CY 37	Gladstone St	Woodstock	5	CE 30
Gabriel Rd	Manenberg	32	CP 45	Gelder Ct	Marina Da Gama	64	DC 33	Glamis Cl.	Maitland	7	CD 34
Gabriel Rd	Plumstead	40	CS 32	Geloof Way	Steenberg	64	DB 33	Glaren Rd	Wynberg	40	CR 33
Gaff	Strandfontein	69	DA 48	Geluks Rd	Sybrand Pk	18	CK 37	Glasgow	Rondebosch	28	CL 33
Gaff Cl.	Strandfontein	69	DA 48	Gemini Rd	Surrey Est.	31	CM 43	Glass Furnace Way	Glencairn Hgts	83	DO 27
Gaika St	Strandfontein	69	DB 49	Gemini Rd	Wittebloomen	38	CS 26	Glastonbury Dr.	Bishopscourt	26	CP 28
Gail Rd	Retreat	52	CY 33	Gemini Way	Elfindale	52	CW 33	Glastonbury Rd	Kenilworth	28	CP 34
Galaxy Cl.	Ocean View	79	DO 16	Gemini Way	Ocean View	79	DN 16	Glebe Rd	Rondebosch	28	CL 34
Galaxy Way	Salberau	11	CE 47	Gemsbok Ave	Lotus River	55	CV 41	Gledholt Rd	Mowbray	17	CH 35
Galena Rd	Belthorn Est.	30	CO 40	Gemsbok St	Strandfontein	69	DB 49	Gleemoor Rd	Athlone	30	CL 39
Galilee Rd	Steenberg	64	DB 32	General St	Athlone	29	CL 37	Glen Alpine Way	Bergvliet	52	CX 31
Galilee Rd	Steenberg	64	DB 33	Geneva Dr.	Camps Bay	12	CH 21	Glen Ave	Bel Ombre	39	CS 28
Galilee Wk	Hanover Pk	43	CQ 41	Geneva Rd	Coniston Pk	64	DB 34	Glen Ave	Gardens	13	CG 23
Galiot Cl.	Glen Rdg	83	DO 28	Geneva Rd	Muizenberg	64	DE 33	Glen Avon	Pinelands	9	CE 40
Galleon Cr.	Sun Valley	72	DJ 22	Genevieve Cl.	Meadowsteads	72	DG 20	Glen Avon Cl.	Belle Constantia	51	CV 29
Galleon Rd	Strandfontein	68	DA 45	Genoa Ave	Fish Hoek	74	DK 26	Glen Beach Way	Glencairn Hgts	83	DO 27
Gallinule Cl.	Pelikan Pk	55	CX 40					Glen Cl.	Grassy Pk	54	CW 37

STREET NAME	SUBURB NAME	PG	GRID
Glen Cr.	Gardens	13	CG 24
Glen Darroch Rd	Rondebosch	16	CK 32
Glen Devon	Pinelands	9	CE 40
Glen Eagles Rd	Fish Hoek	83	DN 28
Glen Esk	Pinelands	18	CF 39
Glen Garry	Pinelands	18	CF 39
Glen Lily Rd	Richmond	11	CB 47
Glen Rd	Bishopscourt	27	CP 30
Glen Rd	Goodwood Est.	10	CA 43
Glen Rd	Simon's Town	82	DO 25
Glen Roy	Pinelands	18	CF 39
Glen Thorne La.	Rondebosch	28	CL 34
Glen Wk	Rondebosch	16	CK 32
Glenalpine Rd	Welcome Glen	81	DO 23
Glenavon Rd	Welcome Glen	82	DO 24
Glenbrae Ave	Tokai	63	DA 29
Glenbrae Rd	Welcome Glen	81	DO 23
Glencairn Rd	Mowbray	16	CH 33
Glencoe Ave	Gardens	13	CG 23
Glencoe Ave	Oranjezicht	13	CG 24
Glencoe Rd	Oranjezicht	13	CG 24
Glencraig Cl.	Westlake	63	DC 30
Glencraig Cl.	Westlake	63	DE 31
Glendale Cr.	Claremont	28	CM 33
Glendyrr Wk	Barbarossa	40	CT 31
Gleneagle Rd	Simon's Town	82	DO 24
Gleneagle Rd	Welcome Glen	82	DO 24
Glenferrie Rd	Crawford	30	CN 38
Glengariff Rd	Sea Point	3	CC 23
Glengariff Ter.	Three Anchor Bay	3	CB 23
Glenhaven Cl.	Welcome Glen	82	DO 24
Glenhof Rd	Newlands	28	CN 32
Glenhurst Rd	Welcome Glen	82	DO 24
Glenjennifer St	Brooklyn	7	CC 35
Glenoak Rd	Welcome Glen	81	DO 23
Glenook Ave	Wetton	42	CQ 39
Glenpine Way	Matroosfontein	21	CG 47
Glenside Rd	Greenpoint	4	CB 25
Glenugie Ave	Tokai	51	CZ 29
Glenwood Way	Pinelands	18	CG 38
Glider Cr.	Factreton	9	CA 40
Glindon Rd	Fish Hoek	82	DL 26
Glossderry Rd	Claremont	29	CO 35
Gloucester Ave	Bishopscourt	27	CP 29
Gloucester Rd	Lakeside	63	DD 31
Gloucester Rd	Mowbray	17	CH 34
Gloucester St	Claremont	28	CO 33
Gloxinia St	Charlesville	21	CH 46
Gluck St	Steenberg	64	DB 33
Glynn St	Cape Town Central	4	CE 26
Glynn St	Gardens	14	CF 26
Glynville Ter.	Gardens	14	CF 25
Godfrey St	Kalk Bay	75	DK 29
Goede Gift Rd	Simon's Town	88	DU 27
Goede Sq.	Kewtown	19	CJ 40
Golconda St	Glencairn Hgts	83	DN 27
Goldbourne Rd	Kenilworth	41	CQ 34
Golden Gr.	Rondebosch	29	CM 36
Golden Rd	Retreat	52	CY 33
Golders Green Rd	Woodstock	15	CF 30
Goldsmith Rd	Salt River	16	CF 32
Golf Rd	Fairways	41	CT 36
Goliath St	Kensington	8	CC 39
Gondolier Cl.	Crofters Valley	72	DH 21
Gontsana St	Browns Farm	45	CS 48
Gonubie St	Manenberg	32	CM 44
Gonubie St	Surrey Est.	32	CM 44
Good Hope Rd	Strandfontein	69	DB 49
Good Hope St	Wynberg	40	CR 33
Good Hope St	Wynberg	40	CR 31
Goodenough Ave	Epping Ind.	11	CE 46
Goodman Rd	Retreat	53	CZ 34
Goodwood St	Townsend Est.	10	CB 44
Goose Rd	Phumlani	55	CW 41

STREET NAME	SUBURB NAME	PG	GRID
Goran Rd	Wynberg	40	CS 33
Gordon Rd	Crawford	30	CN 38
Gordon Rd	Heathfield	52	CX 33
Gordon Rd	Hout Bay	46	CV 15
Gordon Rd	Kalk Bay	75	DK 29
Gordon Rd	Kenilworth	28	CP 34
Gordon Rd	Lansdowne	42	CQ 39
Gordon Rd	Mowbray	16	CH 33
Gordon Rd	Observatory	16	CG 33
Gordon Searle St	Cafda Village	53	CZ 35
Gordon St	Gardens	14	CF 25
Gordon Ter.	Bantry Bay	2	CE 20
Gore St	District Six	4	CE 27
Gorge Rd	Vredehoek	14	CG 26
Gorlay Rd	Ottery	42	CR 38
Gorleston Rd	Sea Point	2	CD 21
Gosport Rd	Wynberg	40	CR 33
Gothic Rd	Penlyn Est.	31	CN 41
Goud Rd	Vanguard	31	CL 43
Gouda St	Claremont	28	CN 33
Goudblom St	Grassy Pk	53	CW 36
Goudini	Heideveld	20	CK 45
Gougem Rd	Flintdale Est.	53	CW 35
Goulburn St	Townsend Est.	10	CB 44
Gouritz Rd	Manenberg	32	CN 44
Gouritz St	Ruyterwacht	10	CD 45
Gousblom	Bishop Lavis	21	CH 48
Gousblom Rd	Pinelands	18	CF 37
Gousblom St	Charlesville	21	CH 46
Government Ave	Cape Town Cen	4	CE 25
Governor's La.	Newlands	27	CM 30
Governor's Wk	Hout Bay	35	CU 16
Grace Rd	Claremont	27	CO 31
Grace St	Montagu's Gift	54	CV 38
Grace Vulliamy St	Cafda Village	53	CY 35
Graham Rd	Sea Point	3	CC 22
Gramis Cr.	Maitland	7	CE 34
Grampus St	Rugby	7	CA 36
Granada Cl.	Capri	81	DM 21
Grand Bahama Dr.	Capri	81	DL 21
Grand Vue Ave	Salberau	11	CE 47
Grand Vue Rd	Woodstock	15	CF 29
Grande Ave	Newlands	27	CM 31
Grange Ave	Observatory	16	CH 33
Granger Bay Rd	Foreshore	4	CA 25
Granger St	Greenpoint	4	CA 25
Graniet Rd	Vanguard	31	CL 43
Granite Cl.	Lotus River	54	CV 38
Grant St	Kenilworth Pk	29	CP 35
Grant St	Observatory	16	CF 33
Graphite St	Belthorn Est.	30	CO 40
Grasmead Rd	Grassy Pk	54	CX 38
Grasmere	Pinelands	8	CE 39
Grasmere St	Athlone	30	CL 38
Grass St	Bonteheuwel	20	CH 44
Grassfield Rd	Claremont	28	CO 34
Gray Rd	Plumstead	40	CT 32
Gray St	District Six	5	CE 28
Grays Inn Rd	Newlands	27	CN 31
Great Dutch Cr.	Nyanga	33	CO 49
Great Dutch Rd	Nyanga	33	CO 49
Great Fish Ave	Manenberg	32	CN 45
Greatmore St	Woodstock	6	CE 31
Grebe Cl.	Imhoff's Gift	79	DL 17
Grebe Cl.	Pelikan Pk	55	CX 40
Grebe St	Pelikan Pk	67	DD 43
Greef St	Woodstock	6	CE 32
Green	Woodstock	15	CF 30
Green Rd	Bergvliet	52	CY 31
Green St	Cape Town Central	4	CE 25
Green St	Maitland	7	CD 34
Green Valley Cl.	Plumstead	52	CW 33
Green Way	Strandfontein	69	DA 47
Greenacres Cl.	Hout Bay	36	CT 19

STREET NAME	SUBURB NAME	PG	GRID
Greenacres St	Silverhurst	39	CS 28
Greenbank Rd	Rondebosch	17	CK 36
Greenfield Cir.	Ottery East	42	CS 39
Greenfield Cl.	Ottery East	42	CS 39
Greenfield Rd	Dieprivier	52	CV 32
Greenfield Rd	Kenilworth	28	CP 33
Greenford Rd	Newlands	27	CM 31
Greenhawk	Pelikan Pk	55	CX 41
Greenhill Cl.	Peers Hill	74	DK 26
Greenlawn Sq.	Claremont	29	CM 35
Greens Passage	Observatory	16	CG 33
Greenside Cl.	Townsend Est.	10	CA 43
Greenturf Rd	Hanover Pk	31	CP 42
Greenville Rd	Flintdale Est.	53	CV 34
Greenway	Pinelands	18	CF 38
Greenway Cl.	Ottery	43	CR 40
Greenway Rd	Ottery	43	CR 40
Greenway Rd	Schaap Kraal	43	CR 41
Greenways	Rondebosch	29	CL 36
Greenwich Rd	Dieprivier	52	CW 32
Greenwood Rd	Claremont	28	CO 33
Greenwood Wk	Tokai	51	CZ 29
Gregory Rd	Goodwood Est.	10	CA 43
Grens St	Epping Ind.	10	CD 44
Grens St	Steenberg	64	DB 34
Grenville Ave	Epping Ind.	19	CF 42
Gretel Rd	Heathfield	52	CX 33
Grey Rd	Glencairn Hgts	83	DO 27
Grey St	Brooklyn	7	CB 34
Grey St	Richmond	11	CB 48
Grey St	Woodstock	5	CE 29
Greyland Rd	Ottery	42	CS 37
Grey's Pass	Cape Town Central	4	CE 25
Greyton Rd	Bergvliet	51	CW 30
Grieta Rd	Manenberg	32	CP 45
Grimm Rd	Heathfield	52	CX 32
Grimsby Rd	Three Anchor Bay	3	CB 23
Grindal Ave	Lavender Hill	65	DA 35
Grindal Cl.	Lavender Hill	65	DA 35
Grindel Cr.	Lavender Hill	65	DA 35
Grisnez Rd	Vredehoek	14	CG 26
Groenall Wk	Hanover Pk	43	CQ 41
Groenberg Rd	Heideveld	20	CK 45
Groeneveld Rd	Rondebosch	28	CL 33
Groenewald St	Flintdale Est.	53	CV 35
Groenpoort Wk	Hanover Pk	31	CP 42
Groevenbeek Ave	Bel Ombre	39	CS 29
Groot Constantia Rd			
	High Constantia	38	CU 26
Groot Salze	Kirstenhof	63	DC 30
Groot Salze	Kirstenhof	63	DE 31
Grootbosch Cl.	Belle Constantia	51	CV 29
Groote Schuur Ave	Rondebosch	16	CK 32
Groote Schuur Dr.	Observatory	16	CG 32
Grootkop Rd	Manenberg	32	CM 45
Gross	Belthorn Est.	30	CN 40
Grosvener Rd	Rosebank	17	CJ 34
Grosvenor Ave	Oranjezicht	13	CG 25
Grosvenor Ave	Vredehoek	14	CH 25
Grosvenor Rd	Capricorn	65	DE 35
Grosvenor Rd	Dieprivier	52	CV 32
Grotto Rd	Hout Bay	35	CU 18
Grotto Rd	Rondebosch	16	CK 33
Grove Ave	Claremont	28	CN 32
Grove Rd	Churchill	11	CA 48
Grove Rd	Glenlily	11	CA 48
Grove St	Greenpoint	3	CB 24
Grove St	Mowbray	16	CH 33
Grove Rd	Observatory	16	CF 32
Grove Rd	Rondebosch	17	CJ 34
Grove Wk	Claremont	28	CN 32
Grove Wk	Fir Grove	51	CX 29
Grumman St	Kensington	8	CB 38
Grysbok Rd	Lotus River	55	CW 40

Index to Street Names

STREET NAME	SUBURB NAME	PG	GRID
Grysbok Way	Fish Hoek	82	DL 26
Guardian Rd	Heideveld	20	CK 44
Guernsey St	Rondebosch East	29	CM 36
Guildford Rd	Rosebank	16	CJ 33
Guildford St	Capricorn	64	DE 34
Guinea Fowl Cr.	Silverhurst	38	CT 26
Guinea Fowl Rd	Masiphumelele	80	DL 20
Guinea Fowl Way	Noordhaven	72	DF 21
Guinevere Ave	Hout Bay	47	CW 18
Gull Cl.	Flintdale Est.	53	CW 35
Gull Rd	Flintdale Est.	53	CW 35
Gull Rd	Montagu's Gift	54	CV 37
Gull St	Pelikan Pk	67	DD 43
Gulliver Rd	Heathfield	52	CX 32
Gulls Way	Glencairn Hgts	83	DO 28
Gully Rd	Hout Bay	34	CR 15
Gumbo Rd	Nyanga	33	CP 49
Gumtree Cl.	Dreyersdal	52	CY 31
Gumtree La.	Hout Bay	36	CT 20
Gumtree Rd	Dreyersdal	52	CY 31
Gumtree Rd	Steenberg	64	DB 34
Gunners Cir.	Epping Ind.	10	CE 43
Gwalia Rd	Claremont	28	CO 33
Gympie St	Woodstock	5	CE 29
Gypsum Rd	Crawford	30	CN 39

STREET NAME	SUBURB NAME	PG	GRID
Hanover Park Ave	Hanover Pk	31	CP 41
Hanover Rd	Dieprivier	52	CV 32
Hanover Rd	Fresnaye	2	CD 21
Hans Ras Rd	Rondebosch	28	CL 33
Hans Strijdom Ave	Cape Town Cen.	4	CD 26
Hansel Rd	Heathfield	52	CY 33
Hansen Rd	Muizenberg	76	DG 33
Hansen Rd	Muizenberg	76	DH 33
Hants Rd	Lakeside	63	DD 31
Harbour Heights Cl.	Simon's Town	89	DU 29
Harbour Lights	Hout Bay	47	CW 16
Harbour Rd	Hout Bay	47	CX 16
Harbour Rd	Hout Bay Harbour	46	CY 15
Harbour Rd	Kalk Bay	75	DK 30
Harcourt Rd	Claremont	27	CN 31
Hardepeer Rd	Bonteheuwel	20	CH 44
Harding Rd	Claremont	29	CN 36
Harding Rd	Kirstenhof	63	DB 31
Hardwick Rd	Rondebosch	28	CL 33
Hare Rd	Kalk Bay	75	DK 30
Hare Rd	Kalk Bay	75	DJ 29
Hare St	Mowbray	16	CH 33
Hares Ave	Salt River	16	CF 31
Harfield Rd	Claremont	28	CO 33
Harfield Rd	Kenilworth	28	CO 33
Hargraves Rd	Hout Bay	34	CR 15
Haring Rd	Strandfontein	68	DB 45
Harlem Ave	Langa	19	CH 40
Harlequin Rd	Rondebosch	29	CL 36
Harley St	Lavender Hill	65	DB 35
Harman Rd	Claremont	28	CN 33
Harmonica St	Retreat	64	DA 33
Harmonie Rd	Hazendal	18	CK 38
Harmony Rd	Kirstenhof	63	DB 30
Harmony Rd	Retreat	53	CY 34
Harmony Way	Ottery	42	CR 38
Harold Cl.	Hout Bay	36	CT 20
Haroldene Rd	Lansdowne	29	CO 37
Harpenden Rd	Muizenberg Nth	64	DE 32
Harpford Ave	Wynberg	41	CR 34
Harpford Cl.	Wynberg	41	CR 34
Harrier	Dreyersdal	51	CZ 30
Harrier Cir.	Imhoff's Gift	79	DL 17
Harrier Cl.	Imhoff's Gift	79	DL 17
Harrier Rd	Phumlani	55	CW 41
Harrier Way	Montagu's Gift	42	CU 37
Harriers Rd	Mowbray	17	CH 35
Harries St	Plumstead	40	CU 33
Harrington Rd	Tamboerskloof	3	CE 24
Harrington Rd	Fish Hoek	73	DK 23
Harrington Rd	Simon's Town	89	DU 30
Harrington St	District Six	4	CE 26
Harrington St	Gardens	4	CE 26
Harris Dr.	Ottery East	42	CT 39
Harris Rd	Kalk Bay	75	DK 30
Harris St	Mowbray	17	CJ 36
Harrow Ln.	Westlake Est.	62	DC 28
Harrow Rd	Dieprivier	52	CV 32
Harrow Rd	Rondebosch	28	CL 33
Harry de Stadler St	Fish Hoek	73	DK 24
Harry Stodel St	Kenilworth Pk	28	CP 34
Hart Rd	Crawford	30	CN 38
Harvard Dr.	Lansdowne	42	CQ 38
Harvey Rd	Claremont	28	CO 34
Hasme Rd	Masiphumelele	80	DL 20
Hastings Rd	Muizenberg	76	DF 34
Hastings Rd	Wynberg	41	CR 34
Hastings St	Tamboerskloof	13	CF 24
Hatfield Rd	Three Anchor Bay	3	CB 23
Hatfield St	Gardens	14	CF 25
Haupt St	Flintdale Est.	53	CW 34
Hauptville	Barbarossa	40	CT 31
Haute Rd	Belthorn Est.	30	CN 39
Haven Cr.	Gatesville	31	CM 42

STREET NAME	SUBURB NAME	PG	GRID
Haven Dr.	Noordhaven	72	DF 21
Haven Rd	Maitland Gdn Village	7	CE 35
Haven Rd	Ndabeni	7	CE 34
Hawe Sq.	Factreton	9	CC 40
Hawford St	Athlone	30	CL 38
Hawk Cr.	Pelikan Pk	55	CZ 41
Hawk Rd	Montagu's Gift	42	CU 37
Hawkins Ave	Epping Ind.	19	CF 41
Hawks Cl.	Kirstenhof	63	DB 31
Hawkwood La.	Epping Forest	21	CF 48
Hawthorden Rd	Wynberg	40	CQ 31
Hawthorne Cl.	Dennedal	51	CY 29
Hawthorne Cl.	Fairie Knowe	72	DK 21
Hawthorne Cr.	Thornton	9	CE 42
Hawthorne Rd	Claremont	28	CN 32
Hawthorne Rd	Heathfield	52	CX 32
Hawthorne Rd	Lotus River	54	CX 39
Hawthorne Rd	Newlands	27	CN 29
Hawthorne Way	Pinelands	18	CG 39
Hay Rd	Lansdowne	30	CO 38
Hay Rd	Woodstock	15	CF 30
Haydn St	Steenberg	64	DB 33
Hayes Rd	Wynberg	41	CR 34
Haylett Way	Meadowridge	52	CV 31
Hayro Rd	Wynberg	41	CS 34
Haytor Rd	Greenpoint	3	CB 24
Haywood Rd	Crawford	30	CM 38
Hayworth Rd	Kirstenhof	63	DB 31
Hazel Cl.	Valhalla Pk	21	CJ 48
Hazel Rd	Gatesville	31	CL 42
Hazel Rd	Valhalla Pk	21	CJ 48
Hazeldene Cl.	Rondebosch	16	CK 33
Head Rd	Fresnaye	2	CE 21
Heath Ct	Kewtown	18	CK 39
Heath Rd	Heathfield	52	CW 32
Heath Rd	Lotus River	54	CW 39
Heath Rd	Parkwood	41	CU 36
Heath Rd	Rondebosch	17	CJ 36
Heath St	Newlands	27	CN 29
Heathcote Ave	Athlone	30	CL 38
Heather Rd	Claremont	28	CN 34
Heather Way	Meadowridge	52	CV 31
Heatherly Rd	Lansdowne	29	CN 37
Heatherton Rd	Claremont	28	CN 33
Heatherton St	Metro Ind. Township	7	CA 34
Heathfield Rd	Sea Point	3	CC 22
Hebron Ct	Bridgetown	19	CK 42
Hector Ave	Montagu's Gift	43	CU 40
Hector Cl.	Grassy Pk	54	CW 37
Hector Cr.	Grassy Pk	54	CV 37
Hector Petersen	Weltevreden Valley	45	CT 48
Hector Rd	Valhalla Pk	21	CJ 47
Hedge La.	Retreat	64	DA 33
Heere St	District Six	15	CF 28
Heerengracht	Cape Town Cen.	4	CC 27
Heerengracht Rd	Bergvliet	52	CW 31
Heerlik Rd	Kensington	8	CC 38
Heide Rd	Bishop Lavis	21	CH 49
Heide St	Bridgetown	19	CJ 41
Heideveld Rd	Heideveld	20	CK 44
Heideveld Rd	Vanguard	32	CL 44
Heifer St	Rondebosch East	29	CM 36
Hek St	Lavender Hill	65	DA 35
Helder Rd	Athlone	18	CK 37
Helderberg Rd	Bishop Lavis	21	CH 48
Heldersig Rd	Thornton	10	CD 43
Heldray St	Chapman's Peak	71	DF 19
Helen Joseph	Weltevreden Valley	45	CS 48
Helena Rd	Montagu's Gift	54	CV 38
Helgarda Rd	Hout Bay	34	CU 15
Hellenburgh Rd	Claremont	28	CM 33
Helliger La.	Cape Town Central	4	CD 25
Hely Hutchinson Ave	Bakoven	12	CJ 21
Hely St	Maitland	7	CE 35

Index to Street Names

Hemlock St North   Humberstone Rd

STREET NAME	SUBURB NAME	PG	GRID
Hemlock St North ...	Newlands	28	CM 32
Hemyock Rd	Plumstead	40	CS 33
Hendon Rd	Athlone	30	CM 38
Hendon Rd	Wynberg	40	CQ 32
Hendricks Ave	Athlone	18	CK 38
Hendrik St	Ottery	42	CS 37
Henley Rd	Lotus River	54	CW 39
Henley Rd	Marina Da Gama	64	DC 33
Henley Rd	Muizenberg	76	DF 33
Henry Thomson Cl. ..	Heathfield	52	CW 33
Henschell Rd	Hout Bay	34	CU 15
Henshawe Rd	Plumstead	41	CU 34
Henwick Rd	Muizenberg Nth	64	DD 32
Herbert Rd	Sea Point	3	CC 22
Herbert Rd	Sea Point	3	CD 23
Herbrand St	Hazendal	18	CJ 38
Hercules St ...	Woodstock	5	CE 29
Hercules Way	Ocean View	79	DN 16
Hereford Rd	Claremont	28	CO 34
Hereford St	Montana	21	CJ 47
Herman Rd	Observatory	16	CG 33
Hermes St	Paarden Eiland	6	CC 33
Hermina Ave	Bel Ombre	39	CS 28
Hermina Pl.	Bel Ombre	39	CS 28
Hermitage Ave ...	Rosebank	16	CJ 33
Hermitage Way	Meadowridge	51	CV 30
Herold Rd	Rondebosch	29	CM 36
Heron	Pelikan Pk	66	DA 39
Heron Cir.	Kommetjie	78	DM 14
Heron Cl.	Montagu's Gift	54	CV 37
Heron Cl.	Westlake Est.	62	DB 28
Heron Rd	Marina Da Gama	64	DC 34
Heron Rd	Pelikan Pk	55	CZ 41
Heron Way	Pinelands	18	CG 38
Herschel Cl.	Claremont	28	CO 32
Herschel Rd	Claremont	28	CO 32
Herschel Rd	Fish Hoek	82	DL 25
Herschel Rd	Observatory	16	CG 33
Herschel St	Ruyterwacht	10	CC 45
Herschel Wk	Wynberg	40	CQ 31
Hertford Rd	Wynberg	41	CR 34
Hertslet St	Cafda Village	53	CZ 35
Hertzog Blvd	Foreshore	4	CD 27
Hertzog Rd	Bergvliet	52	CX 32
Hertzog Rd West ..	Bergvliet	52	CX 31
Hertzog St	Ruyterwacht	10	CE 45
Heseldon Rd	Rondebosch	29	CL 35
Hess Rd	Grassy Pk	54	CX 39
Hester St	Valhalla Pk	21	CJ 48
Hewett Ave	Epping Ind.	21	CG 46
Hex Cr.	Manenberg	32	CM 45
Hexagon Cr.	Observatory	16	CH 33
Heytor Rd	Muizenberg	75	DH 31
Hibiscus Ave ...	Newlands	27	CM 31
Hibiscus Cl.	Ocean View	79	DM 16
Hibiscus Cl.	Pinelands	19	CG 40
Hibiscus Cl.	Pinelands	19	CG 41
Hibiscus St	Thornton	9	CD 42
Hickory St	Kewtown	19	CK 40
Hiddingh Ave	Newlands	27	CM 30
Hiddingh Ave	Oranjezicht	14	CF 25
Hiddingh Rd East ..	Bergvliet	52	CX 31
Hiddingh Rd North ...	Bergvliet	52	CX 31
Hiddingh Rd South ...	Bergvliet	52	CX 31
Hiddingh Rd West ...	Bergvliet	52	CW 31
Higgo Cr.	Gardens	13	CG 23
Higgo La.	Gardens	13	CG 23
Higgo Rd	Gardens	13	CG 23
High Cape Ave ...	Devil's Peak Est. ..	14	CF 27
High Level Rd ...	Greenpoint	3	CB 24
High Level Rd	Sea Point	3	CC 22
High Rd	Leonsdale	11	CD 48
High Riding Cl. ...	Noordhaven	72	DF 21
High St	Woodstock	15	CF 29
Highbury Rd	Mowbray	16	CH 33
Highclaire St	Maitland	7	CD 35
Highfield Rd	Greenpoint	4	CC 25
Highfield Rd	Rosebank	16	CJ 33
Highfield St	Greenpoint	4	CC 25
Highgate St	Ndabeni	7	CE 35
Highgrove Rd	Lansdowne	42	CQ 38
Highlands Ave	Tokai	62	DA 28
Highlands Ave	Vredehoek	14	CG 26
Highlands La.	Simon's Town	88	DU 27
Highstead Rd	Rondebosch	16	CK 33
Highway	Fish Hoek	83	DM 27
Highwick Ave	Kenilworth	28	CO 32
Highwick Dr.	Kenilworth	28	CP 32
Highworth Rd	Sea Point	3	CC 22
Hilary Cl.	Lavender Hill	65	DB 35
Hilary Dr.	Lavender Hill	65	DA 35
Hilda Rd	Manenberg	32	CP 45
Hildalan La.	Bishopscourt	27	CO 30
Hildalan Rd	Bishopscourt	27	CO 30
Hildene Rd	Tamboerskloof	3	CE 23
Hill Rd	Da Gama Pk	81	DP 23
Hill Park La.	Mowbray	17	CH 34
Hill Rd	Greenpoint	3	CB 23
Hill Rd	Rosebank	16	CJ 33
Hill St	Woodstock	15	CF 29
Hill Top St	Scarborough	86	DU 19
Hill View Ave ...	Lavender Hill East ..	65	DB 36
Hillbrow Rd	Kenilworth	40	CQ 33
Hillcrest Cr.	Fish Hoek	82	DL 25
Hillcrest Rd	Muizenberg	76	DG 32
Hillcrest Rd	The Vines	40	CU 31
Hillrise	Pinelands	18	CG 37
Hillrise Rd	St James	75	DJ 31
Hills St	Schaap Kraal	43	CQ 42
Hillside Rd	Fish Hoek	83	DM 28
Hillside Rd	Tamboerskloof	3	CE 24
Hillside Ter.	Greenpoint	4	CC 25
Hillstar Ave	Ottery	42	CR 38
Hilltop La.	Newlands	27	CM 30
Hillview Rd	Sybrand Pk	18	CK 37
Hillwood Ave	Bishopscourt	27	CO 30
Hillwood Rd	Claremont	27	CP 31
Hilmar Rd	Dieprivier	52	CV 32
Hilton Rd	Clovelly	74	DK 28
Hilton Rd	Hout Bay	35	CT 18
Hilton Rd	Lotus River	54	CW 38
Hilton Rd	Mowbray	17	CH 35
Hilton Rd	Oranjezicht	14	CG 25
Hilton St	Schaap Kraal	43	CQ 42
Hilyard St	Woodstock	5	CE 30
Hind Ave	Kensington	8	CB 38
Hintsa Ave	Hout Bay	35	CU 17
Hlati St	Nyanga	33	CO 49
Hobbs Steps	Fish Hoek	83	DM 28
Hobhouse St ...	Flintdale Est.	53	CV 35
Hobhouse St ...	Ruyterwacht	11	CE 46
Hockey Cl.	Pinelands	17	CF 36
Hockey Rd	Pinelands	17	CF 36
Hoek Cl.	Lansdowne	42	CQ 39
Hoek St	Chapman's Peak ..	71	DF 19
Hoek St	Lansdowne	42	CQ 39
Hoek St West	Wetton	42	CQ 39
Hof St	Gardens	13	CF 24
Hof St	Oranjezicht	14	CF 25
Hoffman Ave	The Vines	40	CU 31
Hofmeyer La.	Woodstock	5	CE 29
Hofmeyer Rd ...	Richmond Est.	11	CA 46
Hofmeyer Rd	Vasco Est.	10	CA 45
Hofmeyr Rd ...	Three Anchor Bay ...	3	CB 22
Hofmeyr St	Gardens	13	CF 24
Hogsback Rd	Heideveld	32	CL 45
Hohenhort Ave	Hohenort	38	CQ 27
Holderness Rd	Lansdowne	29	CP 37
Holland Rd	Muizenberg	76	DF 33
Holland St	Townsend Est.	9	CA 42
Holley Cr.	The Range	21	CF 47
Holley Way	Matroosfontein	21	CG 47
Hollow Ct	Epping Forest	21	CF 48
Holly Cl.	Fairie Knowe	72	DK 21
Holly St	Newlands	27	CO 29
Holmdene Rd	Plumstead	41	CU 34
Holme Rd	Lansdowne	30	CP 39
Holmfirth Rd	Sea Point	3	CC 22
Homeleigh Ave ...	Vredehoek	14	CG 26
Homeleigh Ave	Vredehoek	14	CH 25
Homer St	Salt River	6	CE 32
Homerton La.	Salt River	16	CF 31
Homestead Ave	Bergvliet	51	CX 30
Homestead Way ..	Pinelands	18	CG 37
Honeyside Rd ...	Belthorn Est.	30	CN 39
Honeyside Rd West ...	Crawford	30	CN 39
Honeysuckle Cl. ...	Hout Bay	47	CV 17
Honeysuckle St ...	Bonteheuwel	20	CH 45
Honeysuckle St ...	Bridgetown	19	CK 40
Honeywell Rd ...	Retreat Ind. Area ...	64	DB 32
Honiton Rd	Plumstead	40	CS 33
Hood Rd	Belgravia	30	CM 40
Hoole Cl.	Plumstead	52	CV 33
Hoopoe La.	Bakoven	24	CL 20
Hoosain Parker St ...	Parkwood	54	CV 37
Hope Rd	Rosebank	16	CJ 33
Hope St	Cape Town Central ..	4	CE 26
Hope St	Claremont	28	CO 34
Hope St	Simon's Town	88	DU 27
Hopeville St	Gardens	14	CF 25
Hopkins St	Salt River	16	CF 31
Hopkirk Way	Simon's Town	88	DQ 27
Horak Ave	Bakoven	12	CJ 21
Horatio Way	Simonskloof	89	DU 28
Horeb St	Kirstenhof	63	DB 30
Horizon Cl.	Salberau	11	CE 47
Hornbill Cr.	Seawinds	64	DB 34
Hornbill Rd	Pelikan Pk	55	CZ 41
Hornsey Rd	Mowbray	17	CH 34
Horseshoe Cr.	Noordhoek		
Manor Retirement ...	Village	73	DG 23
Hospital Rd	Wynberg	40	CR 31
Hospital St ...	Cape Town Central ..	4	CC 26
Hou Moed Ave ...	Sunnydale	72	DJ 21
Houghton Rd	Bakoven	12	CK 20
Houghton Steps ...	Bakoven	12	CK 20
Houmoed Ave	Lekkerwater	72	DJ 21
Hounslow La.	Woodstock	16	CF 31
Hout Bay Rd	Hout Bay	36	CT 19
Hout La.	Cape Town Central ..	4	CD 26
Houwhoek St	Manenberg	32	CM 45
Hove Rd	Bakoven	12	CK 20
Howard Dr.	Meadowridge	52	CV 31
Howard Dr.	Pinelands	18	CF 39
Howe St	Observatory	16	CF 33
Howell Rd	Simon's Town	89	DU 30
Howes Rd	Wynberg	40	CS 31
Hudson Rd	Retreat	52	CZ 33
Hudson St ...	Schotsche Kloof ...	4	CD 25
Hughenden St ...	Hout Bay	35	CU 18
Hugo Ave	Hout Bay	47	CX 18
Hugo Cl.	Hout Bay	47	CX 18
Hugo Naude St ..	Cafda Village	53	CZ 35
Hugo Rd	Montagu's Gift	43	CQ 40
Hugo St	Richmond Est.	11	CA 46
Hugon Rd	Claremont	28	CN 32
Huguenot Ave ...	Oranjezicht	14	CG 25
Huguenot Ave ...	Oranjezicht	14	CH 25
Huguenot St ...	Ruyterwacht	11	CG 46
Huilbos Rd	Bonteheuwel	20	CH 44
Humber St	Manenberg	32	CN 45
Humberstone Rd ...	Plumstead	40	CT 33

STREET NAME	SUBURB NAME	PG	GRID
Humby Rd	Ottery	42	CS 37
Humility Cl.	Retreat	53	CY 34
Hunter Ave	Strandfontein	69	DA 48
Hunters Way	Hout Bay	36	CR 20
Huntingdon Cr.	Ottery East	42	CT 38
Huntingdon Rd	Retreat	64	DA 32
Hurley Rd	Mowbray	17	CH 35
Hurricane St	Factreton	9	CC 40
Hurter Ave	Chapman's Peak	71	DF 18
Huskisson Way	Kommetjie	78	DM 12
Hutchinson Ave	Retreat	52	CY 32
Hutton Rd	Kirstenhof	63	DB 31
Huxley Dr.	Athlone	30	CL 38
Huxley Dr.	Meadowridge	51	CV 30
Hyacinth Ave	Pinelands	18	CG 39
Hyde Park Ave	Noordhoek Manor Retirement Village	73	DG 23
Hyde Park Ave	Noordhoek Manor Retirement Village	73	DJ 24
Hyde Rd	Parkwood	41	CU 36
Hyde St	District Six	5	CE 29
Hydra Ave	Ocean View	79	DN 16
Hydrangea St	Charlesville	21	CH 46

STREET NAME	SUBURB NAME	PG	GRID
I			
Ian Cl.	Barbarossa	40	CU 31
Ian Rd	Rondebosch	29	CM 36
Ian Taylor Rd	Plumstead	52	CV 33
Ibis Cl.	Dreyersdal	51	CY 30
Ibis Cl.	Imhoff's Gift	79	DL 17
Ibis End	The Lakes	72	DJ 20
Ibis Rd	Montagu's Gift	54	CV 37
Ibis St	Pelikan Pk	55	CZ 41
Ibis Way	Sunnydale	72	DK 22
Ibis Way	Westlake Est.	62	DB 28
Ibiza Way	Capricorn	65	DE 35
Ibizi Cl.	Capri	80	DL 20
Idaho St	Brooklyn	7	CC 35
Idalia	Kirstenhof	63	DA 30
Iena St	Strandfontein	68	DA 46
Ilex Ave	Ottery	42	CT 38
Ilex Rd	Claremont	27	CO 31
Ilford St	Sea Point	2	CD 21
Ilkley Cr.	Sea Point	3	CC 23
Impala Cl.	Lotus River	55	CW 40
Impala Way	Pinelands	18	CH 39
Inari Pl.	Hanover Pk	31	CP 42
Incholm Pl.	Cape Town Central	14	CF 26
Indian Rd	Kenilworth	40	CQ 33
Induland Ave	Pinati	30	CO 39
Induland Cr.	Pinati	30	CO 39
Indus La.	Ocean View	79	DN 16
Industry Rd	Paarden Eiland	6	CD 33
Industry St	Paarden Eiland	6	CC 32
Industry Way	Cafda Village	53	CZ 34
Inez Rd	Sea Point	2	CD 21
Infanta Cr.	Strandfontein	68	DA 45
Inga Rd	Manenberg	32	CP 45
Ingle Rd	Claremont	28	CN 32
Ingleside Rd	Camps Bay	12	CK 20
Inkblom St	Charlesville	21	CH 46
Innesfree Cl.	Barbarossa	40	CT 31
Innesfree Cl.	Belthorn Est.	30	CN 40
Innesfree Cl.	Belthorn Est.	30	CO 38
Innesfree Rd	Barbarossa	39	CT 30
Innis Rd	Wynberg	41	CR 34
Innisfree Rd	Belthorn Est.	30	CN 40
Inniskillen Rd	Mowbray	17	CH 34
Internal Rd	Strandfontein	68	DA 44
Invermark Cr.	Gardens	13	CG 23
Inverness Ave	Pinelands	18	CF 39

STREET NAME	SUBURB NAME	PG	GRID
Invery Pl.	Foreshore	5	CE 29
Inyoni St	Ndabeni	8	CE 37
Ipsting Rd	Lavender Hill	65	DA 35
Irene Rd	Claremont	27	CO 31
Irene Rd	Montagu's Gift	54	CV 38
Irene Rd	Rondebosch	28	CL 32
Irene Way	Sunnydale	72	DJ 21
Iris Rd	Grassy Pk	53	CY 36
Iris St	Bridgetown	19	CJ 41
Iris Way	Scarborough	86	DU 20
Irma's La.	Plumstead	52	CV 33
Iron St	Lakeside	63	DD 31
Ironwood St	Bonteheuwel	20	CH 45
Irvine St	Manenberg	32	CN 45
Irwell St	Observatory	16	CF 32
Irwinton Rd	Sea Point	2	CD 21
Isaac Rd	Montagu's Gift	43	CU 40
Isaac Way	Montagu's Gift	43	CU 40
Isabel Ave	Claremont	27	CN 31
Isadore Cohen Pl.	Bakoven	12	CK 20
Isadore Cohen Pl.	Bakoven	12	CJ 19
Ishak Rd	Grassy Pk	54	CY 37
Island Rd	Pelikan Pk	54	CZ 39
Islay Rd	Grassy Pk	54	CW 37
Italian Rd	Grassy Pk	53	CY 36
Ivan Rd	Grassy Pk	54	CX 38
Ivan Rd	Montagu's Gift	43	CU 40
Ivanhoe St	Gardens	13	CF 24
Ivanhoe Way	Matroosfontein	21	CG 47
Ivochunett St	Cafda Village	53	CY 35
Ivory Cl.	Sheraton Pk	64	DC 33
Ivory St	Bonteheuwel	20	CH 45
Ivy La.	Tokai	51	CZ 29
Ivy Price Rd	Retreat	53	CY 35
Ivy Rd	Parkwood	41	CU 36
Ivy St	Gardens	13	CF 24
Ivy St	Observatory	16	CF 33
Ivydene Ave	Rondebosch	28	CL 34
Ixia Ave	Devil's Peak Est.	14	CF 27
Ixia Ave	Kommetjie	78	DL 13
Ixia Ct	Kewtown	18	CK 39
Ixia St	Hout Bay	47	CW 18

STREET NAME	SUBURB NAME	PG	GRID
J			
J.F.Celliers St	Townsend Est.	10	CB 43
J.Nontulo St	Nyanga	33	CP 48
J.Z.Fuku Way	Langa	19	CH 42
Jabavi St	Langa	19	CH 40
Jacana La.	Pelikan Pk	55	CX 40
Jacaranda Ave	Grassy Pk	54	CY 37
Jacaranda Ave	Pinelands	18	CF 39
Jacaranda Cl.	Fairie Knowe	72	DK 21
Jacaranda Cr.	Thornton	10	CD 43
Jacaranda Way	Matroosfontein	21	CG 47
Jacaranda Way	Nova Constantia	50	CW 27
Jacht St	Sun Valley	72	DJ 22
Jack Craig St	Cape Town Cen.	4	CD 27
Jackhalsvlei Rd	Nyanga	33	CO 48
Jackson Cr.	Penlyn Est.	31	CO 41
Jackson Rd	Simon's Town	89	DU 29
Jackson's Steps	Simon's Town	89	DU 29
Jacob Ave	Kommetjie	78	DM 13
Jacobs Ladder	St James	75	DJ 31
Jacobs Rd	Grassy Pk	53	CX 36
Jacobus St	Athlone	30	CL 38
Jacomina Way	Wetton	42	CR 39
Jade La.	Sheraton Pk	64	DC 32
Jagger Rd	Elsies River Ind.	11	CB 48
Jahr Cr.	Manenberg	32	CN 45
Jakkalsvlei Ave	Bonteheuwel	20	CH 44
Jamaica Cl.	Capri	81	DL 21

STREET NAME	SUBURB NAME	PG	GRID
Jamaica Dr.	Capri	80	DL 20
James Barry Ave	Alphen	39	CS 29
James Cl.	Grassy Pk	54	CW 38
James Rd	Observatory	16	CG 33
James St	Woodstock	6	CE 31
Jameson Rd	Goodwood Est.	10	CB 45
Jameson Rd	Vasco Est.	11	CA 46
Jamieson Rd	Rondebosch	29	CL 35
Jamieson St	Gardens	4	CE 25
Jan Smuts Dr.	Athlone	30	CL 38
Jan Smuts Dr.	Epping Ind.	19	CF 40
Jan Smuts Dr.	Kewtown	18	CG 39
Jan Smuts Dr.	Lansdowne	30	CP 39
Jan Smuts Dr.	Pinelands	8	CE 39
Jan Smuts Rd	Simon's Town	89	DU 29
Jan Smuts Rd	Wynberg	40	CR 32
Jan Smuts St	Cape Town Central	4	CD 27
Jan Smuts St	Plumstead	53	CV 34
Jan van Riebeeck Ave	Ruyterwacht	10	CD 45
Janari Rd	Grassy Pk	53	CY 36
Jandy Cl.	Kenilworth	28	CO 34
Jane Ave	Gatesville	31	CM 41
Janet	Barbarossa	40	CT 31
Janey Cl.	Montana	21	CK 48
Jangada St	Sun Valley	72	DJ 22
Janni Rd	Plumstead	52	CV 33
Janssens Rd	Maitland	8	CD 37
Jarvis St	Greenpoint	4	CC 25
Jarvis Way	Montagu's Gift	43	CU 40
Jasmine Ave	Fish Hoek	83	DL 27
Jasmine Cir.	Ocean View	79	DM 17
Jasmine St	Bonteheuwel	20	CH 45
Jasmyn Rd	Ottery	42	CS 38
Jasper St	Oranjezicht	14	CF 25
Jasper St	Sheraton Pk	64	DC 32
Jasper Way	Noordhoek Manor Retirement Village	73	DF 23
Java Cl.	Capri	81	DM 22
Javier St	District Six	5	CE 28
Jay Rd	Montagu's Gift	54	CV 38
Jay St	Sunnydale	72	DK 22
Jean Rd	Strandfontein	69	DB 48
Jean Rd	Valhalla Pk	21	CJ 48
Jebel Cl.	Penlyn Est.	31	CN 41
Jebel St	Penlyn Est.	31	CN 41
Jeffcoat Ave	Bergvliet	52	CX 31
Jefferson Rd	Claremont	29	CN 36
Jefferson Rd	Sunnydale	72	DK 21
Jellicoe Ave	Epping Ind.	19	CF 41
Jenkins Rd	Elfindale	52	CW 33
Jenny Schreiner St	Manenberg	32	CN 46
Jeram Ave	Gatesville	31	CM 42
Jerry St	Cape Town Central	4	CD 27
Jersey St	Montana	21	CK 47
Jersey St	Woodstock	5	CE 30
Jesmond Rd	Kenilworth Pk	28	CP 34
Jessica Rd	Valhalla Pk	21	CJ 48
Jet St	Kensington	8	CB 38
Jetty St	Cape Town Central	4	CD 27
Jill Rd	Surrey Est.	31	CM 43
Jim Francis Rd	Newfields	31	CO 42
Joan St	Valhalla Pk	21	CJ 47
Joan Way	Lavender Hill	65	DB 35
Joanna Rd	Montagu's Gift	54	CV 38
Joanne Rd	Lansdowne	42	CQ 39
Joe Gqabi	Weltevreden Valley	45	CT 48
Joe Slovo Cr.	Weltevreden Valley	45	CT 48
Joe Slovo St	Manenberg	32	CN 45
Johan Rd	Hout Bay	47	CW 17
Johanna Rd	Manenberg	32	CP 45
Johannes St	Valhalla Pk	21	CJ 47
Johanneson Rd	Penlyn Est.	31	CO 40
John Heddon St	Brooklyn	7	CB 34
John Jansen Rd	Charlesville	21	CK 47

STREET NAME	SUBURB NAME	PG	GRID
John Laguma Rd ...	Elfindale	52	CW 33
John St	Mowbray	16	CH 33
John Tyres Rd	Ottery	42	CS 37
Johndown Rd	Hanover Pk	31	CP 42
Johns Rd	Grassy Pk	53	CX 36
Johnson Rd	Grassy Pk	54	CW 37
Johnston Rd	Doornhoogte	30	CN 40
Johnturf Wk	Hanover Pk	31	CP 42
Johnvlei Wk	Hanover Pk	31	CP 42
Jonathan Rd	Hazendal	18	CK 38
Jonkershoek Rd ...	Heideveld	32	CL 45
Joolay Rd	Gatesville	31	CM 42
Jordaan St	Schotsche Kloof	4	CD 25
Jordan St	Manenberg	32	CM 45
Jordan Wk	Manenberg	32	CM 45
Joseph Anderson St ...	Steenberg	64	DA 32
Joseph Ave	Grassy Pk	53	CW 36
Joseph Cl.	Grassy Pk	54	CW 37
Josephine Rd	Claremont	27	CO 31
Joubert Rd	Greenpoint	3	CC 24
Joubert St	Vasco Est.	11	CA 46
Joy Ave	Wetton	42	CR 39
Joy Cl.	Valhalla Pk	21	CJ 48
Joyce Rd	Goodwood Est.	10	CA 43
Joyce St	Valhalla Pk	21	CJ 47
Jubilee Rd	Welcome	20	CK 44
Jubilee St	Simon's Town	88	DT 27
Juliana Veld North ...	Pinelands	18	CF 38
Juliana Veld South ...	Pinelands	18	CF 38
Julius Cr.	Retreat	64	DA 32
Junction Rd	Woodstock	6	CE 32
June St	Claremont	29	CO 35
Jungle Wk	Langa	19	CH 41
Juniper Rd	Bonteheuwel	20	CH 45
Juniper Rd	Nova Constantia	50	CW 27
Juniper Way	Fairie Knowe	72	DK 21
Jupiter Ave	Ocean View	79	DO 16
Jupiter Cl.	Salberau	11	CE 47
Jupiter Rd	Kirstenhof	63	DA 30
Jupiter Rd	Surrey Est.	31	CN 43
Jurgens Ave	Kenilworth	28	CO 32
Jurgens Rd	Simon's Town	88	DQ 27
Justice Wk	District Six	14	CF 27
Justin St	Brooklyn	7	CB 34
Justin Way	Montagu's Gift	43	CU 40
Jutland	Gardens	14	CF 26

K

STREET NAME	SUBURB NAME	PG	GRID
Kaag Cr.	Sun Valley	72	DJ 22
Kabeljou Rd	Strandfontein	68	DB 45
Kakapo Cl. ..Belvedere (Noordhoek)..		72	DF 21
Kalkoen Cr.	Bridgetown	19	CK 42
Kalkoen Rd	Bridgetown	19	CK 42
Kalman St	Brooklyn	7	CB 35
Kalo Rd	Browns Farm	45	CR 47
Kamassi Ave	Pinelands	18	CF 39
Kameellboom St ...	Bonteheuwel	20	CH 45
Kamfer Rd	Wynberg	40	CQ 31
Kamiesberg Rd ..Lavender Hill East ..		65	DB 37
Kamiesberg Rd ..Lavender Hill East ..		65	DD 37
Kamieskroon Rd ...	Heideveld	32	CL 45
Kanana	Masiphumelele	71	DK 19
Kanarie Rd	Lansdowne	30	CP 38
Kaneelblom St ...	Pelikan Pk	55	CX 41
Kani Cl.	Nyanga	45	CQ 48
Kannemeyer St ...	Grassy Pk	54	CX 38
Kanti Ave	Gatesville	31	CN 41
Kappie St	Charlesville	21	CG 46
Karakal Rd	Hout Bay	34	CU 15
Karakul St	Rondebosch East	29	CN 36
Karatara Ave	Kenilworth	28	CP 33
Karbonkel Rd . Hout Bay Harbour ...		46	CY 15
Karen Rd	Manenberg	32	CP 45
Karen Rd	Montagu's Gift	54	CV 38
Kariega Rd	Manenberg	32	CN 44
Karoo Rd	Crawford	30	CN 38
Karpas St	Richmond	11	CB 48
Karper St	Muizenberg Nth	64	DD 32
Karree Rd	Bonteheuwel	20	CH 45
Karreeboom Rd	Thornton	9	CE 42
Kasouga Rd	Manenberg	32	CN 45
Kasteel Rd	Wynberg	40	CR 32
Kasteel Steps	Clifton	12	CF 20
Kasteells Rd	Oudekraal	24	CL 20
Katberg St	Heideveld	20	CK 44
Katberg St	Ruyterwacht	10	CD 45
Katie Martin Way ...	Kirstenhof	63	DB 31
Katz Cl.	Masiphumelele	80	DL 19
Katzenellenbogen St ...			
	Chapman's Peak ...	71	DG 19
Katzenellenbogen St ... Wynberg		40	CQ 31
Kayser Ave	Athlone	30	CL 38
Kayter Rd	Athlone	30	CL 39
Keating Way	Ocean View	79	DN 17
Kedah Rd	Rondebosch	29	CL 35
Keerom St .. Cape Town Central ...		4	CE 25
Keert-de-Koe .. Rondebosch		17	CK 36
Kei Apple Gr.	Sea Point	2	CD 21
Kei Apple Rd	Sea Point	2	CD 21
Kei St	Manenberg	32	CN 45
Keith Rd	Montagu's Gift	43	CU 40
Keizersgracht	District Six	15	CF 28
Kelp Rd	Kommetjie	78	DL 12
Kelvin Cl.	Fairie Knowe	72	DK 21
Kelvin Cl.	Fairie Knowe	72	DH 20
Kelvin Rd	Bergvliet	52	CY 31
Kelvin Rd	Greenpoint	3	CC 23
Kelvin Rd	Rondebosch	28	CL 33
Kelvin St	Gardens	13	CF 24
Kemms Rd	Wynberg	40	CS 33
Kempenfelt Rd .. Paarden Eiland		6	CD 32
Kemps Way	Simon's Town	88	DQ 27
Ken Cl.	Barbarossa	40	CU 31
Kendal Rd	Dieprivier	52	CV 32
Kendal Rd	Meadowridge	39	CU 30
Kendal Service Rd ... Meadowridge ..		52	CV 31
Kendall Ave	Maitland	8	CD 37
Kendall Rd	Lansdowne	30	CO 38
Kenhardt Rd	Wynberg	40	CR 32
Kenilworth Cr.	Kenilworth	28	CP 33
Kenilworth Rd	Kenilworth	28	CP 34
Kenmar Cr.	Claremont	28	CO 32
Kenmore Rd	Lotus River	54	CV 38
Kenmore Rd .. Tamboerskloof		3	CE 24
Kenmuir Steps .. Simon's Town		83	DP 27
Kenneth Rd	Plumstead	40	CU 33
Kensington Cr.	Gardens	13	CG 24
Kensington Rd ... Kensington		8	CE 37
Kensington Rd	Maitland	7	CD 36
Kensington Rd	Mowbray	17	CH 34
Kensington Rd	Muizenberg	76	DF 34
Kent Cr.	The Range	21	CF 47
Kent Rd	Lotus River	54	CV 39
Kent Rd	Newlands	27	CM 31
Kent Rd	Rosebank	17	CH 35
Kent Rd	Wynberg	41	CS 34
Kent St	Maitland	7	CD 36
Kent St	Woodstock	6	CE 31
Kent Way .... Matroosfontein		21	CG 47
Kenwood Rd	Fish Hoek	82	DL 26
Kenwood Rd	Lansdowne	42	CQ 38
Kenya Gr.	Lansdowne	42	CQ 37
Kerk St	Simon's Town	89	DU 28
Kerner Cl.	Westlake	63	DC 31
Kerry Rd	Fairways	41	CT 36
Kersboom St	Bonteheuwel	20	CH 45
Kershout Rd	Farmsteads	59	DD 19
Kershout St	Lotus River	54	CV 39
Kestel St	Plumstead	41	CU 35
Kestrel	Bergvliet	51	CV 29
Kestrel Cl.	Westlake Est.	62	DB 28
Kestrel Way	Montagu's Gift	42	CU 37
Keswick Rd	Flintdale Est.	52	CW 33
Keswick Way	Pinelands	8	CE 39
Ketch Cl.	Strandfontein	68	DB 45
Ketch Rd	Strandfontein	68	DB 45
Ketch St	Sun Valley	72	DK 22
Keur	Bonteheuwel	20	CH 45
Keurboom	Pinelands	17	CF 36
Keurboom Rd	Bergvliet	51	CX 30
Keurboom Rd .. Chapman's Peak ...		71	DF 18
Keurboom Rd	Claremont	28	CM 34
Keurboom Rd	Thornton	9	CD 42
Kevin Rd	Montagu's Gift	43	CU 40
Kew Rd	Gardens	13	CF 23
Kew Rd	Mowbray	17	CH 35
Key Link	Avon	11	CD 47
Keyser River Dr. ... Dreyersdal		51	CZ 30
Keysers Rd ...... Retreat Ind. Area ...		63	DA 31
Khalfe Rd	Gatesville	31	CM 42
Khanya Cr.	Gugulethu	32	CO 46
Khayalethu	Gugulethu	32	CM 46
Kiaat Rd	Bonteheuwel	20	CJ 45
Kiewiet Cl.	Westlake Est.	62	DB 28
Kiewiet Cl.	Westlake Est.	62	DB 28
Kiewiet La.	Greenpoint	3	CA 23
Kiewiet Rd	Bridgetown	19	CJ 42
Kiewiet Rd	Pelikan Pk	55	CZ 41
Kildare	Newlands	27	CM 31
Kildare La.	Newlands	27	CM 31
Kildare Rd	Wynberg	41	CQ 34
Kildonan Rd	Mowbray	17	CH 34
Kilgetty Rd	Rondebosch	29	CL 35
Killarney Rd	Muizenberg	76	DG 33
Killarney Rd	Muizenberg	76	DH 33
Kim Rd	Surrey Est.	31	CM 43
Kimberley Rd	Observatory	16	CG 33
Kimberley Rd	St James	75	DJ 31
Kimberley Rd ... Townsend Est.		10	CB 43
Kinders Rd	Belthorn Est.	30	CO 39
Kinewood Ct	Elnor	21	CF 48
King George St ... Ruyterwacht		10	CC 45
King St	Gardens	13	CF 24
King St	Hout Bay	47	CW 18
King St	Manenberg	44	CQ 45
King St	Woodstock	15	CF 30
Kingfisher	Seawinds	64	DB 34
Kingfisher Cl.	Pelikan Pk	66	DA 38
Kingfisher La.	Bergvliet	52	CW 32
Kingfisher La. .. Hout Bay Harbour ..		46	CY 15
Kingfisher Rd	Flintdale Est.	53	CW 35
Kingfisher Rd	Kommetjie	78	DL 14
Kingfisher St	Pelikan Pk	55	CZ 41
Kingfisher St	Westlake Est.	62	DB 28
Kingfisher Wk	Pinelands	18	CH 38
Kinghall Ave ...... Epping Ind.		21	CG 46
King's Pl.	Pinelands	17	CG 36
Kings Rd	Brooklyn	7	CB 35
Kings Rd	Mowbray	17	CH 35
Kings Rd	Sea Point	2	CD 20
Kings St	Newlands	27	CM 31
Kings Way	Pinelands	18	CF 38
Kingsburypark Rd ... Rondebosch ...		28	CL 33
Kingsley Rd	Salt River	16	CF 32
Kingston Rd	Rosebank	17	CJ 35
Kingsway Rd .. Flintdale Est.		41	CU 36
Kinkleway Ave ... Claremont		28	CM 33
Kinkleway La. ...... Claremont		28	CM 33
Kinnoull Rd	Camps Bay	12	CJ 20

STREET NAME	SUBURB NAME	PG	GRID
Kinross Cr.	Fish Hoek	82	DL 26
Kinsale Rd	Fairways	41	CS 36
Kipling St	Observatory	16	CF 32
Kirch St	Bonteheuwel	20	CJ 45
Kirkwood Rd	Plumstead	40	CT 33
Kirsten Ave	Kommetjie	78	DM 19
Kirsten Rd	Kirstenhof	63	DB 31
Kirstenbosch Dr.	Bishopscourt	27	CO 30
Kirstenbosch Dr.	Bishopscourt	27	CO 29
Kirun Rd	Retreat	52	CZ 32
Kismet Ave	Gatesville	31	CM 41
Kitchener Rd	Woodstock	15	CF 30
Kittyhawk Rd	Factreton	8	CB 39
Klaas Rd	Browns Farm	45	CR 47
Klaasenbosch Rd	Hohenort	38	CR 27
Klaasenbosch Dr.	Hohenort	39	CR 28
Klaassens Rd	Alphen	27	CP 29
Klaassens Rd	Hohenort	26	CP 28
Klapperbos St	Kewtown	18	CK 39
Klaproos St	Plumstead	40	CU 32
Klarinet La.	Retreat	64	DA 34
Klaver St	Sybrand Pk	18	CK 37
Klavier St	Retreat	64	DA 34
Klein Constantia Rd	Huis-in-bos	50	CV 27
Klein Constantia Rd			
	Nova Constantia	50	CV 26
Klein St	District Six	5	CE 28
Klein Tuin Rd	Simon's Town	89	DU 30
Klein Wassenaar Rd	Westlake	63	DC 31
Kleinsmidt St	Grassy Pk	54	CW 38
Klip Rd	Grassy Pk	54	CW 37
Klip Rd	Knole Pk	55	CV 41
Klip Rd	Lotus River	54	CV 39
Klip St	Scarborough	86	DU 20
Klipfontein Rd	Airport Industria	33	CN 49
Klipfontein Rd	Athlone	18	CK 37
Klipfontein Rd	Belgravia	30	CL 40
Klipfontein Rd	Doornhoogte	31	CL 41
Klipfontein Rd	Manenberg	32	CM 45
Klipfontein Rd	Mowbray	17	CH 35
Klipfontein Rd	Nyanga	33	CN 48
Klipfontein Rd	Rondebosch	17	CJ 35
Klipfontein Rd	Surrey Est.	32	CL 44
Klipfontein Rd	Sybrand Pk	18	CK 37
Klipper Cr.	Sun Valley	72	DJ 22
Klipper Rd	Rondebosch	28	CL 32
Kloof Ave	Gardens	13	CF 24
Kloof Nek Rd	Gardens	13	CF 23
Kloof Rd	Clifton	12	CG 20
Kloof Rd	Fresnaye	2	CD 21
Kloof St	Gardens	13	CF 24
Knightsbridge Ave	Noordhoek		
Manor Retirement Village		73	DG 23
Knightsbridge Ave	Noordhoek		
Manor Retirement Village		73	DJ 24
Knole Park Ave	Knole Pk	43	CU 41
Knutsford Rd	Plumstead	40	CS 32
Koala St	Brooklyn	7	CB 35
Kob Rd	Hout Bay Harbour	46	CY 15
Koeberg Rd	Brooklyn	7	CB 35
Koeberg Rd	Maitland	7	CD 34
Kohling St	Gardens	3	CE 24
Kolanisi St	Nyanga	33	CO 49
Kolara Cr.	Kenilworth	28	CP 34
Kolobe	Masiphumelele	71	DK 19
Komlossy St	Cafda Village	53	CZ 35
Kommetjie Blvd.	Kommetjie	78	DM 19
Kommetjie Rd	Fish Hoek	73	DK 24
Kommetjie Rd	Kommetjie	78	DM 14
Kommetjie Rd	Sunnydale	72	DK 22
Kontiki Rd	Penlyn Est.	30	CM 40
Koodoo St	Kewtown	18	CK 39
Koornhof St	Nyanga	33	CP 48
Koornhoop Rd	Mowbray	17	CH 34

STREET NAME	SUBURB NAME	PG	GRID
Koosani Ave	Sea Point	2	CD 20
Koperkring	Vanguard	20	CK 43
Koppiesdam Rd	Bishop Lavis	21	CH 48
Koraal St	Ottery	42	CT 38
Koring Rd	Belthorn Est.	30	CN 39
Korne Cl.	Belgravia	30	CN 39
Kornet	Steenberg	64	DB 34
Kort St	Greenpoint	3	CC 23
Kort St	Maitland	8	CD 38
Korvette Cl.	Strandfontein	68	DB 45
Korvette Cl.	Strandfontein	68	DE 45
Korvette Rd	Strandfontein	68	DB 45
Korvette Rd	Strandfontein	68	DE 45
Korvette Rd	Strandfontein	68	DB 45
Kotze St	Gardens	13	CF 24
Kotzee Rd	Observatory	16	CG 33
Kowie Rd	Mowbray	17	CH 35
Kraal Rd	Knole Pk	55	CV 42
Kraal Rd	Schaap Kraal	56	CW 43
Krag Rd	Ottery East	42	CS 38
Kranskop Ct	Townsend Est.	10	CA 43
Kremer Rd	Salt River	6	CE 31
Kreupelbosch Way	Belle Constantia	51	CV 29
Kreupelhout La.	Devil's Peak Est.	14	CG 27
Krieger Rd	Heathfield	52	CY 33
Krieket Rd	Penlyn Est.	30	CN 40
Kritzinger Rd	Lansdowne	30	CO 38
Kritzwald Rd	Lansdowne	30	CP 38
Krom Elbow La.	Cape Town Cen.	4	CE 26
Krom Rd	Bergvliet	52	CX 32
Krom St	Rondebosch East	29	CN 36
Kromboom Parkway	Lansdowne	29	CP 36
Kromboom Parkway	Mowbray	17	CJ 36
Kromboom Parkway			
	Rondebosch East	29	CL 36
Kromboom Rd	Belgravia	30	CM 39
Kromboom Rd	Rondebosch East	29	CM 37
Kromendal Rd	Kirstenhof	63	DB 30
Kruger Rd	Lansdowne	30	CP 38
Kruis St	District Six	5	CE 28
Kruyer St	Ottery	42	CR 38
Krynauw St	Gardens	13	CF 24
Kudu Ave	Lotus River	55	CW 40
Kuils Rd	Hazendal	18	CJ 38
Kukhanya St	Nyanga	45	CQ 48
Kunene Rd	Primrose Pk	32	CN 44
Kurper Cl.	Pelikan Pk	55	CX 40
Kuyper St	District Six	14	CF 27
Kweper Ave	Bridgetown	19	CJ 41
Kylemore Rd	Woodstock	15	CG 30

L

STREET NAME	SUBURB NAME	PG	GRID
L.Eleni Rd	Nyanga	33	CO 49
L.R. Glen Steps	Gardens	13	CG 24
La Cases Rd	Newlands	27	CM 31
La Dauphine	Kirstenhof	63	DB 30
La Gratitude	Pinelands	19	CF 40
La Rhone	Kirstenhof	63	DB 30
La Sacra Rd	Montana	21	CK 48
La Scala Rd	Strandfontein	69	DA 49
Labounere St	Oranjezicht	14	CG 25
Lacre Rd	Lansdowne	30	CP 39
Ladan Rd	Kalk Bay	75	DK 30
Ladbrook Rd	Lansdowne	29	CP 37
Ladies Mile Rd	Bergvliet	51	CW 30
Ladies Mile Rd	Bergvliet	51	CV 30
Ladies Mile Rd Ext.	Gaylands	39	CT 29
Ladies Mile Service Rd	Bergvliet	51	CW 30
Lady Anne Ave	Newlands	27	CM 31
Lady Annes Wk	Brooklyn	7	CC 35
Lady Grey Rd	Fish Hoek	73	DK 25

STREET NAME	SUBURB NAME	PG	GRID
Lady May St	Athlone	29	CL 37
Laidlaw Rd	Rondebosch	28	CM 34
Laindon St	Lansdowne	30	CP 38
Lainsberg Rd	Heideveld	32	CL 46
Lair Ave	Hout Bay	35	CU 16
Lake Rd	Frogmore Est.	63	DC 31
Lake Rd	Grassy Pk	54	CW 38
Lake View Rd	Bergvliet	51	CX 30
Lakeshore Dr.	The Lakes	72	DH 21
Lakeside Pl.	Capricorn	65	DE 35
Lakeside Rd	Capricorn	65	DD 35
Lakeside St	Ruyterwacht	11	CC 46
Lakeview Dr.	Retreat	52	CZ 32
Lakeview La.	Muizenberg	76	DF 32
Lambert Rd	Vredehoek	14	CG 27
Lancashire Cl.	Kirstenhof	63	DB 31
Lancashire Cl.	Kirstenhof	63	DE 31
Lancashire Rd	Lansdowne	30	CP 39
Lancaster Rd	Kenilworth Pk	28	CP 34
Lancaster Rd	Mowbray	17	CH 35
Lancaster Rd	Rondebosch	28	CL 34
Lancaster St	Claremont	28	CO 33
Lancaster St	Hout Bay	47	CV 16
Lancelot Rd	Fish Hoek	74	DK 26
Landdros Ave	Salberau	11	CE 47
Landdrost St	Brooklyn	7	CB 36
Landers Cl.	Fairie Knowe	72	DK 21
Landseer Rd	Mowbray	17	CH 34
Langeberg Rd	Lavender Hill East	65	DC 36
Langenhoven St	Flintdale Est.	53	CV 35
Langenhoven St	Ruyterwacht	11	CC 45
Langevlei Rd	Retreat	52	CY 33
Langham St	Maitland	7	CD 35
Langley Rd	Wynberg	40	CR 32
Langton Rd	Mowbray	17	CH 34
Languedoc	Pinelands	19	CF 40
Lansburg Rd	Hanover Pk	31	CO 42
Lansdowne Rd	Browns Farm	45	CQ 47
Lansdowne Rd	Claremont	28	CN 34
Lansdowne Rd	Lansdowne	29	CO 37
Lansdowne Rd	Schaap Kraal	43	CQ 43
Lansia Wk	Hanover Pk	31	CP 42
Lansing Rd	Grassy Pk	53	CY 36
Lansman Wk	Hanover Pk	43	CQ 41
Lansport Rd	Hanover Pk	31	CP 42
Lansry Wk	Hanover Pk	43	CQ 40
Lansta Wk	Lansdowne	30	CO 38
Lansur Rd	Hanover Pk	31	CP 41
Lantana St	Ottery	42	CS 38
Lanyon Rd	Rondebosch	29	CL 35
Larch Rd	Bonteheuwel	20	CJ 45
Largo Rd	Newlands	27	CN 31
Lark Cr.	Pelikan Pk	55	CZ 41
Lark Ct	Bridgetown	19	CK 42
Lark La.	Montagu's Gift	54	CV 38
Larne Rd	Heathfield	52	CX 32
Las Palmas Dr.	Capri	81	DM 22
Lascelles St	Rondebosch East	29	CL 37
Lasswade Rd	Belle Constantia	51	CV 29
Lategan Rd	Hout Bay	47	CV 17
Latin St	Strandfontein	69	DA 49
Latvan Rd	Gatesville	31	CM 42
Laura Rd	Retreat	52	CY 32
Laurel	Pinelands	19	CG 40
Laurel La.	Claremont	28	CN 32
Laurentia Way	Hout Bay	34	CU 15
Laurier Cl.	Claremont	29	CN 36
Laurier Rd	Claremont	29	CN 36
Lava Cl.	Salberau	11	CE 47
Lavender Pl.	Pelikan Pk	55	CY 41
Lavendon Cl.	Fish Hoek	74	DK 26
Lavendon Rd	Rondebosch	28	CL 34
Lavis Cr.	Brooklyn	7	CB 35
Law Rd	Three Anchor Bay	3	CB 23

STREET NAME	SUBURB NAME	PG	GRID
Lawley Rd	Woodstock	16	CF 31
Lawrence Cl.	Athlone	30	CM 38
Lawrence Rd	Athlone	18	CK 38
Lawrence Rd	Diepriver	52	CV 32
Lawrence St	Maitland	7	CD 35
Lawson Rd	Belthorn Est.	30	CN 39
Lawson Rd	Crawford	30	CN 38
Lawson Rd	Lansdowne	29	CN 37
Layallee Way	Meadowridge	51	CV 31
Le Breton Ave	Steenberg	64	DB 32
Le Grange Rd	Grassy Pk	54	CX 37
Le Provence	Pinelands	19	CF 40
Le Roux Ave	Grassy Pk	53	CY 36
Le Roux La.	Belle Constantia	51	CW 29
Le Sueur Ave	Hohenort	39	CR 29
Lea Rd	Muizenberg Nth	64	DE 32
Lea Rd	Ottery	42	CS 37
Lea Rd	Rondebosch	29	CL 35
Leader St	Vanguard	32	CL 44
Leadwood St	Bonteheuwel	21	CH 46
Leafmore Rd	Lansdowne	29	CP 37
Leah St	Schotsche Kloof	4	CC 25
Leander Pl.	Kirstenhof	63	DB 31
Leander Rd	Strandfontein	69	DB 49
Leballo Rd	Masiphumelele	72	DK 20
Leballo Rd	Masiphumelele	72	DH 20
Lebombo	Lavender Hill East	65	DB 36
Ledore Rd	Plumstead	41	CU 35
Lee Rd	Claremont	29	CN 35
Leepark Rd	Fish Hoek	74	DK 26
Leerdam Rd	Chapman's Peak	71	DF 19
Leerdam St	Wynberg	40	CR 31
Leervis Cr.	Marina Da Gama	64	DC 34
Leeufontein Rd	Kirstenhof	63	DB 30
Leeukloof Dr.	Tamboerskloof	3	CF 23
Leeukop Rd	Hout Bay	35	CU 16
Leeukop St	Tamboerskloof	13	CF 23
Leeukoppie Rd	Hout Bay	34	CR 15
Leeuloop	Hout Bay	35	CU 16
Leeuwen St	Cape Town Central	4	CD 25
Leeuwendal Cr.	Gardens	13	CF 24
Leeuwenhof	Pinelands	19	CF 40
Leeuwenhof Cr.	Gardens	13	CG 24
Leeuwenhof Rd	Gardens	13	CG 24
Leeuwenvoet Rd	Tamboerskloof	3	CE 24
Legas Rd	Flintdale Est.	53	CW 35
Leicester Dr.	Ottery	43	CS 40
Leicester Gr.	Greenpoint	3	CB 24
Leicester Rd	Lakeside	63	DD 31
Leicester St	Claremont	28	CO 33
Leighton Rd	St James	75	DJ 31
Leinster Rd	Greenpoint	3	CB 24
Leith Hill Rd	Tamboerskloof	3	CE 24
Leith Rd	Alphen	39	CR 29
Leith St	Rondebosch	28	CM 34
Lekkerwater Rd	Capri	72	DK 20
Lekoma Way	Langa	19	CH 41
Lelia Rd	Claremont	28	CO 32
Lelie St	Cape Town Central	4	CE 26
Lelieblom Cr.	Silvertown	19	CK 41
Lelieveld Way	Belthorn Est.	30	CN 40
Lemoen Cr.	Silvertown	19	CK 41
Lemon La.	Newlands	28	CM 32
Lena Cl.	Valhalla Pk	21	CJ 48
Lena Cl.	Valhalla Pk	21	CH 47
Lennox St	Woodstock	5	CE 30
Lens Rd	Observatory	16	CG 33
Lensie Rd	Retreat	53	CY 35
Lente Rd	Sybrand Pk	18	CJ 37
Lente St	Kirstenhof	63	DA 31
Lentedal Rd	Hout Bay	35	CU 16
Leo Rd	Elfindale	53	CW 34
Leo Rd	Ocean View	79	DN 16
Leon Ter.	Wynberg	40	CS 32

STREET NAME	SUBURB NAME	PG	GRID
Leonard St	Plumstead	41	CU 34
Leoni Cl.	Dreyersdal	51	CZ 30
Leopard Cl.	Strandfontein	68	DA 46
Leopard St	Paarden Eiland	6	CC 33
Lepanto	Strandfontein	69	DB 47
Lepanto Cl.	Strandfontein	68	DB 46
Lepanto Cl.	Strandfontein	68	DB 47
Lepelhout St	Bonteheuwel	21	CJ 46
Leraar St	Claremont	28	CO 34
Lerotholi Ave	Langa	19	CG 41
Leslie La.	Cape Town Central	4	CD 26
Leslie Rd	Claremont	28	CN 33
Lester Rd	Wynberg	40	CR 33
Letaba Rd	Manenberg	32	CN 44
Letchworth Rd	Pinelands	18	CG 38
Letsatsi Mosala			
	Weltevreden Valley	45	CS 48
Letterstedt Rd	Newlands	28	CM 32
Levendal Cl.	Ocean View	79	DN 17
Lever Rd	Kalk Bay	75	DK 30
Lever St	District Six	15	CF 29
Lewies Rd	Matroosfontein	21	CG 47
Lewin St	Foreshore	5	CE 28
Lewis Dr.	Barbarossa	40	CU 31
Lewis Dr.	Bergvliet	51	CX 30
Lexi Cl.	Salberau	11	CE 47
Ley Rd	St James	75	DJ 31
Leyden Rd	Bergvliet	51	CX 30
Leyte	Strandfontein	68	DB 46
Leytonstone Rd	Retreat	53	CY 34
Liberator St	Kensington	8	CB 38
Libertas	Pinelands	19	CF 40
Liberty Rd	Retreat	53	CY 34
Liberty St	Plumstead	53	CV 34
Libisa Cl.	Nyanga	33	CO 48
Libra Rd	Ocean View	79	DO 17
Libra Rd	Surrey Est.	32	CM 44
Library La.	Grassy Pk	54	CX 37
Lichfield Rd	Bishopscourt	26	CP 28
Liddesdale	Pinelands	8	CE 39
Liddle St	Cape Town Central	4	CC 26
Lidford Rd	Plumstead	40	CT 33
Liermans Rd	Hout Bay	34	CR 15
Liesbeeck Parkway	Rosebank	17	CJ 34
Liesbeek Ave	Observatory	17	CG 34
Liesbeek Parkway	Observatory	16	CF 33
Liesbeek Rd	Rosebank	17	CJ 34
Liesbeek Rd West	Rosebank	17	CJ 34
Lighthouse Rd	Kommetjie	78	DN 12
Lighthouse Rd	Witsand	84	DQ 14
Lilac St	Kewtown	19	CK 40
Lilian Ave	Flintdale Est.	53	CV 36
Lilian Rd	Retreat	53	CY 34
Lillian Ngoyi St	Manenberg	32	CN 45
Lilian Ngoyi Dr.	Weltevreden Valley	45	CT 48
Lily Cl.	Bridgetown	19	CK 42
Lily Cl.	Hanover Pk	31	CO 42
Lily Cl.	Ocean View	79	DM 17
Lily Cl.	Ottery East	42	CT 39
Lily Rd	Retreat Ind. Area	64	DA 32
Lily St	Kewtown	19	CK 40
Lily Way	Lavender Hill East	65	DB 36
Lily Way	Lavender Hill East	65	DD 37
Lilydale Rd	Lotus River	54	CW 39
Lime Rd	Parkwood	41	CU 36
Limerick Rd	Crawford	30	CM 39
Limpopo Ave	Belthorn Est.	30	CO 39
Limpopo Rd	Bishop Lavis	21	CH 47
Linaria Cr.	Bridgetown	31	CL 42
Lincoln Dr.	Bishopscourt	27	CP 29
Lincoln Fields Cr.	Lakeside	63	DE 31
Lincoln Rd	Camps Bay	12	CH 20
Lincoln Rd	Claremont	28	CO 33
Lincoln Rd	Lakeside	64	DD 32

STREET NAME	SUBURB NAME	PG	GRID
Lincoln Rd	Oranjezicht	14	CG 25
Lincoln Rd	Sea Point	3	CC 22
Lincoln Way	Meadowridge	52	CV 31
Linda Ave	Valhalla Pk	21	CJ 47
Linda Cl.	Hout Bay	35	CU 16
Linda Rd	Claremont	28	CO 32
Linda Rd	Montagu's Gift	54	CV 38
Linda St	Hout Bay	47	CV 16
Lindela Rd	Nyanga	33	CP 49
Linden St	Ottery	42	CT 38
Linden Way	Pinelands	18	CF 39
Lindeshof Rd	Sweet Valley	51	CX 29
Lindevista La.	Hout Bay	47	CX 18
Lindewa St	Nyanga	33	CP 49
Lindley Rd	Wynberg	40	CS 32
Lindsay Cr.	Meadowridge	52	CV 31
Liner Cl.	Strandfontein	68	DC 44
Linga Rd	Masiphumelele	80	DL 20
Lingen St	Gardens	13	CF 24
Lingfield Cr.	Ottery	43	CR 40
Lingfield Rd	Ottery	43	CR 40
Link	Strandfontein	69	DB 47
Link Rd	Capricorn	65	DE 36
Link Rd	Flintdale Est.	53	CV 36
Link Rd	Grassy Pk	53	CX 36
Link Rd	Ottery East	42	CS 38
Link Rd	Paarden Eiland	6	CD 33
Link St	Bakoven	12	CJ 20
Linkoping Rd	Rondebosch	16	CK 33
Links Dr.	Mowbray	17	CH 36
Links Dr.	Pinelands	18	CH 37
Links Rd	Rondebosch	17	CK 35
Linnet Way	Pinelands	18	CG 38
Linray Rd	Rosebank	16	CJ 33
Lion Cl.	Strandfontein	68	DA 46
Lion St	Schotsche Kloof	4	CD 25
Lionel Rd	Wynberg	40	CS 32
Lions Paw	Hout Bay Harbour	46	CY 14
Lipton Rd	Wynberg	40	CR 33
Lisboa St	Ruyterwacht	10	CC 45
Liscard Rd	Lansdowne	29	CP 37
Lismore Rd	Dennedal	51	CY 29
Lismore Rd	Tokai	51	CZ 29
Lismore Ter.	Greenpoint	3	CB 24
Lister Rd	Rondebosch	29	CM 35
Lister Way	Meadowridge	52	CW 31
Listowell Rd	Salt River	16	CF 31
Little Rd	Athlone	18	CK 38
Little St	Kensington	8	CC 38
Liverpool St	Hout Bay	47	CW 16
Liverpool St	Wynberg	41	CR 34
Livingstone Ave	Ruyterwacht	11	CD 46
Livingstone Rd	Claremont	28	CN 34
Livingstone St	Langa	19	CG 41
Lizo Nkonki	Weltevreden Valley	45	CS 47
Llandudno Rd	Hout Bay	34	CR 15
Loader St	Greenpoint	4	CC 25
Loanda St	Brooklyn	7	CB 35
Locarno Rd	Rondebosch	28	CL 34
Loch Rd	Camps Bay	12	CH 21
Loch Rd	Claremont	29	CO 35
Loch Rd	Kalk Bay	75	DK 29
Loch Rd	Kalk Bay	75	DJ 29
Loch Rd	Retreat	53	CY 35
Loch Rd	Rondebosch	17	CJ 36
Lochiel Rd	Masiphumelele	80	DL 19
Lochiel Rd	Rondebosch	29	CL 35
Lochner Rd	Barbarossa	40	CT 31
Lock Rd	Capri	80	DL 19
Lockerby Rd	Lansdowne	29	CN 37
Lockwood Rd	Lansdowne	28	CN 34
Loco Rd	Woodstock	6	CE 33
Lodestar St	Kensington	8	CB 38

STREET NAME	SUBURB NAME	PG	GRID
Lodewyk Cr.	Newfields	31	CN 42
Lodewyk Rd	Newfields	31	CN 42
Lodge Rd	Oranjezicht	14	CF 25
Lodge Rd	Ottery	42	CS 38
Lodwar St	Charlesville	21	CK 46
Loerie Ave	Pinelands	18	CG 39
Loerie Cl.	Barbarossa	40	CT 31
Loerie Rd	Bridgetown	19	CJ 40
Loerie Rd	Pelikan Pk	67	DA 41
Loerie Rd	Silvertown	21	CK 41
Logan Way	Pinelands	18	CF 39
Loganberry Cl.	Strandfontein	69	DD 48
Loganberry Pl.	Strandfontein	69	DA 47
Loganberry St	Bonteheuwel	20	CJ 45
Logies Rd	Hout Bay	34	CR 15
Loman Rd	Retreat	52	CZ 32
Lombardie Ave	Bel Ombre	38	CR 27
Lomond Cr.	Coniston Pk	64	DB 34
Lomond St	Claremont	29	CO 35
London Rd	Observatory	16	CG 33
London Rd	Sea Point	3	CC 22
London Rd	Woodstock	6	CE 32
London St	Athlone	30	CL 38
Londonderry Rd	Royal Cape	41	CS 36
Lonedown Rd	Hanover Pk	31	CP 41
Long Pl.	Pinelands	18	CF 38
Long St	Cape Town Central	4	CE 25
Long St	Maitland	7	CD 36
Long St	Mowbray	16	CH 33
Long St	Observatory	16	CG 33
Long St	The Vines	40	CU 31
Longboat Rd	Sunnydale	72	DJ 21
Longboat St	Sun Valley	72	DK 22
Longdon Ave	Athlone	30	CL 38
Longhorn Rd	Rondebosch East	29	CN 36
Longkloof Cir.	Heideveld	32	CL 46
Longkloof Rd	Hout Bay	36	CR 21
Longmarket St	Cape Town Central	4	CD 26
Longmarket St	Schotsche Kloof	4	CC 25
Longueville Way	Bergvliet	52	CW 31
Lonsdale Rd	Wynberg	40	CR 32
Lonsdale Way	Pinelands	18	CF 38
Lonston Rd	Hanover Pk	31	CP 42
Loods Sq.	Factreton	8	CB 40
Lookout Wk	Kommetjie	78	DN 12
Looksmart Ngudle St	Weltevreden Valley	45	CT 48
Loop St	Cape Town Central	4	CD 25
Loop St	Maitland	7	CD 36
Loop St	Vanguard	31	CL 43
Loos Cr.	Kensington	8	CB 38
Loret Ave	Silverhurst	39	CT 28
Lorraine Ave	Woodstock	16	CG 31
Lorrimer St	Brooklyn	7	CB 35
Losack Ave	Epping Ind.	20	CG 45
Lothian Rd	Newlands	27	CN 31
Lothian Rd	Rondebosch	17	CK 35
Lotus Rd	Lansdowne	30	CP 39
Lotus Rd	Lotus River	54	CV 39
Lotus Way	Matroosfontein	21	CG 47
Lotus Way	Thornton	9	CE 41
Loubser Cr.	Kensington	8	CC 39
Loughton Ave	Epping Forest	21	CF 48
Louis Ave	Ottery East	42	CT 39
Louis Botha Ave	Ruyterwacht	10	CE 45
Louis Glassman Rd	Paarden Eiland	7	CC 34
Louis Gradner St	Cape Town Cen.	5	CD 28
Louis Trichard St	Flintdale Est.	53	CV 35
Louis Trichardt Sq.	Ruyterwacht	10	CD 45
Louis Trichardt St	Goodwood Est.	10	CA 44
Louis Trichardt St	Ruyterwacht	10	CD 45
Louise St	Valhalla Pk	21	CJ 47
Louisvale Rd	Athlone	30	CM 38
Lourier St	Flintdale Est.	53	CV 35
Louw Ave	Grassy Pk	54	CX 37
Louw Rd	Hout Bay	47	CV 17
Louw Rd	Wetton	43	CQ 40
Louw Rd	Wetton	43	CT 41
Lovat Rd	Ottery	42	CS 38
Lovedale Ave	Athlone	30	CL 38
Lovedale Cl.	Riverton	11	CC 46
Lovers Wk	Lansdowne	29	CO 36
Lovers Wk	Rondebosch	16	CJ 33
Lovers Wk	Wynberg	28	CP 32
Loviso Ave	Nyanga	33	CP 48
Low Rd	Pelikan Pk	54	CY 38
Low St	Observatory	16	CG 33
Lower 5th Ave	Manenberg	44	CQ 45
Lower Bath Rd	Wynberg	41	CS 34
Lower Botha St	Vasco Est.	11	CB 47
Lower Burg St	Cape Town Central	4	CD 26
Lower Burg St	Rosebank	17	CK 34
Lower Church St	Wynberg	40	CQ 33
Lower Collingwood Rd	Observatory	16	CJ 33
Lower De Wet St	Elsies River Ind.	11	CB 47
Lower Hope Rd	Rosebank	17	CJ 34
Lower Kelvin Rd	Rondebosch	28	CL 33
Lower Kildare Cr.	Fish Hoek	82	DL 26
Lower Klipfontein Rd	Silvertown	18	CK 39
Lower Kloof Rd	Clifton	12	CG 20
Lower Long St	Cape Town Central	4	CC 27
Lower Main Rd	Observatory	16	CF 32
Lower Maynard Rd	Wynberg	40	CR 33
Lower Nursery Rd	Rosebank	16	CJ 33
Lower Piers Rd	Wynberg	40	CR 33
Lower Plein St	Cape Town Central	4	CD 26
Lower Pypies Sq.	Devil's Peak Est.	14	CF 27
Lower Trill Rd	Observatory	16	CG 33
Lower Wrensch Rd	Observatory	16	CG 33
Lower York Rd	Lansdowne	42	CQ 39
Lowestoft St	Paarden Eiland	7	CC 34
Lowlands Ave	Tokai	51	CZ 28
Lucerne Cr.	Coniston Pk	64	DB 34
Lucerne Rd	Retreat	52	CY 32
Lucius Way	The Vines	40	CU 31
Lucy's La.	Wynberg	40	CQ 32
Ludgate Rd	Lansdowne	42	CQ 37
Ludlow Rd	Vredehoek	14	CG 26
Lugard St	Observatory	16	CF 33
Lugmag Ave	Factreton	9	CA 40
Luisa Way	Hout Bay	35	CT 17
Lukannon Dr.	Strandfontein	68	DD 46
Lukas St	Valhalla Pk	21	CJ 48
Lukwart Cir.	Silvertown	31	CL 42
Lulworth Rd	Rondebosch	16	CK 33
Lulworth Way	Pinelands	8	CE 39
Lunar Cl.	Salberau	11	CE 47
Luntu	Masiphumelele	72	DK 20
Lupin St	Bonteheuwel	21	CJ 46
Lute La.	Retreat	64	DA 34
Lutgens Rd	Rondebosch	29	CL 36
Luthango Cr.	Nyanga	45	CQ 48
Luthering Rd	Montagu's Gift	43	CU 40
Luthuli Ave	Hout Bay	35	CU 18
Luton Rd	Heathfield	52	CW 32
Luton St	Vredehoek	14	CF 26
Luttrel	Fish Hoek	83	DL 27
Luvuyo	Guguletu	32	CN 46
Luxmi St	Sand Industria	31	CO 43
Luzon Cl.	Strandfontein	68	DB 48
Luzon Cl.	Strandfontein	68	DE 45
Lydia St	Valhalla Pk	21	CJ 48
Lydia Way	Wetton	42	CQ 39
Lyle Rd	Rosebank	16	CJ 33
Lymington St	District Six	14	CF 27
Lympleigh Rd	Plumstead	41	CS 34
Lynath Wk	Pinati	30	CO 40
Lynburg Rd	Pinati	30	CO 40
Lyndale Rd	Sybrand Pk	18	CJ 37
Lyndhurst Rd	Kenilworth	28	CP 33
Lyndon Cr.	Pinati	30	CP 39
Lyne Rd	Manenberg	32	CN 44
Lynette Cl.	Fish Hoek	73	DK 23
Lynfrae Ave	Claremont	28	CM 34
Lyngean Rd	Pinati	30	CP 40
Lynn St	Norwood	11	CD 48
Lynton Rd	Observatory	16	CG 33
Lynwood Rd	Claremont	28	CM 34
Lynx Ave	Ocean View	79	DN 16
Lynx Cl.	Muizenberg Nth	64	DE 32
Lynx Rd	Paarden Eiland	7	CA 34
Lynx Way	Westlake Est.	62	DB 28
Lyra	Retreat	52	CY 32
Lyra Rd	Ocean View	79	DO 16
Lysander	Factreton	9	CC 40
Lysander Way	Meadowridge	51	CV 30
Lyton Way	Capricorn	65	DE 35
Lytton St	Observatory	16	CF 32
Lytton St	Townsend Est.	9	CA 42

STREET NAME	SUBURB NAME	PG	GRID
M. Mabinda Ave	Hout Bay	35	CU 17
M.E.Rothman St	Townsend Est.	10	CC 43
M.Goniwe Ave	Hout Bay	35	CU 17
M.H.Goldshmidt	Vredehoek	14	CG 26
M.Kotane Rd	Hout Bay	35	CU 17
M.Mbewana St	Nyanga	33	CO 49
M.Oliphant Rd	Nyanga	33	CO 49
Maasbanker Rd	Strandfontein	68	DB 45
Mabel Rd	Doornhoogte	31	CM 41
Mabel Way	Wetton	42	CQ 38
Maclear Rd	Bishopscourt	27	CO 30
Maclear St	Ruyterwacht	10	CC 45
Madaka Cr.	Browns Farm	45	CQ 47
Madeira Dr.	Capricorn	65	DE 35
Madison Rd	Claremont	29	CM 35
Madrid Rd	Airport Industria	33	CL 49
Mafeking Rd	Retreat	52	CY 32
Mafunga Cr.	Langa	19	CH 42
Magalies Rd	Manenberg	32	CP 45
Magaliesberg Rd	Lavender Hill East	65	DB 36
Magaliesberg Rd	Lavender Hill East	65	DB 37
Magcanya Rd	Browns Farm	45	CR 47
Magda Rd	Montagu's Gift	54	CV 38
Magda Rd	Retreat	52	CY 32
Magnolia Cr.	Thornton	9	CD 42
Magnolia Rd	Newlands	27	CM 30
Mahatma Gandhi Ave	Gatesville	31	CN 41
Mahlatini St	Nyanga	33	CP 48
Mahogany St	Bonteheuwel	21	CH 46
Maidstone Rd	Dieprivier	52	CV 32
Maidstone Rd	Heathfield	52	CX 33
Mail St	Epping Ind.	10	CE 44
Main Ave	Athlone	30	CL 39
Main Dr.	Sea Point	3	CC 23
Main Rd	Dieprivier	40	CU 32
Main Rd	Fish Hoek	83	DL 28
Main Rd	Greenpoint	3	CB 24
Main Rd	Heathfield	52	CX 32
Main Rd	Hout Bay	47	CV 17
Main Rd	Kenilworth	40	CQ 33
Main Rd	Lakeside	63	DD 31
Main Rd	Misty Cliffs	86	DU 19
Main Rd	Muizenberg	76	DF 33
Main Rd	Muizenberg Nth	64	DE 32
Main Rd	Newlands	28	CM 32
Main Rd	Observatory	16	CG 32
Main Rd	Plumstead	40	CT 33
Main Rd	Retreat	52	CY 32

STREET NAME	SUBURB NAME	PG	GRID	STREET NAME	SUBURB NAME	PG	GRID	STREET NAME	SUBURB NAME	PG	GRID
Main Rd	Retreat Ind. Area	63	DB 31	Margate Rd	Muizenberg	76	DF 34	Maslamoney Rd	Sand Industria	31	CO 43
Main Rd	Simon's Town	83	DO 29	Marico St	Manenberg	32	CO 44	Masonwabe	Masiphumelele	71	DK 19
Main Rd	Simon's Town	83	DO 28	Marie Cr.	Valhalla Pk	21	CJ 48	Massey Ave	Athlone	30	CM 38
Main Rd	St James	75	DJ 31	Marie St	Rondebosch	28	CL 32	Massinger Rd	Plumstead	52	CV 33
Main Rd Service	Bergvliet	52	CX 32	Mariendahl Ave	Claremont	28	CM 33	Masterman Cr.	Newfields	31	CN 42
Main St	Newlands	28	CM 32	Marigold Ct	Kewtown	18	CK 39	Masters Way	Strandfontein	69	DA 47
Maindy Rd	Athlone	30	CL 39	Marigold St	Silvertown	19	CK 40	Matanzima Rd	Nyanga	33	CP 49
Mainstay	Strandfontein	68	DA 45	Marinda Ave	Montana	21	CK 48	Matapan Ave	Strandfontein	68	DA 46
Maitland Rd	Bishop Lavis	21	CG 48	Marine Dr.	Paarden Eiland	7	CA 34	Matapan Rd	Rondebosch	29	CM 36
Majorca Way	Capri	81	DL 21	Marine Dr.	Woodstock	6	CC 32	Mathew Rd	Claremont	28	CO 34
Makana Sq.	Langa	19	CG 41	Marine Dr. Service Rd				Mathies St	Pinati	30	CP 40
Makholwa Cr.	Nyanga	45	CQ 48		Paarden Eiland	7	CA 34	Matilla Pl.	Leonsdale	11	CD 48
Malamba Way	Langa	19	CH 41	Marine Rd	Strandfontein	68	DB 46	Matolengwe Cr.	Nyanga	33	CP 48
Malan Cr.	Brooklyn	7	CC 35	Marine Rd	Three Anchor Bay	3	CB 22	Matopo Rd	Mowbray	16	CH 33
Malan Cr.	Grassy Pk	54	CW 38	Mariner Way	Heathfield	52	CW 33	Matopo Rd	Thornton	9	CE 41
Malan St	Gardens	13	CF 24	Mariners Cl.	Bayview Hgts	88	DS 26	Matroos Sq.	Factreton	9	CB 40
Malawi Rd	Retreat	52	CZ 32	Mariner's Cl.	Kommetjie	78	DM 13	Matruh Rd	Lansdowne	42	CQ 37
Malcolm Rd	Rondebosch	29	CM 35	Marinus Ave	Grassy Pk	54	CX 37	Mattheus St	Valhalla Pk	21	CJ 48
Malgas St	Flintdale Est.	53	CW 36	Marion Ave	Flintdale Est.	53	CV 35	Matthews Rd	Ocean View	79	DN 17
Malherbe Rd	Elsies River Ind.	11	CB 48	Maritz St	Flintdale Est.	53	CV 36	Mauritius Cr.	Capri	81	DM 21
Malines Ave	Claremont	28	CM 34	Marius Rd	Montagu's Gift	43	CU 40	Mavis Rd	Doornhoogte	31	CM 42
Malleson Rd	Mowbray	17	CH 34	Marivy St	Sybrand Pk	18	CJ 37	Mawson St	Maitland Gdn Village	17	CF 35
Mallow St	Hazendal	18	CK 38	Mark Rd	Claremont	28	CN 32	May St	Avonwood	11	CD 48
Malmesbury St	Ruyterwacht	10	CD 45	Market	Plumstead	40	CT 33	May St	Claremont	28	CO 34
Malone Ave	Claremont	28	CN 33	Market Sq.	Grassy Pk	54	CX 37	Maybank Rd	Flintdale Est.	52	CW 33
Malta Rd	Observatory	6	CE 33	Market St	Grassy Pk	54	CX 37	Maybury Rd	Lansdowne	42	CQ 37
Malta Rd	Ottery	42	CQ 38	Markham Rd	Claremont	28	CN 34	Maydon St	Three Anchor Bay	3	CB 23
Malton Rd	Wynberg	40	CS 33	Marlborough Dr.	Noordhoek			Mayfair Ave	Claremont	28	CM 33
Malunga	Gugulethu	32	CN 45	Manor Retirement Village		73	DG 23	Mayfair Cr.	Noordhoek Manor		
Maluti St	Lavender Hill East	65	DC 36	Marlborough Dr.	Noordhoek			Retirement Village		73	DG 23
Manatoka Ave	Pinelands	18	CG 39	Manor Retirement Village		73	DJ 24	Mayfield Ave	Rondebosch	29	CL 35
Manatoka Ave	Thornton	9	CD 42	Marlborough Rd	Kenilworth	28	CP 32	Mayflower Way	Sun Valley	73	DJ 23
Manatoka Rd	Bonteheuwel	20	CJ 45	Marlbrook Way	Fir Grove	51	CX 28	Maynard Cl.	Pinelands	18	CH 38
Manchester St	Hout Bay	47	CV 16	Marlin Cr.	Hout Bay Harbour	46	CY 15	Maynard Rd	Muizenberg	76	DF 33
Mandel Rd	Newfields	31	CO 42	Marlin Cr.	Strandfontein	68	DA 45	Maynard St	Gardens	14	CF 26
Mandoline Sq.	Steenberg	64	DB 34	Marlin St	Strandfontein	68	DA 45	Mbekweni	Masiphumelele	71	DK 19
Manenberg Ave	Manenberg	32	CN 45	Marlowe Rd	Kenilworth	28	CP 34	Mcaphukiso Ave	Nyanga	33	CP 48
Mangaan St	Vanguard	31	CL 43	Marmion Ave	Clovelly	74	DK 28	Mcaphukiso Ave	Nyanga	33	CM 48
Manhattan St	Airport Industria	33	CM 49	Marmion Rd	Oranjezicht	14	CG 25	McBrides La.	Claremont	28	CO 34
Manitoba Ave	Coniston Pk	64	DB 34	Marne Ave	Claremont	28	CM 34	McClean Rd	Heathfield	52	CX 32
Manitoba Rd	Retreat	52	CZ 32	Marne Rd	Strandfontein	69	DC 49	McDonald St	Goodwood Est.	10	CC 44
Manly Rd	Athlone	29	CL 37	Maroela Way	Pinelands	18	CG 39	McGregor St	Maitland	7	CE 35
Manlyn Wk	Pinati	30	CP 40	Maroon Rd	Parkwood	54	CV 37	McKenzie St	District Six	14	CF 27
Manor Ave	Noordhoek			Mars Cl.	Salberau	11	CE 47	McKenzie St	Gardens	14	CF 26
Manor Retirement Village		73	DG 23	Mars Cl.	Salberau	11	CE 46	McKinley Rd	Kenilworth Pk	29	CO 35
Manor House	Silverhurst	38	CT 27	Mars Rd	Manenberg	32	CM 44	McManus St	Kensington	8	CC 38
Manrose St	Salt River	16	CF 31	Mars Rd	Wynberg	40	CS 33	Mdolombo St	Langa	19	CH 40
Mansfield Rd	Lansdowne	42	CQ 38	Mars Way	Ocean View	79	DO 16	Mdubi St	Browns Farm	45	CS 48
Manson Cl.	Dreyersdal	52	CY 31	Marsden Rd	Hout Bay	35	CU 18	Mead Way	Pinelands	18	CG 37
Manson Rd	Newlands	27	CM 31	Marsden Rd	Woodstock	15	CF 29	Meadow Ave	Hout Bay	36	CT 19
Manta Way	Strandfontein	68	DB 45	Marsh Rd	Rondebosch	29	CL 36	Meadow Ave	Silverhurst	39	CT 29
Manyano Ave	Nyanga	45	CQ 48	Marshall Ave	Wynberg	27	CP 31	Meadow Rd	Ottery	42	CQ 38
Maori Rd	Hout Bay	34	CR 15	Marshall Rd	Richmond Est.	11	CA 47	Meadow Rd	Rosebank	16	CJ 33
Mapasa St	Nyanga	33	CO 49	Marshall Rd	Vasco Est.	10	CA 45	Meadow Way	Plumstead	40	CS 31
Maple Ave	Gardens	13	CF 24	Marston Rd	Dieprivier	52	CV 32	Mechau St	Cape Town Central	4	CC 26
Maple La.	Bergvliet	51	CW 30	Martello Rd	Simon's Town	89	DU 29	Medburn Rd	Camps Bay	12	CJ 21
Maple St	Fairie Knowe	72	DK 21	Martin Adams Rd	Ruyterwacht	10	CE 45	Medina St	Kirstenhof	63	DB 30
Maprin Rd	Flintdale Est.	53	CW 35	Martin Cr.	Pelikan Pk	55	CZ 41	Medlar	Bonteheuwel	20	CJ 45
Mara Ave	Athlone	30	CL 38	Martin Hammerschlag Way				Medway Rd	Plumstead	41	CT 34
Marais Rd	Hout Bay	47	CV 18	Cape Town Central		5	CD 28	Meerendal Rd	Townsend Est.	10	CA 43
Marais Rd	Sea Point	3	CC 22	Martin Luther St	Belgravia	30	CL 40	Meerhof	Kirstenhof	63	DB 30
Marais St	Richmond	11	CB 48	Martin Rd	Barbarossa	40	CT 31	Meerlust	Pinelands	19	CF 40
Marathon Rd	Silvertown	19	CK 40	Martindale Ave	Pinelands	18	CG 39	Meersig Rd	Elfindale	53	CX 34
Marchmont Ave	Oranjezicht	14	CG 25	Martingale Ave	Hout Bay	35	CS 17	Meeu St	Flintdale Est.	53	CW 35
Marchmont Rd	Muizenberg	76	DF 32	Martius Way	The Vines	52	CV 31	Meiring St	Ruyterwacht	10	CD 45
Marconi Way	Meadowridge	52	CW 31	Maryland Ave	Dennedal	51	CY 29	Melba Rd	Newlands	28	CN 32
Mare St	Strandfontein	69	DA 47	Maryland St	Factreton	8	CB 39	Melbourne Rd	Rondebosch East	29	CM 37
Maree Cl.	Kommetjie	78	DM 14	Masakane	Masiphumelele	71	DK 19	Melbourne Rd	Woodstock	15	CF 30
Maree St	Kommetjie	78	DM 14	Masebulele	Masiphumelele	72	DK 20	Melck St	Ndabeni	7	CE 36
Margaret Ave	Pinelands	8	CE 39	Masemola	Masiphumelele	71	DK 19	Melkboom Rd	Muizenberg Nth	64	DD 32
Margaret Pl.	Pinelands	8	CE 39	Masemola Rd	Masiphumelele	72	DK 20	Melkhout Ave	Kommetjie	78	DL 12
Margaret Rd	Bishop Lavis	21	CH 48	Masemola St	Weltevreden Valley	45	CT 48	Melkhout Cr.	Hout Bay	47	CW 17
Margaret St	Constantia Vale	39	CT 28	Masiza St	Gugulethu	33	CN 47	Melkhout Rd	Bonteheuwel	20	CJ 45

Index to Street Names

STREET NAME	SUBURB NAME	PG	GRID	STREET NAME	SUBURB NAME	PG	GRID	STREET NAME	SUBURB NAME	PG	GRID
Melkhout St	Hout Bay	47	CW 17	Miles Rd	Ottery East	42	CT 38	Mocke Rd	Flintdale Est.	52	CV 33
Melkhout St	Scarborough	86	DU 19	Milford Rd	Plumstead	41	CT 34	Modderdam Rd	Montana	21	CJ 48
Melle St	Hout Bay	47	CW 18	Military Rd	Frogmore Est.	63	DB 31	Modena Rd	Greenpoint	3	CB 24
Mellheim	Lansdowne	30	CP 39	Military Rd	Hout Bay	47	CX 18	Moeder Crassula	Charlesville	21	CG 46
Mellish Rd	Vredehoek	14	CG 26	Military Rd	Lavender Hill East	65	DB 36	Moeli St	Nyanga	33	CN 48
Melo Ave	Athlone	29	CL 37	Military Rd	Schotsche Kloof	3	CD 24	Moerdyk St	Townsend Est.	10	CA 43
Melodie Rd	Kirstenhof	63	DB 30	Military Rd	Sheraton Pk	64	DB 33	Moffat Cir.	Ruyterwacht	11	CD 46
Melody Sq.	Retreat	64	DA 34	Military Rd	Tamboerskloof	3	CE 24	Moffat Putego	Weltevreden Valley..	45	CT 48
Melon St	Maitland	7	CD 35	Milkwood Cl.	Kalk Bay	75	DK 29	Moffat St	Langa	19	CH 41
Melrose Ave	Muizenberg	76	DG 33	Milkwood Cl.	Kalk Bay	75	DJ 29	Mohale Rd	Browns Farm	45	CR 47
Melrose Wk	Claremont	28	CN 33	Milky Way	Ocean View	79	DO 16	Mohan Ave	Gatesville	31	CN 41
Melville Rd	Ottery East	42	CT 39	Milky Way	Ocean View	79	DN 16	Mohr Rd	Dennedal	51	CZ 29
Melville Rd	Plumstead	40	CU 33	Milky Way	Salberau	11	CE 47	Moira Rd	Surrey Est.	31	CN 43
Memani Ave	Nyanga	45	CQ 48	Mill St	Brooklyn	7	CB 34	Moka St	Claremont	28	CN 33
Memel Rd	Claremont	28	CN 32	Mill St	Newlands	28	CM 32	Mokobe Rd	Browns Farm	45	CR 47
Mendi Ave	Langa	19	CG 41	Mill St	Oranjezicht	14	CF 25	Molenvliet Rd	Observatory	17	CG 34
Menin Ave	Claremont	28	CM 34	Mill St	Vredehoek	14	CF 26	Moletsani Cr.	Nyanga	33	CP 48
Menton Rd	St James	75	DJ 31	Mill St	Woodstock	6	CE 31	Molinera Way	Meadowridge	51	CV 30
Mercury Cl.	Salberau	11	CE 47	Milldene Ave	Rondebosch	29	CM 35	Molopo Rd	Manenberg	32	CN 44
Mercury Cl.	Salberau	11	CE 46	Miller Rd	Claremont	28	CN 33	Molteno Rd	Claremont	28	CO 33
Mercury Cr.	Ottery	42	CR 37	Miller Rd	Knole Pk	55	CV 41	Molteno Rd	Oranjezicht	13	CG 24
Merino St	Rondebosch East	29	CN 36	Miller Rd	Simon's Town	89	DU 30	Molteno St	Richmond Est.	11	CB 46
Merlin Rd	Phumlani	55	CW 41	Miller St	Guguletu	33	CN 47	Mona Cr.	Claremont	28	CM 33
Mermaid La.	Strandfontein	68	DA 45	Miller St	Nyanga	33	CN 49	Monastery Rd	Fresnaye	3	CD 22
Merrick St	Observatory	16	CG 32	Milne St	Salt River	16	CF 32	Monica Way	Montagu's Gift	54	CV 39
Merriman Rd	Foreshore	3	CC 24	Milner Ave	Hout Bay	47	CV 16	Monkwood Rd	Epping Forest	21	CF 47
Merriman Rd	Goodwood Est.	10	CB 45	Milner Rd	Claremont	29	CN 35	Monmouth Ave	Claremont	27	CO 31
Merriman Rd	Richmond Est.	11	CB 46	Milner Rd	Maitland	7	CE 35	Monowarr Rd	Ottery	42	CR 39
Merriman Rd	Townsend Est.	10	CB 43	Milner Rd	Muizenberg	76	DF 33	Monroe Rd	Claremont	29	CM 36
Merriman St	Langa	19	CG 41	Milner Rd	Observatory	16	CG 33	Mons Ave	Claremont	28	CM 34
Mersa St	Penlyn Est.	30	CN 40	Milner Rd	Rondebosch	17	CJ 35	Montagu St	Ruyterwacht	10	CD 45
Mervyn Rd	Fish Hoek	74	DK 26	Milner Rd	Sea Point	3	CC 22	Montagu Way	Pinelands	18	CH 38
Merwe St	Ottery	42	CS 37	Milner Rd	Tamboerskloof	3	CE 24	Montague Rd	Bergvliet	52	CW 31
Meset Rd	Montana	33	CL 48	Milner Rd	Woodstock	16	CF 31	Montague Rd	Maitland	7	CE 34
Mesfort Cl.	Hout Bay Harbour	46	CY 14	Milner St	Metro Ind. Township	7	CA 34	Montagu's Gift Rd	Montagu's Gift	54	CU 38
Metal La.	Gardens	4	CE 25	Milner St	Paarden Eiland	7	CA 34	Montana Rd	Camps Bay	12	CH 21
Meteor Cl.	Salberau	11	CE 48	Milner St	Ruyterwacht	10	CE 45	Montefleur Ave	Townsend Est.	10	CA 43
Meteor Way	Lansdowne	42	CQ 38	Milton Cl.	Kirstenhof	63	DA 30	Monterey Ave	Bishopscourt	27	CP 30
Metropolitan Rd	Retreat	52	CY 33	Milton Rd	Goodwood Est.	10	CA 45	Monterey Dr.	Bel Ombre	38	CR 26
Meulen Ct	Marina Da Gama	64	DD 34	Milton Rd	Observatory	16	CG 32	Monterey Rd	Hout Bay	35	CT 17
Meyer St	Claremont	28	CO 34	Milton Rd	Sea Point	2	CC 21	Monton St	Lansdowne	29	CP 37
Meyer St	Plumstead	40	CU 33	Milton Rd	Townsend Est.	10	CB 43	Montreal Ave	Oranjezicht	14	CG 25
Meyrick Ave	Plumstead	40	CU 33	Milton Rd	Vasco Est.	11	CA 46	Montreal Ave	Oranjezicht	14	CH 25
Mghayi St	Langa	19	CG 41	Mimosa Cl.	Fairie Knowe	72	DK 21	Montreal Rd	Mowbray	17	CH 35
Mgooi Cl.	Langa	19	CJ 42	Mimosa Cr.	Thornton	10	CD 43	Montrose Ave	Claremont	28	CN 33
Mgoqi Cl.	Nyanga	45	CQ 48	Mimosa Rd	Misty Cliffs	86	DU 19	Montrose Ave	Clovelly	74	DJ 27
Mguqulwa Cl.	Langa	19	CJ 42	Mimosa St	Plumstead	40	CU 32	Montrose Ave	Klassenbosch	26	CP 28
Micawber Rd	Salt River	16	CF 31	Mimosa Way	Pinelands	18	CG 39	Montrose Ave	Oranjezicht	14	CG 25
Michael Mapongwana				Mincing La.	Foreshore	5	CE 28	Montrose Cl.	Sunnydale	72	DJ 22
	Weltevreden Valley	45	CT 48	Minnow St	Brooklyn	7	CC 35	Montrose St	Newlands	28	CM 32
Michael Richmond St	Nyanga	33	CP 48	Minor St	Vanguard	31	CL 43	Montrose Ter.	Klassenbosch	26	CP 28
Michael Storer Ave	Silverhurst	39	CT 28	Minorca Ave	Capricorn	64	DE 34	Monty Rd	Flintdale Est.	53	CV 36
Michaels Rd	Strandfontein	69	DC 47	Minos Rd	Ottery	42	CQ 38	Moody Ave	Epping Ind.	19	CF 41
Michell St	Ruyterwacht	10	CD 45	Mira Rd	Ocean View	79	DN 16	Moody Cr.	Epping Ind.	19	CF 41
Middel Rd	Doornhoogte	31	CM 41	Miramonte St	Maitland	7	CD 36	Moolenberg Rd	Rondebosch	17	CK 35
Middelbank Rd	Strandfontein	69	DC 48	Miranda Ngculu	Weltevreden Valley..	45	CS 48	Moon Cl.	Salberau	11	CE 48
Middelberg Cl.	Claremont	27	CO 31	Miranda Way	Meadowridge	51	CV 30	Moonstone Cr.	Sheraton Pk	64	DB 33
Middle Ave	Schaap Kraal	55	CV 41	Mirbey Rd	Lavender Hill	65	DA 35	Moore Rd	Wynberg	40	CR 32
Middleton Rd	Claremont	28	CM 33	Miriam St	Athlone	28	CK 38	Moore Rd	Wynberg	40	CR 31
Midhurst Way	Barbarossa	39	CT 30	Misrole Ave	Grassy Pk	54	CX 37	Moore St	Kenilworth Pk	29	CP 35
Midmar Rd	Coniston Pk	64	DC 34	Mission Rd	Wynberg	40	CR 33	Moorgate St	Woodstock	5	CE 29
Midsea Way	Ruyterwacht	11	CC 46	Mistletoe Rd	Pelikan Pk	55	CX 41	Moorhen Rd	Marina Da Gama	64	DC 34
Midway Rd	Ottery	42	CS 38	Mistral Cl.	Lakeside	63	DD 31	Moorhen Rd	Pelikan Pk	55	CX 41
Midwood Ave	Bergvliet	51	CX 30	Mitcham St	Wynberg	40	CR 33	Moorland Cr.	Dreyersdal	51	CZ 30
Midwood Ave	Claremont	28	CM 33	Mitchell Rd	Athlone	30	CL 38	Moorsom Ave	Epping Ind.	20	CG 45
Mignon	Elfindale	52	CW 33	Mitre Cl.	Leonsdale	11	CD 48	Moosa Wk	Parkwood	54	CV 37
Mikro St	Goodwood Est.	10	CA 44	Mjekula	Langa	19	CH 41	Moray Pl.	Oranjezicht	14	CF 25
Milagro La.	Noordhaven	72	DF 21	Mkhonto Rd	Masiphumelele	80	DL 20	Moray Way	Strandfontein	68	DB 45
Milan Rd	District Six	15	CF 29	Mkondweni Ave	Nyanga	33	CP 48	Moreland Ter.	Greenpoint	4	CC 25
Milan St	Airport Industria	33	CM 49	Mlokothi Rd	Masiphumelele	72	DK 20	Morgenrood Rd	Kenilworth	40	CQ 32
Milano Way	Strandfontein	69	DA 49	Mlokoti	Masiphumelele	72	DK 20	Morkel Rd	Dreyersdal	52	CY 31
Milbank Rd	Wynberg	40	CR 33	Mndayi Cl.	Nyanga	45	CQ 48	Morkel St	Gardens	14	CF 25
Mile End Rd	Dieprivier	52	CV 32	Mngeele St	Browns Farm	45	CR 48	Morley Rd	Observatory	16	CG 33
				Mobile Rd	Airport Industria	33	CL 49	Mornay St	Schaap Kraal	43	CQ 42

STREET NAME	SUBURB NAME	PG	GRID
Morningside Rd	Ndabeni	8	CE 37
Morningside Rd	Pinelands	18	CF 38
Morom Rd	Wynberg	40	CQ 33
Morpeth Rd	Plumstead	40	CT 33
Morris Cl.	Airport Industria	33	CN 49
Morris La.	Schotsche Kloof	4	CD 25
Morris Rd	Claremont	27	CN 31
Morris Way	Retreat	52	CZ 33
Mortimer Rd	Wynberg	40	CR 32
Mortlake Rd	Wynberg	41	CR 34
Morton Rd	Plumstead	40	CT 33
Morven Rd	Lotus River	54	CV 39
Moselle Rd	St James	75	DH 31
Moser Rd	Strandfontein	69	DC 49
Moses Kotane Wk			
....	Weltevreden Valley ...	45	CS 48
Moses Kotane Wk			
....	Weltevreden Valley ...	45	CT 47
Moses Madiba Cr.			
....	Weltevreden Valley ...	45	CT 48
Moses Madiba Cr.			
....	Weltevreden Valley ...	45	CT 47
Moses St	Welcome	20	CK 44
Mosheshi Ave	Langa	19	CH 41
Mosman Rd	Athlone	29	CL 37
Mosque Rd	Grassy Pk	53	CW 36
Mosque Rd	Wynberg	40	CR 33
Moss St	Newlands	27	CN 29
Mossel St	Churchill	11	CA 47
Mosselbaai St ..	Paarden Eiland	6	CC 33
Mossie	Seawinds	65	DB 35
Mossie Cr.	Pelikan Pk	55	CZ 40
Mossie La.	Montagu's Gift	54	CV 38
Mossop Steps ...	Fish Hoek	83	DM 28
Mostert St ..	Cape Town Central ...	4	CE 26
Mothapeng	Masiphumelele	72	DK 20
Mount Cl.	Noordhoek Manor		
Retirement Village		73	DG 23
Mount Clare St ..	Sybrand Pk	18	CK 37
Mount Nelson Rd ...	Sea Point	3	CC 22
Mount Pleasant Rd ...	Rondebosch ..	27	CL 31
Mount Pleasant Steps ...	Clifton	12	CG 20
Mount Prospect Dr. ...	Huis-in-bos ...	38	CU 27
Mount Rd	Mowbray	16	CH 33
Mount Rd	Muizenberg	76	DF 33
Mount Rd	Rondebosch	28	CL 32
Mount Rhodes Dr. ...	Hout Bay	35	CS 16
Mount Royal Way ...	Pinelands	8	CE 39
Mount St	District Six	4	CE 27
Mountain Cl.	Capricorn	65	DE 35
Mountain Cr. ...	Montagu's Gift	54	CU 38
Mountain Pl.	Kommetjie	78	DM 14
Mountain Rd ...	Chapman's Peak	59	DE 17
Mountain Rd ...	Claremont	27	CO 31
Mountain Rd ...	Clovelly	74	DK 28
Mountain Rd	Farmsteads	59	DE 19
Mountain Rd ...	Fish Hoek	83	DM 27
Mountain Rd ...	Kommetjie	78	DM 13
Mountain Rd ...	Matroosfontein	24	CL 47
Mountain Rd ...	Woodstock	15	CF 30
Mountain Rise ...	Scarborough	86	DU 19
Mountain St ...	Hout Bay	47	CV 16
Mountain View	Pinelands	17	CG 36
Mountain View Rd ...	Wynberg	40	CS 32
Mountainview Cr.	Tokai	63	DA 29
Mountbatten Ave ...	Pinelands	18	CF 39
Mourne Rd	Royal Cape	41	CS 36
Mowbray Rd	Maitland	7	CD 36
Mozart Cl.	Retreat	64	DA 34
Mpetha Rd ...	Masiphumelele	80	DL 20
Msence	Browns Farm	45	CS 48
Mshumpela Way	Langa	19	CJ 42
Msingizane St ...	Browns Farm	45	CR 48
Much Binding Rd ...	Wetton	43	CQ 40

STREET NAME	SUBURB NAME	PG	GRID
Muir Cl.	Rondebosch	29	CL 35
Muir Rd	Rondebosch	29	CL 35
Muir St	District Six	5	CE 28
Mulberry Cr.	Fairie Knowe	72	DK 21
Mulberry St ...	Bonteheuwel	21	CJ 46
Mulder Cl.	Tokai	51	CZ 29
Mullberry Way ..	Strandfontein ...	69	DA 47
Muller Rd	Wetton	42	CR 39
Mullet Cl.	Marina Da Gama ...	64	DC 33
Mulvihal Rd	Rondebosch	29	CL 36
Munich Rd	Airport Industria ...	33	CL 49
Munnik	District Six	15	CF 28
Munster Rd	Royal Cape	41	CS 36
Murdine St	Flintdale Est.	53	CV 35
Murida Rd	Retreat	52	CY 33
Muriel Cl.	Montana	21	CK 47
Muritz Cl.	Coniston Pk	64	DC 34
Muritz Pl.	Coniston Pk	64	DC 34
Muritz Way	Coniston Pk	64	DC 34
Murray Rd	Kenilworth	28	CP 33
Murray Rd	Penlyn Est.	31	CO 41
Murton Rd	Doornhoogte	31	CM 41
Murtz Cl.	Grassy Pk	53	CY 36
Musca Cl.	Ocean View	79	DO 17
Muscat La. ...	South ..Nova Constantia..	51	CW 28
Muscat Way	Huis-in-bos	51	CV 28
Music Rd	Capricorn	65	DD 35
Musket Rd	Wynberg	41	CR 34
Mustang St	Factreton	8	CA 39
Muswell Rd	Mowbray	17	CH 35
Mutley Rd	Three Anchor Bay ...	3	CB 23
Mutual Way	Bergvliet	51	CX 30
Mutual Way	Pinelands	8	CD 39
Mvundla St	Browns Farm	45	CS 48
Myburgh Rd	Dieprivier	52	CV 32
Myer Rd	Retreat	52	CY 32
Myeza	Masiphumelele	71	DK 19
Myeza Rd	Masiphumelele	72	DK 20
Myhof Rd	Claremont	29	CO 36
Mymona Cr.	Primrose Pk	31	CO 43
Myn Rd	Vanguard	32	CL 44
Mynderd St	Plumstead	53	CV 35
Mynie Rd	Wetton	42	CQ 38
Myoli St	Masiphumelele	72	DK 20
Myrtle Rd	Bishop Lavis	21	CH 47
Myrtle Rd	Kenilworth	28	CP 33
Myrtle Rd	Ottery	42	CS 38
Myrtle Rd	Parkwood	41	CU 36
Myrtle Rd	Rondebosch	16	CK 33
Myrtle Rd	Tokai	51	CZ 28
Myrtle St	Oranjezicht	14	CF 26
Myrtle Way	Lekkerwater	72	DJ 21
Myrtle Way	Newlands	28	CM 32
Mzamo	Guguletu	32	CM 46
Mzamo Cr.	Nyanga	33	CP 48
Mzar Cr.	Ocean View	79	DO 16
Mzomtsha Cl.	Nyanga	33	CP 48
Mzonke Jack ...	Weltevreden Valley..	45	CT 48
Mzukisi Skweyiya Rd			
....	Weltevreden Valley ...	45	CS 48
Mzukisi Skweyiya Rd			
....	Weltevreden Valley ...	45	CT 47

── **N** ──

STREET NAME	SUBURB NAME	PG	GRID
N.R.Mandela Rd ...	Hout Bay	35	CU 18
N.R.Mandela Rd ...	Hout Bay	35	CS 18
N.R.Mandela Rd ...	Hout Bay	35	CU 17
Nabucco Rd ...	Strandfontein	69	DA 49
Naggett Ave ...	Hout Bay	35	CU 17
Nahoon Ave ...	Silverhurst	39	CS 28
Nahoon St	Manenberg	32	CN 44

STREET NAME	SUBURB NAME	PG	GRID
Nahum St	Ysterplaat	7	CA 36
Namaqua St ...	Flintdale Est.	53	CV 35
Nansen Rd	Claremont	28	CN 33
Nansen St	Observatory	16	CF 32
Nantes	Kirstenhof	63	DB 30
Napier Rd	Royal Cape	41	CS 35
Napier St	Cape Town Central ..	4	CC 26
Naples St	Observatory	16	CF 32
Napoli Ave	Strandfontein	69	DA 49
Nares St	Observatory	16	CF 32
Naruna Cr.	Plumstead	41	CU 34
Narwahl St	Rugby	7	CA 35
Nassau Ave	Pinelands	9	CE 40
Nassau Rd ..	Chapman's Peak ..	72	DF 20
Nassau Rd	Wynberg	40	CR 31
Nassau St	Ruyterwacht	10	CC 45
Natal St	Paarden Eiland	7	CC 34
Natmeat Rd	Factreton	9	CC 40
Nautilus St ..	Paarden Eiland	6	CB 33
Nautilus St ...	Strandfontein	69	DB 49
Nazareth House Cl. ...	Avon	11	CD 47
Nceba Ave	Nyanga	33	CP 48
Ndabaninzi Ave ...	Nyanga	45	CQ 48
N'dabeni Rd	Langa	19	CH 40
Ndabeni St	Ndabeni	17	CF 36
Ndamane Ave	Nyanga	33	CP 48
Ndamane Ave	Nyanga	33	CM 48
Ndamane Ave	Nyanga	33	CM 48
Ndiki Cl.	Nyanga	33	CP 48
Ndima St	Nyanga	33	CP 48
Ndlela Cl.	Nyanga	45	CQ 48
Ndumiseni Cl.	Nyanga	45	CQ 48
Neath Rd	Observatory	16	CG 33
Neave St	Claremont	28	CO 32
Nebula Ave	Salberau	11	CE 48
Nebula Way	Ocean View	79	DO 16
Nectar Rd	Steenberg	64	DA 32
Nederburg	Kirstenhof	63	DC 30
Nehru Ave	Gatesville	31	CN 41
Neil Cl.	Montagu's Gift	43	CU 40
Nellie Spilhaus St ...	Cafda Village ...	53	CY 35
Nelson Dr.	Simonskloof	89	DU 28
Nelson Rd	Fish Hoek	73	DK 24
Nelson Rd	Observatory	16	CF 33
Nelson St	Foreshore	5	CE 28
Nelson St	Vasco Est.	10	CA 45
Nemesia Cl.	Ottery East	42	CT 39
Nemesia Rd	Silvertown	19	CK 41
Neptune Cl. ...	Simon's Town	88	DS 26
Neptune St ..	Hout Bay Harbour ...	46	CY 15
Neptune St	Paarden Eiland	6	CC 33
Neptune St	Salberau	11	CE 47
Nereide St	Woodstock	6	CD 32
Nerina Ave	Fish Hoek	83	DL 27
Nerina Ave	Kommetjie	78	DN 12
Nerina Cr.	Fish Hoek	74	DK 27
Nerina St	Woodstock	15	CF 30
Nerina Way	Thornton	20	CE 42
Nerine Ave	Pinelands	18	CG 39
Nerine Cl.	Ottery East	42	CT 39
Nerine St	Hout Bay	47	CW 17
Nerine Steps ...	Simon's Town	89	DU 29
Nethi Cl.	Langa	19	CJ 42
Netreg Rd	Bonteheuwel	21	CJ 46
Nettleton Rd	Clifton	12	CF 20
Neva Cl.	Fir Grove	51	CW 28
Nevada Rd	Montana	21	CL 48
Nevin St	Athlone	30	CL 38
New Baden Powell Dr. ...	Capricorn ..	77	DF 36
New Church St ..	Cape Town Cen. ..	4	CE 25
New Church St ...	Gardens	4	CE 24
New Cl.	Valhalla	11	CD 46
New Market St	Foreshore	5	CE 28
New Ottery Rd ...	Ottery East	42	CS 39
New Park Rd	Claremont	28	CM 34

STREET NAME	SUBURB NAME	PG	GRID	STREET NAME	SUBURB NAME	PG	GRID	STREET NAME	SUBURB NAME	PG	GRID
New St	Valhalla	11	CD 46	Norfolk St	Claremont	28	CO 33	NY112	Guguletu	33	CM 47
New Way	Pinelands	18	CF 38	Norfolk St	Maitland	7	CD 36	NY113	Guguletu	33	CM 47
Newark Rd	Kenilworth	28	CP 34	Norfolk St	Newlands	27	CM 31	NY114	Guguletu	33	CM 47
Newbery La.	Newlands	27	CM 31	Norma Rd	Silvertown	19	CK 41	NY115	Guguletu	33	CM 47
Newent St	Lansdowne	42	CQ 37	Norma Way	Montagu's Gift	54	CV 39	NY116	Guguletu	33	CM 47
Newfields Cr.	Newfields	31	CN 42	Norman Ave	Wetton	42	CQ 39	NY117	Guguletu	33	CN 47
Newfields Rd	Newfields	31	CN 42	Norman Cl.	Montagu's Gift	43	CU 40	NY118	Guguletu	33	CL 47
Newlands Ave	Newlands	27	CM 30	Norman Gr.	Fresnaye	2	CD 21	NY119	Guguletu	33	CL 47
Newlands Ave	Rondebosch	27	CL 31	Norman Rd	Greenpoint	3	CB 24	NY12	Guguletu	32	CN 46
Newlands Rd	Claremont	27	CO 31	Norman Rd	Kalk Bay	75	DK 30	NY120	Guguletu	33	CL 47
Newlands Wk	Kenilworth	27	CP 31	Norman St	Hout Bay	47	CV 16	NY121	Guguletu	33	CL 47
Newmans Ave	Belthorn Est.	30	CO 39	Normandie Cl.	Dreyersdal	52	CY 31	NY122	Guguletu	32	CL 46
Newmarket Rd	Ottery	43	CR 40	North Ave	Kewtown	19	CK 40	Ny123	Guguletu	32	CM 46
Newport St	Gardens	13	CF 24	North Cl.	Montagu's Gift	42	CU 38	NY124	Guguletu	32	CM 46
Newry St	Claremont	28	CN 32	North End	Strandfontein	69	DB 47	NY125	Guguletu	33	CL 47
Newton Ave	Athlone	30	CL 38	North Link	Athlone	18	CK 38	NY126	Guguletu	33	CL 47
Newton Dr.	Meadowridge	52	CV 31	North Rd	Sunnydale	72	DK 21	NY127	Guguletu	33	CL 47
Ngawa St	Browns Farm	45	CR 48	North St	Rosebank	17	CJ 34	NY128	Guguletu	33	CL 47
Ngxobongwana	Nyanga	45	CQ 48	North Star Rd	Surrey Est.	32	CN 44	Ny129	Guguletu	33	CL 47
Niblick St	Lakeside	63	DD 31	North Way	Pinelands	17	CG 36	NY13	Guguletu	32	CN 46
Nice Rd	Plumstead	52	CV 33	North Wk	Fish Hoek	74	DK 27	NY130	Guguletu	33	CM 47
Nicholas Cl.	Plumstead	52	CV 33	North Wk	Pinelands	18	CF 37	NY131	Guguletu	33	CM 47
Nicholette St	Plumstead	52	CV 33	Northbridge Rd	Rondebosch East	29	CM 37	NY132	Guguletu	33	CM 47
Nicholi Ave	Kommetjie	78	DM 14	Northoaks Ave	Hout Bay	36	CS 21	NY133	Guguletu	33	CM 47
Nico Cl.	Crawford	30	CM 39	Northshore Dr.	Hout Bay	47	CX 16	NY134	Guguletu	33	CM 47
Nicol St	Gardens	13	CF 24	Northumberland Ave	Lakeside	63	DD 31	NY135	Guguletu	33	CM 48
Niekerks La.	Claremont	28	CN 32	Northumbria Rd	Sea Point	3	CD 22	NY136	Guguletu	33	CM 48
Nightingale Rd	Pelikan Pk	55	CZ 40	Norton Dingle Cl.	Bel Ombre	38	CR 27	NY137	Guguletu	33	CM 47
Nightingale Rd	Wingfield	9	CC 42	Norton Dingle Dr.	Bel Ombre	38	CR 27	NY138	Guguletu	33	CM 47
Nightingale Way	Pinelands	18	CG 38	Norton Way	Rondebosch	29	CL 36	NY139	Guguletu	33	CM 47
Nightjar St	Pelikan Pk	67	DC 43	Norway St	Maitland	7	CD 36	NY14	Guguletu	32	CN 46
Nile St	District Six	15	CF 29	Norwich Ave	Observatory	16	CG 33	NY140	Guguletu	33	CM 48
Nimbus Way	Elfindale	52	CW 33	Norwich Dr.	Bishopscourt	27	CO 29	Ny141	Guguletu	33	CM 47
Nineteenth Ave	Salberau	11	CE 47	Norwood Cl.	Valhalla	11	CD 46	NY142	Guguletu	33	CM 48
Nineteenth Ave	Silverglade	73	DK 25	Norwood Rd	Avonwood	11	CE 48	NY143	Guguletu	33	CM 48
Nineteenth St	Elsies River Ind.	11	CC 47	Norwood Rd	Leonsdale	11	CD 48	NY144	Guguletu	32	CM 46
Ninth Ave	Avon	11	CD 47	Norwood Rd	Norwood	11	CE 48	NY145	Guguletu	33	CM 47
Ninth Ave	Da Gama Pk	81	DP 23	Norwood St	Athlone	30	CL 38	NY146	Guguletu	33	CN 47
Ninth Ave	Fairways	41	CU 36	Nottingham Rd	Lakeside	64	DD 32	NY147	Guguletu	33	CN 47
Ninth Ave	Fish Hoek	82	DL 26	Nourse Ave	Epping Ind.	20	CG 44	NY148	Guguletu	33	CN 48
Ninth Ave	Hazendal	18	CJ 38	Nova Constantia Rd				NY149	Guguletu	33	CN 48
Ninth Ave	Kensington	8	CB 38		Nova Constantia	50	CV 27	NY15 St	Guguletu	32	CN 46
Ninth Ave	Leonsdale	11	CD 48	Ntansiso Rd	Masiphumelele	80	DL 20	NY150	Guguletu	33	CN 47
Ninth Ave	Pelikan Pk	54	CX 39	Ntantala Rd	Masiphumelele	72	DK 20	NY151	Guguletu	33	CN 47
Ninth Ave	Retreat	53	CY 34	Nthombeni Way	Farmsteads	60	DE 20	NY152	Guguletu	33	CN 47
Ninth Ave	Schaap Kraal	55	CX 41	Ntlakohlaza Cl.	Nyanga	33	CP 48	Ny153	Guguletu	33	CN 47
Ninth St	Elnor	21	CF 48	Ntlanganisela Cl.	Nyanga	33	CP 48	NY154	Guguletu	32	CM 46
Ninth St	Kensington	8	CC 37	Ntlangano Cr.	Nyanga	33	CO 49	NY155	Guguletu	32	CM 46
Nirvana Way	Silverhurst	39	CT 29	Ntongana Cr.	Nyanga	45	CQ 48	NY156	Guguletu	33	CM 47
Nita Rd	Montagu's Gift	54	CV 39	Ntukwane St	Browns Farm	45	CS 48	NY157	Guguletu	33	CM 47
Nkomo Way	Langa	19	CH 42	Nukanuka St	Browns Farm	45	CR 48	NY158	Guguletu	33	CL 47
Nkqubela St	Guguletu	32	CP 46	Nursery Rd	Rosebank	16	CJ 33	NY159	Guguletu	33	CL 47
Nkunzane St	Browns Farm	45	CS 48	Nursery Way	Epping Forest	21	CF 48	NY16	Guguletu	32	CN 46
Nobel Way	Meadowridge	52	CW 31	Nursery Way	Epping Forest	21	CH 47	NY17	Guguletu	32	CO 46
Noble Cir.	Ottery East	42	CS 39	Nursery Way	Pinelands	18	CG 38	NY18	Guguletu	32	CO 46
Noll Ave	Newfields	31	CN 42	Nuttall Rd	Observatory	16	CG 33	NY19	Guguletu	32	CO 46
Nolwana Way	Langa	19	CH 41	NY Rd	Claremont	27	CO 30	NY2	Guguletu	33	CO 46
Nomthandazo Peter Cl.	Nyanga	33	CP 48	NY Rd 1	Guguletu	32	CM 46	NY20	Guguletu	32	CO 46
Nongauza Cr.	Langa	19	CH 41	NY1	Guguletu	45	CQ 46	NY21	Guguletu	32	CO 46
Nonguase Rd	Nyanga	33	CP 49	NY1 Rd	Guguletu	33	CP 47	NY22	Guguletu	33	CO 46
Nonkqubela	Masiphumelele	72	DK 20	NY10	Guguletu	32	CN 46	NY23	Guguletu	33	CN 47
Nooitgedacht Dr.	Hout Bay	35	CT 16	NY100	Guguletu	33	CN 48	NY25	Guguletu	33	CO 47
Noord Cl.	Glen Rdg	83	DO 28	NY101	Guguletu	33	CN 48	NY27	Guguletu	33	CN 46
Noordelik Ave	Devil's Peak Est.	14	CG 27	NY102	Guguletu	33	CN 48	NY28	Guguletu	33	CN 47
Noordhoek Rd	Crofters Valley	72	DG 20	NY103	Guguletu	33	CN 48	NY29 St	Guguletu	33	CN 47
Noordhoek Rd	Sunnydale	72	DJ 21	NY104	Guguletu	33	CN 48	NY3	Guguletu	32	CO 46
Noreen Ave	Claremont	27	CN 31	NY105	Guguletu	33	CN 48	NY30	Guguletu	33	CO 46
Norfolk Cl.	Newlands	27	CM 31	NY106	Guguletu	33	CN 48	NY37	Guguletu	33	CN 47
Norfolk La.	Rosebank	17	CJ 34	NY107	Guguletu	33	CO 47	NY38	Guguletu	33	CN 47
Norfolk Rd	Lakeside	63	DD 31	NY108	Guguletu	33	CO 48	NY39	Guguletu	33	CN 47
Norfolk Rd	Observatory	16	CG 33	NY109	Guguletu	32	CM 46	NY4	Guguletu	32	CN 46
Norfolk Rd	Sea Point	3	CC 22	NY11	Guguletu	32	CN 46	NY40	Guguletu	33	CN 46
Norfolk Rd	Tokai	51	CZ 29	NY110	Guguletu	33	CL 47	NY41	Guguletu	33	CN 47
Norfolk Rd	Tokai	51	CY 28	NY111	Guguletu	32	CL 46				

STREET NAME	SUBURB NAME	PG	GRID
NY42	Guguletu	32	CO 46
NY43	Guguletu	33	CO 48
NY44	Guguletu	33	CO 47
NY45	Guguletu	33	CO 47
NY46	Guguletu	32	CO 46
NY47	Guguletu	32	CO 46
NY48	Guguletu	33	CO 47
NY49	Guguletu	33	CO 47
NY5	Guguletu	33	CN 47
NY50	Guguletu	32	CP 46
NY52	Guguletu	33	CP 47
NY53	Guguletu	33	CP 47
NY54	Guguletu	32	CP 46
NY55	Guguletu	33	CP 47
NY56	Guguletu	33	CP 47
NY57	Guguletu	33	CP 47
NY58	Guguletu	32	CP 46
NY59	Guguletu	32	CP 46
NY6	Guguletu	33	CN 48
NY60	Guguletu	33	CP 47
NY61	Guguletu	32	CP 46
NY62	Guguletu	32	CP 46
NY63	Guguletu	32	CP 46
NY64	Guguletu	45	CQ 46
NY65	Guguletu	45	CQ 46
NY66	Guguletu	32	CQ 46
NY67	Guguletu	32	CQ 46
NY69	Guguletu	45	CQ 47
NY7	Guguletu	32	CN 46
NY70	Guguletu	45	CQ 47
NY71	Guguletu	45	CQ 47
NY72	Guguletu	45	CQ 46
NY74	Guguletu	45	CQ 46
NY75	Guguletu	45	CQ 46
NY76	Guguletu	45	CQ 47
NY77	Guguletu	33	CO 47
NY78	Guguletu	33	CP 48
NY78	Nyanga	33	CO 47
NY79	Guguletu	33	CO 47
NY8	Guguletu	32	CM 46
NY80	Guguletu	33	CP 47
NY81	Guguletu	33	CP 47
NY82	Guguletu	33	CP 47
NY83	Guguletu	33	CP 47
NY84	Guguletu	33	CP 47
NY85	Guguletu	33	CP 47
NY86	Guguletu	33	CP 47
NY87	Guguletu	33	CP 47
NY88	Guguletu	33	CP 47
NY89	Guguletu	33	CP 47
NY9	Guguletu	32	CN 46
NY90	Guguletu	33	CP 48
NY91	Guguletu	33	CP 47
NY92	Guguletu	33	CP 47
NY93	Guguletu	45	CQ 47
NY94	Guguletu	45	CQ 47
NY95	Guguletu	45	CQ 47
NY96	Guguletu	45	CQ 47
NY97	Guguletu	45	CQ 47
NY99	Guguletu	33	CN 48
Nyala Cr.	Silvertown	19	CK 41
Nyala Rd	Pelikan Pk	55	CW 40
Nyasa Rd	Retreat	52	CY 32
Nyman St	Maitland	8	CC 39
O.R.Tambo Rd	Hout Bay	35	CU 17
Oak Ave	Chapman's Peak	71	DF 18
Oak Ave	Claremont	27	CH 31
Oak Ave	Grassy Pk	54	CY 37
Oak Ave	Hohenort	39	CQ 29
Oak Ave	Kenilworth	28	CP 32
Oak Ave	Newlands	27	CM 31
Oak Ave	Rondebosch	28	CL 33
Oak Ave	Thornton	9	CD 42
Oak Ave	Wynberg	40	CR 32
Oak Farm Cr.	The Vines	52	CV 31
Oak St	Observatory	16	CF 33
Oak Way	Lekkerwater	72	DJ 21
Oakburn Rd	Hout Bay	34	CR 15
Oakdale	Pinelands	18	CF 38
Oakdale Rd	Newlands	28	CN 32
Oakdale Ter.	Newlands	28	CN 32
Oakfield Rd	Claremont	28	CN 33
Oakhurst Ave	Hout Bay	36	CT 19
Oakhurst Ave	Rondebosch	28	CL 34
Oakhurst Cl.	Rondebosch	28	CL 34
Oakley Ave	Tokai	63	DA 29
Oakley Pl.	Ocean View	79	DN 16
Oakley Rd	Rondebosch	29	CL 36
Oakridge Ave	Meadowridge	52	CW 31
Oakridge Cl.	Meadowridge	52	CW 32
Oaktree Rd	Devil's Peak Est.	14	CG 27
Oakvale Rd	Rondebosch	29	CL 35
Oakwood Rd	Bonteheuwel	20	CJ 44
Oasis Rd	Hazendal	18	CJ 38
Oasis St	Riverton	11	CC 47
Oban St	Hazendal	18	CK 38
Oban Rd	Rondebosch	29	CM 36
Obelisk Rd	Claremont	27	CN 31
Oberon Way	Meadowridge	51	CV 30
Oboe St	Cafda Village	53	CZ 35
Observatory Rd	Observatory	17	CF 34
Ocean	Foreshore	5	CD 30
Ocean View Dr.	Bantry Bay	2	CE 20
Ocean View Dr.	Fresnaye	2	CE 21
Ocean View Dr.	Greenpoint	4	CC 25
Ocean View Dr.	Sea Point	3	CC 24
Ocean View Dr.	Sea Point	3	CC 23
Oceana Amethyst Way	Hout Bay Harbour	46	CY 15
Oceana Emerald Way	Hout Bay Harbour	46	CY 15
Oceana Ruby Way	Hout Bay Harbour	46	CY 15
Oceana Sapphire	Hout Bay Harbour	46	CY 15
Odin Dr.	Thornton	9	CE 41
Ohio Ave	Primrose Pk	32	CN 44
Ohlsson Way	Newlands	27	CM 31
Okinawa Cl.	Strandfontein	68	DB 46
Okinawa Cl.	Strandfontein	68	DE 45
Old Bear Rd	Silverhurst	38	CT 27
Old Boyes Dr.	Muizenberg	76	DF 32
Old Cape Farm Rd	Crofters Valley	72	DG 21
Old Cottage Rd	Silverhurst	38	CT 27
Old Farm Rd	Rondebosch	17	CK 36
Old Farm Rd	Silverhurst	38	CT 27
Old Kendal Cl.	Dieprivier	52	CV 32
Old Kendal Rd	Dieprivier	40	CU 32
Old Kendal Rd	The Vines	40	CU 31
Old Klipfontein Rd	Athlone	18	CK 38
Old Kommetjie Rd	Sunnydale	72	DK 22
Old Lansdowne Rd	Schaap Kraal	44	CR 44
Old Marine Dr.	Foreshore	4	CD 27
Old Mill Rd	Pinelands	18	CF 37
Old Rhodes Dr.	Bishopscourt	26	CO 28
Old Rhodes Dr.	Wittebomen	38	CR 25
Old Strandfontein Rd	Wetton	43	CR 40
Oldfield Rd	Sea Point	3	CC 22
Oleander Cl.	Fir Grove	51	CX 28
Oleander Cr.	Thornton		CE 42
Oleander St	Bonteheuwel	21	CJ 46
Oleander Way	Sweet Valley	51	CX 28
Olga Ncivata	Weltevreden Valley	45	CS 48
Olga Rd	Manenberg	32	CO 45
Olga Rd	Montagu's Gift	54	CV 38
Olieboom Rd	Schaap Kraal	44	CR 43
Oliehout Rd	Bonteheuwel	21	CK 46
Olienhout Pl.	Leonsdale	11	CD 48
Olienhout Pl.	Leonsdale	11	CC 47
Olifants Rd	Manenberg	32	CN 44
Olifants Rd	Primrose Pk	32	CN 44
Olive Cl.	Huis-in-bos	38	CU 27
Olive Schreiner Rd	Bergvliet	51	CW 30
Oliver Rd	Sea Point	2	CC 21
Oliver St	Valhalla Pk	21	CJ 47
Oliver Tambo Ave	Manenberg	32	CN 46
Oliver Tambo Dr.	Weltevreden Valley	45	CT 48
Olivia Way	Meadowridge	51	CV 30
Olivine Rd	Lansdowne	29	CN 37
Olympic Cr.	Bridgetown	31	CL 42
Ombersley Rd	Muizenberg Nth	64	DE 32
Onderbos St	Bonteheuwel	21	CJ 46
Ondine Cl.	Manenberg	32	CP 45
Onse Jan Sq.	Brooklyn	7	CC 35
Ontario Rd	Retreat	52	CZ 32
Ontong Way	Grassy Pk	54	CW 37
O'Okiep Rd	Lansdowne	29	CN 37
Oosterzee Heights	Bishopscourt	27	CP 30
Opal La.	Sheraton Pk	64	DC 33
Opal Rd	Lansdowne	29	CN 37
Opal Way	Matroosfontein	21	CG 47
Opal Way	San Michel	72	DF 22
Ophir Rd	Plumstead	41	CT 34
Orange Ave	Belthorn Est.	30	CN 39
Orange Rd	Kirstenhof	63	DB 30
Orange Rd	Newlands	27	CM 30
Orange St	Cape Town Central	4	CE 25
Orange St	Hout Bay	47	CW 18
Oranje Ave	Pinelands	8	CE 39
Oranje Rd	Bishop Lavis	21	CH 47
Oranje Rd	Chapman's Peak	72	DF 20
Oranje St	Ruyterwacht	10	CE 45
Oranje St	Wynberg	40	CR 31
Orbea Cl.	Hout Bay	46	CV 15
Orca Cl.	Kommetjie	78	DL 14
Orchard Ave	Westlake	63	DC 31
Orchard Cl.	Westlake	63	DC 31
Orchard Cl.	Westlake	63	DE 31
Orchard Heights	Newlands	27	CM 29
Orchard Pl.	Pinelands	18	CG 37
Orchard Rd	Bergvliet	51	CW 30
Orchard St	Lavender Hill East	65	DC 36
Orchard St	Lavender Hill East	65	DD 37
Orchard St	Newlands	27	CM 30
Orchard Way	Pinelands	18	CG 37
Orchestra St	Steenberg	64	DB 33
Orchid Cr.	Silvertown	19	CK 41
Orchid St	Hanover Pk	31	CO 42
Oribi Ave	Lotus River	55	CW 41
Oriele Cr.	Montagu's Gift	54	CV 38
Orient Rd	Muizenberg Nth	64	DE 32
Orient Rd	Wynberg	40	CS 32
Oriole	Fish Hoek	74	DK 26
Oriole Cl.	The Lakes	72	DJ 20
Orion Rd	Lansdowne	30	CO 39
Orion Rd	Ocean View	79	DN 16
Orion Rd	Surrey Est.	31	CM 43
Orion St	Kirstenhof	63	DA 30
Orkney St	Rondebosch	28	CM 34
Orlando Rd	Fish Hoek	82	DL 26
Orlando Rd	Grassy Pk	54	CW 38
Orlando Way	Meadowridge	51	CV 30
Orleans Ave	Bel Ombre	38	CR 27
Ormskirk St	Woodstock	6	CE 31
Orpen La.	Kenilworth	28	CP 33
Orpen Rd	Sweet Valley	50	CY 27
Orphan La.	Cape Town Central	4	CE 25

Index to Street Names

STREET NAME	SUBURB NAME	PG	GRID
Orphan La.	Schotsche Kloof	4	CE 25
Orphan St	Cape Town Central	4	CE 25
Orrel La.	Cafda Village	53	CZ 34
Orrscroft Rd	Rondebosch	29	CL 36
Osborne Rd	Claremont	28	CN 32
Osborne Rd	Mowbray	16	CH 33
Osborne St	Foreshore	5	CE 26
Osborne St	Kommetjie	78	DM 14
Oscar Mpetha	Weltevreden Valley..	45	CT 48
Osmond Cl.	Simon's Town	88	DS 26
Osprey St	Pelikan Pk	68	DD 44
Ossian Rd	Observatory	17	CG 34
Osterley Rd	Crawford	30	CN 33
Ostrich Rd	Phumlani	55	CW 41
Oswald Pirow St	Foreshore	5	CD 28
Otela Rd	Nyanga	33	CP 49
Ottawa Rd	Bakoven	24	CL 20
Otter Cr.	Westlake Est.	62	DB 28
Otters Creek	Pelikan Pk	54	CY 38
Ottery	Hanover Pk	44	CQ 43
Ottery Rd	Ottery	42	CS 37
Ottery Rd	Ottery East	42	CS 38
Ottery Rd	Royal Cape	41	CS 35
Ottery Rd	Schaap Kraal	43	CT 42
Ottery Rd	Wynberg	41	CS 34
Otto Cl.	Westlake Est.	63	DC 29
Ou Kaapse Rd	Westlake Est.	62	DD 27
Ou Kaapse Rd Ext.	Sunnydale	72	DK 22
Ou Wingerd Rd	High Constantia	38	CU 26
Ouberg Rd	Heideveld	20	CK 45
Oude Hout St	Bonteheuwel	21	CK 46
Oude Molen Cl.	Pinelands	17	CF 36
Oude Molen Rd	Ndabeni	17	CF 36
Oude Skip Rd	Hout Bay Harbour	46	CY 14
Oudekraal Rd	Bakoven	24	CL 20
Oudevlei Rd	Marina Da Gama	64	DC 34
Outeniqua St	Lavender Hill East	65	DC 36
Outspan Steps	Fish Hoek	83	DM 27
Ovambo St	Langa	19	CG 40
Overton Cl.	Silvertown	19	CK 41
Overton Rd	Silvertown	31	CL 41
Owen Dr.	Meadowridge	52	CV 31
Owen Dr.	Nyanga	33	CN 49
Owen La.	Grassy Pk	54	CY 38
Owen Rd	Matroosfontein	21	CF 48
Owen Rd	Silvertown	19	CK 41
Owl Cl.	Westlake Est.	62	DB 28
Owl St	Pelikan Pk	68	DC 44
Oxenham Ct	Rondebosch	29	CL 36
Oxford Rd	Observatory	16	CG 33
Oxford St	Claremont	28	CO 34
Oxford St	Hout Bay	47	CW 16
Oxford St	Maitland	7	CD 35
Oxford St	Richmond Est.	11	CA 46
Oxford St	Woodstock	6	CE 31
Oxford St	Wynberg	40	CQ 32
Oxford Way	Noordhoek Manor Retirement Village	73	DG 23
Oxford Way	Noordhoek Manor Retirement Village	73	DJ 24
Oxley Ave	Athlone	30	CL 38
Oyster Cl.	Kommetjie	78	DM 13
Oystercatcher Cl.	Kommetjie	78	DL 14

STREET NAME	SUBURB NAME	PG	GRID
Packer	Epping Ind.	20	CG 44
Paddington Rd	Dieprivier	52	CV 32
Paddock Ave	Cape Town Central	4	CE 25
Paddock Ave	Noordhoek Manor Retirement Village	73	DG 23
Paddock Cl.	Noordhoek Manor Retirement Village	73	DF 23
Paddock Cl.	Strandfontein	69	DA 48
Paddock La.	Dennedal	51	CZ 29
Paddock Rd	Montagu's Gift	42	CU 38
Paddock St	Strandfontein	69	DA 47
Paddy Cl.	Ottery East	43	CT 40
Padrone	Strandfontein	68	DB 45
Pagasvlei Rd	Huis-in-bos	38	CU 27
Pagasvlei Rd	Huis-in-bos	50	CV 27
Pagasvlei Rd	Sillery	39	CU 28
Page La.	Woodstock	5	CE 29
Page St	Woodstock	5	CE 29
Palace Hill Rd	Simon's Town	88	DT 26
Palatine Rd	Plumstead	40	CT 33
Palermo Cr.	Strandfontein	69	DA 49
Pall Mall	Noordhoek Manor Retirement Village	73	DG 23
Pall Mall	Noordhoek Manor Retirement Village	73	DJ 24
Pallotti Rd	Montana	21	CK 47
Palm Ave	Fairie Knowe	72	DK 21
Palm Gr.	Peers Hill	73	DK 25
Palm St	Newlands	27	CN 30
Palm St	Thornton	9	CD 42
Palm St	Tokai	51	CZ 29
Palmboom Cl.	Newlands	27	CM 31
Palmboom Cr.	Newlands	27	CM 31
Palmboom Rd	Newlands	27	CM 31
Palmer Rd	Muizenberg	76	DG 33
Palmerston Rd	Woodstock	15	CF 30
Palmetto Cl.	Rugby	7	CA 35
Palmetto St	Rugby	7	CA 35
Palmiet Ave	Belthorn Est.	30	CN 39
Palmtree Ct	Bridgetown	19	CJ 41
Palmyra Cl.	Sunnydale	72	DK 21
Palmyra Rd	Claremont	28	CN 33
Palmyra St	Sunnydale	72	DK 21
Palmyra St	Sunnydale	72	DH 20
Pampas St	Bonteheuwel	21	CH 46
Panoster Sq.	Charlesville	21	CG 46
Panton Rd	Fairways	41	CT 36
Papenboom Gr.	Newlands	27	CL 31
Papillon Rd	Strandfontein	68	DA 46
Papkuilsvlei Rd	Schaap Kraal	44	CR 44
Papu St	Langa	19	CG 41
Parade Cr.	Fir Grove	51	CX 28
Parade St	Cape Town Central	4	CE 26
Paradise Rd	Newlands	27	CN 30
Paradise Rd	Simon's Town	88	DT 26
Paradise View Rd	Claremont	28	CP 32
Parakeet St	Sunnydale	72	DK 22
Paris	Fish Hoek	82	DL 25
Parish St	Constantia Vale	39	CT 28
Parish St	Rust-en-vrede	39	CT 28
Park Ave	Camps Bay	12	CH 20
Park Ave	Dreyersdal	51	CZ 29
Park Ave	Hout Bay	35	CT 16
Park Cl.	Capricorn	64	DD 34
Park Cr.	Montagu's Gift	42	CU 39
Park House Rd	Gardens	3	CE 24
Park Island Way	Marina Da Gama	64	DD 34
Park La.	Rondebosch	28	CL 32
Park La.	Rosebank	16	CJ 33
Park La.	Silverhurst	39	CT 28
Park Rd	Grassy Pk	54	CW 37
Park Rd	Mouille Point	3	CA 23
Park Rd	Observatory	17	CF 34
Park Rd	Rondebosch	17	CK 35

STREET NAME	SUBURB NAME	PG	GRID
Park Rd	Rosebank	17	CJ 35
Park Rd	Woodstock	15	CF 29
Park Rd	Wynberg	40	CS 33
Park St	Gardens	4	CE 25
Park Villa Rd	Observatory	16	CG 33
Parkchester Ave	Pinelands	8	CE 39
Parker Ave	Gatesville	31	CM 42
Parkers Wk	Parkwood	54	CV 37
Parkview Pl.	Avon	11	CD 47
Parkview Ter.	Silverhurst	38	CT 27
Parkway Cl.	Rondebosch East	29	CM 37
Parkwood Ave	Parkwood	53	CV 36
Parkwood Wk	Parkwood	53	CV 36
Parliament St	Cape Town Central	4	CE 26
Parow Rd	Maitland	7	CB 36
Parry Rd	Claremont	28	CN 34
Partridge St	Sunnydale	72	DK 22
Partridge Way	Penlyn Est.	31	CN 41
Pasadena Sq.	Heathfield	52	CW 33
Pasadena Way	Ottery East	42	CT 38
Pascall La.	Oranjezicht	14	CG 25
Pass Rd	Fish Hoek	82	DL 25
Pasteur St	Wynberg	40	CQ 31
Paterson St	Newlands	27	CM 31
Paton Rd	Claremont	28	CN 33
Patriot St	Maitland	7	CD 35
Patrol St	Lansdowne	29	CO 37
Patrys Sq.	Factreton	9	CB 40
Patton St	Maitland	7	CD 35
Paul Andrew Cl.	Nyanga	33	CP 48
Paul Kruger Ave	Ruyterwacht	10	CC 45
Paul Kruger St	Plumstead	53	CV 33
Paulsberg Rd	Heideveld	20	CK 45
Paulus St	Newfields	31	CO 42
Paulus St	Valhalla Pk	21	CH 48
Paulus Way	Grassy Pk	53	CX 36
Pavo St	Surrey Est.	32	CM 44
Payne Rd	Hout Bay	47	CV 17
Payne St	Ocean View	79	DN 17
Peace St	Schotsche Kloof	3	CE 24
Peach La.	Newlands	27	CM 31
Peach Rd	Capricorn	65	DD 35
Peacock Rd	Phumlani	55	CW 41
Peak Dr.	Pinelands	17	CG 36
Peak Rd	Devil's Peak Est.	14	CF 27
Peak Rd	Fish Hoek	82	DM 26
Pear La.	Newlands	27	CM 31
Pear La.	Wittebomen	38	CS 26
Pearce Rd	Claremont	28	CN 32
Pearl Cr.	San Michel	72	DG 22
Pearl St	Kensington	8	CC 39
Pearl St	Pelikan Pk	67	DA 42
Pearl Way	Matroosfontein	21	CG 47
Pearly Shell Rd	Strandfontein	68	DD 46
Pearson Ave	Kenilworth	28	CP 34
Pearston St	Ruyterwacht	10	CD 45
Pecos Way	Manenberg	32	CP 45
Pecos Wk	Manenberg	32	CP 45
Peddie Rd	Penlyn Est.	31	CO 41
Peerboom Ave	Thornton	10	CE 43
Peers Hill	Peers Hill	73	DK 25
Peffers St	Kenilworth	28	CO 34
Pegasus	Retreat	52	CY 32
Pegasus Way	Ocean View	79	DO 16
Pelican Path	Montagu's Gift	42	CU 37
Pelican Pl.	Kommetjie	78	DL 14
Pelican St	Ocean View	79	DM 17
Pelican Way	Pelikan Pk	54	CX 39
Pelikan	Marina Da Gama	64	DC 34
Pelikan Cir.	Ruyterwacht	10	CC 45
Pelikan Rd	Bridgetown	19	CJ 42
Pelkalmy Rd	Bergvliet	51	CX 30
Pembroke La.	Capricorn	77	DF 35
Pembroke La.	Newlands	27	CM 31

Index to Street Names

STREET NAME	SUBURB NAME	PG	GRID	STREET NAME	SUBURB NAME	PG	GRID	STREET NAME	SUBURB NAME	PG	GRID
Pembroke St	Claremont	28	CO 33	Phlox St	Charlesville	21	CJ 46	Pitt St	Plumstead	40	CU 33
Penarth Rd	Three Anchor Bay	3	CB 22	Phoenix Way	Glencairn Hgts	83	DO 27	Pittosporum Ave	Thornton	10	CD 43
Pendennis Pl.	Dreyersdal	51	CZ 30	Phoenix Way	Glencairn Hgts	83	DN 27	Plakkies St	Charlesville	21	CJ 47
Pendoring Ave	Lotus River	54	CX 39	Phyllis Rd	Claremont	27	CO 31	Plane Ave	Thornton	9	CD 42
Pendoring Rd	Bonteheuwel	21	CJ 46	Phyllis Way	Wetton	42	CQ 39	Plane Cr.	Peers Hill	73	DK 25
Penelope Cl.	Bakoven	24	CL 20	Picardie Ave	Bel Ombre	38	CS 27	Planet Cl.	Salberau	21	CF 48
Pengem St	Flintdale Est.	53	CW 35	Picaroon Cr.	Sun Valley	72	DK 22	Plantation Rd	Devil's Peak Est.	14	CF 27
Penguin	Seawinds	65	DB 35	Piccolo St	Retreat	64	DA 34	Plantation Rd	Ottery	42	CQ 38
Penguin Cr.	Lotus River	55	CX 40	Pickerill St	Retreat	64	DA 33	Plate Rd	Manenberg	32	CP 45
Penguin Dr.	Simon's Town	88	DQ 27	Pickwick Rd	Salt River	16	CF 31	Platoon Rd	Wynberg	41	CS 34
Penguin Rd	Flintdale Est.	53	CW 35	Pieke Rd	Thornton	9	CD 42	Platteklip Sq.	Bakoven	12	CJ 21
Peninsula Rd	Pelikan Pk	54	CZ 38	Pierneef St	Goodwood Est.	10	CA 44	Platteklip Sq.	Bakoven	12	CJ 19
Penlyn Ave	Belthorn Est.	30	CN 40	Piers Rd	Wynberg	40	CR 32	Play St	Strandfontein	69	DA 47
Penrith Rd	Kenilworth	41	CQ 34	Piet Grobelaar St	Brooklyn	7	CB 35	Pleasant Pl.	Pinelands	18	CG 38
Penrose Rd	Muizenberg	76	DG 32	Piet Joubert St	Ruyterwacht	11	CE 46	Pleasant Pl.	Tokai	51	CZ 30
Penryn St	Woodstock	6	CE 32	Piet Retief Sq.	Brooklyn	7	CB 35	Pleasant Way	Newfields	31	CN 42
Pentrich	St James	75	DJ 31	Piet Retief St	Flintdale Est.	53	CV 35	Plein St	Cape Town Central	4	CE 26
Penyano St	Nyanga	33	CP 49	Piet Retief St	Goodwood Est.	10	CA 43	Plein St	Woodstock	5	CE 30
Penzance Rd	Hout Bay	47	CV 17	Piet Uys Cir.	Ruyterwacht	10	CC 45	Plender Ave	Athlone	30	CL 38
Penzance Rd	Observatory	16	CG 33	Pieters Rd	Strandfontein	69	DC 49	Plettenberg Rd	Doornhoogte	31	CM 41
Peperbos Cir.	Grassy Pk	53	CW 36	Pieterse Cl.	Retreat	53	CY 35	Plimplol Cr.	Newfields	31	CN 42
Pepper St	Cape Town Central	4	CD 25	Pilanesberg Rd	Lavender Hill East	65	DB 36	Pliny St	Athlone	30	CL 38
Pepper Way	Sunnydale	72	DJ 21	Pilanesberg Rd	Lavender Hill East	65	DD 37	Plover Pl.	Imhoff's Gift	79	DM 16
Peppertree Rd	Devil's Peak Est.	14	CG 27	Pillans Rd	Rosebank	17	CJ 34	Plover St	Brooklyn	7	CC 34
Percy	Edward	43	CT 40	Pilot Way	Kommetjie	78	DK 14	Plover St	Pelikan Pk	67	DC 43
Percy Rd	Rosebank	16	CJ 33	Pilot Way	Strandfontein	68	DB 46	Plover Way	Montagu's Gift	42	CU 38
Percy St	Salt River	6	CE 32	Pilot Way	Strandfontein	68	DB 45	Plum Cl.	Peers Hill	73	DK 25
Perelberg Rd	Bishop Lavis	21	CH 48	Pinaok Rd	Weltevreden Valley	45	CU 48	Plum La.	District Six	5	CE 29
Perfecta Rd	Paarden Eiland	6	CD 33	Pincushion Way	Scarborough	86	DU 20	Plum Rd	Capricorn	65	DD 36
Peri Rd	Clovelly	74	DJ 27	Pine	Simon's Town	89	DU 29	Plumbago Cl.	Ottery East	42	CT 39
Peridot Cr.	Pelikan Pk	67	DA 42	Pine Ave	Devil's Peak Est.	14	CG 27	Plumbago Rd	Bonteheuwel	21	CJ 46
Perivale Rd	Lotus River	54	CV 39	Pine Ave	Westlake Est.	62	DB 28	Plumer Gr.	Woodstock	15	CF 30
Periwinkle Cl.	Kommetjie	78	DM 14	Pine Cl.	Hanover Pk	43	CQ 41	Plumtree Ave	Hout Bay	35	CU 18
Periwinkle Pl.	Kommetjie	78	DM 13	Pine Rd	Doornhoogte	31	CM 41	Plumtree Cl.	Hout Bay	35	CT 18
Perrault Rd	Hout Bay	35	CU 16	Pine Rd	Greenpoint	3	CB 24	Pluto Rd	Ocean View	79	DN 16
Pers Rd	Parkwood	54	CV 37	Pine Rd	Kenilworth	28	CO 33	Pluto Rd	Plumstead	41	CT 34
Perseverance Rd				Pine Rd	Tokai	51	CZ 28	Pluto Rd	Surrey Est.	32	CM 44
	Maitland Gdn Village	17	CF 35	Pine St	Woodstock	5	CE 29	Pluto St	Salberau	11	CE 47
Pershof	Parkwood	54	CV 37	Pine St	Hout Bay	36	CT 20	Plympton Rd	Plumstead	40	CS 33
Perth Ave	Cape Town Central	4	CE 25	Pine St	Peers Hill	73	DK 25	Pochard Rd	Pelikan Pk	55	CY 40
Perth Rd	District Six	15	CF 28	Pine St	Pelikan Pk	55	CX 40	Poets Cnr	Woodstock	5	CE 30
Perth Rd	Grassy Pk	53	CX 35	Pine Way	Pinelands	18	CF 37	Poinsettia St	Bonteheuwel	21	CH 46
Perth Rd	Observatory	16	CG 33	Pinedene Rd	Hout Bay	47	CW 18	Point Rd	Witsand	84	DR 15
Perth Rd	Pelikan Pk	54	CY 37	Pinehill Ave	Plumstead	40	CU 33	Point St	Glenlily	11	CA 47
Perth Rd	Rondebosch	28	CM 33	Pinehurst Cl.	Silverhurst	39	CS 28	Pointer Cl.	Salberau	11	CE 47
Perth Rd	Rondebosch East	29	CM 37	Pinehurst Rd	Lansdowne	29	CO 37	Pointer Way	Strandfontein	68	DA 46
Perth Rd	Tokai	51	CZ 28	Pinehurst Way	Constantia Vale	39	CT 28	Pokela Rd	Masiphumelele	72	DK 20
Perth Rd	Woodstock	15	CF 29	Pinelaw Rd	Dieprivier	40	CU 32	Polacca St	Sun Valley	72	DK 22
Perth Rd	Wynberg	41	CR 34	Pineoak Rd	Devil's Peak Est.	15	CG 28	Polaris Rd	Lansdowne	30	CP 39
Perth St	Maitland	7	CE 34	Pinetree Cr.	Ruyterwacht	10	CC 45	Polaris Rd	Ocean View	79	DO 16
Petal St	Retreat	52	CZ 32	Pinetree Cl.	Vredehoek	14	CG 27	Poleman St	Lansdowne	30	CP 39
Peteni Cl.	Langa	20	CJ 43	Pinetree La.	Bergvliet	52	CW 31	Pollen Rd	Retreat	64	DA 32
Peter Charles St	Cafda Village	53	CY 35	Pinetree Rd	Claremont	29	CO 35	Pollsmoor Rd	Kirstenhof	63	DB 30
Peter Cloete Ave	Alphen	39	CR 29	Pinewood Dr.	Pinelands	19	CG 40	Pollux Rd	Lansdowne	30	CP 39
Peter Rd	Grassy Pk	54	CW 37	Pinewood Rd	Bonteheuwel	20	CJ 44	Pollux Way	Ocean View	79	DN 16
Peter St	Athlone	30	CL 38	Pinewood Rd	Newlands	27	CM 30	Polo Rd	Observatory	16	CF 32
Peterhof Cl.	Hout Bay	36	CU 19	Pinewood Rd	Rondebosch	28	CL 33	Ponder Rd	Kalk Bay	75	DK 30
Petrea St	Ottery	42	CT 38	Pinnacle Cr.	Strandfontein	68	DA 46	Pondicherry Ave	Hout Bay	46	CV 15
Petrel Cl.	Bakoven	24	CL 20	Pinnacle Cr.	Strandfontein	68	DE 45	Pondicherry Cl.	Hout Bay	46	CW 15
Petrel Way	Pelikan Pk	55	CY 40	Pinoak	Alphen	39	CS 29	Pontac St	District Six	5	CE 29
Petricia Rd	Barbarossa	40	CU 32	Pinoak	Rust-en-vrede	39	CS 29	Pooke Rd	Gatesville	31	CM 42
Petunia Cr.	Peers Hill	73	DK 25	Pinoak Cr.	Peers Hill	73	DK 25	Pooke Rd	Newfields	31	CN 42
Petunia Rd	Bridgetown	31	CL 42	Pinscher	Strandfontein	69	DA 47	Poole St	Brooklyn	7	CB 35
Petunia Rd	Silvertown	31	CL 42	Pintail Cr.	Pelikan Pk	54	CY 37	Pope St	Salt River	16	CF 32
Petunia St	Hanover Pk	31	CO 42	Pioneer St	Lansdowne	30	CP 39	Poplar Ave	Bergvliet	52	CX 31
Petunia St	Ocean View	79	DM 17	Piper St	Kensington	8	CB 38	Poplar Ave	Westlake Est.	62	DB 28
Phalo Ave	Hout Bay	35	CU 18	Pipers Cl.	Kommetjie	78	DL 13	Poplar Rd	Silverglade	73	DK 25
Phambile	Gugulethu	32	CM 46	Pippit Cl.	Ottery	43	CR 40	Poplar Rd	Chapman's Peak	71	DF 18
Pheiffer Rd	Ocean View	79	DN 17	Pisa Way	Strandfontein	69	DA 49	Poplar St	Newlands	27	CN 29
Philips Rd	Rondebosch	16	CK 33	Pisces Rd	Surrey Est.	32	CN 44	Poplar Way	Pinelands	18	CG 39
Phillans Wk	Hanover Pk	31	CP 41	Pitlochry Rd	Bakoven	12	CK 19	Poplar Way	Thornton	10	CE 43
Phillip Rd	Montagu's Gift	54	CV 39	Pitlochry Rd	Rondebosch	21	CL 35	Porath Wk	Hanover Pk	31	CP 42
Philmau Rd	Lavender Hill	65	DB 35	Pitt St	Maitland	8	CD 37	Poros Pl.	Capricorn	64	DE 34
				Pitt St	Observatory	6	CE 32	Port Jackson La.	Leonsdale	11	CD 48

Index to Street Names

STREET NAME	SUBURB NAME	PG	GRID
Port Jackson La. ..	Leonsdale	11	CC 47
Port Jackson Rd ...	Belgravia	30	CN 40
Port Jackson Rd ...	Bishop Lavis ...	21	CH 48
Port Rd	Cape Town Central ...	4	CC 26
Port Rd	Foreshore	4	CB 26
Portadown Rd	Heathfield	52	DB 36
Portavue Dr.	Surrey Est.	31	CM 43
Porter Rd	Fir Grove	51	CX 28
Porter St	Woodstock	5	CE 29
Portia Wk	Hanover Pk	31	CO 42
Portland Rd	Rondebosch	29	CL 35
Portland Rd	Woodstock	6	CE 32
Portman Rd	Sea Point	2	CE 20
Portswood Rd	Foreshore	4	CB 25
Portswood Rd	Royal Cape	41	CS 35
Possen Rd	Newlands	27	CM 30
Postern Rd	Heideveld	32	CL 45
Postern Rd	Oudekraal	24	CL 20
Potberg	Lavender Hill East ...	65	DB 36
Potomac Cl.	Crofters Valley ...	72	DG 17
Powell Rd	Steenberg	64	DB 32
Powerful St	Paarden Eiland	6	CC 33
Poyser Rd	Tamboerskloof	3	CE 24
Premier Rd	Woodstock	15	CG 29
Prenton Rd	St James	75	DJ 30
Presence Rd	Retreat	52	CY 32
President Brand St ..	Ruyterwacht ...	10	CD 45
President Kruger St ..	Paarden Eiland..	7	CB 34
President Reitz St ...	Ruyterwacht ...	10	CD 45
President Steyn St ...	Flintdale Est. ...	53	CV 35
Prestige Dr.	Ndabeni	8	CD 37
Prestwich St .	Cape Town Central ..	4	CC 26
Pretorius St	Flintdale Est. ...	53	CV 35
Price Dr.	High Constantia ...	38	CT 26
Prideaux Rd	Rondebosch	29	CL 36
Prieska Rd	Athlone	18	CK 37
Prieska Rd	Sybrand Pk ...	18	CJ 37
Prima Ave	Bakoven	12	CJ 21
Primrose Ave	Claremont	27	CP 31
Primrose St	Bridgetown	31	CL 42
Primrose St	District Six	4	CE 27
Primrose St	Hanover Pk ...	31	CO 42
Prince Arthur Rd ...	Lansdowne	30	CO 37
Prince Ave	Plumstead	40	CU 33
Prince Charles Rd ..	Flintdale Est. ...	53	CV 36
Prince George Dr. ...	Lavender Hill	65	DA 35
Prince George Dr. ..	Marina Da Gama..	64	DC 34
Prince George Dr. ...	Muizenberg	64	DE 34
Prince George Dr. ...	Plumstead	41	CT 35
Prince George Dr. ...	Retreat	53	CY 35
Prince George Dr. ..	Wynberg	41	CR 34
Prince George Dr. Service Rd ...			
....	Plumstead	41	CT 35
Prince Henry Cr. ...	Flintdale Est. ...	41	CU 36
Prince Sq.	Claremont	28	CO 34
Prince St	Oranjezicht	14	CG 25
Prince William St ...	Flintdale Est. ...	41	CU 36
Princes Ave	Claremont	28	CO 34
Princess Alice Ave ...	Brooklyn ...	7	CC 35
Princess Anne Ave ...	Rondebosch ...	27	CL 31
Princess Ave	Bishopscourt ...	27	CN 30
Princess Margaret St ..	Ruyterwacht..	10	CD 44
Princess Path	Pinelands	18	CG 38
Princess Rd	Fresnaye	2	CE 21
Princess Rd	Ottery	43	CR 40
Princess Rd	Retreat	52	CY 32
Princess Royal St ...	Flintdale Est. ...	41	CU 36
Princess St	Hout Bay ...	47	CW 16
Princess St	Mowbray	16	CH 33
Princess St	Woodstock	15	CF 29
Princessvlei Rd	Elfindale	53	CW 35
Princessvlei Rd	Plumstead	40	CU 33
Pringle Cl.	Ruyterwacht	10	CC 45
Pringle Pl.	Strandfontein	68	DB 44
Prinia Cl.	Fish Hoek	74	DK 27
Prinskasteel Cl. ...	Belle Constantia ..	51	CV 29
Printzia Cl.	Hout Bay ...	46	CV 15
Prion Way	Pelikan Pk ...	55	CY 40
Prior Roger Cl.	Nyanga	33	CP 48
Priory Rd	Mowbray	17	CH 35
Pritchard Steps	Fish Hoek ...	83	DM 27
Private Rd	Rondebosch	28	CL 32
Privateer Rd	Strandfontein	68	DB 44
Privet Ave	Grassy Pk ...	54	CY 37
Privet St	Bonteheuwel	21	CJ 46
Product St	Ndabeni	7	CE 36
Promenade Rd	Muizenberg	76	DF 33
Promenade Rd ...	Muizenberg Nth ...	64	DD 32
Prospect Hill Rd ...	Wynberg	40	CS 32
Prospect Rd	Newlands	26	CN 28
Prospect Ter.	Huis-in-bos ...	50	CV 27
Protea Ave	Fish Hoek ...	83	DL 27
Protea Ave	Fresnaye	2	CD 21
Protea Ave	Kommetjie	78	DM 12
Protea Cir.	Ocean View	79	DM 16
Protea Cl.	Pinelands	18	CG 39
Protea Rd	Bergvliet	51	CX 30
Protea Rd	Claremont	28	CN 32
Protea Rd	Oudekraal	23	CL 19
Protea Rd	Thornton	10	CE 43
Protea Rd	Townsend Est. ...	10	CC 43
Protea St	Chapman's Peak ...	71	DF 18
Protea St	Kewtown	18	CJ 39
Protea Way	Ruyterwacht	10	CC 45
Protea Way ...	Lavender Hill East ...	65	DB 36
Protea Way ...	Lavender Hill East ...	65	DD 37
Provence	Bel Ombre ...	38	CS 27
Prudence Way ...	Montagu's Gift ...	54	CV 39
Pruim Kring Cr. ...	Silvertown ...	19	CK 41
Prunus St	Bonteheuwel	20	CJ 44
Puffin	Seawinds	65	DB 35
Pula	Masiphumelele	80	DL 19
Pula Rd	Nyanga	33	CP 49
Puma Rd	Ocean View	79	DN 17
Puma St	Paarden Eiland	7	CC 34
Punt Cl.	Flintdale Est. ...	53	CW 34
Punt Rd	Schaap Kraal ...	56	CX 44
Punt Rd	Strandfontein	67	DB 43
Punt St	Flintdale Est. ...	53	CW 34
Punters Cl.	Kenilworth Pk ...	29	CP 36
Punters Way	Kenilworth Pk ...	29	CP 36
Pupil St	Strandfontein	69	DB 47
Purcell Way	Bergvliet	51	CW 29
Pyrley St	Kenilworth	28	CO 34
Putney St	Kenilworth	41	CQ 34
Putter Rd	Lakeside	63	DD 30
Pyrite Rd	Belthorn Est. ...	30	CO 40
Qagane Rd	Browns Farm	45	CR 47
Quail	Seawinds	65	DB 35
Quail Rd	Montagu's Gift ...	42	CU 37
Quality St	Maitland	7	CD 36
Quantock Rd	Sea Point ...	2	CD 20
Quarry Hill Rd ...	Tamboerskloof ...	13	CF 23
Quarry Rd	Fish Hoek ...	82	DL 24
Quarry Rd	Kalk Bay ...	83	DL 29
Quarry Rd	Simon's Town ...	88	DU 27
Quarterdeck Rd	Kalk Bay ...	75	DJ 30
Quartz	Belthorn Est. ...	30	CO 40
Quartz	Belthorn Est. ...	30	CO 38
Quasar Cr.	Surrey Est. ...	32	CM 44
Quebec Rd	Camps Bay ...	12	CJ 21
Queen Bess Rd ...	Lansdowne	29	CO 37
Queen St	District Six	5	CE 28
Queen St	Mowbray	16	CH 33
Queen Victoria Rd ...	Claremont ...	28	CN 33
Queen Victoria St ..	Cape Town Cen. ..	4	CE 27
Queens Cl.	Flintdale Est. ...	41	CU 36
Queens Park Ave ...	Salt River ...	16	CF 31
Queens Rd	Rondebosch	16	CK 33
Queens Rd	Sea Point ...	2	CD 20
Queens Rd	Simon's Town ...	89	DU 29
Queens Rd	Tamboerskloof ...	3	CE 24
Queens Rd	Woodstock	5	CE 30
Queens Way	Matroosfontein ...	21	CG 47
Queens Way	Pinelands	18	CF 39
Queens Way	Ruyterwacht	10	CD 45
Quendon Rd	Sea Point ...	2	CD 21
Quick Rd	Lansdowne	30	CP 38
Quiet St	Claremont	28	CN 32
Quince Cr.	Noordhaven ...	72	DF 21
Quincy Cr.	Norwood	11	CE 47
Quintus Way	The Vines ...	40	CU 31
Quoin Cr.	Strandfontein	68	DA 44
R.Sibukwe St	Hout Bay ...	35	CU 18
Raapenberg Rd	Mowbray	17	CH 35
Raapkraal Cr.	Kirstenhof ...	63	DC 30
Raapkraal Rd	Kirstenhof ...	63	DC 30
Rabbi Mirvish Ave ...	Vredehoek ...	14	CF 26
Race Course Rd ..	Lansdowne	29	CO 37
Rachel Dick St ...	Cafda Village ...	53	CY 35
Rachel St	Avonwood	11	CE 44
Radiant Cl.	Heathfield	52	CX 33
Rael St	Tamboerskloof ...	13	CF 23
Raft Rd	Penlyn Est. ...	30	CM 40
Raglan Ave	Athlone	30	CM 38
Railway St	Woodstock	6	CD 31
Rainbow La.	Silvertown ...	19	CK 41
Rainbow St	Pelikan Pk ...	54	CX 39
Rainham La.	Woodstock	16	CF 31
Raleigh Rd	Mowbray	17	CH 35
Ralph St	Claremont	28	CN 32
Rambler Rd	Plumstead	52	CW 32
Rameron St	Imhoff's Gift ...	79	DL 17
Ramola Ave	Gatesville	31	CM 41
Ramone Ave	Riverton	11	CC 46
Ramone Rd	Nyanga	33	CP 49
Ramsey Rd	Rondebosch	28	CL 33
Rand Rd	Heathfield	52	CY 33
Ranelagh Rd	Claremont	29	CN 35
Ranelagh Rd	Rondebosch	29	CM 35
Range Rd	Lansdowne	30	CP 38
Range Rd	The Range ...	21	CF 47
Ranger Cr.	Elfindale	53	CW 34
Ranger Rd	Fish Hoek ...	73	DK 24
Rankie Rd	Retreat	64	DA 32
Ranunculus St	Charlesville ...	21	CJ 46
Rapide St	Factreton	9	CB 40
Rarabe Ave	Hout Bay ...	35	CU 18
Rateklip St ...	Chapman's Peak ...	59	DE 17
Rathfelder Ave ...	Bel Ombre ...	38	CS 27
Rathfelder Rd	Fresnaye	2	CE 21
Ravel St	Steenberg	64	DB 33
Raven St	Grassy Pk ...	54	CX 39
Ravens Cl.	Ottery	43	CR 40
Ravensberg Ave ...	Newlands	27	CM 30
Ravenscraig Rd ...	Greenpoint ...	3	CB 24
Ravenscraig Rd ...	Woodstock	5	CE 29
Ravensteyn Rd ...	Bakoven	12	CK 21
Ravensworth Rd ...	Claremont	28	CN 33
Ravine Cl.	Bantry Bay ...	2	CE 20
Ravine Steps	Bantry Bay ...	2	CE 20

STREET NAME	SUBURB NAME	PG	GRID
Ravine Steps	Fish Hoek	83	DM 27
Rawbone St	Greenpoint	4	CC 25
Rawson St	Observatory	16	CF 33
Ray Alexander St	Manenberg	32	CN 46
Rayden St	Gardens	13	CF 24
Raymond Cir.	Montagu's Gift	54	CV 39
Rayner Rd	Surrey Est.	31	CN 43
Read St	Ottery East	42	CT 39
Reagon Cr.	Bridgetown	19	CJ 42
Rebus Ave	Fish Hoek	83	DM 27
Recife Cr.	Strandfontein	68	DB 44
Recreation Rd	Fish Hoek	83	DM 27
Recreation Rd	Muizenberg	76	DF 34
Red Cross Dr.	Strandfontein	69	DC 47
Red Hill Rd	Redhill	87	DU 24
Red Hill Rd	Simon's Town	88	DS 25
Red River Cr.	Manenberg	32	CO 45
Red River St	Manenberg	32	CO 44
Red River Wk	Manenberg	32	CO 45
Red Roman Way	Marina Da Gama	64	DC 33
Redberry Cl.	Bonteheuwel	20	CK 45
Redberry St	Bonteheuwel	20	CK 45
Reddam Ave	Westlake Est.	62	DB 27
Reddy Ave	Grassy Pk	54	CX 37
Redgum Ave	Thornton	10	CD 43
Redgum Rd	Bonteheuwel	20	CJ 45
Redhawk	Pelikan Pk	55	CX 41
Redpoll St	Rondebosch East	29	CN 36
Redthorn	Bonteheuwel	20	CJ 45
Reef Rd	Vanguard	32	CL 44
Reen Ave	Newfields	31	CN 42
Refinery Rd	Paarden Eiland	6	CC 32
Reform Rd	Rondebosch	28	CL 32
Reform St	District Six	5	CE 28
Regan Cl.	Valhalla Pk	21	CJ 48
Regan Cl.	Valhalla Pk	21	CH 47
Regent Circus	Tamboerskloof	13	CF 23
Regent Sq.	Woodstock	5	CE 30
Regent St	Sea Point	2	CD 21
Regent St	Weltevreden Valley	45	CU 48
Regent St	Woodstock	6	CE 31
Regents Park Dr.	Noordhoek Manor Retirement Village	73	DG 23
Regina Way	Pinelands	9	CE 40
Regis Rd	Frogmore Est.	64	DC 32
Reids Way	Simon's Town	88	DQ 27
Reiger Rd	Ruyterwacht	10	CC 45
Rembrandt Rd	Claremont	29	CN 35
Rembrandt Rd	Welcome	20	CK 44
Remington Rd	Wynberg	40	CQ 32
Rene? Ave	Flintdale Est.	53	CX 33
Renfrew Cl.	Heathfield	52	CW 33
Renfrew St	Athlone	18	CK 37
Renoster Rd	Manenberg	32	CO 45
Renoster Wk	Manenberg	32	CO 45
Renosterbos Pl.	Leonsdale	11	CC 48
Renosterbos Pl.	Leonsdale	11	CC 47
Repulse Rd	Belgravia	30	CN 39
Repulse Rd	Penlyn Est.	30	CN 40
Resandon Ave	Fresnaye	3	CD 22
Residence Rd	Rondebosch	16	CJ 31
Resthaven Dr.	Tokai	51	CZ 29
Restio Cr.	Westlake Est.	62	DB 28
Retief La.	Fish Hoek	82	DM 26
Retreat Rd	Cafda Village	53	CY 35
Retreat Rd	Retreat	52	CZ 33
Reunion Mews	Capri	81	DL 21
Revel Fox Cl.	Guguletu	33	CP 48
Reyger Rd	Thornton	10	CE 43
Rheede St	Gardens	4	CE 25
Rheezicht	Pinelands	19	CF 40
Rhine Rd	Bishop Lavis	21	CG 47
Rhine Rd	Sea Point	3	CC 22
Rhino St	Ocean View	79	DN 17
Rhode Vos Rd	Hout Bay Harbour	46	CY 15
Rhodes Ave	Mowbray	16	CH 33
Rhodes Ave	Newlands	27	CN 29
Rhodes Ave	Woodstock	15	CG 30
Rhodes Dr.	Bel Ombre	38	CR 26
Rhodes Dr.	Bishopscourt	26	CO 28
Rhodes Dr.	Glen Alpine	37	CR 24
Rhodes Dr.	Mowbray	16	CJ 32
Rhodes St	Langa	19	CH 41
Rhodesia Rd	Muizenberg	76	DG 33
Rhodesia St	Woodstock	5	CE 30
Rhone	Pinelands	19	CF 40
Rhone Way	Manenberg	32	CP 44
Rhynheath Way	Elfindale	53	CW 34
Ribbok Way	Fish Hoek	83	DL 27
Rica Louw Ave	Barbarossa	40	CU 31
Ricardo Rd	Lansdowne	30	CO 39
Rice La.	Fish Hoek	83	DM 27
Richard Cr.	Valhalla Pk	21	CJ 47
Richard Lakey Rd	Lotus River	54	CW 39
Richard Rd	Sunnydale	72	DK 21
Richmond	Noordhoek Manor Retirement Village	73	DG 23
Richmond Ave	Pinelands	8	CE 39
Richmond Cl.	Sweet Valley	51	CX 29
Richmond La.	Capricorn	77	DF 35
Richmond Rd	Kenilworth	28	CP 33
Richmond Rd	Mowbray	17	CH 34
Richmond Rd	Three Anchor Bay	3	CB 23
Richmond St	Ruyterwacht	10	CD 45
Richmond Way	Sweet Valley	51	CX 29
Rickard La.	Fish Hoek	82	DM 26
Ricketts Cl.	Simon's Town	89	DU 28
Ridge Way	Pinelands	18	CG 37
Ridge Wk	Hohenort	26	CP 27
Ridgedale Cr.	Airlie	51	CW 28
Ridgeway	Townsend Est.	10	CA 43
Riebeeck St	Goodwood Est.	10	CB 45
Riebeeck St	Wynberg	40	CR 32
Riebeek La.	Cape Town Central	4	CD 26
Riebeek St	Cape Town Central	4	CD 26
Riesling Rd	The Vines	40	CU 31
Rietbok Ave	Lotus River	55	CW 41
Rifle Range Rd	Thornton	9	CD 42
Rifle Rd	Lansdowne	42	CQ 37
Rifstone Rd	Lavender Hill	65	DB 35
Rigel Rd	Lansdowne	30	CP 39
Rigel Rd	Ocean View	79	DN 16
Ring Cr.	Penlyn Est.	31	CO 41
Ringwood Cl.	Bel Ombre	38	CS 27
Ringwood Dr.	Pinelands	18	CG 39
Rio Grande Rd	Manenberg	32	CO 44
Rio Grande Wk	Heideveld	32	CL 44
Rio Grande Wk	Manenberg	32	CP 44
Ripelby Rd	Claremont	28	CO 32
Ripple Cl.	Rondebosch	27	CL 31
Risi Rd	Fish Hoek	82	DL 24
Rita St	Montagu's Gift	54	CV 39
Ritchie Ave	Kenilworth	28	CP 34
Ritchie St	Woodstock	16	CG 31
Ritters Rd	Belthorn Est.	30	CO 39
River Cl.	Meadowsteads	72	DG 20
River St	Brooklyn	7	CC 34
River St	Rosebank	17	CJ 34
Rivers End Rd	Plumstead	40	CT 32
Riversdale Rd	Brooklyn	7	CB 34
Riversdale Rd	Crawford	30	CN 38
Riverside	Pinelands	18	CG 38
Riverside Cl.	Westlake	63	DC 30
Riverside Cl.	Westlake	63	DE 31
Riverside Dr.	Kommetjie	78	DM 14
Riverside Rd	Bishopscourt	27	CN 30
Riverside Rd	Fish Hoek	73	DK 25
Riverside Rd	Lansdowne	29	CN 37
Riverside Rd	Lotus River	55	CW 40
Riverside Rd	Peers Hill	73	DK 25
Riverside Rd	Rondebosch	28	CL 33
Riverside Ter.	Hout Bay	35	CT 18
Riverstone	Hout Bay	48	CW 19
Riverstone Rd	Wynberg	40	CQ 32
Riverton Cr.	Ruyterwacht	10	CC 45
Riverton Cl.	Riverton	11	CC 46
Riverton Cr.	Rondebosch	29	CL 36
Riverton Cr.	Riverton	11	CC 46
Riverton Rd	Rondebosch	17	CK 35
Riviera Rd	Claremont	28	CO 32
Roan Ave	Hout Bay	36	CS 21
Roan Rd	Lotus River	55	CW 40
Roath St	Lansdowne	29	CP 37
Robert Ave	Lotus River	54	CV 39
Robert Carr La.	Dennedal	51	CZ 29
Robert Sobukhwe	Weltevreden Valley	45	CT 48
Roberts Rd	Woodstock	15	CF 30
Robertson La.	Retreat	53	CZ 34
Robertson Rd	Brooklyn	7	CB 34
Robin Cir.	Ocean View	79	DM 17
Robin Cr.	Penlyn Est.	31	CN 41
Robin Ct	Bridgetown	19	CJ 41
Robin La.	Bergvliet	52	CX 31
Robin Rd	Montagu's Gift	42	CU 37
Robin St	Valhalla Pk	21	CJ 47
Robindale	Pinelands	18	CG 39
Robins St	Observatory	16	CF 32
Robinson Ave	Bishopscourt	27	CN 30
Robinson Ave	Hout Bay	34	CR 15
Robinson Rd	Kenilworth	40	CQ 33
Robor Cr.	Mowbray	17	CJ 35
Rochea	Hout Bay	46	CV 15
Rochester Rd	Heathfield	52	CX 33
Rochester Rd	Observatory	16	CF 32
Rochester Rd	Sea Point	2	CE 20
Rock Rd	Rondebosch	17	CJ 36
Rockcliff Cr.	Bantry Bay	2	CE 20
Rockcliff Cr.	Bantry Bay	2	CE 19
Rockdale Ct	Ocean View	79	DN 16
Rockford Rd	Lansdowne	29	CP 37
Rockford Rd	Lotus River	55	CW 40
Rockhill Way	Retreat	64	DA 33
Rocklands Ave	Vredehoek	14	CG 26
Rocklands Rd	Sea Point	3	CB 22
Rockley Rd	Wynberg	40	CS 33
Rocky Cl.	Salberau	11	CE 47
Rod La.	Lotus River	55	CV 40
Roderick Way	Gaylands	39	CU 29
Rodgers Ave	Fir Grove	51	CX 28
Roding Cl.	Epping Forest	21	CF 47
Rodwell Rd	St James	75	DJ 31
Roeland St	Gardens	14	CF 26
Roeland Ter.	Cape Town Central	4	CE 26
Roger St East	District Six	5	CE 28
Roggebaai Sq.	Cape Town Cen.	4	CD 27
Roggeberg Rd	Heideveld	32	CL 46
Roggeberg Rd	Heideveld	32	CL 44
Rohm Rd	Goodwood Est.	10	CA 43
Rokeby Rd	Crawford	30	CM 38
Rolen Cr.	Belgravia	30	CM 40
Roman La.	Hout Bay Harbour	46	CY 14
Roman Rd	Observatory	16	CG 32
Romany Wk	Fir Grove	51	CX 28
Romney Rd	Greenpoint	3	CB 23
Rompe St	Lansdowne	30	CP 38
Ronald Rd	Camps Bay	12	CJ 20
Rondeberg Rd	Heideveld	32	CL 45
Rondeberg Rd	Heideveld	32	CL 44
Ronell Cr.	Plumstead	52	CV 33
Ronleigh Rd	Muizenberg	76	DF 33

Index to Street Names

STREET NAME	SUBURB NAME	PG	GRID
Rontree Ave	Bakoven	12	CK 20
Rontree Cl.	Bakoven	24	CL 20
Roodebloem Rd	Woodstock	15	CF 30
Roodehek St	Gardens	14	CF 26
Roodekranz Rd	Townsend Est.	10	CA 43
Rooiberg Cr.	Heideveld	20	CK 45
Rooiels Rd	Bonteheuwel	20	CK 45
Rooiels Rd	Farmsteads	60	DE 20
Rooihout Rd	Bonteheuwel	20	CK 45
Rooikrans	Thornton	9	CD 42
Rooikrans Rd	Muizenberg Nth	64	DD 32
Rooikrans Rd	Pelikan Pk	54	CY 38
Roome Rd	Brooklyn	7	CA 36
Roos Rd	Lavender Hill	65	DA 35
Roos Rd	Sea Point	3	CC 24
Roosevelt Rd	Claremont	29	CN 36
Rorke Rd	Plumstead	41	CU 34
Rosalind St	Valhalla Pk	21	CJ 47
Rosalyn Rd	Meadowsteads	72	DG 20
Roscommon Rd	Elfindale	52	CW 33
Roscommon Rd	Heathfield	52	CW 32
Roscommon St	Claremont	28	CN 32
Rose Ave	Kirstenhof	63	DA 31
Rose Cl.	Bridgetown	31	CL 42
Rose Innes St	Langa	19	CG 41
Rose La.	Wynberg	40	CR 32
Rose Mount Ave	Oranjezicht	14	CG 25
Rose Rd	Bergvliet	52	CX 31
Rose Rd	Goodwood Est.	10	CA 44
Rose St	Bishopscourt	27	CO 29
Rose St	Cape Town Central	4	CD 25
Rose St	Kewtown	19	CK 40
Rose St	Lavender Hill East	65	DD 36
Rose St	Lavender Hill East	65	DD 37
Rose St	Mowbray	16	CH 33
Rose St	Newlands	27	CO 29
Rose St	Ocean View	79	DM 17
Rose Way	Belle Constantia	51	CW 28
Rose Way	Matroosfontein	21	CG 47
Rose Way	Pinelands	18	CF 38
Rosebank Pl.	Oranjezicht	14	CF 25
Roseberry Ave	Oranjezicht	13	CG 24
Roseberry Rd	Mowbray	17	CH 35
Rosedene Rd	Sea Point	3	CC 22
Rosedene Rd	Sea Point	3	CD 23
Rosedon Rd	Lansdowne	29	CN 36
Roseland Rd	Rondebosch	16	CK 33
Rosendale Rd	Rondebosch	16	CK 33
Rosequartz St	Sheraton Pk	64	DB 33
Roseville Rd	Claremont	28	CO 33
Rosewood Rd	Hanover Pk	43	CQ 41
Rosewood St	Bonteheuwel	21	CJ 46
Roslyn La.	Bakoven	12	CK 20
Roslyn Rd	Rondebosch	16	CK 33
Rosmead Ave	Claremont	28	CO 34
Rosmead Ave	Gardens	13	CG 24
Rosmead Ave	Kenilworth Pk	28	CP 34
Rosmead Ave Service Rd			
	Claremont	28	CO 34
Rosmead Ave Service Rd			
	Kenilworth	28	CO 34
Rosmead Rd	Kalk Bay	75	DJ 30
Ross La.	Fish Hoek	82	DL 26
Ross Rd	Rondebosch	28	CL 34
Ross Rd	Salt River	16	CF 32
Ross Rd	Wynberg	41	CS 34
Ross St	Maitland	7	CD 36
Ross St	Valhalla Pk	21	CJ 47
Rossal Rd	Athlone	30	CL 39
Rossini St	Steenberg	64	DB 33
Rossouw La.	Tokai	51	CZ 29
Rotherfield Rd	Plumstead	41	CS 34
Rothesay Pl.	Greenpoint	3	CA 23
Rottingdean Rd	Bakoven	12	CK 20
Rouen Ave	Plumstead	52	CV 33
Rough Moor Rd	Mowbray	16	CH 33
Round House Rd	Clifton	12	CG 20
Rouwkoop Ave	Rondebosch	28	CL 34
Rouwkoop Rd	Rondebosch	28	CL 33
Rouxton Cr.	Lansdowne	30	CO 38
Rouxton Rd	Lansdowne	30	CP 38
Rouxville Rd	Kalk Bay	75	DJ 30
Rover Rd	Rondebosch	29	CL 36
Rowan La.	Kenilworth	28	CP 32
Rowan Rd	Kenilworth	28	CP 32
Roxana Rd	Mowbray	17	CH 35
Roy Dewar Cl.	Capri	81	DL 22
Roy Rd	Lansdowne	42	CQ 39
Roy Rd East	Lansdowne	42	CQ 39
Royal Ave	Hout Bay	47	CW 16
Royal Cr.	Gatesville	31	CL 42
Royal Rd	Maitland	7	CD 34
Royal Rd	Muizenberg	76	DF 34
Royal Tern Cl.	Kommetjie	70	DK 14
Royland Cr.	Hout Bay	35	CU 16
Royston Rd	Muizenberg Nth	64	DE 32
Roytston Cl.	Ottery	43	CR 40
Rubbi Rd	Kommetjie	78	DM 14
Rubens Rd	Welcome	20	CJ 43
Rubicon Rd	Rondebosch	29	CM 36
Rubusana Ave	Langa	19	CH 40
Ruby Cr.	San Michel	72	DG 22
Ruby Cr.	Sheraton Pk	64	DC 33
Ruby Rd	Lansdowne	29	CO 37
Ruby St	Belgravia	30	CL 40
Ruby Way	San Michel	72	DG 22
Ruchill Rd	Dieprivier	52	CV 32
Ruff Cr.	Pelikan Pk	55	CY 40
Rugby Cl.	Westlake Est.	62	DC 28
Rugby Rd	Oranjezicht	13	CH 24
Rugley Rd	Vredehoek	14	CG 26
Ruimte Rd	Manenberg	32	CN 45
Ruimte Rd	Primrose Pk	32	CN 44
Rule St	Plumstead	41	CU 34
Runciman Dr.	Simon's Town	88	DU 27
Rune Way	Silvermine Village	72	DG 22
Runge St	Cafda Village	53	CZ 35
Ruritania Ave	Ottery East	42	CS 38
Rusacre Rd	Rondebosch	29	CM 36
Rushmore Way	Tokai	51	CZ 29
Rushy Cl.	Epping Forest	21	CF 47
Ruskin Rd	Dreyersdal	51	CX 30
Rusper St	Maitland	8	CD 37
Russel Cl.	Barbarossa	39	CT 30
Russel Cl.	Nyanga	33	CP 48
Russel St	District Six	5	CE 28
Russel St	Foreshore	5	CE 28
Russel St	Montana	21	CK 48
Rust St	Belgravia	30	CN 39
Rust St	Belthorn Est.	30	CN 39
Rusten Ct	Marina Da Gama	64	DD 34
Rustenberg	Pinelands	19	CF 40
Rustenburg Ave	High Constantia	38	CU 26
Rustenburg Ave	Rondebosch	16	CK 33
Rust-en-Vrede	Pinelands	19	CF 40
Rust-en-Vrede Ave	Alphen	39	CT 29
Rustic Rd	Gardens	13	CG 23
Ruth First	Weltevreden Valley	45	CT 48
Ruth Rd	Doornhoogte	31	CM 41
Ruth St	Manenberg	32	CP 44
Rutherford Way	Meadowridge	51	CW 30
Rutherglen Ave	Newlands	27	CM 30
Rutherglen Ave	Newlands	27	CM 29
Rutherglen Cl.	Newlands	27	CM 30
Rutherglen Cl.	Newlands	27	CM 29
Rutherglen Rd	Rondebosch	17	CK 35
Rutland St	Claremont	28	CO 34
Rutter Rd	Lakeside	64	DD 32
Rutvale Rd	Belthorn Est.	30	CN 40
Ryan Rd	Rosebank	16	CJ 33
Ryan St	Churchill	11	CA 48
Ryan St	Glenlily	11	CA 48
Ryburg	Hanover Pk	31	CP 42
Rye Rd	Mowbray	17	CH 34
Ryger St	Ndabeni	7	CE 36
Ryk St	Brooklyn	7	CC 35
Rylands Rd	Doornhoogte	31	CL 42
Rylands Rd	Schaap Kraal	43	CQ 42
Ryston Rd	Hanover Pk	31	CP 42
Rywood Rd	Hanover Pk	30	CP 42

S

STREET NAME	SUBURB NAME	PG	GRID
S.Biko St	Hout Bay	35	CU 17
S.Karnovetz Rd	Nyanga	33	CP 49
S.Saba Cr.	Nyanga	33	CO 48
Sabatha Dalinyebo			
	Weltevreden Valley	45	CS 48
Sabie Rd	Manenberg	32	CP 45
Sabie Wk	Manenberg	32	CO 45
Sable Rd	Lotus River	55	CV 40
Sable Rd	Ysterplaat	8	CA 38
Sabre St	Kensington	8	CB 38
Sachs St	Schotsche Kloof	4	CD 25
Saddle Cl.	Noordhoek Manor		
	Retirement Village	73	DG 23
Saddle Rd	Devil's Peak Est.	14	CF 27
Saddlers Cl.	Hout Bay	35	CS 17
Saddlers Row	Hout Bay	35	CS 17
Safari Rd	Thornton	9	CE 41
Saffraan Rd	Bonteheuwel	20	CJ 45
Sagewood Dr.	Hout Bay	47	CV 18
Sail	Strandfontein	69	DA 47
Sakabula Cir.	Ruyterwacht	10	CC 45
Sakela Cl.	Nyanga	33	CP 48
Salazar Plain	Cape Town Central	4	CD 27
Salberau Ave	Salberau	11	CE 48
Saldanha St	Ruyterwacht	10	CD 45
Salem Way	Steenberg	64	DB 33
Salerna Way	Strandfontein	69	DB 47
Salford Rd	Mowbray	16	CH 33
Salisbury Ave	Bishopscourt	27	CO 30
Salisbury Rd	Kenilworth	40	CQ 33
Salisbury St	Woodstock	15	CF 30
Sally Rd	Sunnydale	72	DK 21
Sally-Ann Ave	Oudekraal	24	CM 20
Salmander Sq.	Factreton	9	CB 40
Salmon Rd	Pelikan Pk	55	CX 40
Salmon St	Woodstock	5	CE 29
Salmon Way	Strandfontein	68	DB 45
Salt River Rd	Salt River	6	CE 31
Saltire Rd	Belgravia	30	CM 40
Salvia St	Charlesville	21	CH 46
Samba Cr.	Retreat	64	DA 33
Samora Machel	Weltevreden Valley.	45	CT 48
San Juan Ave	Fir Grove	51	CW 28
San Remo Ave	Strandfontein	69	DA 49
Sanatorium Rd	Claremont	29	CN 35
Sanctuary Rd	Pelikan Pk	66	DB 38
Sandberry Ave	Tokai	51	CZ 29
Sandgate Ave	Athlone	30	CL 38
Sandhurst Rd	St James	75	DJ 31
Sandhurst Rd	Wynberg	40	CR 33
Sandle Ave	Langa	19	CG 41
Sandown Dr.	Ottery	43	CR 40
Sandown Rd East	Rondebosch East.	29	CL 37
Sandpiper Ave	Grassy Pk	54	CX 38

Index to Street Names

STREET NAME	SUBURB NAME	PG	GRID
Sandpiper Cl.	Hout Bay	46	CV 15
Sandpiper Rd	Flintdale Est.	53	CV 35
Sandringham Cl.	Pinelands	19	CG 41
Sandstone Rd	Kommetjie	78	DM 14
Sandy Bay Rd	Hout Bay	34	CS 14
Sandy Cl.	Hout Bay Harbour	46	CY 14
Sandy La.	Bishop Lavis	21	CH 48
Sangrove Dr.	Rondebosch	29	CL 36
Sans Souci Rd	Newlands	28	CM 32
Santa Cruz St	Ruyterwacht	10	CD 45
Santana La.	Elfindale	53	CW 35
Santos Ave	Nyanga	45	CQ 48
Sapphire Way			
....	Belvedere (Noordhoek)..	72	DF 22
Saratoga Ave	Ottery	43	CR 40
Sardinia Dr.	Capri	81	DL 21
Sardinia Dr.	Sunnydale	72	DK 22
Sardyn Rd	Strandfontein	68	DB 45
Sarel Celliers St	Churchill	11	CA 48
Sarel Celliers St	Glenlily	11	CA 48
Sasmeer Rd	Retreat	53	CY 35
Saturn Cl.	Salberau	11	CE 47
Saturn Cl.	Salberau	11	CE 46
Saturn Cl.	Surrey Est.	31	CM 43
Saturn Rd	Surrey Est.	31	CM 43
Saturn Way	Ocean View	79	DN 16
Sauer Rd	Ottery	42	CR 38
Saul St	Rugby	7	CA 36
Saunders Cl.	Fish Hoek	74	DK 26
Saunders Rd	Bantry Bay	2	CE 20
Saunders Rd	Wetton	43	CQ 40
Sawkins Rd	Mowbray	17	CH 35
Sawkins Rd	Rondebosch	17	CJ 35
Sawle Rd	Plumstead	41	CT 34
Saxo St	Retreat	64	DA 34
Saxon Rd	Rondebosch	29	CM 36
Scala Cl.	Nyanga	33	CP 48
Scala Rd	Simon's Town	88	DQ 25
Scarboro Rd	Muizenberg	76	DF 34
Sceptre La.	Leonsdale	11	CD 48
Schaap Rd	Knole Pk	55	CV 41
Schaap Rd	Schaap Kraal	55	CW 42
Schaapkraal Rd	Schaap Kraal	55	CW 41
Schaay Rd	Dieprivier	52	CV 32
Scheldt St	Manenberg	32	CO 45
Schiebe St	Cape Town Central	4	CC 26
Schilpadvlei Rd	Barbarossa	39	CT 30
Schoenstatt Ave	High Constantia	38	CT 26
Scholtz Rd	Three Anchor Bay	3	CB 23
School Cl.	Strandfontein	69	DB 47
School End	Riverton	11	CC 46
School Rd	Bishop Lavis	21	CH 48
School Rd	Claremont	27	CO 31
School Rd	Muizenberg	76	DG 32
School Side	Meadowridge	51	CV 30
School St	Strandfontein	69	DB 47
School Way	Retreat	52	CZ 33
Schools La.	Pinelands	18	CF 38
Schoonder St	Gardens	14	CF 26
Schoonder St	Oranjezicht	14	CF 26
Schooner Ave	Sun Valley	73	DJ 23
Schooner Cl.	Lakeside	63	DD 31
Schooner Rd	Strandfontein	68	DA 44
Schoonvrucht Ave	The Vines	40	CU 31
Schreiner St	Brooklyn	7	CB 35
Schroeder Rd	Pinati	30	CP 40
Schuilhoek Rd	Kenilworth	28	CP 33
Schumann St	Cafda Village	53	CZ 33
Scobel Rd	Wynberg	40	CR 31
Scopus Rd	Muizenberg	76	DF 33
Scorpio Rd	Ocean View	79	DO 17
Scott Rd	Churchill	11	CA 48
Scott Rd	Claremont	28	CO 32
Scott Rd	Glenlily	11	CA 48

STREET NAME	SUBURB NAME	PG	GRID
Scott Rd	Hout Bay	47	CW 18
Scott Rd	Observatory	16	CF 32
Scott St	Gardens	14	CF 26
Scottsville Cir.	Hout Bay	47	CW 18
Scottsville Rd	Retreat	53	CY 35
Scout Rd	Lansdowne	29	CO 37
Scouts Pl.	Pinelands	18	CF 37
Sea Breeze Cr.	Crofters Valley	72	DG 22
Sea Breeze Pl.	Kirstenhof	63	DB 31
Sea Breeze Rd	Kirstenhof	63	DB 31
Sea Cottage Dr.	Crofters Valley	72	DH 21
Sea Cottage Dr.	Meadowsteads	72	DG 20
Sea View Rd	Muizenberg	76	DG 32
Seacliff Rd	Bantry Bay	2	CE 20
Seacliffe Rd	Hout Bay	46	CX 15
Seafarer Dr.	Strandfontein	69	DB 49
Seaforth Dr.	Simon's Town	89	DU 30
Seagull Cl.	Hout Bay Harbour	46	CY 15
Seagull Rd	Scarborough	86	DU 19
Seagull St	Ocean View	79	DM 17
Seagull St	Pelikan Pk	67	DC 43
Searle Cl.	Lansdowne	29	CN 37
Searle St	Woodstock	5	CE 29
Seascape Rd	Crofters Valley	72	DG 22
Seaton St	Plumstead	53	CV 34
Seaview Rd	Fish Hoek	73	DK 24
Seaview Rd	Wynberg	40	CS 32
Sebastian Rd	Sunnydale	72	DJ 21
Sebastian St	Constantia Vale	39	CT 28
Second Ave	Belgravia	30	CL 39
Second Ave	Claremont	28	CO 34
Second Ave	Da Gama Pk	81	DO 24
Second Ave	Elsies River Ind.	11	CC 47
Second Ave	Fairways	41	CT 36
Second Ave	Fish Hoek	83	DM 27
Second Ave	Glenlily	11	CA 48
Second Ave	Grassy Pk	53	CX 36
Second Ave	Hazendal	18	CJ 38
Second Ave	Kenilworth	28	CP 34
Second Ave	Kensington	8	CC 37
Second Ave	Knole Pk	55	CV 41
Second Ave	Lotus River	54	CV 39
Second Ave	Maitland	8	CD 37
Second Ave	Manenberg	32	CP 45
Second Ave	Retreat	52	CY 33
Second Ave	Rondebosch East	29	CM 37
Second Ave	Vanguard	31	CL 43
Second Ave	Woodlands	82	DP 25
Second Cr.	Fish Hoek	83	DL 27
Second Gate Green	Strandfontein	69	DB 47
Second Rd	Heathfield	52	CX 33
Second St	Bishop Lavis	21	CG 48
Second St	Maitland	8	CD 38
Second St	Welcome	20	CK 43
Section Rd	Brooklyn	7	CC 34
Section Rd	Paarden Eiland	6	CC 33
Sedgemoor Rd	Camps Bay	12	CH 20
See Sq.	Factreton	9	CB 38
Seeliger Rd	Kommetjie	78	DL 13
Seemeeu Cr.	Seawinds	65	DB 35
Seemeeu St	Simon's Town	88	DQ 27
Seemeeu St	Sunnydale	72	DK 22
Seemeeu St	Thornton	9	CB 40
Seil Sq.	Factreton	9	CB 38
Seine Wk	Manenberg	32	CO 45
Selbourne Rd	Claremont	27	CN 31
Selbourne Rd	Mowbray	16	CH 33
Selbourne Rd	Sea Point	3	CC 22
Selbourne Rd	Woodstock	16	CG 31
Selby Rd	Mowbray	17	CH 34
Selby Rd	Plumstead	40	CU 33
Selica Cl.	Glencairn Hgts	83	DO 27
Selkirk St	District Six	5	CE 28
Selous Rd	Claremont	28	CN 34

STREET NAME	SUBURB NAME	PG	GRID
Selous St	Observatory	6	CE 32
Selwyn St	Foreshore	5	CE 29
Selwyn Ter.	Kenilworth	28	CP 33
Sentinal Cl.	Ocean View	79	DN 17
Sentinal Cl.	Ocean View	79	DP 17
Sentinel Cl.	Hout Bay Harbour	46	CY 14
Sentinel Rd	Heideveld	32	CL 45
Sequoia Rd	Bonteheuwel	20	CJ 44
Serenade Rd	Steenberg	64	DB 34
Sergeant St	Rondebosch East	29	CN 37
Serissa St	Ottery	42	CT 38
Serpentine Rd	Oranjezicht	14	CH 25
Serpentine Rd	Pinelands	18	CG 39
Serv Rd	Kalk Bay	75	DK 30
Service Rd	Lakeside	63	DD 30
Service Rd	Pinelands	17	CG 36
Service Way	Wetton	42	CR 39
Sessel St	Plumstead	53	CV 34
Seth Rd	Browns Farm	45	CR 47
Settler St	Ruyterwacht	11	CC 46
Settlers Way	Bridgetown	19	CJ 41
Settlers Way	Guguletu	32	CL 48
Settlers Way	Heideveld	20	CK 45
Settlers Way	Kewtown	18	CH 39
Settlers Way	Mowbray	16	CH 33
Seven Sleepers St	Kirstenhof	63	DA 30
Sevenoaks Rd	Heathfield	52	CX 33
Sevenoaks Rd	Plumstead	40	CS 33
Seventeenth Ave	Avon	11	CD 47
Seventeenth Ave	Fish Hoek	82	DL 25
Seventeenth Ave	Maitland	9	CC 40
Seventeenth Ave	Norwood	11	CE 47
Seventeenth Ave	Schaap Kraal	55	CY 42
Seventeenth St	Avon	11	CD 47
Seventeenth St	Kensington	8	CB 38
Seventh Ave	Belgravia	30	CL 40
Seventh Ave	Da Gama Pk	81	DP 23
Seventh Ave	Elsies River Ind.	11	CC 47
Seventh Ave	Fairways	41	CT 36
Seventh Ave	Fish Hoek	83	DL 27
Seventh Ave	Grassy Pk	53	CY 36
Seventh Ave	Hazendal	18	CJ 38
Seventh Ave	Kensington	8	CB 38
Seventh Ave	Lotus River	54	CW 39
Seventh Ave	Maitland	8	CC 38
Seventh Ave	Retreat	52	CY 33
Seventh Ave	Rondebosch East	29	CM 37
Seventh Ave	Schaap Kraal	55	CW 41
Seventh St	Kensington	8	CC 37
Severn Rd	Dieprivier	52	CW 32
Severn Rd	Plumstead	41	CT 34
Seychelles Ave	Capri	81	DL 21
Seymour Ave	Vredehoek	14	CG 26
Seymour Rd	Wynberg	40	CQ 32
Seymour St	Observatory	16	CF 33
Shaanti Cr.	Gatesville	31	CM 42
Shaddock St	Brooklyn	7	CB 34
Shaftesburg Rd	Wetton	42	CR 39
Shako Pl.	Leonsdale	11	CC 48
Shallcross Rd	Bel Ombre	39	CS 28
Shanklin Cr.	Camps Bay	12	CH 21
Shannon St	Salt River	16	CF 31
Sharon Rd	Browns Farm	45	CR 47
Sharpeville	Weltevreden Valley	45	CS 48
Shaun Rd	Pinati	30	CP 40
Shaw Rd	Rondebosch	29	CL 36
Shawcamp Rd	Ottery	42	CS 37
Shearwater Dr.	Marina Da Gama	64	DC 34
Sheeda Rd	Hout Bay	34	CU 15
Sheerness Rd	Kenilworth	28	CP 33
Sheffield Rd	Browns Farm	45	CR 47
Sheldon Rd	Crawford	30	CM 39
Shelduck Cr.	Pelikan Pk	67	DC 43
Shelduck Rd	Pelikan Pk	55	CX 41

Index to Street Names

STREET NAME	SUBURB NAME	PG	GRID
Shell Rd	Steenberg	64	DB 34
Shelley Rd	Salt River	16	CF 32
Shellsby	Newfields	31	CO 42
Sheperd St	District Six	15	CF 28
Shepherd Way	Lavender Hill	65	DA 35
Sheppard St	District Six	5	CE 28
Sherard Sq.	Wynberg	40	CS 33
Sherborne Cl.	Sun Valley	81	DL 23
Sheridan St	Brooklyn	7	CB 35
Sherwood Ave	Kenilworth	28	CP 34
Shetland Dr.	Capri	80	DL 20
Shetland St	Rondebosch	28	CM 34
Shilling St	Ruyterwacht	10	CC 45
Shiplake Rd	Wynberg	40	CR 33
Shipman Rd	Elfindale	52	CW 33
Shiraz Cr.	Constantia Village	39	CT 29
Shiraz Cl.	Elfindale	52	CW 33
Shiraz Rd	Hout Bay	47	CW 17
Shire Rd	Kirstenhof	63	DB 31
Shire Rd	Kirstenhof	63	DE 31
Shirley Rd	Bishop Lavis	21	CH 48
Shirley Rd	Claremont	28	CO 32
Shiryan Cl.	Alphen	39	CR 29
Short	Ottery	42	CS 37
Short Rd	Barbarossa	40	CU 31
Short Rd	Montagu's Gift	42	CU 39
Short Rd	Sunnydale	72	DK 21
Shortmarket St	Cape Town Cen.	4	CD 26
Shoveller Way	Pelikan Pk	55	CX 41
Showground Ave	Epping Ind.	10	CE 44
Shrewbury Way	Westlake Est.	62	DC 28
Shrike Cr.	Seawinds	64	DB 34
Shropshire St	Paarden Eiland	6	CC 33
Sibelius Ave	Retreat	64	DA 33
Sibiya Rd	Browns Farm	45	CS 47
Sicily Rd	Ottery	42	CQ 38
Sicily Way	Rondebosch East	29	CM 37
Sidbury Rd	Plumstead	40	CS 33
Siddique Ave	Salberau	11	CE 47
Sidmouth	Muizenberg	76	DG 33
Sidmouth	Muizenberg	76	DH 33
Sidmouth Ave	Claremont	27	CO 31
Sidmouth Ave	Oranjezicht	14	CH 25
Sidmouth Ave	Oranjezicht	14	CG 25
Sidmouth Ave	Vredehoek	14	CH 25
Sierra Rd	Montana	33	CL 48
Sigcawu Ave	Langa	19	CH 41
Signal Hill Rd	Sea Point	3	CD 23
Signal St	Schotsche Kloof	4	CD 25
Sihlanu Ave	Nyanga	33	CO 49
Sikhinkili Cl.	Nyanga	33	CP 48
Silica Rd	Sand Industria	31	CO 43
Sillery Rd	Bergvliet	52	CX 32
Sillery Rd	Sillery	39	CU 28
Silva St	Brooklyn	7	CB 34
Silverdale	Pinelands	8	CE 39
Silverdale Way	Pinelands	18	CF 39
Silvergang	Silverhurst	38	CT 27
Silverhill Cr.	Kenilworth	28	CP 33
Silverhurst Cl.	Wynberg	27	CP 31
Silverhurst Dr.	Silverhurst	38	CT 27
Silverhurst Way	Bergvliet	52	CX 31
Silverhurst Way	Wynberg	40	CQ 31
Silverlea Rd	Wynberg	40	CS 32
Silvermine Rd	San Michel	72	DF 21
Silveroak Ave	Thornton	10	CD 43
Silverstream Rd	Manenberg	32	CM 45
Silverton Rd	Plumstead	40	CT 33
Silvertree	Farmsteads	60	DD 20
Silvertree Cl.	Hout Bay	35	CT 16
Silvertree La.	Bergvliet	52	CW 31
Silvertree La.	Bergvliet	52	CZ 31
Silvertree La.	Silverhurst	38	CT 26
Silvertree St	Silvertown	18	CK 39

STREET NAME	SUBURB NAME	PG	GRID
Silverwater St	Kirstenhof	63	DA 31
Silverwood Cl.	Westlake Est.	62	DC 28
Silwood Rd	Rondebosch	17	CK 35
Silwood Way	Matroosfontein	21	CG 47
Simon Cl.	Glen Rdg	83	DO 28
Simon Rd	Montagu's Gift	55	CV 40
Simon Rd	Newfields	31	CN 42
Simon van der Stel Freeway			
	Dennedal	51	CY 30
Simons Way	Noordhoek Manor		
Retirement Village		73	DG 23
Simonsberg Rd	Heideveld	32	CL 45
Simonsberg St	Ocean View	79	DN 17
Simonsberg St	Ocean View	79	DP 17
Simonstown Rd	Fish Hoek	83	DM 28
Simpson Rd	Athlone	18	CK 39
Sine Ave	Nyanga	33	CP 49
Singolamthi St	Browns Farm	45	CS 48
Sipho Hashe	Weltevreden Valley	45	CS 48
Sipho Hashe	Weltevreden Valley	45	CT 47
Sipres Ave	Bridgetown	19	CJ 41
Sipres Ave	Thornton	10	CD 43
Sipres St	Bridgetown	19	CJ 41
Sir Alfred Ave	Lansdowne	29	CO 37
Sir George Grey St	Oranjezicht	14	CG 25
Sir George Grey St	Ruyterwacht	10	CE 45
Sir Lowry Rd	District Six	4	CE 27
Sir Lowry Rd	Foreshore	5	CE 28
Sirius Way	Ocean View	79	DN 16
Siros St	Ottery	42	CR 38
Sirus Rd	Surrey Est.	31	CN 43
Sisulu Rd	Masiphumelele	80	DL 20
Sithandatu Ave	Nyanga	33	CP 49
Sithembele Matiso St			
	Weltevreden Valley	45	CT 48
Siviwe St	Nyanga	45	CQ 48
Sixteenth Ave	Da Gama Pk	82	DP 24
Sixteenth Ave	Fish Hoek	82	DL 26
Sixteenth Ave	Leonsdale	11	CD 48
Sixteenth Ave	Maitland	9	CC 40
Sixteenth Ave	Schaap Kraal	55	CY 42
Sixteenth St	Elsies River Ind.	11	CC 47
Sixteenth St	Kensington	8	CB 38
Sixth Ave	Athlone	29	CL 37
Sixth Ave	Belgravia	30	CL 40
Sixth Ave	Da Gama Pk	81	DO 23
Sixth Ave	Elsies River Ind.	11	CC 47
Sixth Ave	Fairways	41	CT 36
Sixth Ave	Fish Hoek	83	DM 27
Sixth Ave	Grassy Pk	53	CY 36
Sixth Ave	Hazendal	18	CJ 38
Sixth Ave	Kensington	8	CB 38
Sixth Ave	Lotus River	54	CW 39
Sixth Ave	Maitland	8	CD 38
Sixth Ave	Retreat	52	CY 33
Sixth Ave	Rondebosch East	29	CM 37
Sixth Ave	Schaap Kraal	55	CW 41
Sixth St	Bishop Lavis	21	CG 48
Sixth St	Kensington	8	CC 37
Sixth St	Valhalla	11	CC 46
Skaife St	Hout Bay	47	CW 18
Skep Sq.	Factreton	9	CB 40
Skew St	Plumstead	53	CV 35
Skina Rd	Masiphumelele	72	DK 20
Skip Rd	Surrey Est.	31	CN 43
Skipper's End	Pelikan Pk	66	DA 38
Skool St	Montana	21	CK 47
Skua Cr.	Pelikan Pk	67	DC 43
Skuller Sq.	Factreton	9	CB 40
Skutter Sq.	Factreton	9	CB 40
Skye Way	Sea Point	3	CC 24
Slanghoek Rd	Manenberg	32	CM 45
Slangkop Rd	Ocean View	79	DN 15
Slangoolie Ave	Oudekraal	23	CL 19

STREET NAME	SUBURB NAME	PG	GRID
Slangoolie Pl.	Oudekraal	24	CM 20
Slangoolie Way	Oudekraal	24	CM 20
Sleepy Hollow La.	Chapman's Peak..	71	DF 19
Sloop St	Strandfontein	68	DB 44
Sloster Ave	Grassy Pk	53	CX 36
Sluysken Rd	Hout Bay	47	CX 16
Smal St	Rondebosch East	29	CN 36
Smalblaar Rd	Bonteheuwel	20	CJ 44
Small St	Grassy Pk	54	CY 37
Small St	Valhalla	11	CD 46
Smartt Rd	Goodwood Est.	10	CA 44
Smartt Rd	Townsend Est.	10	CA 44
Smartt Rd	Vasco Est.	10	CA 44
Smith Rd	Rosebank	17	CJ 34
Smith St	Bishop Lavis	21	CG 48
Smith St	Simon's Town	89	DU 28
Smithers Rd	Kenilworth	40	CU 33
Smiths Rd	Plumstead	40	CU 33
Smuts Rd	Lansdowne	29	CN 37
Snaffle Ave	Hout Bay	35	CS 17
Snapdragon St	Bridgetown	31	CL 42
Snapdragon St	Bridgetown	31	CP 43
Snares Brook Rd	Epping Forest	21	CF 48
Sneeuberg Rd	Heideveld	32	CL 46
Sneeuberg Rd	Lavender Hill East	65	DB 34
Sneeuberg Rd	Lavender Hill East	65	DD 37
Snipe Rd	Pelikan Pk	55	CY 40
Snowdrop Sq.	Bridgetown	19	CJ 41
Sobukwe Rd	Masiphumelele	72	DK 20
Socony Rd	Elsies River Ind.	11	CB 48
Soetdoring Rd	Bonteheuwel	20	CJ 44
Soetkop St	Charlesville	21	CH 46
Soetvlei Ave	Porter Est.	51	CX 29
Soetvlei Ave	Sweet Valley	51	CX 29
Sohland Ave	Belle Constantia	39	CU 29
Sol Cohen Rd	Heathfield	52	CW 32
Solan Rd	Gardens	14	CF 26
Solar Cl.	Salberau	11	CE 47
Soldaat Sq.	Factreton	9	CB 40
Soliter St	Kirstenhof	63	DA 30
Sollum Rd	Greenpoint	3	CB 23
Solo St	District Six	15	CF 28
Solo St	Retreat	64	DA 33
Solomon Mahlangu			
	Weltevreden Valley	45	CT 48
Solomons Ave	Grassy Pk	54	CX 37
Solomons Link	Ocean View	79	DN 17
Solomons Rd	Sea Point	2	CD 20
Sombo St	Nyanga	33	CO 49
Somer St	Surrey Est.	31	CM 43
Somerset Cr.	Lakeside	64	DE 32
Somerset Rd	Greenpoint	4	CC 24
Somerset St	Claremont	28	CO 33
Somerset St	Claremont	28	CP 32
Somerset Way	Kommetjie	78	DM 12
Somme Cl.	Strandfontein	68	DB 46
Somme Cl.	Strandfontein	68	DE 45
Son St	Lansdowne	29	CP 36
Sonata St	Retreat	64	DA 34
Sonderend Rd	Manenberg	32	CO 45
Sondou La.	Silvertown	19	CK 41
Soni St	Athlone	30	CM 38
Sonneblom Cr.	Bridgetown	19	CK 41
Sonnedou Rd	Pelikan Pk	55	CX 41
Sonnet Quay	Marina Da Gama	64	DD 34
Sonny Leon Rd	Charlesville	21	CK 46
Sophia St	Oranjezicht	14	CG 25
Sopwith Rd	Kensington	8	CC 38
Sorrel Way	Pelikan Pk	55	CX 41
Sorrento Rd	St James	75	DJ 31
South Arm Rd	Foreshore	5	CB 27
South Ave	Athlone	18	CK 39
South Ave	Kewtown	19	CK 40
South Cl.	Montagu's Gift	42	CU 38

STREET NAME	SUBURB NAME	PG	GRID
South Link	Athlone	30	CL 38
South Rd	Plumstead	41	CS 34
South Way	Pinelands	18	CH 37
South Wk	Pinelands	18	CH 37
Southern Cross Dr.	Bel Ombre	38	CS 26
Southern Cross Dr.	Silverhurst	39	CS 28
Southern Cross Dr.	Witteboomen	38	CS 26
Southern Cross St	Salberau	11	CE 47
Southern Hills Dr.	Lavender Hill	65	DB 35
Southern Right Cir.	Kommetjie	70	DK 15
Southfield Rd	Plumstead	40	CT 33
Southgate Rd	Retreat	53	CY 34
Southgate St	Woodstock	5	CE 29
Soutpansberg Rd	Lavender Hill East	65	DC 37
Sovereign	Plumstead	53	CV 34
Spaanschemat River Rd	Barbarossa	39	CT 29
Spaanschemat River Rd	Fir Grove	50	CX 27
Spaarman Ave	Alphen	39	CS 30
Span St	Lakeside	63	DD 31
Spaniel	Strandfontein	69	DA 47
Sparrow Mkhonto	Weltevreden Valley	45	CT 48
Sparrow St	Penlyn Est.	31	CN 41
Sparrowhawk Rd	Pelikan Pk	55	CY 41
Spearhead Quay	Marina Da Gama	64	DD 34
Spectra Rd	Retreat	52	CY 32
Spekboom Pl.	Leonsdale	11	CD 48
Speke St	Observatory	16	CF 33
Spencer Rd	Claremont	28	CN 33
Spencer St	Woodstock	6	CE 32
Spencer St	Maitland	7	CD 36
Spey Rd	Manenberg	32	CP 45
Spilhaus Ave	Hohenort	39	CQ 28
Spin St	Cape Town Central	4	CE 26
Spin St	Rosebank	17	CH 34
Spine Rd	Strandfontein	68	DB 46
Spinnaker Ave	Lakeside	63	DD 31
Spinnaker Cl.	Pelikan Pk	54	CY 38
Spinner Cl.	Hout Bay Harbour	46	CY 15
Spioenkop Rd	Heideveld	32	CL 46
Spitfire St	Factreton	8	CA 39
Spitskop St	Heideveld	21	CK 46
Spitz Cl.	Strandfontein	68	DA 46
Spitz Way	Strandfontein	68	DA 46
Spoon St	Lakeside	63	DD 31
Spoonbill Cl.	Imhoff's Gift	79	DM 16
Spoonbill Cl.	Pelikan Pk	55	CY 41
Spoonbill Cr.	Pelikan Pk	55	CY 41
Spoonbill Cr.	Seawinds	65	DB 35
Spooner Rd	Strandfontein	68	DA 46
Spoor La.	Maitland	7	CE 35
Spoorbaan St	Woodstock	6	CE 33
Sport Pienaar Rd	Newlands	28	CM 33
Sprig Rd	Rondebosch East	29	CM 36
Spring Cl.	Montagu's Gift	42	CU 39
Spring Gdns	Pinelands	18	CF 38
Spring St	Woodstock	5	CE 30
Springbok Rd	Pinelands	18	CH 38
Springbok Rd	Sea Point	3	CC 23
Springbok St	Silvertown	18	CK 39
Springbok Way	Fish Hoek	82	DL 26
Springer Cl.	Marina Da Gama	64	DC 34
Springfield Cl.	Rondebosch	17	CK 35
Springfield Rd	Rondebosch	17	CK 35
Springfield St	Schaap Kraal	43	CR 41
Springfield Ter.	District Six	5	CE 28
Springwood Cir.	Westlake	63	DC 30
Spurwing Ave	Marina Da Gama	64	DC 34
Squaw Rd	Steenberg	64	DB 34
Squires Cr.	Heathfield	52	CW 32
Squires Rd	Heathfield	52	CW 32
Squirrel Ave	Westlake Est.	63	DB 29
Squirrel Cl.	Fir Grove	51	CX 28
Squirrels Way	Rondebosch	28	CM 34
St Agatha Cr.	Lavender Hill	65	DA 36
St Agnes St	Lavender Hill	65	DA 36
St Aidan Rd	Lavender Hill	65	DA 36
St Aidans Rd	Lansdowne	30	CO 38
St Alban	Lavender Hill	65	DB 36
St Albert Rd	Capricorn	65	DD 36
St Albert Rd	Lavender Hill	65	DB 36
St Alexander Cir.	Lavender Hill	65	DA 36
St Alexander Rd	Lavender Hill	65	DA 36
St Alexander Rd	Lavender Hill	65	DD 36
St Alexis Rd	Lavender Hill	65	DA 36
St Alexis Rd	Lavender Hill	65	DA 36
St Ambrose Cir.	Lavender Hill	65	DA 36
St Ambrose Rd	Lavender Hill	65	DA 36
St Ambrose Rd	Lavender Hill	65	DD 36
St Andrew Rd	Lavender Hill	65	DA 36
St Andrews	Rondebosch	16	CK 33
St Andrews Rd	Claremont	28	CN 34
St Andrews Rd	Rondebosch	16	CK 33
St Andrews Rd	Sea Point	2	CD 21
St Anne St	Lavender Hill	65	DA 36
St Anthony Rd	Heathfield	52	CX 33
St Anthony Rd	Lavender Hill	65	DB 36
St Athans Rd	Athlone	30	CL 38
St Augustine Rd	Lavender Hill	65	DB 36
St Augustine Rd	Lavender Hill	65	DB 36
St Barbara Rd	Lavender Hill	65	DB 36
St Barnabas Rd	Lavender Hill	65	DB 36
St Bartholomew Rd	Lavender Hill	65	DB 36
St Basil St	Lavender Hill	65	DB 36
St Beatrice Rd	Lavender Hill	65	DB 36
St Bede St	Lavender Hill	65	DB 36
St Bede's Rd	Three Anchor Bay	3	CB 23
St Benedict St	Lavender Hill	65	DB 36
St Bernard Cr.	Lavender Hill	65	DB 36
St Bernard Rd	Belgravia	30	CL 39
St Blaise Cr.	Lavender Hill	65	DA 36
St Blaise St	Lavender Hill	65	DA 36
St Blaize	Strandfontein	68	DA 44
St Blaize St	Ruyterwacht	11	CD 46
St Bonaventure St	Lavender Hill	65	DB 36
St Boniface Rd	Lavender Hill East	65	DB 36
St Brendan Rd	Lavender Hill	65	DB 36
St Bridget St	Lavender Hill	65	DB 36
St Bruno Rd	Lavender Hill	65	DA 36
St Catherine Rd	Lavender Hill East	65	DB 36
St Catherine Rd	Plumstead	40	CT 32
St Cecilia St	Lavender Hill	65	DB 36
St Charles Rd	Grassy Pk	54	CW 37
St Charles Rd	Lavender Hill East	65	DB 36
St Clair Rd	Plumstead	40	CT 32
St Clements Way	Lotus River	54	CW 39
St Conute St	Lavender Hill	65	DB 36
St David's Rd	Claremont	28	CN 34
St Dennis Rd	Claremont	28	CN 34
St Edward Rd	Lavender Hill East	65	DB 36
St Francis Pl.	Strandfontein	68	DA 45
St Francis Rd	Grassy Pk	54	CW 37
St Francis Rd	Heathfield	52	CW 32
St Frusquin Rd	Belgravia	30	CL 39
St George St	Simon's Town	89	DU 28
St Georges Mall	Cape Town Cen.	4	CE 26
St George's Rd	Claremont	28	CN 34
St George's Rd	Greenpoint	3	CB 24
St Gothas Rd	Belgravia	30	CL 39
St Heiler's Rd	Muizenberg	76	DF 33
St Helena Cl.	Strandfontein	68	DB 44
St Helena St	Strandfontein	68	DB 44
St Irene Rd	Lavender Hill East	65	DB 36
St Irene Rd	Lavender Hill East	65	DD 37
St James Rd	Sea Point	3	CB 22
St James St	Vredehoek	14	CG 26
St Joan's Rd	Plumstead	40	CT 32
St Johns Rd	Cape Town Central	4	CE 25
St John's Rd	Kalk Bay	75	DK 30
St John's Rd	Lansdowne	30	CP 38
St John's Rd	Sea Point	2	CD 21
St Johns Ter.	Claremont	28	CO 33
St John's Ter.	Wynberg	40	CQ 31
St Joseph Rd	Plumstead	40	CT 32
St Joseph's Rd	Lansdowne	42	CQ 39
St Julian Rd	Belgravia	30	CL 39
St Kilda Rd	Crawford	30	CM 38
St Lawrence Cl.	Seawinds	65	DC 35
St Lawrence Cl.	Seawinds	65	DB 35
St Leger Rd	Claremont	28	CN 33
St Linus Cl.	Seawinds	65	DC 35
St Louis Cl.	Seawinds	65	DC 35
St Louis Way	Grassy Pk	53	CX 36
St Lucia Pl.	Strandfontein	68	DB 44
St Lucia Pl.	Strandfontein	68	DE 45
St Lucina Cl.	Seawinds	65	DC 35
St Lucina Cl.	Seawinds	65	DD 36
St Lucy Cl.	Seawinds	65	DC 35
St Lucy Cl.	Seawinds	65	DC 35
St Luke Cl.	Seawinds	65	DC 35
St Luke Cl.	Seawinds	65	DD 36
St Luke's Rd	Claremont	28	CM 34
St Marks Rd	Claremont	28	CN 34
St Marks Rd	Hout Bay	34	CR 15
St Mark's St	District Six	4	CE 27
St Mary Rd	Plumstead	40	CT 32
St Mauri Rd	Belgravia	30	CL 39
St Michael's Rd	Claremont	28	CN 34
St Michael's Rd	Grassy Pk	54	CX 38
St Michael's Rd	Observatory	16	CF 33
St Michael's Rd	Tamboerskloof	13	CF 23
St Michael's St	Capricorn	64	DE 34
St Pancras Rd	Belgravia	30	CL 39
St Patrick Ave	Lavender Hill	65	DC 36
St Patrick Ave	Lavender Hill East	65	DC 36
St Patrick Ave	Seawinds	65	DC 35
St Patrick Rd	Fresnaye	2	CE 21
St Patrick's Rd	Claremont	28	CM 34
St Patrick's St	Capricorn	65	DE 35
St Paul's Cr.	Rondebosch	16	CK 33
St Peter Ave	Seawinds	65	DB 36
St Peters Rd	Mowbray	16	CH 33
St Phillips St	District Six	5	CE 28
St Quintons Rd	Oranjezicht	14	CF 25
St Ralph Rd	Seawinds	65	DD 36
St Ralph Rd	Seawinds	65	DB 35
St Raymond Rd	Seawinds	65	DB 35
St Regis Rd	Seawinds	65	DB 35
St Richard Rd	Seawinds	65	DC 35
St Robert La.	Seawinds	65	DC 35
St Robert La.	Seawinds	65	DD 36
St Robert Rd	Seawinds	65	DC 35
St Sebastion St	Seawinds	65	DC 35
St Silas Rd	Belgravia	30	CL 39
St Simon St	Lavender Hill	65	DB 36
St Simon's Rd	Belgravia	30	CM 39
St Stainlas St	Seawinds	65	DB 35
St Stephen Ave	Seawinds	65	DC 35
St Stephens Rd	Pinelands	18	CG 37
St Stephen's Rd	Claremont	29	CN 35
St Stephen's Rd	Lavender Hill East	65	DB 36
St Swithin Rd	Lavender Hill East	65	DB 36
St Theresa Cr.	Seawinds	65	DC 35
St Thomas Rd	Claremont	28	CM 34
St Thomas St	Lavender Hill	65	DB 36
St Timothy St	Seawinds	65	DC 35
St Titus Cr.	Seawinds	65	DC 35
St Urban St	Lavender Hill	65	DB 36
St Valentine Cl.	Seawinds	65	DD 36
St Valentine Cl.	Seawinds	65	DC 35
St Victor Cl.	Seawinds	65	DC 35

STREET NAME	SUBURB NAME	PG	GRID
St Victor Cl. .... Seawinds		65	DD 36
St Vincent La. ... Lavender Hill East .		65	DB 36
St Vincent La. ... Lavender Hill East .		65	DD 37
St Wenceslas St ... Seawinds		65	DC 35
St William Cr. ...... Seawinds		65	DC 35
St William Rd ...... Seawinds		65	DC 35
St Winifred St ...... Seawinds		65	DB 35
St.Albans Cl. ...... Bishopscourt		27	CO 29
St.James Rd ...... St James		75	DJ 31
St.James St ...... Vredehoek		14	CG 27
St.Kilda Rd ...... Crawford		30	CO 38
St.Lawrence Cl. ... Seawinds		65	DD 36
St.Linus Cl. ...... Seawinds		65	DD 36
St.Louis Cl. ...... Seawinds		65	DD 36
St.Lucia Cr. ...... Coniston Pk		64	DC 34
St.Lucia St ...... Coniston Pk		64	DB 34
St.Ursula Cl. ...... Seawinds		65	DC 35
St.Ursula Cl. ...... Seawinds		65	DD 36
Stable Cl. .... Noordhoek Manor			
Retirement Village		73	DG 23
Stable Rd .... Grassy Pk		53	CY 36
Stables .... Schaap Kraal		45	CS 46
Stadzicht St ..... Schotsche Kloof ...		4	CD 25
Staff Rd ...... Rondebosch East		29	CN 37
Stafford St .... Claremont		28	CO 33
Staines Rd ...... Plumstead		40	CT 32
Stal St .... Cape Town Central ..		4	CE 26
Stamen St .... Retreat		52	CZ 32
Stamford Rd ...... Grassy Pk		54	CX 37
Stamford Rd ...... Kenilworth		28	CP 32
Stanberry Rd ...... Rugby		7	CA 35
Standard La. ...... Wynberg		40	CR 32
Stanford Rd ...... Rondebosch		29	CM 35
Stanhope Rd ...... Claremont		28	CN 32
Stanley Onasi St ... Manenberg		32	CN 46
Stanley Pl. ...... Mouille Point		3	CB 23
Stanley Rd .... Claremont		28	CN 33
Stanley Rd .... Observatory		16	CF 33
Stanley Rd ...... Rondebosch		16	CK 32
Stanley St ..... Cape Town Central ..		4	CC 26
Star Cl. .... Salberau		11	CE 47
Star Effort .... Noordhoek Manor			
Retirement Village		73	DG 23
Starck Rd .... Elsies River Ind.		11	CB 48
Starke Rd .... Bergvliet		51	CW 30
Starke Rd .... Dreyersdal		52	CY 31
Starling St ...... Penlyn Est.		31	CN 41
Statice Sq. ...... Kewtown		19	CJ 40
Statice St ...... Kewtown		19	CK 40
Station Rd ...... Athlone		18	CK 37
Station Rd .... Claremont		28	CN 32
Station Rd ...... Fish Hoek		83	DL 27
Station Rd ...... Heathfield		52	CX 32
Station Rd .... Lakeside		64	DD 32
Station Rd .... Maitland		7	CD 35
Station Rd ...... Mowbray		16	CH 33
Station Rd ...... Observatory		16	CF 33
Station Rd .... Retreat		52	CY 32
Station Rd ..... Retreat Ind. Area ...		52	CZ 32
Station Rd ...... Rondebosch		16	CK 33
Station Rd ...... Simon's Town		88	DT 27
Station Rd ..... Townsend Est.		10	CA 44
Station Rd ...... Wynberg		40	CR 33
Station St ...... Woodstock		5	CE 30
Steamboat Cl. ... Strandfontein		68	DB 45
Steamboat Cl. ... Strandfontein		68	DE 45
Steamboat Rd ... Strandfontein		68	DB 45
Steed Cl. .... Grassy Pk		53	CX 36
Steen St .... Maitland		8	CD 37
Steenberg Blvd ... Westlake Est.		62	DC 28
Steenberg Cl. ... Frogmore Est.		64	DB 32
Steenberg Rd ..... Frogmore Est.		64	DB 32
Steenberg Rd .... Tokai		51	CZ 28
Steenberg Rd .... Westlake		63	DC 31
Steenberg Rd .... Westlake Est.		62	DC 27
Steenberg Rd .... Westlake Est.		63	DC 29
Steenbok Ave .... Westlake Est.		63	DB 29
Steenbok Cl. ...... Pinelands		18	CH 38
Steenbok Rd ...... Lotus River		55	CV 40
Steenbok Way ..... Fish Hoek		83	DL 27
Steenbras St ...... Brooklyn		7	CB 34
Steengroef Rd ...... Pinelands		17	CF 36
Steensway Rd .... Hout Bay		34	CR 15
Stegman Rd ...... Claremont		28	CN 32
Stegman Way ... Glencairn Hgts		83	DO 27
Stella Rd ...... Montagu's Gift		54	CV 39
Stella Rd ...... Plumstead		41	CT 34
Stella Rd .... Thornton		9	CD 42
Stella Rd .... Wetton		42	CQ 39
Stellen Cl. ...... Marina Da Gama ..		64	DD 34
Stellenberg .... Pinelands		18	CF 39
Stellenberg Ave .... Kenilworth		28	CP 33
Stellenberg St ...... Salberau		11	CE 47
Stemmet Rd ...... Penlyn Est.		30	CN 40
Stephan Way ...... Greenpoint		3	CA 24
Stephen Rd ..... Montagu's Gift		55	CV 40
Stephen Rd .... Tokai		63	DA 29
Stephen St .... Gardens		13	CF 24
Sterket .... Pelikan Pk		55	CY 41
Sterlig .... Kirstenhof		63	DA 30
Stern Cl. .... Bakoven		23	CL 19
Stethoek .... Vredehoek		14	CG 26
Stetson Rd ...... Leonsdale		11	CD 48
Steve Biko Cr. ...Weltevreden Valley ..		45	CS 47
Stevens Cl. .... Grassy Pk		54	CW 38
Stevens Rd .... Grassy Pk		54	CW 37
Stewart St ..... Townsend Est.		10	CA 43
Stewart St .... Tygerdal		9	CA 42
Steyn Rd .... Brooklyn		7	CB 35
Steyning St ...... Woodstock		5	CE 29
Stibitz St ...... Westlake Est.		63	DC 29
Stignant Cr. ...... Claremont		29	CO 35
Stignant Rd ...... Claremont		29	CO 35
Stilton Rd .... Wynberg		40	CS 33
Stingel Rd .... Retreat		64	DA 32
Stinkwood Dr. ..... Farmsteads		68	DD 20
Stint Rd ...... Montagu's Gift		42	CU 38
Stirling Rd ...... Newlands		27	CN 31
Stirling Rd ...... Royal Cape		41	CS 35
Stirling St ...... District Six		14	CF 27
Stirrup Cl. ..... Noordhoek Manor			
Retirement Village		73	DG 23
Stirrup La. ...... Hout Bay		35	CS 17
Stock St ...... Charlesville		21	CJ 46
Stockley Rd ...... Lansdowne		29	CP 37
Stone Cl. .... Dennedal		51	CZ 29
Stone Cl. .... Salberau		11	CE 47
Stone Rd ...... Sea Point		3	CB 22
Stonehill .... Hout Bay		48	CW 19
Stonelands Rd .... Hanover Pk		31	CP 41
Stork St ...... Ocean View		79	DN 17
Stork Way ...... Sunnydale		72	DK 22
Storms River Way ... Manenberg		32	CO 45
Storms River Wk ... Manenberg		32	CO 45
Stowe Cl. ...... Westlake Est.		62	DC 28
Stowe La. ...... Westlake Est.		62	DC 28
Stowe St ...... Woodstock		6	CE 31
Straalen Cl. ...... Barbarossa		40	CS 31
Strand Cl. ...... Cape Town Central ..		4	CD 26
Strand St ...... Greenpoint		4	CC 25
Strand St ...... Woodstock		6	CE 31
Strandfontein Rd ... Lotus River		55	CV 41
Strandfontein Rd ... Montagu's Gift ..		43	CU 41
Strandfontein Rd ... Pelikan Pk		55	CV 41
Strandfontein Rd ... Schaap Kraal ..		43	CS 40
Strandfontein Rd ... Strandfontein ...		67	DB 43
Strandloper Rd ... Sunnydale		72	DK 22
Stranton Rd .... Wynberg		40	CS 33
Stratford Path ...... Pinelands		18	CG 38
Stratford Way ... Meadowridge		51	CV 30
Strathallan Rd ... Rondebosch		17	CK 36
Strathcona Rd .... Oranjezicht		14	CH 25
Stratheam Ave ... Camps Bay		12	CJ 20
Strathmore Rd ... Camps Bay		12	CH 20
Strauss Ave .... Retreat		64	DA 34
Strawberry La. ... Belle Constantia ..		51	CV 29
Strelitzia Rd ...... Kommetjie		78	DN 12
Struben Rd .... Claremont		27	CO 30
Strubens Rd ...... Observatory		16	CF 34
Stuart Cl. .... Dennedal		51	CZ 28
Stuart Rd ...... Rondebosch		29	CM 35
Stuartfield Ave ...... Wynberg		27	CP 31
Stuckeris St ...... District Six		5	CE 28
Student Way ...... Strandfontein		69	DB 48
Students Way ...... Plumstead		40	CS 32
Stuka St .... Factreton		9	CA 40
Suddie Cl. .... Steenberg		62	DA 29
Suffolk Rd .... Lakeside		63	DD 31
Suffolk St .... Claremont		28	CO 34
Suffolk St .... Maitland		7	CD 35
Sugarbird Cr. ...... Seawinds		64	DB 34
Sugarloaf Rd ...... Manenberg		32	CM 45
Suikerbos .... Oudekraal		24	CL 20
Suikerbos La. ...... Westlake Est.		62	DB 28
Suikerbos St ...... Bridgetown		19	CJ 41
Sullivan Rd .... Retreat		64	DA 34
Summer Cl. ...... Montagu's Gift		42	CU 39
Summer Pl. ...... Kirstenhof		63	DA 30
Summerley Rd ... Kenilworth		28	CP 33
Summerseat Cl. .... Gardens		13	CG 23
Summit Rd ...... Hanover Pk		30	CP 40
Summit Way ... Nova Constantia ..		50	CV 27
Sun Valley Ave ... Hohenort		39	CR 28
Sunbird Cir. .... Kommetjie		78	DM 14
Sunbird Cl. .... Kommetjie		78	DM 14
Sunbird Ct ...... Bridgetown		19	CJ 42
Sunbird Link ...... Pelikan Pk		55	CY 41
Sunbury Rd .... Elfindale		52	CX 33
Sunbush Cl. ...... Hout Bay		47	CV 17
Sunday Peak Rd ... Heideveld		32	CL 45
Sunderland St ...... Factreton		8	CB 39
Sunderland St .... Kensington		8	CB 39
Sundew Rd ...... Lotus River		54	CW 39
Sundown Wk .... Pinati		30	CO 40
Sunflower Cl. ...... Bridgetown		19	CK 42
Sunflower Rd ... Lavender Hill East ..		65	DB 36
Sunflower Rd ... Lavender Hill East ..		65	DD 37
Sunlands Ave ...... Lansdowne		42	CQ 37
Sunningdale Rd ... Kenilworth		28	CP 32
Sunninghill Rd ... Wynberg		40	CQ 33
Sunny Way .... Pinelands		17	CF 36
Sunny Way ...... Surrey Est.		31	CM 43
Sunnybrae Rd ... Rondebosch		28	CL 34
Sunnybrook Way ... Elfindale		53	CW 34
Sunnycove Steps ... Fish Hoek		83	DN 28
Sunnydale Rd ...... Sunnydale		72	DK 22
Sunnyside Cr. ...... Woodstock		7	CD 34
Sunnyside Rd .... Crawford		30	CM 38
Sunray Rd ...... Fish Hoek		83	DL 28
Sunrise .... Pinelands		8	CE 38
Sunrise Cir. ...... Capricorn		76	DF 34
Sunrise Cir. .... Ndabeni		8	CE 38
Sunrise Cl. ...... Barbarossa		39	CU 30
Sunset .... Fish Hoek		82	DL 25
Sunset Ave ...... Hout Bay		34	CS 14
Sunset Cl. .... Pinelands		17	CF 36
Sunset Cl. .... Salberau		11	CE 47
Sunset Cr. .... Pinelands		17	CF 36
Sunwood Dr. .... Tokai		62	DA 28
Supermarine St ... Kensington		8	CB 39
Surbiton Rd .... Rosebank		17	CJ 34

STREET NAME	SUBURB NAME	PG	GRID
Surcingle Ave	Hout Bay	35	CT 17
Surf Rd	Strandfontein	69	DC 47
Surf St	Sea Point	2	CD 21
Surf Way	Kommetjie	78	DL 13
Suria Wk	Hanover Pk	31	CP 42
Suring St	Plumstead	40	CU 32
Surran Rd	Hanover Pk	31	CO 42
Surran Rd	Newfields	31	CO 41
Surrey Pl.	Greenpoint	3	CA 24
Surrey Rd	Mowbray	17	CH 35
Surrey St	Claremont	28	CO 34
Surrey St	Townsend Est.	10	CB 44
Surwood Wk	Hanover Pk	31	CP 41
Susan Ave	Bakoven	12	CK 21
Susan Way	Tokai	63	DA 30
Susanne Ave	Bel Ombre	39	CR 28
Sussex Rd	Observatory	16	CG 33
Sussex Rd	Tokai	62	DA 28
Sussex Rd	Wynberg	40	CR 33
Sussex St	Claremont	28	CO 33
Sussex St	Woodstock	5	CE 30
Suther Cl.	Hout Bay	35	CT 16
Sutherland St	Claremont	28	CO 33
Sutherland St	Claremont	28	CP 32
Sutherland St	Ruyterwacht	10	CD 45
Sutton Rd	Fairways	41	CU 36
Suzanne Ave	Hout Bay	47	CX 18
Swakop Rd	Manenberg	32	CO 45
Swallow Cr.	Seawinds	65	DB 35
Swallow La.	Dreyersdal	51	CZ 30
Swallow La.	Kommetjie	78	DM 14
Swallow Rd	Phumlani	55	CW 41
Swallow St	Maitland Gdn Village	7	CE 35
Swallow St	Ocean View	79	DM 17
Swan Cir.	Ocean View	79	DM 17
Swan Cl.	Plumstead	52	CV 33
Swan La.	Bergvliet	52	CX 32
Swan St	Pelikan Pk	67	DC 43
Swanmore Rd	Rondebosch	29	CM 35
Swansea Rd	Newlands	27	CM 31
Swanson St	Woodstock	6	CE 32
Swart Rd	Athlone	30	CL 38
Swartberg St	Ruyterwacht	10	CD 44
Swartdam Rd	Belthorn Est.	30	CN 39
Swartysterhout Rd	Bonteheuwel	20	CJ 44
Sweet Home Way	Heathfield	52	CW 32
Sweet Valley Rd	Bergvliet	52	CW 31
Sweetwater Cl.	The Lakes	72	DJ 20
Swift	Seawinds	65	DB 35
Swift Cl.	Montagu's Gift	42	CU 37
Swift St	Salt River	16	CF 32
Swiss Rd	Lansdowne	30	CP 39
Sword Dancer Cl.	Crofters Valley	72	DG 21
Sybil La.	Camps Bay	12	CJ 20
Sybil Rd	Ottery	42	CR 38
Sybrand Rd	Sybrand Pk	18	CJ 37
Sycamore Cr.	Silverglade	73	DK 25
Sycamore St	Fairie Knowe	72	DK 21
Sycamore Way	Bridgetown	19	CJ 41
Sydney Rd	Mowbray	17	CH 34
Sydney Rd	Wynberg	40	CR 33
Sydney St	District Six	4	CE 27
Sydney St	Greenpoint	3	CB 24
Sydow St	Maitland	7	CE 34
Syfret Rd	Rondebosch	17	CK 35
Sylvan Cl.	Oranjezicht	14	CG 25
Sylvan Rd	Wynberg	40	CR 32
Sylvester Rd	Retreat	53	CY 35
Sylvia Rd	Claremont	27	CO 31
Symphony Ave	Steenberg	64	DA 33
Syringa Cr.	Thornton	9	CD 42
Syringa Rd	Bergvliet	52	CY 31
Syringa St	Bonteheuwel	20	CJ 44
Syringa St	Hanover Pk	31	CO 42

STREET NAME	SUBURB NAME	PG	GRID
Taaibos	Leonsdale	11	CD 48
Taaibos Rd	Bonteheuwel	20	CJ 44
Table Bay Blvd.	Woodstock	6	CD 32
Tabora Way	Newlands	27	CN 30
Tafelberg Rd	Bishop Lavis	21	CH 48
Tafelberg Rd	Lavender Hill East	65	DC 36
Tafelberg Rd	Oranjezicht	13	CH 24
Tagus Way	Manenberg	32	CP 44
Tahiti Cl.	Capri	81	DL 21
Talana Cl.	Claremont	27	CO 31
Talana Cl.	Leonsdale	11	CC 48
Talana Rd	Claremont	27	CN 31
Talc St	Belthorn Est.	30	CO 40
Talent St	Plumstead	52	CV 33
Tallent St	Churchill	11	CA 48
Talma Rd	Muizenberg	76	DG 32
Tamani Rd	Browns Farm	45	CR 47
Tamarisk Cl.	Nova Constantia	50	CW 27
Tamarisk La.	Nova Constantia	50	CW 27
Tamarix Rd	Thornton	9	CD 42
Tambo Rd	Masiphumelele	80	DL 20
Tamboekie Pl.	Leonsdale	11	CC 48
Tamboekie Pl.	Leonsdale	11	CC 47
Tamboerskloof Rd	Tamboerskloof	3	CE 24
Tambotie Rd	Thornton	9	CD 42
Tambourine St	Cafda Village	53	CZ 35
Tamo Rd	Retreat	52	CZ 32
Tana Rd	Retreat	52	CZ 32
Tanabaru Rd	Schotsche Kloof	4	CD 25
Tancred St	Athlone	30	CL 38
Tanel Rd	Pinati	30	CP 40
Tango Cr.	Retreat	52	CZ 32
Tanja Rd	Hohenort	39	CR 28
Tanner Ave	Athlone	30	CM 38
Tantalon Rd	Rondebosch	16	CK 32
Taranto	Strandfontein	69	DB 47
Tarentaal Rd	Bridgetown	19	CJ 41
Tarley Rd	Wynberg	41	CR 34
Taronga Rd	Crawford	30	CM 38
Tasman Rd	Observatory	16	CF 33
Tasman St	Claremont	28	CN 34
Tatum Rd	Retreat	52	CZ 33
Taunton Rd	Wynberg	40	CR 33
Taurus Cl.	Ocean View	79	DO 16
Taurus Rd	Surrey Est.	32	CM 44
Taurus Way	Ocean View	79	DN 16
Tay St	Woodstock	5	CE 30
Teachers Way	Strandfontein	69	DB 47
Teak Rd	Bonteheuwel	20	CJ 43
Teal Cl.	Crofters Valley	72	DG 21
Teal Cl.	Imhoff's Gift	79	DL 17
Teal Rd	Montagu's Gift	42	CU 37
Teck	Woodstock	5	CE 30
Tecno Cr.	Epping Ind.	10	CD 44
Tecoma Cr.	Thornton	10	CE 43
Tecoma Rd	Flintdale Est.	53	CW 35
Tecoma Way	Pinelands	18	CG 39
Tedder Ave	Simon's Town	89	DU 30
Teddington Rd	Rondebosch	16	CK 33
Tee St	Westlake	63	DC 30
Tees Rd	Manenberg	32	CP 44
Telford Ave	Athlone	30	CL 38
Tembe St	Athlone	18	CK 38
Temperance Rd	Retreat	53	CY 34
Temple St	Gatesville	31	CL 42
Tenby Rd	Wynberg	40	CR 33
Tennant St	District Six	4	CE 27
Tennant St	Kenilworth	28	CP 32
Tennent Rd	Athlone	30	CM 39

STREET NAME	SUBURB NAME	PG	GRID
Tennyson St	Salt River	6	CE 32
Tenth Ave	Avon	11	CD 47
Tenth Ave	Cafda Village	53	CZ 34
Tenth Ave	Da Gama Pk	82	DP 24
Tenth Ave	Fairways	41	CU 36
Tenth Ave	Fish Hoek	82	DL 26
Tenth Ave	Hazendal	18	CJ 38
Tenth Ave	Kensington	8	CB 38
Tenth Ave	Leonsdale	11	CD 48
Tenth Ave	Retreat	53	CY 34
Tenth Ave	Schaap Kraal	55	CX 41
Tenth St	Kensington	8	CC 37
Terblans Rd	Bonteheuwel	20	CJ 43
Tercentenary Way	Glen Rdg	83	DO 28
Teremain Rd	Ottery	42	CS 37
Terminus Rd	Nyanga	33	CO 48
Terminus Steps	Bakoven	12	CK 19
Tern Cr.	Pelikan Pk	54	CY 38
Tern Rd	Montagu's Gift	42	CU 38
Tern St	Pelikan Pk	67	DC 43
Terrace Hill	Silverhurst	38	CT 26
Teubes Rd	Kommetjie	78	DM 13
Texel Ct	Marina Da Gama	64	DC 34
Texel St	Ruyterwacht	10	CD 45
Thames Ave	Bishop Lavis	21	CG 47
Thames Ave	Manenberg	32	CO 44
Thames La.	Manenberg	32	CO 45
Thames Wk	Manenberg	32	CO 45
Thamsanqa Rubusana			
	Weltevreden Valley	45	CT 48
Thandeka	Guguletu	32	CN 46
Thatch Rd	Tokai	63	DA 29
Thatcher St	Constantia Vale	39	CT 28
Thaxter Rd	Muizenberg Nth	64	DE 32
The Aloes Cl.	Peers Hill	74	DK 26
The Avenue	Salt River	16	CF 31
The Avenue	Silverhurst	38	CT 27
The Bend	Bergvliet	52	CY 32
The Bend	Pinelands	17	CG 36
The Cheviots	Camps Bay	12	CH 21
The Close	Dreyersdal	52	CZ 31
The Close	Fish Hoek	74	DK 27
The Cobbles	Rondebosch	28	CL 33
The Crescent	Pinelands	18	CG 38
The Crossing	Pinelands	17	CF 36
The Dale	Fish Hoek	73	DK 25
The Dale	Silverglade	73	DK 25
The Dell	Dreyersdal	51	CZ 30
The Dell	Pinelands	18	CG 38
The Downs Rd	Manenberg	32	CP 45
The Drive	Camps Bay	12	CJ 20
The Fairway	Camps Bay	12	CH 20
The Fairway	Pinelands	18	CG 37
The Glade	Silverglade	73	DK 25
The Glen	Pinelands	18	CG 37
The Glen	Sea Point	3	CC 22
The Glen	Silverglade	73	DK 25
The Grange Ave	Rondebosch	16	CK 32
The Grange Rd	Camps Bay	12	CH 20
The Lane	Rondebosch	29	CL 36
The Link	Noordhoek Manor		
Retirement Village		73	DG 23
The Mead	Pinelands	18	CG 37
The Meadows	Camps Bay	12	CH 20
The Meadway	Camps Bay	12	CJ 20
The Needles Way	Hout Bay	36	CR 21
The Old Rd	Hout Bay	47	CW 18
The Oval	Pinelands	17	CF 36
The Promenade	Hout Bay	47	CX 16
The Ridge	Clifton	12	CG 19
The Row	Marina Da Gama	64	DE 33
The Row	Muizenberg	64	DE 33
The Sanctuary	Kirstenhof	63	DB 30
The Stables	Strandfontein	69	DD 48

STREET NAME	SUBURB NAME	PG	GRID
The Steps	Newlands	27	CL 31
The Triangle	Pinelands	17	CF 36
The Valley Wk	Silverhurst	39	CS 29
The Woods	Newlands	27	CL 31
Thelma Rd	Claremont	28	CO 32
Thembani Rd	Guguletu	32	CO 46
Thembisa	Guguletu	33	CN 47
Theomar Ct	Hohenort	39	CR 29
Theresa Ave	Bakoven	12	CK 21
Theresa Ave	Oudekraal	24	CL 20
Thibault Ave	Newlands	27	CN 31
Thibault Rd	Marina Da Gama	64	DD 34
Thibault St	Ruyterwacht	10	CD 45
Thicket Rd	Mowbray	17	CH 35
Thicket St	Newlands	28	CM 32
Thiele Rd	Ottery East	42	CS 38
Third Ave	Belgravia	30	CL 40
Third Ave	Claremont	28	CO 34
Third Ave	Da Gama Pk	81	DP 23
Third Ave	Elsies River Ind.	11	CC 47
Third Ave	Fairways	41	CT 36
Third Ave	Fish Hoek	83	DM 27
Third Ave	Glenlily	11	CA 48
Third Ave	Grassy Pk	53	CX 36
Third Ave	Hazendal	18	CJ 38
Third Ave	Kenilworth	28	CO 34
Third Ave	Kensington	8	CC 37
Third Ave	Lotus River	54	CW 39
Third Ave	Maitland	8	CD 37
Third Ave	Manenberg	32	CP 45
Third Ave	Nyanga	33	CP 49
Third Ave	Retreat	52	CY 33
Third Ave	Rondebosch East	29	CM 37
Third Ave	Schaap Kraal	55	CV 41
Third Ave	Vanguard	32	CL 44
Third Cr.	Fish Hoek	83	DL 27
Third Rd	Heathfield	52	CX 33
Third St	Bishop Lavis	21	CG 48
Third St	Maitland	8	CD 38
Third St	Welcome	20	CK 44
Thirlmere Rd	Plumstead	40	CT 33
Thirteenth Ave	Da Gama Pk	82	DP 24
Thirteenth Ave	Factreton	8	CB 39
Thirteenth Ave	Fish Hoek	82	DL 26
Thirteenth Ave	Schaap Kraal	55	CX 42
Thirteenth Ave	Valhalla	11	CD 46
Thirteenth St	Avon	11	CD 47
Thirteenth St	Kensington	8	CC 37
Thirtieth Ave	Elnor	21	CF 48
Thirty-First Ave	Elnor	21	CF 48
Thirty-Third Ave	Elnor	21	CF 48
Thistle St	Newlands	27	CN 29
Thomas Cr.	Grassy Pk	53	CY 36
Thomas Cr.	Montagu's Gift	55	CV 40
Thomas Rd	Kenilworth	28	CP 33
Thomas Rd	Ndabeni	18	CF 37
Thomas St	Simon's Town	89	DU 28
Thomas St	Valhalla Pk	21	CJ 47
Thompson Cl.	Ocean View	79	DN 17
Thomson Rd	Claremont	28	CN 34
Thor Cir.	Thornton	9	CE 41
Thor Cl.	Salberau	11	CE 46
Thor St	Valhalla	11	CD 46
Thorn St	Newlands	27	CN 29
Thornbury Rd	Plumstead	40	CT 33
Thorne Cl.	Barbarossa	40	CS 31
Thornhill Rd	Greenpoint	3	CB 24
Thornhill Rd	Rondebosch	17	CK 36
Thornton Cl.	Dieprivier	52	CW 32
Thornton Rd	Athlone	30	CL 39
Thornton Rd	Belthorn Est.	30	CO 39
Thornton Rd	Crawford	30	CN 39
Thornton Rd	Dieprivier	52	CW 32
Thornwick Rd	Plumstead	40	CS 32
Thorpe Cl.	Steenberg	61	DA 25
Three Anchor Bay Rd			
	Three Anchor Bay	3	CB 23
Thrush	Bridgetown	19	CK 42
Thrush La.	Montagu's Gift	42	CU 37
Tiara Way	Leonsdale	11	CD 48
Tiber St	Manenberg	32	CP 44
Tico's Way	Crofters Valley	72	DG 21
Tide St	Woodstock	5	CD 30
Tiffany Cl.	Rust-en-vrede	39	CT 29
Tiller Arm Wk	Marina Da Gama	64	DD 34
Timber La.	Retreat	52	CZ 32
Timber Way	Bergvliet	51	CX 30
Timberlost La.	Hout Bay	36	CS 21
Timmerman Cl.	Glen Rdg	83	DO 28
Timour Hall Rd	Plumstead	40	CT 32
Tindale Rd	Dieprivier	52	CW 32
Tisbury Cl.	Sun Valley	81	DL 23
Tissot Rd	Heathfield	52	CY 33
Titania Way	Meadowridge	51	CV 30
Titus Way	The Vines	40	CU 31
Tiverton Rd	Plumstead	40	CT 33
Tobago Way	Capri	81	DL 22
Tobruk	Strandfontein	68	DB 46
Tobruk Rd	Plumstead	40	CS 32
Toby Rd	Surrey Est.	31	CM 43
Toeskouer Rd	Belthorn Est.	30	CN 39
Toffie La.	Claremont	28	CN 32
Tokai Ct	Marina Da Gama	64	DD 33
Tokai Rd	Kirstenhof	63	DA 31
Tokai Rd	Steenberg	50	CZ 27
Tokai Rd	Tokai	51	CZ 29
Toledo Rd	Montana	33	CL 48
Toleni Rd	Kenilworth	28	CP 32
Tolerance Rd	Lansdowne	42	CQ 38
Tolerance Rd	Retreat	53	CY 34
Toll Rd	Rondebosch	16	CK 33
Tolpen Rd	Pinati	30	CP 40
Tom St	Nyanga	45	CQ 48
Tomahawk St	Kensington	8	CB 38
Tomson St	Goodwood Est.	10	CA 44
Tonbridge Rd	Heathfield	52	CY 33
Top Rd	Fresnaye	2	CE 21
Topaz Cl.	Kommetjie	78	DM 14
Topaz Cl.	Pelikan Pk	67	DA 42
Topaz St	Sheraton Pk	64	DC 33
Topaz Ter.	San Michel	72	DF 22
Topaz Way	San Michel	73	DF 23
Topsham Rd	Ottery East	42	CT 39
Topsham Rd	Plumstead	41	CS 34
Torbay Rd	Grassy Pk	54	CX 37
Torbay Rd	Greenpoint	3	CB 24
Toring Rd	Retreat	53	CY 35
Torquay Ave	Claremont	27	CP 31
Torrens Rd	Royal Cape	41	CS 36
Torrid Rd	Surrey Est.	32	CM 44
Tortuga Cl.	Barbarossa	39	CU 30
Totem Rd	Lansdowne	29	CO 37
Totius Rd	Townsend Est.	10	CA 43
Totnes Rd	Plumstead	41	CT 35
Totness Ave	Bakoven	12	CK 20
Toulon Ave	Plumstead	52	CV 33
Touraine St	Bel Ombre	38	CS 27
Tousberg Rd	Manenberg	32	CM 45
Tower Quay	Marina Da Gama	64	DE 34
Towers Rd	Muizenberg	76	DF 33
Townsend Ave	The Vines	52	CV 31
Townsend St	Townsend Est.	10	CA 43
Trafalgar Cr.	Simon's Town	89	DU 29
Trafalgar Dr.	Strandfontein	68	DB 46
Trafalgar Pl.	Simonskloof	89	DU 28
Trafalgar Sq.	Sea Point	3	CD 22
Trafalgar St	Cape Town Central	4	CD 26
Tralee Rd	Heathfield	52	CY 32
Tramore Rd	Plumstead	41	CU 35
Tramway Rd	Sea Point	2	CD 20
Transvaal St	Paarden Eiland	6	CC 33
Travers Rd	Newlands	28	CM 33
Treaty Rd	Woodstock	5	CE 30
Tredree Steps	Simon's Town	89	DU 29
Tree Rd	Camps Bay	12	CJ 20
Treehaven Rd	Claremont	29	CO 35
Trek Rd	Gardens	13	CD 24
Trellis Rd	Tokai	51	CZ 28
Trematon Rd	Athlone	18	CK 37
Trenance Rd	Ottery	42	CR 39
Trent Rd	Gardens	13	CF 24
Trent Rd	Plumstead	52	CV 33
Trentham Rd	Plumstead	41	CU 34
Trevor Rd	Lansdowne	29	CN 37
Trevor Siljeur Rd	Capricorn	65	DC 35
Trevor Vilakazi	Weltevreden Valley.	45	CS 48
Trevor Way	Matroosfontein	21	CG 47
Trigg Rd	Capri	80	DL 19
Trill Rd	Observatory	16	CG 33
Trimaran Cl.	Sun Valley	73	DK 23
Trinidad Cl.	Capri	80	DM 20
Trinity La.	Rondebosch	29	CL 35
Tripper Way	Epping Ind.	21	CF 43
Tristan Cr.	Strandfontein	68	DB 44
Tristania Ave	Ottery	42	CS 38
Trompet St	Steenberg	64	DB 34
Troop Rd	Wynberg	41	CS 34
Trotter Rd	Strandfontein	69	DA 47
Trout Cl.	Pelikan Pk	55	CX 40
Trout Way	Strandfontein	68	DA 44
Trovato Link	Wynberg	40	CQ 33
Trovato Rd	Wynberg	39	CQ 30
Truman Rd	Claremont	28	CN 34
Truro Cr.	Westlake Est.	62	DC 28
Tsessebe Rd	Lotus River	55	CV 40
Tsitsikamma Way			
	Lavender Hill East	65	DC 36
Tsitsikamma Way			
	Lavender Hill East	65	DD 37
Tucana Cl.	Ocean View	79	DO 17
Tudor Ave	Tokai	51	CZ 29
Tudor Cl.	Bergvliet	51	CX 30
Tugela La.	Manenberg	32	CP 45
Tugela St	Manenberg	32	CP 45
Tuin Sq.	Cape Town Central	4	CE 26
Tuin St	Gardens	13	CF 24
Tulbagh St	Brooklyn	7	CB 34
Tulip	Bishop Lavis	21	CH 48
Tulip Cl.	Ottery East	42	CS 38
Tulip Cl.	Grassy Pk	54	CX 38
Tulip Rd	Retreat	52	CZ 32
Tullyallen Rd	Rondebosch	28	CL 34
Tunny Cr.	Strandfontein	68	DB 45
Tunny St	Strandfontein	68	DA 45
Turf Hall Rd	Lansdowne	30	CO 38
Turf Hall Rd	Manenberg	32	CN 45
Turf Hall Rd	Newfields	31	CN 40
Turf Hall Rd	Primrose Pk	31	CN 43
Turf Way	Strandfontein	69	DA 47
Turfburg Wk	Hanover Pk	43	CQ 42
Turflyn Wk	Pinati	30	CO 40
Turkey Rd	Phumlani	55	CW 41
Turkeyberry La.	Hout Bay	47	CX 18
Turks Head Cl.	Marina Da Gama	64	DE 34
Turksvy Rd	Bonteheuwel	20	CJ 43
Turnstone Way	Pelikan Pk	55	CV 40
Turquoise Cl.	San Michel	72	DF 22
Turquoise Cr.	Sheraton Pk	64	DC 33
Turquoise Way	San Michel	72	DF 21
Tussen Rd	Doornhoogte	31	CM 41
Tussendal Ave	Dreyersdal	52	CY 31

STREET NAME	SUBURB NAME	PG	GRID
T'wagen Rd	Marina Da Gama	64	DD 34
Tweed Rd	Rondebosch	28	CL 33
Twelfth Ave	Avon	11	CD 47
Twelfth Ave	Cafda Village	53	CZ 35
Twelfth Ave	Da Gama Pk	82	DP 24
Twelfth Ave	Fish Hoek	82	DL 26
Twelfth Ave	Hazendal	18	CJ 38
Twelfth Ave	Kensington	8	CB 39
Twelfth Ave	Schaap Kraal	55	CX 41
Twelfth St	Elsies River Ind.	11	CC 47
Twelfth St	Kensington	8	CC 37
Twent Pl.	Westlake	63	DC 30
Twent Rd	Westlake	63	DC 30
Twentieth Ave	Fish Hoek	73	DK 24
Twentieth Ave	Norwood	11	CE 48
Twentieth St	Elsies River Ind.	11	CC 47
Twenty Steps	Bakoven	12	CK 19
Twenty-Eighth Ave	Norwood	11	CE 48
Twenty-Eighth St	Norwood	11	CE 48
Twenty-Fifth Ave	Norwood	11	CE 48
Twenty-First Ave	Avonwood	11	CD 48
Twenty-First Ave	Fish Hoek	73	DK 24
Twenty-First Ave	Norwood	11	CD 48
Twenty-First Cl.	Avonwood	11	CD 48
Twenty-First St	Avon	11	CD 47
Twenty-First St	Elsies River Ind.	11	CC 47
Twenty-Fourth Ave	Norwood	11	CE 48
Twenty-Ninth Ave	Elnor	21	CF 48
Twenty-Ninth St	Avonwood	11	CD 48
Twenty-Second Ave	Avonwood	11	CD 48
Twenty-Second Ave	Norwood	11	CE 48
Twenty-Seventh Ave	Norwood	11	CE 48
Twenty-Seventh St	Norwood	11	CE 48
Twenty-Sixth Ave	Norwood	11	CE 48
Twenty-Sixth St	Leonsdale	11	CC 48
Twenty-Third Ave	Norwood	11	CE 48
Twenty-Third St	Elsies River Ind.	11	CC 48
Twickenham Rd	Mowbray	17	CH 35
Twilley St	Kenilworth Pk	29	CP 35
Twine Rd	Plumstead	40	CT 33
Twyford Rd	Rondebosch	29	CL 36
Tygerberg St	Elsies River Ind.	11	CB 47
Tygerberg St	Richmond Est.	11	CA 47
Tyne Ave	Riverton	11	CC 46
Tyne Rd	Wynberg	40	CS 33
Tynemouth Rd	Plumstead	41	CT 35
Typhoon St	Factreton	9	CB 40
Tyrone Rd	Wynberg	41	CR 34

U

STREET NAME	SUBURB NAME	PG	GRID
Uintjie St	Charlesville	21	CH 46
Uithof St	Frogmore Est.	63	DC 31
Uitsig Cl.	Fir Grove	50	CW 27
Uitsig Rd	Marina Da Gama	64	DC 33
Uitsig Rd	Silverhurst	39	CT 29
Uitvlugt Rd	Pinelands	18	CF 37
Ukhuni Cl.	Tygerdal	9	CA 42
Ullswater	Pinelands	8	CE 39
Ullswater Rd	Coniston Pk	64	DB 34
Ulm Cl.	Strandfontein	69	DB 47
Ulm Way	Strandfontein	69	DB 47
Ulster St	Royal Cape	41	CS 35
Ulunthu St	Guguletu	32	CN 46
Ummah Cl.	District Six	5	CD 24
Umnga	Langa	19	CG 41
Union Ave	Newlands	27	CL 30
Union Ave	Pinelands	18	CF 37
Union Rd	Fairways	41	CT 36
Union Rd	Pinelands	18	CF 37
Union St	Gardens	14	CF 25
Union St	Hout Bay	47	CW 18
Union St	Kenilworth Pk	29	CP 35
Union St	Simon's Town	89	DU 28
Union Way	Matroosfontein	21	CG 47
Unity Rd	Belgravia	30	CM 40
Unity Rd	Retreat	53	CY 34
University Dr.	Pinelands	19	CF 40
University St	Cape Town Central	4	CE 25
Upper 5th Ave	Manenberg	32	CP 46
Upper Adelaide Rd	Woodstock	15	CF 30
Upper Adelaide Rd	Woodstock	15	CG 29
Upper Albert Rd	Tamboerskloof	3	CE 23
Upper Alma Rd	Rosebank	16	CJ 33
Upper Angelina Ave	Bishopscourt	27	CN 30
Upper Balfour St	Salt River	16	CF 31
Upper Bebington Ave	Bishopscourt	27	CP 30
Upper Bloem St	Schotsche Kloof	4	CD 25
Upper Bowwood Rd	Claremont	27	CO 31
Upper Buitengracht St	Tamboerskloof	3	CE 24
Upper Cambridge St	Woodstock	15	CF 29
Upper Camp Rd	Ndabeni	7	CE 34
Upper Canterbury St	Gardens	4	CE 25
Upper Chamberlain St	Salt River	16	CF 31
Upper Clarens Rd	Fresnaye	2	CD 21
Upper Coventry Rd	Woodstock	15	CF 29
Upper Coventry Rd	Woodstock	15	CG 29
Upper Duke St	Woodstock	15	CF 29
Upper Duke St	Woodstock	15	CG 29
Upper Durban Rd	Mowbray	16	CH 33
Upper Grove Ave	Claremont	28	CN 32
Upper Hillwood Rd	Bishopscourt	27	CP 30
Upper Holly St	Newlands	27	CN 29
Upper Isabel Ave	Bishopscourt	27	CN 30
Upper Keppel St	Woodstock	15	CF 29
Upper Keppel St	Woodstock	15	CG 29
Upper Kildare Cr.	Fish Hoek	82	DL 26
Upper Kinrae Cr.	Fish Hoek	82	DL 26
Upper Kloof Ave	Gardens	13	CF 23
Upper Leeuwen St	Schotsche Kloof	4	CD 25
Upper Liesbeek Rd	Rosebank	16	CJ 33
Upper Maynard St	Vredehoek	14	CF 26
Upper Melbourne Rd	Woodstock	15	CF 30
Upper Mill St	Vredehoek	14	CF 26
Upper Mountain Rd	Woodstock	15	CF 30
Upper Noreen Ave	Bishopscourt	27	CN 30
Upper Orange St	Oranjezicht	14	CG 25
Upper Paradise Rd	Newlands	27	CM 30
Upper Paradise Rd	Newlands	27	CN 30
Upper Park La.	Strandfontein	69	DD 48
Upper Park La.	Strandfontein	69	DA 47
Upper Pepper St	Schotsche Kloof	4	CD 25
Upper Portswood Rd	Greenpoint	4	CB 25
Upper Primrose Ave	Bishopscourt	27	CP 30
Upper Pypies Plain	Devil's Peak Est.	14	CF 27
Upper Quarterdeck Rd	St James	75	DJ 30
Upper Queens Rd	Woodstock	15	CF 29
Upper Queens Rd	Woodstock	15	CG 29
Upper Rd	Rosebank	16	CJ 32
Upper Recreation Rd	Fish Hoek	74	DK 26
Upper Rhine Rd	Sea Point	2	CC 23
Upper Roodebloem Rd	Woodstock	15	CG 30
Upper Rose St	Newlands	26	CN 28
Upper School St	Strandfontein	69	DA 47
Upper Sidmouth Ave	Bishopscourt	27	CO 30
Upper Silva St	Brooklyn	7	CB 35
Upper Station Rd	Ndabeni	7	CE 35
Upper Thistle Ave	Newlands	26	CN 28
Upper Torquay Ave	Bishopscourt	27	CO 30
Upper Tree Rd	Camps Bay	12	CJ 20
Upper Union St	Gardens	14	CF 24
Upper Warwick St	Woodstock	5	CE 29
Upper Wheelan St	Newlands	27	CM 31
Upshire Cl.	Epping Forest	21	CF 47
Uranuim	Vanguard	31	CL 43
Uranus Cl.	Salberau	11	CE 47
Uranus Cl.	Salberau	11	CE 46
Urfield Rd	Lavender Hill	65	DB 35
Urmarah Ave	Bel Ombre	39	CS 28
Urmarah Cl.	Bel Ombre	39	CS 28
Ursa Cl.	Ocean View	79	DO 17
Ursina Cl.	Hout Bay	46	CV 15
Ursula Rd	Valhalla Pk	21	CJ 47
Usk Rd	Manenberg	32	CP 45
Utah Cl.	Retreat	52	CZ 32
Utica Way	Strandfontein	69	DB 47
Uxbridge Rd	Muizenberg Nth	64	DE 32

V

STREET NAME	SUBURB NAME	PG	GRID
Vaal La.	Belthorn Est.	30	CN 39
Vaal Rd	Bishop Lavis	21	CG 47
Vaalbos Rd	Bonteheuwel	20	CJ 45
Vale Rd	Rondebosch	28	CL 33
Valentino Dr.	Kirstenhof	63	DB 30
Valhalla Dr.	Charlesville	21	CH 47
Valhalla Dr.	Charlesville	21	CK 47
Valhalla Dr.	Matroosfontein	21	CG 47
Valk Way	Bridgetown	19	CJ 42
Valley Rd	Hout Bay	35	CT 17
Valley Rd	Kenilworth	28	CO 32
Valley Rd	Sweet Valley	51	CX 28
Valley St	Riverton	11	CC 46
Valley View	Retreat	52	CZ 33
Valley View Dr.	Hout Bay	35	CT 16
Valley Walk Cl.	Bel Ombre	39	CS 29
Valley Wk	Silverglade	73	DK 25
Van Arckel St	Wynberg	40	CR 31
Van Breda St	Barbarossa	40	CT 31
Van de Leur St	Brooklyn	7	CC 36
Van der Heever St	Goodwood Est.	10	CA 44
Van der Horst Ave	Kommetjie	78	DM 12
Van der Poel Way	Bergvliet	51	CW 30
Van der Poll Ave	Kommetjie	78	DM 13
Van der Stel Ave	Tokai	51	CZ 28
Van der Stel Ave	Brooklyn	7	CC 35
Van der Stel St	Townsend Est.	10	CA 43
Van Goen St	Maitland Gdn Village	7	CE 35
Van Holdt St	Newlands	27	CM 31
Van Hoogstraten Rd	Hout Bay	47	CV 17
Van Imhoff Way	Kommetjie	78	DM 12
Van Kampz St	Camps Bay	12	CJ 20
Van Kemp St	Ruyterwacht	10	CD 45
Van Oudtshoorn Rd	Hout Bay	47	CV 17
Van Reenen Cl.	Newlands	27	CM 30
Van Reenen Cl.	Newlands	27	CM 29
Van Reenen Rd	Constantia Vale	39	CT 28
Van Reenen St	Newlands	27	CM 30
Van Reenen St	Richmond	11	CB 47
Van Rensburg Rd	Goodwood Est.	10	CA 43
Van Riebeeck St	Brooklyn	7	CC 35
Van Riebeeck St	Richmond Est.	11	CA 47
Van Rooyen Rd	Retreat	52	CY 33
Van Ryn St	Barbarossa	40	CT 31
Van Ryneveld Ave	Devil's Peak Est.	14	CF 27
Van Schalkwyk Rd	Rondebosch East	29	CM 36
Van Vuuren St	Plumstead	53	CV 34
Van Wyk Rd	Retreat	64	DA 33
Van Wyk St	Maitland	7	CD 35
Van Zyl Way	Bergvliet	51	CW 30
Vancouver St	Capri	81	DL 21
Vancouver Cr.	Capri	81	DL 21
Vanguard	Foreshore	5	CD 30
Vanguard Dr.	Bonteheuwel	20	CH 43
Vanguard Dr.	Epping Ind.	20	CF 43

Index to Street Names

STREET NAME	SUBURB NAME	PG	GRID	STREET NAME	SUBURB NAME	PG	GRID	STREET NAME	SUBURB NAME	PG	GRID
Vanguard Dr.	Hanover Pk	31	CO 43	Victoria Rd	Woodstock	5	CE 29	Voortrekker Rd	Parow	11	CB 48
Vanguard Dr.	Schaap Kraal	44	CQ 44	Victoria Rd	Wynberg	40	CR 32	Voortrekker Rd	Ruyterwacht	11	CD 46
Vanguard Dr.	Surrey Est.	31	CN 43	Victoria Rd	Wynberg	40	CR 31	Voortrekker Rd	Townsend Est.	10	CC 44
Vanguard Dr.	Thornton	10	CD 43	Victoria St	Gardens	4	CE 25	Voortrekker Rd	Vasco Est.	11	CB 46
Vanguard Dr.	Vanguard	31	CL 43	Victoria St	Retreat	52	CZ 32	Voortrekker Rd	Woodstock	6	CE 33
Vanguard Dr.	Wingfield	9	CB 42	Victoria Wk	Woodstock	5	CE 30	Vooruitsig Rd	Surrey Est.	31	CM 43
Vans Rd	Dreyersdal	52	CZ 31	Victorskloof Rd	Hout Bay	35	CS 17	Vorster Ave	Wetton	42	CQ 39
Varkensvlei Rd	Schaap Kraal	44	CU 43	Victory Ave	Pinelands	8	CE 38	Vos St	Cape Town Central	4	CC 25
Varney's Rd	Greenpoint	3	CB 24	Victory Cl.	Victoria	88	DU 27	Vo?l St	Belgravia	30	CL 40
Varsity St	Tamboerskloof	13	CF 23	Victory La.	Simon's Town	88	DU 27	Vrede Rd	Frogmore Est.	63	DC 31
Vasco Blvd	Vasco Est.	10	CA 45	Victory Rd	Retreat	53	CY 34	Vrede St	Cape Town Central	4	CC 24
Vasco da Gama Blvd				Victory St	Wynberg	41	CS 34	Vredehoek Ave	Vredehoek	14	CF 26
	Cape Town Central	4	CD 27	Victory Way	Victoria	88	DU 27	Vredenburg Ave	Rosebank	17	CH 34
Vasco St	Brooklyn	7	CB 35	Vidal Cr.	Strandfontein	68	DB 44	Vredenburg Circus	Rosebank	17	CJ 34
Vcqunta Way	Langa	19	CH 42	Vienna Way	Grassy Pk	53	CX 36	Vredenburg La.			
Vega Cl.	Ocean View	79	DN 16	Viking Way	Epping Ind.	10	CE 44		Cape Town Central	4	CE 25
Vega Rd	Retreat	52	CY 32	Vilakazi Cr.	Masiphumelele	72	DK 20	Vredendal Rd	Athlone	18	CK 39
Veld Rd	Belgravia	30	CM 40	Viljoens Wk	Parkwood	41	CU 36	Vredenhof	Claremont	28	CM 34
Velden Rd	Wynberg	40	CQ 32	Village Green	Kirstenhof	63	DC 31	Vriedenhof Rd	Wynberg	40	CR 32
Veleli	Guguletu	32	CN 46	Village Green	Kirstenhof	63	DE 31	Vriende St	Oranjezicht	14	CF 26
Velma Rd	Retreat	53	CY 35	Village Green Cl.	Plumstead	40	CU 33	Vrygrond Ave	Capricorn	65	DC 35
Velocity	Primrose Pk	31	CO 43	Village La.	Farmsteads	60	DE 20	Vrystaat Rd	Paarden Eiland	7	CB 34
Velocity	Primrose Pk	31	CP 43	Vimy Ridge	Strandfontein	68	DA 46	Vulcan La.	Hout Bay Harbour	46	CY 14
Venice	Marina Da Gama	64	DE 33	Vincent Ave	Rondebosch	29	CM 35	Vulture Rd	Phumlani	55	CW 41
Venster St	Manenberg	32	CM 45	Vincent Cl.	Montagu's Gift	55	CV 40	Vuurpyl Cr.	Thornton	10	CD 43
Ventnor Rd	Claremont	28	CO 33	Vincent Rd	Manenberg	32	CN 44	Vuurpyl Rd	Bonteheuwel	20	CJ 44
Ventnor Rd	Muizenberg	76	DF 34	Vine Rd	Bergvliet	52	CX 31	Vyeboom Rd	Bonteheuwel	20	CJ 44
Ventura Rd	Factreton	8	CB 39	Vine Rd	Woodstock	16	CF 31	Vygie Cl.	Ottery East	42	CT 39
Ventura Rd	Kensington	8	CB 38	Vine Rd	Wynberg	40	CR 33	Vygie Ct	Kewtown	18	CK 39
Ventura St	Wingfield	9	CA 40	Vine St	Gardens	13	CF 24	Vygie Pl.	Pelikan Pk	55	CY 41
Venus Ave	Bel Ombre	39	CS 28	Vineyard Ave	Hout Bay	36	CT 19	Vygie Rd	Bishop Lavis	21	CH 48
Venus Cl.	Bel Ombre	39	CS 28	Vineyard Cl.	Alphen	39	CS 30	Vygie Rd	Charlesville	21	CG 46
Venus Cl.	Salberau	11	CE 47	Vineyard Cl.	Silverhurst	38	CT 26	Vygie St	Hanover Pk	31	CO 42
Venus Cl.	Salberau	11	CE 46	Vineyard Rd	Bergvliet	51	CX 30	Vygiekraal Rd	Primrose Pk	31	CO 43
Venus Way	Matroosfontein	21	CG 48	Vineyard Rd	Claremont	28	CN 32	Vygiekraal Rd	Sand Industria	32	CP 44
Venus Way	Ocean View	79	DN 16	Vineyard Rd	Dreyersdal	51	CY 30				
Venus Way	Ottery	42	CR 38	Vineyard Way	Hout Bay	47	CV 17				
Venus Way	Valhalla Pk	21	CJ 48	Vink Rd	Sunnydale	72	DK 22		[W]		
Verbena St	Paarden Eiland	6	CC 33	Viola St	Retreat	64	DA 33				
Verbena Way	Pinelands	18	CG 39	Violet Rd	Claremont	27	CO 31	W.Songqeqo St	Hout Bay	35	CU 18
Verdi Cl.	Strandfontein	69	DA 49	Viooltjie St	Plumstead	40	CU 32	W.Songqeqo St	Hout Bay	35	CS 18
Verdi St	Steenberg	64	DB 33	Virginia Ave	Vredehoek	14	CF 26	Waaihoek Rd	Heideveld	32	CL 45
Verdun Way	Strandfontein	68	DB 46	Virgo Rd	Surrey Est.	32	CN 44	Waarnemer Sq.	Factreton	9	CB 40
Vereeniging Cir.	Ruyterwacht	10	CD 45	Virgo St	Ocean View	79	DO 17	Wabash Rd	Schaap Kraal	44	CQ 45
Vernon Rd	Plumstead	40	CS 32	Visagie	Oudekraal	23	CL 19	Waboom St	Sunnydale	72	DK 21
Vernon Terrace Cr.	District Six	4	CE 27	Visser Ave	Wynberg	27	CP 31	Waboom St	Sunnydale	72	DH 20
Verster Rd	Belgravia	30	CL 40	Vista Cl.	Capri	80	DL 20	Wade Rd	Claremont	28	CO 33
Versveld Ave	Hohenort	39	CR 28	Vista Rd	Claremont	28	CN 33	Wadham La.	Woodstock	15	CF 30
Versveld Rd	Goodwood Est.	10	CB 45	Vistula La.	Manenberg	44	CQ 44	Wagner Way	Steenberg	64	DB 33
Versveld Rd	Richmond Est.	11	CB 47	Vistula Rd	Manenberg	32	CP 44	Wagtail Cl.	Dreyersdal	51	CZ 30
Versveld Rd	Vasco Est.	11	CB 46	Vita Nova Ave	Tokai	62	DA 28	Wahid St	Penlyn Est.	31	CN 41
Vertrou Rd	Belthorn Est.	30	CN 38	Vlagskip St	Strandfontein	68	DB 44	Wakefield Rd	Rondebosch	29	CL 36
Verwood Rd	Muizenberg	64	DE 32	Vlamboom Rd	Bonteheuwel	20	CJ 44	Wakefield Rd	Wynberg	40	CR 32
Verwood Rd	Muizenberg Nth	64	DE 32	Vlamboom St	Ottery	42	CU 38	Wale St	Cape Town Central	4	CD 25
Vesperdene Rd	Greenpoint	4	CC 25	Vlei Rd	Greenpoint	3	CB 24	Wallace Cl.	Townsend Est.	10	CA 43
Vesuvius Ave	Strandfontein	69	DA 49	Vlei Rd	Heathfield	52	CX 33	Wallace St	Tygerdal	10	CB 43
Via Appia	Strandfontein	69	DA 49	Vlei Rd	Knole Pk	55	CV 42	Wallflower St	Paarden Eiland	6	CD 33
Vibra St	Hanover Pk	43	CQ 42	Vlei Rd	Muizenberg	76	DF 34	Wallis Rd	Hazendal	18	CK 38
Vickers Rd	Kensington	8	CC 38	Vlei Rd	Muizenberg Nth	64	DE 32	Walloon Rd	Barbarossa	39	CU 30
Victor St	Hout Bay	47	CV 16	Vlei Rd	Pelikan Pk	54	CY 39	Walmer Rd	Parkwood	53	CV 36
Victoria Ave	Hout Bay	47	CV 16	Vlei Rd	Schaap Kraal	55	CW 42	Walmer Rd	Woodstock	5	CE 30
Victoria Cl.	Tokai	63	DA 29	Vleihall Rd	Hanover Pk	43	CQ 41	Walmer Wk	Parkwood	41	CU 36
Victoria Mxenge				Vliegtuig St	Factreton	9	CB 40	Walnut Rd	Lansdowne	30	CP 38
	Weltevreden Valley	45	CT 48	Vlier La.	Ottery	42	CT 37	Wals Ave	Cafda Village	65	DA 35
Victoria Rd	Bantry Bay	2	CE 20	Voetboog Rd	Schotsche Kloof	4	CD 25	Walsall Rd	Plumstead	40	CT 32
Victoria Rd	Camps Bay	12	CJ 20	Vogelgezang St	District Six	15	CF 28	Walter Rd	Three Anchor Bay	3	CB 23
Victoria Rd	Flintdale Est.	53	CV 35	Vokwana Way	Langa	19	CH 41	Walters Cl.	Grassy Pk	53	CX 36
Victoria Rd	Grassy Pk	53	CX 36	Volksang St	Cafda Village	53	CZ 35	Walters Way	Bergvliet	51	CW 30
Victoria Rd	Hout Bay	35	CR 16	Volstruis Rd	Bridgetown	19	CK 42	Waltham Rd	Epping Forest	21	CF 48
Victoria Rd	Llanudno	22	CO 16	Volta Rd	Retreat	52	CZ 32	Waltham Rd	Lansdowne	29	CN 36
Victoria Rd	Pelikan Pk	54	CY 38	Voorjaar St	Surrey Est.	31	CM 43	Waltham Way	Meadowridge	51	CV 30
Victoria Rd	Plumstead	40	CT 33	Voorspoed Rd	Surrey Est.	31	CM 43	Walton Rd	Cafda Village	53	CY 35
Victoria Rd	Salt River	17	CF 31	Voortrekker Rd	Maitland	7	CD 36				
Victoria Rd	Sea Point	2	CD 20								

Index to Street Names

Walton Way   Willow Rd

STREET NAME	SUBURB NAME	PG	GRID
Walton Way	Bridgetown	19	CK 42
Walvis Rd	Strandfontein	68	DB 45
Wandel St	Gardens	14	CF 25
Wanderers Cl.	Fir Grove	51	CW 28
Wapiti	Factreton	8	CA 39
Warbler Ct	Bridgetown	19	CJ 42
Warbler Rd	Pelikan Pk	55	CX 41
Warblers Cl.	Bel Ombre	39	CS 29
Warblers Way	Bel Ombre	39	CS 29
Warbreck Rd	Lansdowne	42	CQ 39
Ward La.	Grassy Pk	54	CX 38
Warden Cr.	Penlyn Est.	31	CO 41
Wargrave Rd	Kenilworth	41	CQ 34
Warner Cr.	Riverton	11	CC 46
Warren Cl.	Retreat	52	CZ 33
Warren St	Tamboerskloof	3	CE 23
Warrenside	Retreat	52	CZ 33
Warrenville Ter.			
	Cape Town Central	4	CE 26
Warrington Rd	Claremont	29	CO 35
Warsaw	Strandfontein	69	DB 47
Warwick St	Claremont	28	CN 32
Warwick St	Vredehoek	14	CF 26
Warwick St	Woodstock	5	CE 29
Washington Dr.	Langa	20	CH 43
Washington Rd	Claremont	29	CN 35
Washington St	Langa	19	CG 41
Wassenar Cl.	Westlake	63	DC 31
Wassenar Cl.	Westlake	63	DE 31
Wastonia Cl.	Ottery East	42	CT 39
Water St	Claremont	28	CM 34
Water St	Simon's Town	89	DU 28
Water Way	Marina Da Gama	64	DD 33
Waterberg Rd	Heideveld	32	CL 45
Waterbury Rd	Plumstead	40	CS 33
Watercress La.	Pelikan Pk	54	CX 39
Waterfall La.	Hout Bay	36	CR 21
Waterford Ave	Lotus River	54	CV 39
Waterford Cir.	Kirstenhof	63	DB 31
Waterford Cl.	Plumstead	52	CV 33
Waterford Rd	Elfindale	52	CW 33
Waterford Rd	Plumstead	40	CU 33
Watering St	Parow	11	CB 48
Waterkant St	Cape Town Central	4	CC 26
Waterkant St	Greenpoint	4	CC 25
Waterloo Gr.	Wynberg	40	CQ 32
Waterloo Rd	Lansdowne	29	CP 36
Waterloo Rd	Strandfontein	69	DA 47
Waterloo Rd	Wynberg	40	CR 32
Waterway	Kewtown	18	CJ 39
Watford Ave	Athlone	30	CL 38
Watson Rd	Muizenberg	76	DF 33
Watson St	Cape Town Central	4	CE 25
Watson Wk	Tokai	62	DA 28
Watsonia Cl.	Pinelands	18	CG 39
Watsonia La.	Scarborough	86	DU 20
Watsonia Rd	Thornton	10	CE 43
Watsonia St	Devil's Peak Est.	14	CF 27
Watsonia Way	Lotus River	54	CV 38
Wattle Gr.	Pinelands	8	CE 38
Wattle La.	Parkwood	42	CU 37
Wattle Rd	Chapman's Peak	71	DF 18
Wattle Rd	Grassy Pk	54	CX 38
Wavell Ave	Simon's Town	89	DU 30
Waveren Sq.	Ruyterwacht	10	CC 45
Waverley Cl.	Barbarossa	39	CU 30
Waverley Rd	Observatory	16	CG 33
Wayside Rd	Bishop Lavis	21	CH 47
Wayside Rd	Rondebosch	28	CL 34
Weatherly St	Ruyterwacht	10	CC 44
Weaver Bird Ave	Dennedal	51	CY 29
Weaver Cr.	Bridgetown	19	CJ 41
Weavers End	Kommetjie	78	DM 14
Weber Cr.	Penlyn Est.	30	CO 40
Webster Cl.	The Vines	39	CU 30
Wedge Rd	Fairways	41	CT 36
Wegner Ave	Ottery East	42	CT 39
Weimar Rd	Churchill	11	CA 48
Weimar St	Glenlily	11	CA 48
Weir Rd	Lansdowne	30	CP 39
Welbeloond Ave	Nova Constantia	50	CW 27
Welbevind Way	Hout Bay	35	CT 18
Welby Rd	Surrey Est.	31	CN 43
Welcome La.	Kensington	8	CC 38
Welegemeend	Pinelands	18	CF 39
Welgelee Rd	Fir Grove	51	CX 28
Welgelegen Ave	High Constantia	38	CU 26
Welgelegen Ave	Strandfontein	68	DB 45
Welgelegen Rd	Mowbray	16	CH 33
Welgemeend St	Gardens	13	CF 24
Welkom Rd	Plumstead	52	CV 33
Well Rd	Hout Bay	36	CT 19
Wellesley St	Factreton	8	CB 39
Wellington Ave	Wynberg	40	CS 32
Wellington Rd	Wynberg	40	CR 33
Wellington St	Vasco Est.	10	CA 45
Welmar Rd	Pinati	30	CO 40
Weltevreden Ave	Rondebosch	28	CL 34
Weltevreden Dr.	The Vines	40	CU 31
Weltevreden Rd	Pinelands	18	CF 39
Weltevreden Rd	Schaap Kraal	45	CU 47
Weltevreden St	Gardens	13	CF 24
Welton St	Lavender Hill	65	DB 35
Welwyn Ave	Pinelands	8	CE 39
Wembley Ave	Plumstead	40	CU 33
Wembley Cl.	Weltevreden Valley	45	CU 48
Wembley Dr.	Weltevreden Valley	45	CU 48
Wembley Rd	Gardens	14	CF 26
Wembley Way	Matroosfontein	21	CG 48
Wemyss St	Brooklyn	7	CA 35
Wendy Rd	Heathfield	52	CY 33
Wenlock Rd	Newlands	28	CM 32
Wens Way	Belthorn Est.	30	CN 40
Wentzel Rd	Steenberg	64	DB 33
Wepener St	Plumstead	41	CU 35
Werde St	Flintdale Est.	53	CV 35
Werk St	Ndabeni	7	CE 35
Weskrom Rd	Claremont	29	CN 36
Wesley	Bergvliet	51	CW 30
Wesley Mabuza St	Nyanga	33	CP 48
Wesley Rd	Sunnydale	72	DK 21
Wesley St	Cape Town Central	14	CF 26
Wesley St	Claremont	28	CO 33
Wesley St	Gardens	14	CF 26
Wesley St	Observatory	16	CF 32
Wessel Cir.	Montana	21	CK 48
Wessel Cr.	Retreat	52	CY 33
Wessels	Greenpoint	4	CC 25
Wessels Rd	Kenilworth	28	CP 34
Wessex Rd	Paarden Eiland	6	CD 32
West Cl.	Salberau	11	CE 47
West Flower Cl.	Montagu's Gift	42	CU 38
West Flower Cl.	Montagu's Gift	42	CU 37
West Link	Athlone	18	CK 38
West Quay Rd	Foreshore	4	CB 26
West Rd	Grassy Pk	53	CX 36
West St	Cape Town Central	4	CC 26
Westbrooke Rd	Athlone	30	CL 39
Westbury Circus	Wynberg	41	CR 34
Westbury Rd	Muizenberg	76	DF 33
Westbury Rd	Rondebosch	17	CK 35
Westerford Rd	Rondebosch	28	CL 32
Westerford Way	Hout Bay	35	CU 16
Western Blvd	Greenpoint	3	CB 24
Westfort Rd	Hout Bay	46	CX 15
Westfort St	Woodstock	15	CG 30
Westgate St	Observatory	16	CG 32
Westlake Ave	Westlake	63	DD 30
Westlake Dr.	Westlake Est.	63	DC 29
Westminister Rd	Woodstock	6	CE 32
Westminster Rd	Lansdowne	42	CQ 39
Westminster Rd	Noordhoek Manor Retirement Village	73	DG 23
Westminster Rd	Noordhoek Manor Retirement Village	73	DJ 24
Westmore Rd	Gardens	13	CG 23
Westoe Rd	Observatory	16	CG 33
Westridge Cir.	Sweet Valley	51	CX 29
Westridge Cl.	Sweet Valley	51	CY 29
Wetton Rd	Kenilworth	40	CQ 33
Wetton Rd	Wetton	42	CQ 38
Wetton Rd	Wynberg	41	CQ 34
Wetton Rd	Youngsfield	41	CQ 36
Wetwyn Rd	Ottery	42	CQ 38
Wexford Rd	Vredehoek	14	CG 27
Weyburn Rd	Lotus River	54	CV 39
Weymouth Rd	Observatory	16	CG 33
Wharf St	Cape Town Central	4	CC 27
Wheatfield Rd	Belthorn Est.	30	CN 39
Wheelan St	Newlands	27	CM 31
Wherry Rd	Muizenberg	76	DF 33
Whimbrell Way	Pelikan Pk	55	CX 41
Whippet	Strandfontein	68	DA 46
Whippet Cl.	Strandfontein	68	DA 46
Whippet Cl.	Strandfontein	68	DE 45
Whitby Rd	Plumstead	40	CS 32
White Rd	Retreat Ind. Area	52	CZ 32
White Rd	Rondebosch	28	CL 33
White St	Plumstead	40	CU 33
Whitehouse Way	Epping Forest	21	CF 47
Whitford St	Tamboerskloof	3	CE 24
Whittlers Way	Hout Bay	35	CT 18
Whytes Way	Simon's Town	83	DP 27
Wicht Cr.	District Six	4	CE 27
Wicht St	Lavender Hill	65	DA 35
Wicht St	Richmond	11	CB 48
Wickboom La.	Simon's Town	89	DU 28
Wicklow Rd	Plumstead	40	CT 32
Wicklow Rd	Royal Cape	41	CS 36
Wiener Rd	Newlands	28	CM 32
Wiener St	Vasco Est.	11	CA 46
Wiersma Rd	Rondebosch	16	CK 33
Wigtown Rd	Greenpoint	3	CB 24
Wildebees Rd	Lotus River	55	CW 40
Wilderness Rd	Claremont	28	CO 33
Wildevoëlvlei Rd	Imhoff's Gift	80	DL 18
Wilfred St	Simon's Town	88	DU 27
Wilge Rd	Bishop Lavis	21	CH 48
Wilge Rd	Claremont	29	CO 35
Wilger Sq.	Bridgetown	19	CJ 41
Wilhelmina St	Rondebosch	16	CK 33
Wilhelmus Rd	Surrey Est.	31	CN 43
Wilkinson St	Gardens	14	CF 25
Wilkinson St	Newlands	28	CM 32
Wilkshire St	Belgravia	30	CL 40
Willesden Rd	Camps Bay	12	CJ 20
Willet Cr.	Pelikan Pk	54	CY 37
William Arendse Rd	Penlyn Est.	30	CO 40
William Frederick Rd	Bergvliet	51	CW 30
William Mason St	Ysterplaat	7	CA 36
William Rd	Observatory	16	CG 33
William Rd	Penlyn Est.	30	CN 40
William St	Maitland	7	CD 36
William St	Woodstock	5	CE 30
Williams Ave	Grassy Pk	54	CX 39
Willis St	Athlone	30	CM 39
Willis St	Lotus River	54	CW 38
Williston Rd	Knole Pk	43	CU 41
Willoughby Dr.	Chapman's Peak	71	DF 18
Willow Rd	Belle Constantia	51	CW 28
Willow Rd	Lotus River	54	CV 38
Willow Rd	Newlands	27	CN 29

STREET NAME	SUBURB NAME	PG	GRID
Willow Rd	Observatory	17	CG 34
Willow Rd	Parkwood	41	CU 36
Willow Rd	Wetton	42	CQ 39
Willow St	Chapman's Peak	71	DF 17
Willow St	Sunnydale	72	DJ 21
Willow Way	Hout Bay	35	CU 16
Willow Way	Pinelands	18	CG 39
Willow Wk	Parkwood	41	CU 36
Willowbrooke La.	Alphen	39	CS 30
Willowmere Rd	Elfindale	52	CX 33
Wills Rd	Rosebank	16	CK 33
Wilmar St	Lavender Hill	65	DB 35
Wilson Rd	Wynberg	40	CR 33
Wiltshire Cr.	Kirstenhof	63	DB 31
Wiltshire Pl.	Kirstenhof	63	DB 31
Wiltshire Rd	Kirstenhof	63	DE 31
Wimbledon Cr.	Weltevreden Valley.	45	CU 48
Wimple La.	Ottery East	42	CT 39
Wincester Ln.	Westlake Est.	62	DC 28
Winchester Ave	Bishopscourt	26	CO 28
Winchester Ave	Noordhoek Manor		
Retirement Village		73	DG 23
Winchester Cl.	Dreyersdal	51	CZ 30
Winchester Rd	Observatory	16	CG 33
Windburg Ave	Devil's Peak Est.	14	CF 27
Windell Rd	Goodwood Est.	10	CA 44
Windermere Rd	Muizenberg	76	DF 34
Windhover St	Kirstenhof	63	DA 31
Windsor Cl.	Noordhoek Manor		
Retirement Village		73	DG 23
Windsor Cl.	Ottery East	42	CT 39
Windsor La.	Dennedal	51	CZ 29
Windsor Park Ave	Elfindale	53	CX 34
Windsor Pl.	Ruyterwacht	11	CD 46
Windsor Rd	Dieprivier	52	CV 32
Windsor Rd	Dreyersdal	51	CZ 30
Windsor Rd	Kalk Bay	75	DK 30
Windsor Rd	Lansdowne	29	CO 37
Windsor Rd	Plumstead	40	CS 32
Wingerd Rd	Nova Constantia	50	CW 27
Wingfield	Factreton	9	CC 40
Winkle Way	Clovelly	74	DK 28
Winnipeg Rd	Coniston Pk	64	DB 34
Winstonia Rd	Sea Point	3	CC 22
Winstonia Rd	Sea Point	3	CD 23
Winter Cl.	Montagu's Gift	42	CU 39
Winter Cr.	Surrey Est.	31	CM 43
Winterberg Rd	Heideveld	32	CL 45
Winterberg Rd	Lavender Hill East	65	DC 37
Winterberg Rd	Lavender Hill East	65	DD 37
Winterswynd Way	Bishopscourt	27	CO 29
Wireless Rd	Kommetjie	78	DL 14
Wisbeach Rd	Sea Point	3	CC 22
Wistaria Ave	Pinelands	18	CH 39
Wisteria Cl.	Newlands	28	CM 32
Witberg Rd	Heideveld	32	CL 45
Withycombe Cl.	Barbarossa	39	CT 30
Witneys La.	Newlands	28	CL 32
Witsenberg Rd	Lavender Hill East	65	DC 37
Witteboomen Rd	Silverhurst	38	CS 27
Wodehouse Cr.	The Vines	40	CU 31
Wodin Rd	Newlands	28	CN 32
Wolborough Rd	Kenilworth	28	CP 32
Wolf Power Cl.	Crofters Valley	72	DH 21
Wolfberg Rd	Heideveld	20	CK 44
Wolfe St	Wynberg	40	CR 32
Wolga	Bishop Lavis	21	CH 47
Wolmarans St	Flintdale Est.	41	CU 36
Wolmunster St	Rosebank	16	CJ 33
Wolraad Rd	Maitland	9	CC 40
Wolsey Rd	Lansdowne	29	CN 36
Wood Cl.	Capri	80	DL 20
Wood Cl.	San Michel	72	DF 21
Wood Rd	Capri	80	DL 20

STREET NAME	SUBURB NAME	PG	GRID
Wood Rd	Hout Bay	47	CW 17
Wood Rd	Ottery	42	CS 37
Wood Rd	Rondebosch	29	CL 36
Wood Way	Simon's Town	82	DO 25
Woodbine Rd	Rondebosch	26	CK 32
Woodburn Cr.	Gardens	13	CG 24
Woodbury Ave	Ottery East	42	CT 39
Woodbury Cl.	Lansdowne	29	CP 37
Woodbury La.	Epping Forest	21	CF 48
Woodbury Rd	Lansdowne	29	CO 37
Woodcutters Cl.	Hout Bay	35	CT 18
Wooddale Rd	Ottery East	42	CT 39
Woodford Ave	Camps Bay	12	CJ 21
Woodford Rd	Epping Forest	21	CF 48
Woodford Rd	Epping Forest	21	CH 47
Woodgate Rd	Plumstead	41	CT 34
Woodhead Cl.	Camps Bay	13	CJ 22
Woodlands	Barbarossa	40	CT 31
Woodlands	Bergvliet	52	CX 31
Woodlands Cl.	Pinelands	17	CG 36
Woodlands Rd	Ottery	42	CR 38
Woodlands Rd	Ottery East	42	CT 39
Woodlands Rd	Rondebosch	17	CK 34
Woodlands Rd	Woodstock	5	CE 29
Woodley Rd	Plumstead	41	CT 34
Woodpecker	Fish Hoek	74	DK 26
Woodpecker	Seawinds	65	DB 35
Woodpecker Cl.	Ottery	43	CR 40
Woodpecker Cl.	Ottery	43	CT 41
Woodrow Way	Pelikan Pk	54	CY 38
Woodroyd La.	Rondebosch	16	CK 32
Woodside Cl.	Rondebosch	29	CL 36
Woodside Dr.	Pinelands	18	CF 37
Woodside Rd	Lansdowne	30	CP 38
Woodside Rd	Ottery	42	CR 38
Woodside Rd	Tamboerskloof	3	CE 24
Woodville Rd	Flintdale Est.	52	CW 33
Woodville Rd	Lotus River	54	CV 39
Woodward Cl.	Ocean View	79	DN 17
Woodward Cl.	Ocean View	79	DP 17
Woodwind Cir.	Retreat	64	DA 34
Woody Pl.	Oudekraal	24	CM 20
Woolmore St	Hazendal	18	CJ 38
Woolsack Dr.	Rondebosch	16	CJ 33
Woolsack Dr.	Rosebank	16	CJ 33
Worcester Cl.	Norwood	11	CD 48
Worcester Rd	Claremont	28	CO 33
Worcester Rd	Sea Point	2	CC 21
Worcester Rd	Woodstock	15	CF 29
Worcester St	Hout Bay	47	CV 16
Wormwood La.	Woodstock	15	CF 30
Wraysbury Cl.	Claremont	28	CM 33
Wren Cl.	Montagu's Gift	42	CU 37
Wren St	Brooklyn	7	CB 35
Wren Way	Meadowridge	52	CW 31
Wrensch Rd	Observatory	16	CG 33
Wright St	Woodstock	5	CE 29
Wurzburg Ave	Lansdowne	29	CO 36
Wycombe Ave	Rust-en-vrede	39	CS 29
Wye La.	Manenberg	44	CQ 45
Wye Rd	Manenberg	44	CQ 45
Wye Rd	Schaap Kraal	44	CQ 45
Wyecroft Rd	Observatory	16	CG 33
Wyehill Cl.	Retreat	52	CZ 33
Wyehill Way	Retreat	52	CZ 32
Wynand Rd	Muizenberg Nth	64	DE 32
Wyndover Rd	Claremont	29	CM 35
Wyngaard Link	Ocean View	79	DN 17
Wyngaard Link	Ocean View	79	DP 17
Wynn Rd	Goodwood Est.	10	CA 44
Wynsam Sq.	Flintdale Est.	53	CW 35
Wynyard St	Oranjezicht	14	CG 25
Wytham Ave	Kenilworth	28	CP 32
Wythenshawe Ave	Pinelands	8	CE 39

X

STREET NAME	SUBURB NAME	PG	GRID
Xyris Way	Matroosfontein	21	CG 48

Y

STREET NAME	SUBURB NAME	PG	GRID
Yacht	Strandfontein	69	DA 48
Yanta Ave	Nyanga	33	CP 48
Yardley Cl.	Epping Forest	21	CF 48
Yarmouth Rd	Muizenberg	76	DF 33
Yarrowdale	Pinelands	18	CF 39
Yataghan La.	Crofters Valley	72	DG 21
Yawl Rd	Pelikan Pk	54	CX 39
Yekiso Cl.	Langa	19	CJ 42
Yellowstone Cr.	Coniston Pk	64	DC 34
Yellowvood Cr.	Dieprivier	52	CV 32
Yellowwood Dr.	Farmsteads	60	DE 20
Yellowwood Rd	Bonteheuwel	20	CJ 44
Yeoville Rd	Vredehoek	14	CG 26
Yew St	Salt River	16	CF 31
Yoksal Rd	Lavender Hill	65	DA 35
York	Muizenberg	76	DG 33
York Cl.	Hout Bay Harbour	46	CY 15
York Cr.	Ottery	43	CS 40
York La.	Rosebank	17	CJ 34
York La.	Greenpoint	3	CB 24
York Rd	Lansdowne	42	CQ 39
York Rd	Ottery	43	CR 40
York Rd	Rosebank	16	CJ 33
York Rd	Wynberg	40	CR 33
York St	Claremont	28	CO 34
York St	Manenberg	32	CP 45
York St	Woodstock	6	CE 31
York Way	Matroosfontein	21	CG 48
Yorkshire Cl.	Kirstenhof	63	DB 31
Yorkshire Cl.	Kirstenhof	63	DB 31
Yorkshire St	Lansdowne	42	CQ 38
Yorkton Rd	Grassy Pk	53	CY 36
Young La.	Tokai	63	DA 29
Young La.	Wynberg	40	CR 32
Yselstein St	Glencairn Hgts	83	DO 27
Ysterplaat St	Brooklyn	7	CC 36
Yubel Rd	Retreat	53	CZ 34
Yudelmans La.	Plumstead	40	CT 33
Yusuf Dr.	Schotsche Kloof	4	CD 25
Yusuf Gool Blvd.	Gatesville	31	CL 42
Yusuf Rd	Welcome	20	CK 44
Yvonne Rd	Plumstead	41	CT 34

Z

STREET NAME	SUBURB NAME	PG	GRID
Z.Memani Rd	Nyanga	33	CO 48
Zak St	Schaap Kraal	44	CQ 45
Zambesi Ave	Belthorn Est.	30	CN 39
Zandvliet	Kirstenhof	63	DB 30
Zandwijk Cl.	Sunnydale	81	DL 22
Zarobi Rd	Lotus River	54	CV 39
Zee Ct	Marina Da Gama	64	DC 33
Zeekoe Rd	Lotus River	54	CV 39
Zeekoevlei Rd	Pelikan Pk	55	CY 41
Zeekoevlei Rd	Pelikan Pk	66	DB 40
Zelda St	Elsies River Ind.	11	CB 48
Zenith Rd	Vanguard	31	CL 43
Zenith Way	Matroosfontein	21	CG 48
Zephania Mothopeng			
	Weltevreden Valley	45	CS 48

Index to Street Names

STREET NAME	SUBURB NAME	PG	GRID	STREET NAME	SUBURB NAME	PG	GRID	STREET NAME	SUBURB NAME	PG	GRID
Zinnia Rd	Silvertown	19	CK 41	Zomerlust Rd	Bergvliet	52	CY 31	Zwaans Rd	Retreat	52	CZ 32
Zion Rd	Claremont	27	CO 31	Zonnebloem St	Athlone	18	CK 37	Zwaanswyk Rd	Steenberg	50	CZ 27
Zircon Cir.	Sheraton Pk	64	DB 33	Zorba Rd	Pinati	30	CP 40	Zwartkops Rd	Schaap Kraal	44	CQ 45
Zither St	Steenberg	64	DA 34	Zoutendyk Steps	Fish Hoek	83	DM 27	Zwelonke Ave	Nyanga	33	CO 48
Zodiac Rd	Ocean View	79	DN 16	Zoutman Rd	Hout Bay	46	CW 15	Zwelonke Ave	Nyanga	33	CM 48
Zomerlust Ave	Huis-in-bos	51	CV 28	Zuurberg Rd	Heideveld	32	CL 44				

Index to Suburb Names

SUBURB NAME	PG	GRID	SUBURB NAME	PG	GRID	SUBURB NAME	PG	GRID
A			Dennedal	51	CY 29	Heathfield	52	CX 33
			Devil's Peak Estate	14	CF 27	Heideveld	32	CL 45
Airlie	51	CW 28	Dieprivier	52	CV 32	High Constantia	38	CU 26
Airport Industria	33	CL 49	District Six	15	CF 28	Highlands Estate	44	CS 44
Alphen	39	CR 30	Doornhoogte	31	CM 41	Hohenort	39	CQ 28
Athlone	30	CL 38	Dreyersdal	52	CZ 31	Hope of Constantia	50	CV 26
Avon	11	CD 47				Hout Bay	35	CU 17
			E			Hout Bay Harbour	46	CY 15
B						Huis-in-bos	50	CV 27
			Eagle's Nest	37	CT 24			
Bakoven	12	CK 20	Edward	43	CT 40	**I**		
Bantry Bay	2	CE 20	Elfindale	53	CW 34			
Barbarossa	40	CT 31	Elnor	21	CF 48	Imhoff's Gift	79	DL 17
Bayview Heights	88	DS 26	Elsies River Industrial	11	CC 47			
Bel Ombre	38	CR 27	Epping Forest	21	CF 48	**K**		
Belgravia	30	CM 40	Epping Industrial	20	CF 44			
Belle Constantia	51	CV 29				Kalk Bay	75	DK 29
Belthorn Estate	30	CN 39	**F**			Kenilworth	28	CP 33
Belvedere (Noordhoek)	72	DF 22				Kenilworth Park	29	CP 35
Bergvliet	51	CX 30	Factreton	9	CB 40	Kensington	8	CC 38
Bishopscourt	27	CO 29	Fairie Knowe	72	DK 21	Kewtown	18	CJ 39
Bonteheuwel	20	CH 45	Fairways	41	CT 36	King Edward Rest	88	DU 27
Bridgetown	19	CK 42	Fir Grove	51	CX 28	Kirstenhof	63	DB 30
Brooklyn	7	CB 35	Fish Hoek	82	DL 26	Klein Constantia	50	CV 25
Browns Farm	45	CR 48	Flintdale Estate	53	CW 35	Klein Wassenaar	63	DC 31
			Foreshore	5	CC 28	Knole Park	43	CU 41
C			Forest Glade	50	CZ 27	Kommetjie	79	DL 15
			Fragmoor Estate	63	DC 31			
Cafda Village	53	CZ 35	Fresnaye	2	CE 21	**L**		
Camps Bay	12	CJ 20						
Cape Town Central	4	CD 26	**G**			Lakeside	63	DD 31
Capri	81	DL 21				Langa	19	CH 42
Capricorn	65	DD 36	Gardens	13	CF 24	Lansdowne	30	CP 38
Chapman's Peak	71	DF 18	Gatesville	31	CM 42	Lavender Hill	65	DA 35
Charlesville	21	CK 46	Gaylands	39	CU 29	Lavender Hill East	65	DB 36
Churchill	11	CA 48	Glen Alpine	37	CS 24	Lekkerwater	72	DK 20
Claremont	28	CN 33	Glen Ridge	83	DO 28	Leonsdale	11	CD 48
Clifton	12	CG 20	Glencairn Heights	83	DO 27	Lotus River	54	CW 39
Clovelly	74	DJ 27	Goodwood Estate	10	CA 44			
Clunie	50	CX 25	Grassy Park	54	CX 37	**M**		
Coniston Park	64	DB 34	Greenpoint	3	CB 24			
Constantia Vale	39	CT 28	Grootbosch	37	CU 24	Maitland	8	CD 38
Constantia Village	39	CT 29	Guguletu	33	CN 47	Maitland Garden Village	17	CF 35
Crawford	30	CN 38				Manenberg	32	CO 45
			H			Marina Da Gama	64	DD 33
D						Marine Oil Refinery	88	DQ 27
			Hanover Park	31	CP 41	Masiphumelele	72	DK 20
Da Gama Park	81	DP 23	Harbour Heights	89	DU 29	Matroosfontein	21	CG 47
			Hazendal	18	CJ 38	Meadowridge	52	CV 31

Index to Suburb Names

SUBURB NAME	PG	GRID
Meadowsteads	72	DG 20
Misty Cliffs	86	DT 19
Montagu's Gift	42	CU 39
Montana/Durrheim	21	CK 48
Mouille Point	3	CA 23
Mowbray	17	CH 35
Muizenberg	76	DF 33
Muizenberg North	64	DD 32

N

SUBURB NAME	PG	GRID
Ndabeni	7	CE 36
Newfields	31	CN 42
Noordhaven	72	DF 21
Noordhoek Manor Retirement Village	73	DG 23
Norwood	11	CE 48
Nova Constantia	50	CW 27
Nyanga	33	CP 49

O

SUBURB NAME	PG	GRID
Observatory	16	CG 33
Ocean View	79	DN 16
Oranjezicht	14	CG 25
Ottery	42	CS 38
Ottery	43	CR 40
Ottery East	42	CT 39

P

SUBURB NAME	PG	GRID
Paarden Eiland	6	CC 33
Pagasvlei	38	CU 27
Parkwood	53	CV 36
Peers Hill	74	DK 26
Pelikan Park	54	CZ 38
Pelikan Park	55	CZ 41
Pelikan Park	67	DC 43
Penlyn Estate	31	CN 41
Phumlani	55	CW 41
Pinati	30	CP 40
Pine Haven	88	DS 25
Pinelands	18	CF 38
Plumstead	40	CT 33

SUBURB NAME	PG	GRID
Pollsmoor	63	DA 29
Porter Estate	50	CY 26
Primrose Park	31	CN 43

R

SUBURB NAME	PG	GRID
Retreat	53	CZ 34
Retreat Industrial Area	64	DA 32
Richmond	11	CB 48
Richmond Estate	11	CA 47
Riverton	11	CC 46
Rondebosch	28	CL 34
Rondebosch East	29	CM 37
Rosebank	17	CJ 34
Royal Cape	41	CS 36
Rust-en-vrede	39	CS 29
Ruyterwacht	10	CD 45

S

SUBURB NAME	PG	GRID
Salberau	11	CE 47
Salt River	16	CF 31
San Michel	72	DF 22
Sand Industria	31	CP 43
Schaap Kraal	56	CV 45
Schotsche Kloof	4	CD 25
Sea Point	3	CC 22
Seawinds	65	DB 35
Sheraton Park	64	DB 33
Sillery	39	CU 28
Silverglade	73	DK 25
Silverhurst	39	CT 28
Silvermine Village	72	DG 22
Silvertown	19	CK 41
Simon's Town	88	DS 26
Simonskloof	89	DU 28
St James	75	DJ 31
Steenberg	64	DB 33
Streenberg	62	DB 26
Sun Valley	73	DK 23
Sunnydale	72	DK 21
Surrey Estate	31	CM 43
Sweet Valley	51	CX 29
Sybrand Park	18	CJ 37

T

SUBURB NAME	PG	GRID
Tamboerskloof	3	CE 23
The Lakes	72	DJ 20
The Range	21	CF 47
The Vines	40	CU 31
Thornton	9	CD 42
Three Anchor Bay	3	CB 23
Tokai	51	CZ 29
Townsend Estate	10	CB 43

V

SUBURB NAME	PG	GRID
Valhalla	11	CD 46
Valhalla Park	21	CJ 47
Vanguard	31	CL 43
Vasco Estate	11	CA 44
Victoria	88	DU 27
Vredehoek	14	CG 26

W

SUBURB NAME	PG	GRID
Welcome	20	CK 44
Welcome Glen	82	DO 24
Westlake Estate	62	DB 28
Wetton	42	CR 39
Wingfield	9	CB 41
Witteboomen	38	CS 25
Woodlands	82	DP 25
Woodstock	6	CE 31
Wynberg	40	CR 32

Y

SUBURB NAME	PG	GRID
Youngsfield	41	CR 36
Ysterplaat	8	CA 37

Z

SUBURB NAME	PG	GRID
Zonnebloem (District Six)	15	CF 28

Index to Community Services

NAME	PG	GRID

Airports

NAME	PG	GRID
Ysterplaat Aerodrome	7	CB 36

Courts of Law

NAME	PG	GRID
Athlone Magistrates Court	18	CK 38
Cape Town High Court	4	CE 26
Cape Town Magistrates Court	4	CE 26
Goodwood Magistrates Court	11	CB 46
Simon's Town Magistrates Court	89	DU 28
Valhalla Park Magistrates Court	21	CH 47
Wynberg Magistrates Court	40	CQ 32

Emergency Services

NAME	PG	GRID
Brooklyn Fire Station 021 510 5180	7	CC 34
Cape Town Central Fire Station 021 465 1033	14	CF 27
Cape Town Traffic Department 021 4068700	4	CC 25
Constantia Fire Station 021 794 3430	39	CT 29
Elsies River Traffic Department 021 5921158	11	CC 47
Epping Fire Station 021 534 1387	10	CE 43
Fish Hoek Fire Station 021 782 2222	83	DL 27
Fish Hoek Traffic Department 021 782 1112	83	DL 27
Guguletu Fire Station 021 633 2533	45	CQ 46
Lakeside Fire Station 021 788 1843	63	DD 31

Index to Community Services

NAME	PG	GRID
Ottery Fire Station ... 021 534 1387..	43	CS 40
Ottery Hillside Traffic Department		
.... 021 799 5100	42	CQ 38
Ottery Traffic Department		
.... 021 937 1211	43	CS 40
Salt River Fire Station		
.... 021 447 4747	16	CF 32
Sea Point Fire Station		
.... 021 434 0030	2	CD 21
Simon's Town Fire Station		
.... 021 786 1611	88	DS 26
Wynberg Fire Station		
.... 021 797 6108	41	CR 34

Hospitals & Clinics

NAME	PG	GRID
2 Military Hospital .. 021 799 6911 ..	40	CQ 31
Albow Gardens Municipal Clinic		
.... 021 510 6326	7	CA 36
Alexandra Care and Rehabilitation		
Centre 021 511 2141	7	CE 35
Alphen Municipal Clinic		
.... 021 794 5906	39	CT 32
Bontehewel CHC .. 021 694 5559 ..	20	CH 45
Booth Memorial Hospital		
.... 021 465 4846	14	CF 25
Broad Rd Surgical Clinic		
.... 021 762 0223	40	CQ 33
Brooklyn Chest Hospital		
.... 021 511 2221	7	CA 35
Browns Farm CHC .. 021 386 3663 ..	45	CR 48
Bruce Rd Municipal Clinic		
.... 021 703 3603	42	CU 39
Cape Town Medi-Clinic		
.... 021 464 5500	13	CF 24
Chapel St Municipal Clinic		
.... 021 465 2793	5	CE 29
Chris Barnard Memorial Hospital		
.... 021 480 6111	4	CD 26
Cape Town Civic Centre CHC		
.... 021 400 3980	4	CD 25
Claremont Hospital .. 021 674 4050..	28	CO 32
Claremont Municipal Clinic		
.... 021 671 7102	28	CN 32
Conradie and Karl Bremer Hospital ..		
.... 021 531 1311	9	CD 41
Constantiaberg Medi-Clinic		
.... 021 799 2911	40	CU 32
Crescent Clinic . 021 762 7666	28	CO 33
D.P.Marais SANTA Centre		
.... 021 712 7491	52	CZ 32
Diep River Municipal Clinic		
.... 021 712 9598	52	CV 32
Dirkie Uys CHC .. 021 592 5207	10	CB 44
Dr Abdurahman CHC ..021 617 9071..	19	CK 40
Elsies River CHC ... 021 931 0211 ...	11	CE 48
Factreton CHC .. 021 593 9858	8	CB 39
False Bay Hospital . 021 782 1121 ..	73	DK 25
Fish Hoek Municipal Clinic		
.... 021 782 3847	83	DL 27
G.F.Jooste Hospital .. 021 690 1000..	32	CO 46
Good Hope CHC .. 021 511 8606	7	CB 34
Goodwood CHC ... 021 592 5207	11	CB 46
Grassy Park CHC ... 021 705 3814 ..	53	CW 36
Grassy Park Municipal Clinic		
.... 021 705 0131	54	CX 37
Green Point Clinic ... 021 402 6911 ..	4	CB 25
Groote Schuur Hospital		
.... 021 404 9111	16	CG 32
Guguletu CHC ... 021 637 9075	33	CO 47
Guguletu Municipal Clinic		
.... 021 637 9075	33	CO 47

NAME	PG	GRID
Hanover Park CHC ..021 692 1240 ..	31	CP 41
Hanover Park Municipal Clinic		
.... 021 692 1250	31	CP 41
Hazendal CHC ... 021 696 9920	18	CJ 38
Heideveld CHC ... 021 637 8036	32	CL 44
Heideveld Municipal Clinic		
.... 021 637 8033	32	CL 45
Honeyside Clinic .. 021 697 1922 ...	30	CN 39
Hout Bay (Main Rd) Imizamo Yethu		
Municipal Clinic ... 021 790 3570 ..	35	CU 17
Kenilworth MediCity ..021 889 6902..	28	CP 33
Kenilworth Medicross ..021 683 5867..	28	CO 34
Kensington CHC ... 021 593 1150 ...	8	CC 38
Kingsbury Hospital ..021 670 4000 ..	28	CO 33
Klip Rd Municipal Clinic		
.... 021 705 1947	54	CV 38
Lady Michaelis Orthopaedic Hospital		
.... 021 797 8171	40	CT 32
Langa CHC ... 021 694 1730	19	CG 40
Langa Municipal Clinic		
.... 021 694 1740	19	CH 41
Lansdowne CHC ... 021 797 4217 ...	30	CP 38
Lavender Hill Municipal Clinic		
.... 021 701 9005	65	DA 35
Leonsdale Municipal Clinic		
.... 021 386 3663	11	CD 48
Libertas Hospital ... 021 370 1111 ...	10	CC 43
Lotus River CHC ... 021 703 3131 ...	42	CU 38
Lotus River Municipal Clinic		
.... 021 703 6990	55	CV 41
Maitland CHC ... 021 551 6272	17	CF 35
Maitland Municipal Clinic		
.... 021 511 2523	7	CD 36
Manenberg CHC ... 021 69 10048 ...	32	CO 45
Masincedane Municipal Clinic		
.... 021 386 0725	33	CO 48
Masiphumelele CHC ..021 785 3938..	72	DK 20
Matroosfontein Municipal Clinic		
.... 021 931 0211	21	CG 47
Medical Centre Gatesville		
.... 021 637 8100	31	CL 42
Mowbray Maternity Hospital		
.... 021 685 3026	17	CH 34
Muizenberg Municipal Clinic		
.... 021 788 8940	76	DG 33
Netreg CHC ... 021 694 1733	21	CH 46
Newfields CHC ... 021 692 1307	31	CO 41
Newlands Surgical Clinic		
.... 021 683 1220	28	CM 32
Nyanga CHC ... 021 386 3663	33	CP 49
Ocean View CHC ... 021 783 1688 ...	79	DN 16
Parkwood Clinic ... 021 705 0103 ...	41	CU 36
Pelikan Park Satellite Clinic		
.... 021 396 2343	55	CX 40
Phillipi Municipal Clinic		
.... 021 692 1161	44	CQ 43
Pinelands Satellite Clinic		
.... 021 930 0110	18	CF 37
Princess Alice Orthopaedic Hospital ..		
.... 021 930 0110	16	CG 31
Red Cross Children's Hospital		
.... 021 658 5111	17	CJ 35
Red Hill Satellite Clinic		
.... 021 930 0110	87	DU 24
Retreat CHC ... 021 712 0310	53	CZ 34
Robbie Nurrock CHC ..021 931 0211..	4	CE 26
Ruyterwacht CHC ..021 592 5207 ..	10	CD 45
Sarah Fox Children's Hospital		
.... 021 637 1302	31	CL 42
Seawind Municipal Clinic		
.... 021 701 1348	65	DB 36
Silvertown CHC ... 021 637 1293 ...	31	CL 42
Simon's Town Satellite Clinic		
.... 021 786 1555	89	DU 28

NAME	PG	GRID
Somerset Hospital .. 021 402 6911 .	4	CB 25
Southern Cross Netcare Hospital		
.... 021 862 3176	40	CR 33
Spencer Rd Municipal Clinic		
.... 021 393 9031	6	CE 32
Strandfontein CHC .. 021 393 6226 ..	68	DB 45
Sun Valley Satellite Clinic		
.... 021 931 0211	72	DJ 22
Tokai Medicross ... 021 715 7063 ...	51	CZ 30
UCT Medical Centre ..021 930 0110..	16	CG 32
Valhalla CHC ... 021 934 0101	21	CJ 47
Valkenberg Hospital ..021 440 3111..	17	CG 35
Vanguard CHC (24hr Cas.)		
.... 021 694 5540/1 ...	20	CH 43
Victoria Hospital ... 021 799 1111 ...	40	CS 31
Vincent Pallotti Hospital		
.... 021 506 5111	17	CG 36
Vuyani CHC 021 637 9016	33	CM 47
Westlake Municipal Clinic		
.... 021 930 0110	62	DB 28
Woodstock Hospital ..021 460 9100..	15	CF 30
Wynberg Municipal Clinic		
.... 021 797 5190	40	CQ 33

Municipal Offices

NAME	PG	GRID
Cape Town Civic Centre	4	CD 27
Fish Hoek Civic Centre	83	DL 27
Gatesville Civic Centre	40	CT 33
Goodwood Civic Centre	10	CB 44
Kensington Civic Centre	8	CB 39
Pinelands Municipal Offices	18	CG 37
Plumstead Municipal Offices	31	CL 42
Schotche Kloof Civic Centre	4	CD 26
Simon's Town Municipal Offices	89	DU 28
Three Anchor Bay Civic Centre	3	CB 23

Government Offices

NAME	PG	GRID
Dept. of Home Affairs	4	CE 26
Dept. of Labour	4	CE 26
House of Parliament	4	CE 26
Provincial Administration		
Western Cape	4	CD 26
S.A. Revenue Services	4	CE 26
State Archives	14	CF 26

Police Stations

NAME	PG	GRID
Athlone 021 697 1120	18	CK 38
Bishop Lavis 021 934 1006	21	CH 47
Camps Bay 021 438 8418	12	CJ 20
Cape Town Railway Station Police ..		
.... 021 419 4871	4	CD 27
Cape Town (Central) ..021 467 8000..	4	CE 26
Claremont 021 683 4936	28	CN 33
Diep River 021 712 6448	52	CV 32
Elsiesrivier 021 933 0300	11	CE 46
Fish Hoek 021 782 6333	83	DL 28
Goodwood 021 592 2171	11	CB 46
Grassy Park 021 705 2599	53	CX 36
Guguletu 021 637 5945	32	CM 46
Hout Bay 021 701 1390	47	CX 17
Kensington 021 593 1770	8	CB 39
Kirstenhof 021 701 2426	63	DB 31
Langa 021 694 1817	19	CG 41
Lansdowne 021 696 6011	30	CO 38

Index to Community Services

NAME	PG	GRID	NAME	PG	GRID	NAME	PG	GRID
Maitland 021 511 4365	7	CD 35	Constantia	39	CT 29	Mowbray	16	CH 33
Manenberg 021 637 6224	32	CM 45	Crawford	29	CM 37	Muizenberg	76	DG 33
Mowbray 021 689 1304	16	CH 33	Durrheim	21	CK 47	Newlands	28	CM 32
Muizenberg 021 788 5437	76	DG 32	Elsies River	11	CC 47	Nyanga	33	CP 49
Nyanga 021 386 3432	33	CO 49	Eppindust	9	CE 42	Ottery	43	CT 40
Ocean View 021 783 4130	79	DM 15	Fish Hoek	83	DM 27	Paardeneiland	6	CC 32
Phillipi 021 692 1190	44	CQ 43	G.P.O.	4	CD 26	Phillipi	44	CQ 43
Pinelands 021 531 2826	18	CG 37	Gatesville	31	CL 42	Plumstead	40	CT 32
Rondebosch 021 689 9321	16	CK 33	Glosderry	29	CO 35	Retreat	53	CZ 34
Sea Point 021 683 4936	3	CB 23	Goodwood	10	CC 45	Rhine Rd	3	CB 22
Simon's Town ... 021 786 2118	89	DU 28	Grassy Park	54	CX 37	Rhodes Gift	16	CJ 32
Steenberg 021 701 1390	64	DA 34	Green Point	3	CB 24	Roggebaai	4	CC 27
Table Bay Harbour .. 021 419 4871 .	4	CB 26	Gugulethu	32	CO 46	Rondebosch	16	CK 33
Woodstock 021 447 8900	5	CE 30	Hanover Park	31	CP 41	Sea Point	2	CD 21
Wynberg 021 799 1300	40	CQ 32	Hout Bay	47	CW 17	Seesig	79	DN 16
			Howard Place	18	CF 39	Simon's Town	89	DU 28
			Kenilworth	28	CP 33	Southfield	53	CV 35
			Kenwyn	42	CQ 38	Stalplein	4	CE 26
Post Offices			Kloof St	13	CF 24	Strandfontein	68	DB 44
			Kommetjie	78	DM 12	Sun Valley	72	DJ 22
Bergvliet	52	CW 32	Langa	19	CH 41	Surwell	32	CL 45
Bonteheuwel	20	CH 45	Lansdowne	30	CO 38	Tokai	63	DA 31
Caledon Square	4	CE 26	Lavender Hill	64	DB 34	Valyland	82	DL 26
Camps Bay	12	CJ 20	Lotus	54	CW 39	Vlaeberg	4	CE 25
'Cape Mail'	10	CE 44	Maitland	7	CD 35	Waterfront	4	CA 26
Capricorn	65	DD 35	Manenberg	32	CM 45	Woodstock	5	CE 30
Clareinch	28	CO 33	Matroosfontein	11	CE 48	Wynberg	40	CR 33
Claremont	28	CN 32	Mill Street	14	CF 26	Ysterplaat	7	CB 35

Index to Education

NAME	PG	GRID	NAME	PG	GRID	NAME	PG	GRID
Primary Schools			Cedar	20	CH 44	Golden Grove	29	CM 36
			Central Park	20	CJ 45	Good Hope Jnr	14	CF 26
			Chapel Street	5	CE 29	Goodwood Park	10	CA 43
Abbotts	28	CO 33	Chinese School	16	CH 33	Grassy Park	53	CX 36
Acacia	54	CV 37	Christian David	64	DB 34	Greenfield Girls' Primary	28	CO 33
Alicedale	18	CK 38	Claremont	28	CN 33	Groenvlei	43	CQ 40
Alpha	15	CF 30	Constantia Primary	39	CU 29	Groote Schuur	28	CL 33
Andile	33	CP 48	Constantia Waldorf	39	CU 28	Grove	28	CN 32
Arcadia	20	CH 45	Cypress	19	CJ 40	H.J.Kroneberg	8	CC 38
Athlone North	18	CK 39	Dagbreek	20	CK 45	Harmonie	64	DA 33
Athwood	30	CP 40	De Vrije Zee	11	CB 46	Hazendal	18	CK 38
Auburn House	40	CQ 33	De Waveren	11	CD 46	Heathfield	52	CW 33
Avonwood	11	CE 48	Delta	53	CZ 35	Helderberg	21	CH 48
Battswood	40	CR 33	Dennegeur Ave	68	DB 45	Heritage College	41	CT 34
Bay Jnr. Primary	74	DK 26	Die Duine	55	CV 41	Herschel Jnr.	28	CO 32
Bay Snr. Primary	75	DK 30	Diocesan College (Bishops)	17	CK 34	Hertzlia	40	CU 31
Belmor	43	CQ 41	Disa	20	CJ 45	Herzlia Jnr	14	CG 26
Belthorn	30	CO 39	Douglas Rd	41	CS 34	Hillside	21	CJ 48
Bergsig	20	CH 44	Dryden Street	16	CF 32	Hillwood	65	DB 35
Bergvliet	52	CX 31	Easter Peak	32	CM 45	Holy Cross Convent	15	CF 29
Blomvlei	31	CP 41	Ederdale	32	CO 45	Huis Vredelus	11	CD 48
Blossom St	31	CL 41	Elnor	21	CF 48	Hyde Park	41	CU 36
Bonga Lower Primary	32	CM 46	Elsbury	21	CG 48	Iketlo	32	CO 46
Boundary	20	CJ 44	Elsies River	11	CD 47	Intshinga	33	CM 47
Bramble Way	20	CG 45	Elswood	11	CC 48	Jan van Riebeeck	3	CE 24
Bridgetown-East	20	CK 43	Esangweni	10	CD 45	John Graham	41	CT 35
Bridgeville	19	CJ 42	Factreton	9	CC 40	John Pama	33	CP 49
Buck Road	55	CW 40	Fairview	54	CW 37	John Wyecliff Christian Primary ...	41	CR 34
Cafda	53	CY 35	Ferndale	42	CT 39	Kalksteenfontein	21	CH 47
Camps Bay	12	CK 20	Fish Hoek	82	DL 26	Kannemeyer	53	CX 36
Camps Bay Prep	12	CJ 20	Floreat	64	DA 34	Kenmere	8	CC 39
Canons Creek	18	CF 38	Garden Village	17	CF 35	Kewtown	18	CJ 39
Cecil Rd	16	CF 32	Garlandale	18	CK 37	Khanyisa Waldorf	40	CT 33

Index to Education

NAME	PG	GRID
Khoza Square	72	DK 20
Kirstenhof	63	DA 31
Kleinberg	79	DN 16
Klipfontein	21	CK 46
Kommetjie	78	DM 13
Koos Sadie	10	CB 45
Kronendal	47	CW 17
Lehlohonolo	33	CM 47
Levana Primary	65	DB 36
Litha Lower Primary	32	CO 46
Llandudno	34	CR 15
Lotusrivier	54	CW 38
Lourier	53	CZ 35
Luzuko	32	CN 46
Lwazi Junior	33	CN 48
Maitland	7	CD 35
Manenberg	32	CN 45
Marine	79	DN 17
Matroosfontein	21	CG 48
Micklefield	29	CL 36
Mimosa	20	CJ 44
Mkhanyiseli	33	CP 49
Mkize Senior	33	CP 47
Modderdam	21	CJ 46
Mokane	19	CH 40
Montagu's Gift	54	CV 38
Montevideo	21	CK 47
Morgenson	30	CO 40
Moshesh	19	CG 41
Mountain Rd	15	CF 30
Mseki Junior	33	CO 47
Muhammadeyah	41	CS 34
Muizenberg	76	DF 33
Muslim Assembly Educare	31	CN 42
Nal'uxulo	45	CS 48
Ned Doman	30	CL 38
Nerina	20	CH 45
Newfields	31	CO 42
Nobantu	33	CP 47
Oakhurst Girls' Primary	28	CL 34
Observatory Junior Primary	16	CG 33
Oranje	7	CD 35
Oranjekloof Moraviese	35	CT 18
Ottery Rd.	41	CR 34
Parkfields	31	CO 42
Parkvale	21	CJ 47
Parkwood	42	CU 37
Parow-Wes	11	CA 48
Paul Greyling	83	DL 28
Pelikan Park	55	CX 41
Perivale	54	CV 39
Pinehurst	19	CF 40
Pinelands	18	CF 37
Pinelands North	8	CE 39
Pioneer	20	CG 44
Plantation	54	CV 38
Plumstead Prep.	41	CU 35
Portavue	31	CN 43
Portia	30	CP 39
Prestwich Street	4	CC 26
Primrose Park	32	CN 44
Prince George	53	CZ 35
Protea	20	CJ 44
Rahmaniyeh	5	CE 29
Range	21	CF 47
Red River	32	CO 45
Reddam House	62	DB 27
Rio Grande	32	CP 45
Riverton	21	CH 47
Rondebosch Boys' Prep	17	CK 34
Rondebosch-Oos	29	CM 37
Rosebank	17	CK 36
Rosemead Central	28	CO 34
Rosewood	21	CJ 46
Ruiterwacht	10	CD 45
Rustenburg Girls' Junior School	16	CK 33
Saambou	32	CN 44
Scorpio Road	79	DO 17
Sea Point	3	CC 23
Sid G. Rule	54	CX 38
Silverstroom	32	CM 45
Simon van der Stel	40	CQ 32
Siviwe Primary	33	CP 47
Sokhanyo	33	CO 47
Songeze Lower Primary	32	CO 46
Sonwabo Primary	45	CO 47
South African College (SACS)	27	CL 31
Southfield	53	CV 35
Spes Bona	18	CJ 38
Square Hill	52	CZ 33
St Agnes Dominican Convent	6	CE 31
St Anne's	41	CU 34
St Anthony's RC Primary	52	CX 33
St Augustine's	40	CS 33
St Clements	54	CW 39
St Columba's	30	CL 38
St James Primary	75	DK 30
St John's RC Primary	8	CB 38
St Joseph's Marist Brother's College	17	CK 34
St Louis RC Primary	19	CG 40
St Mary's	4	CE 26
St Mary's	53	CY 34
St Raphael's	30	CL 38
Star of the Sea Convent	75	DJ 31
Starling	31	CN 41
Steenberg	64	DA 34
Stephen Road	55	CV 40
Strandfontein	68	DB 44
Sullivan	64	DA 34
Summit	30	CP 40
Sun Valley	73	DJ 23
Sunlands	42	CQ 37
Sunnyside	30	CL 39
Surrey	32	CM 44
Sweet Valley	51	CW 30
Talfalah	44	CQ 45
Tamboerskloof	3	CE 24
Thomas Wildschutt Jnr Primary	52	CY 33
Thomas Wildschutt Primary	52	CY 33
Thornton	9	CD 42
Timour Hall	40	CT 32
Turfhall	30	CN 40
Valpark	21	CJ 47
Vanguard	31	CL 43
Voorspoed	31	CP 43
Vrijzee	11	CB 46
Vukukhanye	33	CO 48
Vuyani	32	CP 46
W.D.Hendricks	8	CA 39
Walmer Estate	15	CF 29
Welcome	20	CK 44
Westcott	52	CV 32
Willows	32	CL 46
Windermere	11	CC 39
Windsor Prep	29	CO 37
Windsor Primary	30	CO 38
Wittebome	41	CR 34
Wynberg Boys' Jnr	40	CQ 32
Wynberg Girls' Jnr	40	CQ 32
Xolani Lower Primary	33	CM 48
Yorkweg	30	CP 39
Ysterplaat	7	CC 35
Ysterplaat JP	7	CB 35
Zeekoevlei	55	CW 40
Zerildapark	65	DB 35
Zonnebloem Boys'	15	CF 29
Zwaanswyk	52	CZ 31

Secondary Schools

NAME	PG	GRID
Alexander Sinton	30	CM 39
Alexandra Girls	13	CG 24
American International School of Cape Town	51	CX 28
Arcadia	20	CH 45
Athlone	19	CK 40
Beauvallon	21	CJ 48
Belgravia	30	CM 40
Bergvliet	51	CW 30
Bonteheuwel	20	CH 44
Boston House College	4	CD 26
Bridgetown	19	CK 42
Buren	7	CB 35
Camps Bay	12	CG 20
Cape Town Secondary	14	CF 25
Cathkin	44	CK 44
Cedar House	41	CQ 34
Constantia Boys' High / Seunskool	50	CX 27
Constantia Girls' High / Meisieskool	51	CX 28
Constantia Waldorf	39	CU 28
Crestway	53	CZ 34
Crystal	31	CP 43
De.Ruyter	10	CC 45
Deutsche Schule Cape Town	3	CE 23
Diocesan Col. (Bishops)	17	CK 34
Ellerton	3	CB 23
Elsies River Secondary	11	CD 47
Elswood	11	CC 48
Fairbairn	11	CA 46
Fairmount	54	CV 37
Fezeka	33	CO 47
Filia	11	CA 46
Fish Hoek Middle	74	DK 26
Gardens Commercial School	4	CE 25
Garlandale	18	CK 37
Grassdale	54	CW 38
Grassy Park	54	CX 37
Groote Schuur	28	CM 33
Harold Cressey	14	CF 27
Heathfield	52	CY 32
Heideveld	20	CK 44
Heideveld	32	CL 45
Helderberg	21	CH 48
Herschel	28	CO 32
Herzlia	14	CG 26
Herzlia Weizmann	2	CD 21
Hillcrest	16	CH 33
Houtbaai	46	CY 15
Immaculata	40	CS 33
J.G.Meiring	10	CB 44
Jan van Riebeeck	13	CF 24
Kensington	8	CB 38
Kulani	19	CH 42
Langa	19	CH 41
Lavender Hill	65	DA 36
Livingstone	28	CN 34
Manenberg	32	CP 45
Michael Oak Waldorf	28	CP 34
Michaelis Art	4	CE 25
Mount View 2	31	CO 42
Muizenberg	76	DF 34
Nazareth House	14	CF 27
Norman Henshilwood	40	CS 31
Oaklands	29	CO 36
Ocean View	79	DN 16
Ocean View	79	DN 16
Ottery	42	CT 37
Peak View	19	CJ 41
Pelikan Park	55	CX 40
Phoenix	32	CN 45

Index to Education

NAME	PG	GRID
Pinelands	18	CF 38
Plumstead	41	CT 35
President	11	CA 47
Queens Park	16	CF 31
Range	21	CF 47
Reddam House	62	DB 27
Reddam House	3	CB 24
Rhodes	17	CH 35
Rondebosch Boys'	28	CL 34
Rustenburg Girls' Senior School	17	CJ 34
Rylands	31	CM 42
Salt River	16	CF 32
Sans Souci Girl's High	28	CM 32
Sea Point	3	CB 22
Sentinel	46	CY 15
Sibelius	64	DA 33
Silverstream	32	CO 45
Simon's Town	89	DU 30
Sithembele Manso	33	CP 48
Sonderend	32	CO 45
South African College (SACS)	27	CL 31
South African College (SACS)	28	CL 32
South Peninsula	76	DG 33
Springfield	40	CQ 31
St Cyprian's	14	CG 25
St George's Grammar School	17	CH 34
St Owen's	53	CY 35
Star of the Sea Convent	75	DJ 31
Steenberg	64	DA 33
Strandfontein	68	DB 45
Suid-Skiereiland	40	CU 32
Trafalgar	14	CF 27
Valhalla	11	CD 46

NAME	PG	GRID
Voortrekker	40	CQ 33
Walmer Estate	15	CG 29
Westerford	28	CL 32
Windermere	8	CB 39
Wingfield	10	CB 44
Wynberg	41	CS 34
Wynberg Boys'	27	CP 31
Zeekoevlei	55	CW 41
Zwaanswyk	52	CZ 31

Tertiary Schools

NAME	PG	GRID
Athlone Technical College	18	CK 39
Cape Technicon	4	CE 27
Cape Town School of Education	16	CH 33
College of Cape Town (Cape Town)	4	CE 26
College of Cape Town (Central Office)	17	CH 36
College of Cape Town (Crawford Campus)	30	CM 39
College of Cape Town (Gardens Campus)	14	CF 25
College of Cape Town (Guguletu Campus)	32	CM 46
College of Cape Town (Pinelands Campus)	8	CE 38
College of Cape Town (Thornton Campus)	9	CE 42
College of Cape Town		

NAME	PG	GRID
(Wynberg Campus)	40	CQ 33
Damelin College	17	CH 34
George Whitefield Theological	76	DG 33
Glendale Training Centre	52	CX 32
Good Hope Seminary	14	CF 25
Graduate School of Business	4	CB 25
Molenbeek Training Centre	7	CE 35
Northlink College	9	CB 42
Old Mutual Business School	9	CD 40
Oude Molen Technical College	8	CE 38
Tafelberg Training Centre	3	CC 22
U.C.T. Medical School	16	CG 32
University of Cape Town	16	CK 31
Varsity College (Cape Town)	4	CE 25
Varsity College (Rondebosch)	16	CK 33

Special Schools

NAME	PG	GRID
Astra School for the physicaly disabled	21	CK 48
Batavia Special School	29	CN 36
Blouvlei School for Learners with Educational needs	52	CZ 33
Chrysalis Academy	50	CY 26
Dominican Grimley Special School	35	CT 17
Eros School for the Cerebral Palsied	19	CJ 41
Mary Kihn School for Partially hearing children	17	CG 34
Nompumelo Training Centre	33	CN 47
Vista Nova Special	17	CJ 35

Index to General Information

Fauna and Flora

NAME	PG	GRID
Ardene's Public Gardens	28	CO 32
Cape Peninsula National Park (Silvermine)	62	DE 28
Cecelia Forest	37	CR 22
Cecilia Plantation	26	CN 26
Central Square	18	CG 37
Combrink Park	10	CB 43
Company's Gardens	4	CE 26
Coronaton Park	8	CE 39
Delville Park	68	DB 46
Dido Valley	88	DQ 27
Glencairn Vlei	83	DO 27
Hanekom Park	11	CB 47
Imhoff's Park	78	DL 14
Jubilee Square	89	DU 28
Kenilworth Race Course Conservation Area	41	CQ 35
Keurboom Park	28	CM 34
Kirstenbosch National Botanical Gardens	26	CO 27
Newlands Forest	27	CL 29
Park Island	64	DD 33
Rondebosch Common	17	CJ 35
Rondevlei	54	CZ 37
Sandown Park	28	CL 34
Sheldon Park	18	CF 39

NAME	PG	GRID
St Peter's Square	16	CG 32
Table Mountain National Park	48	CY 20
Trafalgar Park	5	CE 29
Vlakkenberg Plantation	37	CT 23
Wildwood Island	64	DC 32
Wynberg Park	39	CQ 30
Zandvlei	64	DC 33

Places of Interest

NAME	PG	GRID
Admiralty House	88	DT 27
Albertyn's House	88	DU 27
Alphen Hotel	39	CS 30
Bay View House	89	DU 28
Bertram House	4	CE 25
Blockhouse	47	CY 18
Bo-Kaap Museum	4	CC 27
Boshof Gateway	27	CN 30
Braeside House	76	DH 32
Cape Medical Museum	4	CB 25
City Hall - Cape Town Central	4	CE 26
Clifton Scenic Reserve	12	CG 19
Coornhoop Dovecot	17	CG 34
De Beer's Building	88	DU 27
De Goede Verwachting	3	CB 24
De Post Huys Museum	76	DG 33
De Tuynhuys	4	CE 26
De Waal Park	14	CF 25

NAME	PG	GRID
Design Museum	4	CC 26
Die Stem Parsonage & Dutch Reformed Church	89	DU 29
District Six Museum	4	CE 26
Eastern Battery	47	CY 18
Education & Centre for Conservation Education	40	CQ 32
Edwardian Beach Houses	76	DH 32
Edwardian Beach Houses	76	DH 32
Egyptian Building	4	CE 25
Ellerslie Girls' School	3	CC 22
Entrance and Gates - Cape Town High School	4	CE 25
Everard Read Art Gallery	4	CA 26
False Bay Fire Museum	74	DK 28
Former Archives Building	4	CE 25
Fort Wynyard Museum	4	CA 25
Gateway & Walls - St Cyprian's School	14	CG 25
Goedgeloof	38	CS 27
Goodwood Museum	10	CB 44
Government Ave	4	CE 25
Green Point	3	CA 23
Greenmarket Square	4	CD 26
Groot Constantia (1865)	38	CU 26
Groote Kerk	4	CE 26
Groote Schuur	16	CK 32
Herschel	28	CO 32
Historic Houses	75	DJ 31
Historic Outbuildings	14	CF 25

Index to General Information

NAME	PG	GRID
Hout Bay Museum	47	CW 17
Huguenot Memorial Building	4	CE 25
Ibeka	88	DU 27
Irma Stern Museum & Gallery	16	CJ 33
Jewish Museum	4	CE 25
Josephine Mill	28	CL 32
King's Blockhouse	15	CH 30
Koopmans de Wet House	4	CD 26
Kronendal	47	CV 17
Leeuwenhof & Bo-Tuin	13	CF 24
Lodge de Goede Hoop	4	CE 26
Malay Museum	4	CD 25
Malay Quarter	4	CD 25
Martin Melck House	4	CD 26
Mast House	89	DU 28
Middle Campus	16	CJ 32
Mostert's Mill	16	CJ 33
Muizenberg Station	76	DG 33
Museum of National Emblems	89	DU 29
Natale Labia	76	DG 32
Naval Museum	89	DU 29
Old Drill Hall	4	CE 26
Old Locomotive	4	CD 26
Old Magistrates Offices & Residence/Simon's Town Museum	88	DT 27
Old Supreme Court (Cultural History Museum)	4	CD 26
Old Town House	4	CD 26
Oude Molen	7	CE 35
Palace Barracks	88	DT 27
Pump House	14	CG 25
Rhodes Cottage	76	DH 32
Robben Island Embarkation Building & Quay	4	CA 26
Rondebosch Common	17	CJ 33
Rondebosch Fountain	16	CK 33
Rustenburg House	16	CJ 32
Rust-en-Vreugd	4	CE 26
S.A.Air Force Museum	7	CB 36
S.A.Maritime Museum	4	CB 26
S.A.Museum/Planetarium	4	CE 25
S.A.National Art Gallery	4	CE 25
S.A.P.S Museum	76	DG 33
SA Maritime Museum SAS Somerset	4	CC 26
SA National Gallery	4	CE 25
SAS Somerset (Museum Ship)	4	CB 26
Sendinggestig Museum	4	CD 26
Sinodale Hall (N.G.K.)	4	CB 25
Somerset Hospital	4	CB 25
South African Library	4	CE 26
St Andrew's Church	27	CM 31
St Paul's Anglican Church	16	CK 33
St.Stephen's Church	4	CD 25
Stone Church	50	CY 25
Table Mountain	14	CK 25
Terrace Houses	5	CE 29
The Castle of Good Hope	4	CE 27
The French Redoubt	5	CE 29
The Grand Parade	4	CE 27
The Woolsack	16	CJ 32
Time Ball Tower Dragon Tree	4	CB 26
Timour Hall Primary School	40	CT 33
Tokai Manor House	50	CY 26
Union Tavern & Stables	89	DU 28
Valkenberg Hospital	17	CG 35
Van Riebeeck Hedge	26	CP 28
Van Riebeeck Square	4	CD 25
Vineyard Hotel	27	CN 31
Warrior Toy Museum	89	DU 28
Waterhof	13	CF 24
Welgelegen	16	CJ 33
Welgemoed	13	CF 24
Westbrooke	16	CK 32

NAME	PG	GRID
Yarra Yarra	88	DT 27
Zonnebloem Cottages	15	CF 29

Shopping Centres

NAME	PG	GRID
Access Park	29	CO 36
Adelphi	3	CB 22
Alfred Mall	4	CB 26
Anton Anrieth	4	CD 27
Blue Route Mall	52	CZ 31
Capricorn	10	CE 44
Capricorn	65	DD 35
Cavendish Sq.	28	CN 32
Constantia Village	39	CT 29
Dean St Arcade	28	CM 32
Durrheim	21	CK 48
Fountain Square	16	CK 33
Galleria	2	CD 21
Gardens	14	CF 25
Gatesville	31	CL 42
Glencairn	83	DO 27
Golden Acre	4	CD 26
Goodwood Mall	10	CB 45
Howard Centre	18	CF 39
Kenilworth Centre	29	CO 35
Kings Warehouse	4	CA 26
Kirstenhof	63	DB 31
Lakeside	63	DD 31
Link	28	CN 32
Longbeach Mall	72	DJ 22
Mainstream Centre	47	CW 17
Makro	43	CT 40
Maynard Mall	40	CQ 33
Melkhout Centre	47	CW 17
Metropolitan Life	21	CK 47
Oriental Plaza	4	CE 27
Ottery	42	CS 38
Park 'n Shop	52	CW 31
Pick 'n Pay (Claremont)	28	CM 32
Pick 'n Pay (Ottery)	43	CT 40
Pick 'n Pay (Kirstenhof)	63	DA 31
Red Shed Craft Warehouse	4	CB 26
Retreat Mall	52	CZ 32
Riverside Centre	16	CK 33
Sanlam Centre	40	CT 32
Silwood	17	CK 34
Stadium on Main	28	CN 32
Steenberg Village	63	DB 29
Stuttafords	4	CD 26
Sun Valley Mall	72	DJ 21
The Arcade	83	DM 27
The Avenue	28	CN 32
Tokai-on-Main	52	CZ 31
Town Square	83	DM 27
Valyland	82	DL 26
Victoria Mall	35	CU 16
Victoria Wharf	4	CA 26
Werdmuller Centre	28	CN 32
Wynberg Centre	40	CR 33

Sports Venues

NAME	PG	GRID
Athlone Stadium	19	CK 40
Bergvliet Sports Club	52	CX 32
Block 50 Strandfontein Sports Complex	68	DC 44

NAME	PG	GRID
Bonteheuwel Central Recreational Area	20	CJ 45
Brookside Sports Grounds	28	CN 33
City Park Rugby Club	30	CN 39
Claremont Sports Fields	28	CO 32
Clovelly Country Club	74	DJ 27
Constantia Sports Ground	39	CS 30
Dale Brook - Swimming Pool	75	DJ 31
De Waal Park	14	CF 25
False Bay Yacht Club	89	DT 28
Fish Hoek Bowling Club	83	DL 27
Fresnaye Sports Club	3	CE 22
Gardens Bowls Club	14	CH 25
Gardens Football	14	CH 25
Gardens Rugby Field	14	CH 25
Goodwood Sports Club	10	CB 44
Goodwood Sports Fields	10	CA 45
Green Point Sports Fields	3	CA 24
Green Point Track	4	CB 25
Hanover Park Swimming Pool	31	CP 41
Heideveld Sports Fields	32	CL 44
Hockey Pitch (UCT)	16	CH 33
Hout Bay Yacht Club	47	CX 16
Howard Bowling Club	18	CF 39
Johnston Rd Sports Fields	31	CL 41
Kalk Bay Tidal Pool	75	DK 30
King David Golf Club	21	CK 48
Lavender East Sports Fields	65	DC 36
Lawn Tennis Western Province	16	CK 32
Liesbeek Park Sports fields	17	CF 34
Maning Sports Fields	7	CD 36
Marists War Memorial Sports Club	17	CK 36
Marlin & Tuna Club	89	DU 28
Mayfield Tennis Club	29	CM 35
Meadowridge Sports Ground	52	CV 31
Metropolitan Golf Course	4	CA 25
Mowbray Golf Course	18	CH 37
Mutual Park Sports Grounds	8	CD 38
Pinelands Bowling Club	18	CG 37
Pinelands Hockey Club	17	CF 36
Pinelands Sports Centre	18	CH 38
Pinelands Tennis Club	18	CG 37
Plumstead Sports Club	41	CU 34
Red River Road Sports Fields	32	CO 44
Retreat Central Recreation Area	64	DA 33
Rhodes Recreation Ground	16	CJ 33
Rondebosch Bowling Club	29	CL 35
Rondebosch Golf Course	17	CJ 36
Rondebosch Hockey Club	29	CM 35
Rosmead Sports Ground	29	CO 35
Royal Cape Golf Course	41	CT 36
Royal Cape Yacht Club	5	CD 29
Shelley Road Sports Fields	16	CF 32
Silverglade Sports Ground	73	DK 24
Sports Field (Rustdale)	30	CM 39
Sports Ground (Valhalla)	11	CD 46
Stan Abbot Park	10	CE 45
Steenberg Golf Estate	50	CZ 27
The Oval	18	CG 37
Thornton Bowling Club	9	CE 42
Thornton Football	9	CE 42
Thornton Tennis Club	9	CE 42
Three Anchor Bay Bowling Club	3	CB 23
Tidal Pool	83	DP 28
Valhalla Park	21	CJ 47
Villagers Sports Club	28	CN 33
Vygekraal Stadium	31	CL 41
W.P. Cricket Club	28	CM 33
W.P. Rugby Union	28	CM 33
W.P. Sports Club	28	CM 33
Westlake Golf Course	63	DC 29
William Herbert Sports Ground	41	CQ 34
Yacht Club	64	DD 33
Zeekoevlei Yacht Club	54	CZ 38

Amendments

Amendments ?

As part of our ongoing product improvement programme, we value your input.

This information together with your personal details (name and address) can be sent

Post Free to the following address.

Freepost CB 11079
Attention: The Research Department
Map Studio
P.O. Box 1144
CAPE TOWN 8000

Tel: 021 462 4360
Fax: 021 461 9378

E-mail Address:
Research@mapstudio.co.za

0860 10 50 50
Visit our Website:
www.mapstudio.co.za

MapStudio

Notes

....
....
....
....
....
....
....
....
....
....
....
....
....
....
....
....
....
....
....
....
....